Horror at
the Drive-In

ALSO BY GARY D. RHODES
AND FROM McFARLAND

Stanley Kubrick: Essays on His Films and Legacy (2008)

*Docufictions: Essays on the Intersection
of Documentary and Fictional Filmmaking* (2006)

White Zombie: *Anatomy of a Horror Film*
(2001; paperback 2006)

*Lugosi: His Life in Films, on Stage, and in the
Hearts of Horror Lovers* (1997; paperback 2006)

Horror at the Drive-In

Essays in Popular Americana

Edited by GARY D. RHODES

McFarland & Company, Inc., Publishers
Jefferson, North Carolina, and London

For Robert Clarke and David Durston

The present work is a reprint of the illustrated case bound edition of Horror at the Drive-In: Essays in Popular Americana, *first published in 2003 by McFarland.*

LIBRARY OF CONGRESS CATALOGUING-IN-PUBLICATION DATA

Horror at the drive-in : essays in popular Americana / edited by Gary D. Rhodes.
    p. cm.
    Includes bibliographical references and index.

    ISBN 978-0-7864-3762-7
    softcover : 50# alkaline paper ∞

    1. Horror films—United States—History and criticism.
2. Drive-in theaters—United States—History. 3. Drive-in theaters—Austraila—History. I. Rhodes, Gary Don, 1972–
PN1995.9.H6H66 2008
791.43'6164—dc21   2002011643

British Library cataloguing data are available

©2003 Gary D. Rhodes. All rights reserved

No part of this book may be reproduced or transmitted in any form or by any means, electronic or mechanical, including photocopying or recording, or by any information storage and retrieval system, without permission in writing from the publisher.

Cover photograph ©2002 Index Stock
Screen image from poster art of the 1958 film *Monster on the Campus*

Manufactured in the United States of America

McFarland & Company, Inc., Publishers
   Box 611, Jefferson, North Carolina 28640
      www.mcfarlandpub.com

Contents

Introduction 1

DRIVING IN

1. Who's Afraid of the Virgin Wolf Man? Or, the Other Meaning
   of Auto-Eroticism 9
   — *Eric Mark Kramer*

2. Drive-In Horror Across the Outback: Surf, Sand and *Sisters*
   in 1970s Australia 25
   — *Graeme Harper*

SITUATING THE HORROR

3. Naked! Screaming! Terror! The Rhetoric of Hype and Drive-In
   Movie Trailers 41
   — *J. Rocky Colavito*

4. A Drive-In Horror by Default, or, The Premiere of *The Hideous
   Sun Demon* 53
   — *Gary D. Rhodes*

5. Ideology and Style in the Double Feature *I Married a Monster from
   Outer Space* and *Curse of the Demon* 67
   — *Michael Lee*

6. The Legacy of *Last House on the Left* 79
   — *Steven Jay Schneider*

BOILING HOT AND COLD: THE PRESSURES OF WAR

7. Apocalypse Here and Now: Making Sense of *The Texas Chain Saw
   Massacre* 97
   — *Mark Bould*

8. In the Science Fiction Name of National Security: *Cat Women
   of the Moon* 113
   — *Tony Williams*

INTERPRETING GENDER AND SEXUALIZED IDENTITIES

9. "Horror Has Its Ultimate, and I Am That": Severing the Bonds of Identity in *The Head* and *The Brain That Wouldn't Die* 129
   —David Annandale

10. Ed Wood, *Glen or Glenda* and the Limits of Foucauldian Discourse 141
    —Chris Cooling

11. *Daughter of Horror:* Low-Budget Filmmaking, Generic Instability and Sexual Politics 155
    —John Parris Springer

12. "Evil, Beautiful, Deadly": Publicity Posters of Drive-In Horror's Monstrous Women! 169
    —Chrystine Berzsenyi

13. Unmasking Patriarchy's Savior: Gender Politics in *Samson versus the Vampire Women* 187
    —Michael Lee

UNDERSTANDING CULTURAL CURRENTS

14. Monsters and Mayhem Below the Mason-Dixon 201
    —Stephen Budney

15. Italian Cinema Goes to the Drive-In: The Intercultural Horrors of Mario Bava 211
    —Karola

EXAMINING TECHNOLOGY IN, BEHIND AND BEYOND THE DRIVE-IN

16. The Threat of Materialism in the Age of Genetics: DNA at the Drive-In 241
    —David A. Kirby

17. Wizards of Gore, Dances of Life and Hidden Dimensions 259
    —Gary D. Rhodes

18. Drinking Blood with Walter Benjamin and David Durston 277
    —Karola

About the Contributors 297
Index 301

Introduction

Gary D. Rhodes

My strongest connection to drive-in theaters is the now-defunct Skyview in Ardmore, Oklahoma. I have the vaguest memories of being there in the back seat of my parents' 1966 Plymouth one summer. For me, the film acted simply as a background to eating and napping. I recall my father backing into a speaker pole, though it hardly made a scratch on that old chrome bumper. But really, as much as anything else, I remember the heat. That old parking lot spent hours baking under the Oklahoma sun; even after dark, it was still stifling.

The only particular film playing at the Skyview that sticks in my mind is *Infra-Man*. After scanning the comics in the local newspaper, I came across an ad promoting it. The film had been released in 1976, but this screening was definitely after I had seen *Star Wars*. It must have been late 1977 or 1978, and it was my first encounter with the problem that has always plagued drive-in theaters: having to exhibit many films long after their initial run at indoor theaters. But to me, *Infra-Man* was new. In fact, it would be new to me even if I saw it today. You see, I remember *Infra-Man* mainly because I *didn't* get to see it. I guess I couldn't persuade my folks to go, and the only car I had at the time was a Jaguar made of plastic with pedal-powered wheels. Not highway material by any means.

By the time I could drive a real eight-cylinder (which regrettably wasn't a Jag), the Skyview was out of business. Later, in high school, I did sneak over the locked gate and barbed wire to shoot a variety of photographs of its aging screen, which by then had several vines growing up its support beams. The speaker posts were all still in place, but the drive-in was silent. With a little mustered courage, I even poked around in the boarded-up projection room and concession stand, grabbing a few small mementos. Mementos of a cultural site that I'd hardly known or experienced. It is funny how we can sometimes have nostalgia for people and places we never knew.

When I later developed my photographs (which I had shot with black-and-white infra-red film), the images emerged starkly onto the photo paper. They were so bleak and lifeless and dark. What had once been a hopping "passion pit" was devoid of any life at all. Outside of maybe a few squirrels or armadillos or rats, the only life there was me, and—on a later occasion—the girlfriend I took along. Even if there was no longer a movie on the screen, I was determined to make out at a drive in theater. But without the glow of the film—well, it just couldn't have been the same thing.

In the months that followed taking those pictures of the Skyview, I traveled through the Southwest looking for old drive-in theaters, snapping pictures of

The deserted Skyview Drive-In Theatre in Ardmore, Oklahoma, shot in infra-red black-and-white.

many. Each had become its own unique kind of cinematic graveyard. One had become the site of a flea market swap meet; another was practically hidden by eons of uncut weeds. And then there was that beautiful drive-in theater sign I found in Topeka, Kansas. It looked so nice and polished, but as I approached it, I realized it was all that was left of a once-proud theater; a Wal-Mart now stood where the screen once did.

Even if I had basically missed the drive-in era, I was born and bred on watching films at indoor theaters and on TV. More than anything, I was fascinated by the horror films. From an early age, I knew Bela Lugosi and Boris Karloff and Lon Chaney by name. By age five, I was buying horror film magazines and books. As time went on, I became entranced by the lower budget horror films of the 1950s and 1960s. Since drive-in theaters did have problems getting new quality products, they opened their arms to B movies. Horror, sci-fi, juvenile delinquent storylines—those played well at drive-ins, especially as the audience demographic shifted from 1950s families to 1960s teenagers. They were fun, and—at least on the surface—they required little thought. And of course for many teens, these films were the secondary attraction at the drive-in. The assembly of the teen group or the passion of a couple alone—that often took

A silent speaker post at the Skyview Drive-In, shot in infra-red black-and-white.

precedence over the particulars of a given film.

But I did pay attention to those films, watching reruns of them on late-night TV and eventually on videocassette in the '70s and '80s. Roger Corman, Herschell Gordon Lewis, Jack Hill, to me, were the kind of directors to respect. Their films were the kind to watch. They were "drive-in horrors," the (none-too-original) name I've given to these kinds of horror films.

Why have I enjoyed these movies so

much? Well, however flawed the "drive-in horrors" are in some ways (e.g., dialogue, acting, cinematography), they represent a unique approach. By design or accident, they often reject many of the norms of the classical Hollywood approach to filmmaking and storytelling. For example, drive-in horror films sometimes draw on pre-existing literature for narrative focus, which—given their low budgets and quickly produced status—can yield important discussions on the art of literary adaptation. They explore various transgressive themes not often addressed in other films of the same era. Drive-in horrors also offer gender representations worthy of study. They examine and often reject cultural norms and moral codes of the period. They act as a cinematic barometer of issues affecting U.S. culture, ranging from nuclear capabilities to fears of Communism. These productions can even offer important re-evaluations of auteur theory.

And yet drive-in horrors have received little coverage in modern print, with the exception of horror film fan magazines and books that generally offer only production histories and plot summaries. The key theoretical questions and issues have hardly been explored. Though I believe that more scholarly works will appear in the future, it seems that there have been few in the past simply because many scholars have viewed drive-in horrors (and often the horror film genre overall) as being of little importance. Some scholars think the films beneath their time; others perhaps think that their peers won't take studies of such films seriously. After all, only a very few drive-in horrors—*Night of the Living Dead* (1968) being a key example—have been graced with much academic attention. All too often, films like *I Married a Monster from Outer Space* (1958) and *The Wizard of Gore* (1970) just haven't been seen as "valuable" or "worthwhile" or "important."

That same mentality of what is and isn't an academically respectable topic may be why so few good materials exist on the drive-in theater era itself. For example, the only major historical work is Kerry Segrave's *Drive-in Theaters: A History Since Their Inception in 1933* (McFarland, 1992). Nostalgic photographs and anecdotes do come to life in a few books like Don and Susan Sanders' *The American Drive-in Theatre* (Motorbooks, 1997) and Elizabeth McKeon and Linda Everett's *Cinema Under the Stars* (Cumberland House, 1998). And there have been a few stellar documentary films like Jan Krawitz's *Drive-in Blues*. But little else of value can be found. At this writing, no major theoretical examination of the drive-in theater era has appeared in book form.

When I taught a course at the University of Oklahoma Department of Film/Video Studies in the summer of 2001 called "Drive in Movies and Theaters," the dearth of material was a particular hindrance to getting deeper inside the world of drive-ins. And existing drive-ins are now of less help too, which is in part why my thirst for that era of great drive-ins has continued to remain unquenched. For example, when my class went to a drive-in for an evening, students understood some of what our limited class texts described: the large indoor concession stand, which once accommodated long lines of moviegoers dying for a barbeque sandwich. And yet the overgrown weeds hardly appeared inviting, and the infinite cracks on the old pavement smacked more of an ailing elder in the hospital than of a lively, spic-and-span 1950s ozoner. Along with the lack of care and the lack of attendance we noticed, we saw how the modern world encroached upon our experience. After all, while my friends Alex and Clay were searching for PIC mosquito repellent, Matt had to go ask the driver of a new minivan to get the key out of their ignition. Its modern daytime running lamps were making it hard for the rest of us to see the screen. This hardly could be the same experience I had longed for with *Infra-Man*. It hardly could be "The Way It Was."

But if the theaters are fewer in number and encumbered with new problems and changes, the old drive-in horrors (even if they now have to be seen on TV, VHS or DVD) are still with us. The essays contained in *Horror at the Drive-In* represent one stab at finally creating a body of work to examine and understand those films. Certainly it is true that much more work will need to be done. So many wonderful films and filmmakers are not covered. Little space is devoted to director-producer Roger Corman in this collection, and yet an entire essay collection could and should be devoted to his films. And a great many non–Corman gems exist that should eventually be studied in print: films like *I Bury the Living* (1958), *The Screaming Skull* (1958), *Night Tide* (1961) and *The Undertaker and His Pals* (1967). Future works will hopefully embrace these and many other drive-in horrors.

For the present, however, we have 18 essays that I believe cumulatively break much new ground on drive-ins and drive-in horrors in an exciting and stimulating way. "Driving In," the first section of the book, features two essays that emphasize the role of the drive-in theater itself. Eric Mark Kramer's "Who's Afraid of the Virgin Wolf Man? Or, the Other Meaning of Auto-Eroticism" may perhaps be the most intellectually engaging and important essay ever written on the U.S. drive-in theater phenomenon. And Graeme Harper's delightful "Drive-In Horror Across the Outback" examines the oft-overlooked importance of the drive-in theater to Australia, seemingly the only country other than the U.S. where it became a major cultural site.

Section Two—"Situating the Horror"—offers four essays that investigate the ways horror operated at the drive-in theater. J. Rocky Colavito's "Naked! Screaming! Terror!" analyzes the rhetoric of the drive-in horror coming attraction trailer. My own "A Drive-In Horror by Default" looks at opening night: the horror film premiere at the drive-in theater. Michael Lee's "Ideology and Style in the Double Feature" considers the teaming of two film narratives at the drive-in. And Steven Schneider's "The Legacy of *Last House on the Left*" analyzes the preproduction, production and marketing of one of the last and still best known drive-in horrors.

"Boiling Hot and Cold: The Pressures of War" offers Mark Bould's fascinating "Apocalypse Here and Now," which looks at the importance of both Vietnam and U.S. counterculture to *The Texas Chain Saw Massacre*. And Tony Williams' excellent "In the Science Fiction Name of National Security" offers a Cold War reading of *Cat Women of the Moon*.

Williams' essay also examines gender issues, thus acting as a segue into the largest section of the text, "Interpreting Gender and Sexualized Identities." Gender and sexuality have been among the most common and most important subjects of horror film analysis, and the present book is no exception. David Annandale's "Horror Has Its Ultimate, and I Am That" provides an investigation of sexualized identity and severed heads; Chris Cooling's "Ed Wood, *Glen or Glenda*, and the Limits of Foucauldian Discourse" offers new insight into the world of Edward D. Wood, Jr.; and John Parris Springer's "*Daughter of Horror*" discerns generic (in)stability through sexual politics. The section continues with Chrystine Berzsenyi's "Evil, Beautiful, Deadly," a feminist reading of publicity posters and their depiction of women, and concludes with Michael Lee's "Unmasking Patriarchy's Savior," an examination of gender politics in the wild and crazy world of El Santo and *Samson versus the Vampire Women*.

"Understanding Cultural Currents," the fifth section in this volume, gives us two different lenses through which to view culture and the drive-in horror. Stephen Budney's "Monsters and Mayhem Below the Mason-Dixon" scrutinizes the depiction of both the South and Southerners through works as varied as *Hush…Hush, Sweet Charlotte* and *2000 Maniacs*. And Karola's monumental "Italian Cinema Goes to the Drive-in" offers an intercultural analysis of the works of Mario Bava in which she probes both the origins of his visual style and its translation onto U.S. theater screens.

The final section of the text, "Examining Technology In, Behind and Beyond the Drive-In" offers three essays that inspect a variety of issues in the drive-in horror film. David A. Kirby's "The Threat of Materialism in the Age of Genetics" offers a scientific treatise on the drive-in horror's narrative embrace of DNA. My own "Wizards of Gore, Dances of Life and Hidden Dimensions" examines the use of cinematic form to create a definitely non–Hollywood spatio-temporal zone in Herschell Gordon Lewis's *Wizard of Gore*. And Karola's "Drinking Blood with Walter Benjamin and David Durston" provides an important closure (and opening) for *Horror at the Drive-In*. She examines the many different prints and running times of the film *I Drink Your Blood* by engaging with Benjamin's landmark "The Work of Art in the Age of Mechanical Reproduction." Karola does truly take us (as the section title suggests) beyond our drive-in in many ways, including down the road of future work that will need to consider a topical byproduct of her essay: the role of the auteur, if any, in creating a/the drive-in horror film.

As with any book, a large number of people have given freely of their time and help. Many thanks to the friends who helped in various capacities on this volume: Robert Clarke, William Clarke, David Durston, Andrew H. Horton, Michael Lee, Amy Nicholson, Michael F. Price, Don and Phyllis Rhodes, Karola, John Parris Springer, Bob Stovall, Tom Weaver, Alex Webb and Clay Withrow. And of course my thanks to Mom and Pop for those few, fleeting memories I have of the old Skyview. And to Melissa for making my life so wonderful, and for making our own trips to an aging drive-in theater so much fun.

Special thanks for the photos in this volume go to Robert Brosch of Archival Photography and film collector Lynn Naron. And special thanks to my dear friend Coco Kiyonaga at *Cult Movies* magazine, who found the bulk of the images seen herein.

My thanks also to all of the contributors of the essays, each of whom found new and important vantage points from which to examine their chosen topics. And with that said, this introduction has finally found twilight, and it's now dark enough for the movie to begin.

Gary Rhodes
Norman, Oklahoma
Fall 2002

Driving In

1

Who's Afraid of the Virgin Wolf Man? Or, the Other Meaning of Auto-Eroticism

Eric Mark Kramer

> Live dangerously. Build your cities on the slopes of Vesuvius.
> —*Nietzsche*

Pretext

Websites, books and articles dedicated to the accounting of the drive-in industry are readily available. They dutifully record how the number of drive-ins exploded during the optimistic 1950s and declined in the 1960s and '70s, nearly dying-out altogether in the 1980s with the advent of home video machines, cable television and the like. They reveal how audience demographics changed over these decades. How World War II with its rationing of rubber, gasoline and other essentials to auto-mobility forced many drive-ins to close for the good of the collective. Other articles describe the efforts of some loyalists to the form trying to "keep hope alive" with a pseudo-revival at the turn of the millennium. Optimists anxiously chart progress with about 11 DIs reopening and fully four new ones built since 1995! They mark the rebirth with special showings featuring "classic cars" carrying equally, though not so classically, aging "Baby Boomers." More and more literature and documentary text is appearing as a manifest ersatz nostalgia for the old "ozoners." Boomers miss them but they were precisely the people who abandoned them in the first place and for reasons selective memory censors.

Since several chapters in this volume have set out to recount the technological and political-economic history of the drive-in theater form along with its retroactively glorified "B-grade" contents, this chapter seeks to take a different path. In this chapter, I attempt a very cursory survey of the phenomenology of the drive-in theater experience, the necessary conditions for its birth and the romantic memories it has spawned in the wake of its decline. In this chapter, I focus on the folk phenomenon and its essentially local form, for in the instance of the drive-in theater the form competes with the content for significance, asserting locale as a meaningful part of personal geography. With the continual individuation of the American psyche, the great "people's palaces" that showcased the Depression

era cinema have become minimalized in size and décor. At the center of the entire shift is the emergence of what Jean Gebser has called hypertrophic egocentrism, perspectivism as an ironic ideal.[1] For both the grandiosity of the big outdoor screen and the reductionism of the palace to the strip mall "multiplex" owe everything to the superabundance of personal motorized transportation in the form of the automobile, which in turn presupposes an attitude of increasing individualism and at the same time neocolonial resource consumption on a scale never before seen in human history. While one may argue that all art is a wasteful luxury, the drive-in is a perfect example of kitsch art, a moment in time where the mob can afford extravagance, where high production values occasionally meet an adulterous medium, where the rubber meets the gravel.

Being Here

Museum space is a special, modern form of sacrality.[2] It is quintessentially modern in that it deploys objects in a form of space created primarily for display. Rarely can one touch. Modern space is space for looking. And with the ocular distance comes a cool reverence. Once put in a museum, a thing becomes "culture" sui generis, an object revered but no longer part of daily life. The magic of the museum is the attempt to get as close to authenticity as possible even if you can't touch it. But it is also a sort of death sentence as it reduces a relationship to pure objectivity. Despite our idealistic attempts to flee this fleshy world of unwashed horde into the realm of transcendental truths, still presence has magic power. For instance, visitors of all ilk to the

British Museum spend hours staring into glass cases peering at "actual," handwritten texts by Charles Dickens, Charles Darwin, James Joyce, Winston Churchill and so forth.

Once, while at the museum in London, I noticed a crowd of people gathered around one display case in particular, leaving hundreds of others practically unnoticed. Indeed, it was not the form of display, but the "contents" that were supposed to be the point of focus. And so it was that some content was particularly alluring at drawing a crowd. The cases that displayed English manuscripts by Sigmund Freud, Karl Marx and other "greats" drew no attention except for me looking at something by Emily Brontë. What could be in the case that commanded such interest? When I finally got close enough to peek over someone's shoulder, there below were handwritten poems and cartoons by the pop legend John Lennon.

Locale as a Particular Split-Infinity

For all our post–60s sophistication and college-educated abstractionism, do we not now recognize that as one "progresses," one progresses away from things as well as toward others? And as we were taught that "movies" were an "art form" to be properly called "cinema," what was left behind? Look how we have developed into homeless cosmopolitans (global citizens). The old human, that inferior anachronism, just had to die to make room for the evolved post-human. Superior in every way, the "New Man" dwells in the realm of scientific abstractions, formulaic truths and perfect forms.

In the pre-modern (yet extant) world, performance happens *now*. "Live" means real. But for Plato (the first true modern), all representational art, in fact this entire mortal world, is merely a shadowy mimic of true forms. Of course the post-modernists protest. I have seen them quiver, despite their self-loathing, with the excitement of seeing the "real live" Jacques Derrida enter a conference room. He is not a trace or a graft after all even though some consider his work a type of intellectual fraud (graft of another sort). They rush to get *his* autograph on *his* books and then jealously protect *their* prizes like religious relics. Maybe it is the trace that authenticates the origin.

Despite logic, watching taped or filmed performance somehow makes us, the viewers, seem less real too as compared with watching a live performance. Passivity, the modus of the couch potato, means to act like a vegetable passively following the Sun through phototropic reflexes without really seeing it. We switch on the television, not so much to see a specific show but to watch *it*. The act of being a potato is meaningful in and of itself. We bask in the glow of the tube, lackadaisically relaxing. We rarely turn it off even when "nothing's on." We just keep grazing, hunting and gathering. We switch away from performers in mid-verse, with impunity, because they aren't really real anyway. Maybe we do this more and more in face-to-face interaction too. To appreciate dissociation, we must return to the beginning of drama when the ancient Greeks built lenses, amphitheaters with rows of passive observers focusing on a new kind of staged space with "actors." Thus we have the birth of the "actor" and the "reactors." When this happened, the magic and mythic holism of ritual was fragmented.[3] The dance no longer included everyone. Some, in fact most, just watch now, even too ashamed to dance when asked. Thus we have the modern individual with her heightened self-consciousness isolating her from everything and everyone else. This is why communications has taken on a millenarian status. "Communications," not informatics with its high speed data transmission, but talking and listening have become "central" only because we sense that we are failing at it. The dissociative gaps are expanding everywhere. In part, this is because of the modern sense of chronic urgency and hyper-individualism.[4] In the drive-in, you have to wait until it's dark.

Why do we like the new solipsism? For one thing, we can hide while we watch and so the oft-mentioned sense of voyeurism in the modern technotronic gaze. Participants cannot be voyeurs. Removal, distanciation is a necessary condition for voyeurism to exist. This is so not just for the disinterested gaze but also for the momentary identification that can mythically and magically work. Moving from being a participant to an observer involves a shift from magic idolic communication to perspectival signalic communication, a process manifesting an increase in dimensional accrual and dissociation.[5]

In the taped version, the performer can't look back at us or hear our meager responses, our jeers, coughs and applause, and see us dozing and laughing and weeping. By contrast, in the case of live performance, even taking into account theatrical distance, the audience is yet an essential part of the happening. The actor can modify her presentation to fit the mood of the audience. But in a film, the actors go about their efforts oblivious to the fact that the seats are empty.

There is a profound difference between being at a live performance to which one is embodied, physically present and watching a memorial device (film, tape, hard disk, silicon chip, etc.). It's like comparing a painting reproduced in a book to standing in the presence of the "original." In the presence of the "real thing," the brush strokes, hacks, smudges, scrapes and pokes, which constitute the "actual" places where the artist's personal touch is preserved, we are inexplicably excited. The original is worth far more money than the reproduction and it's not simply because it is rare, the "brightest" or oldest version. Thanks to mass reproduction, the image is available in various media sizes, and qualities. For instance, one can wear a Dali on a t-shirt or open a Cezanne on an umbrella. What is missing is the object as more than just an image, but as a thing-in-itself with a unique history. Locale is not merely a spatio-temporal coordinate. It is a place that is constituted of a unique set of relationships. To touch the canvas that Picasso touched is something special. To hold and read a marked-up script that Orson Welles held and scribbled on is special. We revel in the imperfection, the contingency, the uniqueness of a convergence of human relationships. While the new "constant," space, has no semantic dimension, place is thick with mood. But now an air of perfect cynicism, what Friedrich Nietzsche calls the "gloomy vapors" that surround universal "positive systems," a fragrance that inspires the sophisticated sniff that announces cosmopolitan sensibility, have spread and gained the status of expert knowledge.[6] All places are the same for I am a "world citizen" who transcends all parochial limitations.[7]

The perfection of the modern illusion that distanced us from the world occurred with the invention of photography. That most modern of all inventions, chemical picture processing and the fruition of optics marks the culmination of the modern Enlightenment philosophes and their Neo-Platonic utopianism. We can now watch wars and famine from the comfort of our living rooms switching away to a game show or music video if the visage proves disturbing to our precious "equilibrium." Mathematics blossoms into a new Pythagorian religion, the *mathesis universalis*. As Plato and Pythagorus had taught, virtue is in the virtual while the actual is nothing but shadows on cave walls, or across screens. But "act" is the root of "actual." With the ascendance of the virtual as more real than the actual, first in religion and then in mathematics, this world of real men and women becomes a "shame."[8] The virtually derived average is more "significant," more powerful (exhibiting more "epistemic force") than a single actual "subject." The ideal world is the self-reinforced world "generalized" globally, the realm of transcendental law. It is truth for the "positive" yet "objective" man of "disinterested knowledge." According to this ideology masquerading as absolute truth (or is it the other way around?), the good human, the best human:

> Is only an instrument let us say a mirror—he is not an "end in himself." And the objective man is in fact a mirror: accustomed to submitting to whatever wants to be known, by "mirroring" – he waits until something comes along and then gently spreads himself out, so that not even the lightest footsteps and the fluttering of ghostly beings shall be lost on his surface and skin. Whatever still remains to him of his "own person" seems to him accidental, often capricious, more often disturbing: so completely has he become a passage and reflection of forms and events not his own.[9]

In his pure transcendental world of ideal (positive) objectivism, the self, with its disgraceful perspective and interpretive ambiguity is rightly reduced to nothing but a self-polishing mirror. But wait— there are blasphemers like the impressionists who keep roaring back demanding that the embodied subjective fallible self, with all its animalistic defilements, be celebrated rather than despised. Rather than worshiping death, the pure realm of absolute referential perfection, which once achieved spells the blessed end of pain and striving, of living, many rebel in favor of this world of mere mortal failings and endless heterogeneity that defies generalizability. They note how the light constantly changes and the mood with it. We find meaning in those who champion this world that is unabashedly "mine," rather than the pure world of forms and formulations. They include from painting artists such as Vincent Van Gogh, Gustave Clillebotte, Claude Monet, Paul Gauguin, Pierre-Auguste Renoir; in philosophy Soren Kierkegaard and Nietzsche; and in literature the troubadours, Wolfgang Goethe, Marie Rainer Rilke, Dickens, Mark Twain, etc. Actually, already with Pieter Bruegel and Rembrandt we find a shift into mood and the intimate lives of the "common man."

Already gone are the idealized neoclassicisms and the obsession with religious and royal forms. The paint thickens and the brush strokes become more pronounced. Style emerges as a content all its own. Light and shading become unreally real in diaphaneity. They represent nothing but themselves in their own immediate givenness, which can be no more true or false than saying a cloud in the sky is true or false. Their indubitability, their self-evidentness, is in their being. While Rene Descartes became so abstractly confused as to doubt his own senses and his god, the mundane lifeworld paid his grand philosophical angst little heed. He presupposed its existence even while doubting it. So too, in its new confidence to stand alone from the tyranny of the referent as defined by the dominant culture, painting became an object in its own right, on its own terms, here and now, neither true nor false but yet undeniable. Causing disturbance and disequilibrium is the goal of art. It strives to de-familiarize the "normative" view, to create difference and thus meaning from scratch performing the miracle of giving sight, helping us all to see again.

The modern world remains a place of tension between the degenerate beast and the heavenly spirit: the body and the mind. This is a false dichotomy created by one who worshipped purity, pure mathematics: perfect circles. The realm of the contingent and distorted subject remains "low." It is the realm of the base motive and instinct where passion threatens order and reason, de-coherence threatens the myth of identical things (for no two things are actually identical, a metaphysical faith necessary for the existence of numbers, the redundancy of 1, 2, 3....) Worldly sin defiles timeless paradise.

Thus we have the St. Simonians and Neo-Hegelians engineering a perfect irony, the "positive" order dictated by what Nietzsche calls "pessimistic philosophers."[10] These "positivists" who fear all suffering, promise the "New Man" that escapes antique thinking, becoming the *ne plus ultra* of human development.[11] For them, life is a disease. Perfection is to be found in the transcendental system and its final solution, the end of the line, the end of time. With the final epiphany comes "equilibrium," zero movement: nihilism. Pure continuity spells the end of difference. Finally we have the ambiguous accomplishment of self-denial, what Nietzsche calls a "Buddhism for Europeans," the nirvanic end of suffering, the end of (life) rebirth; the glory of "no mind" going beyond the illusion of this world of opposites.[12] Instead of calling this body, this world an illusion and those who embrace it "ignorant," Nietzsche says a "tender yes" to this world of taste and odor, contingency and folly, ecstasy and suffering. If you eliminate one, you've eliminated the other.

Such fear and trembling toward life is the origin of priestly penance and *ressentiment*; revenge against vitality and action. It marks a "disease of the will" manifested as a weariness at living and its inherent struggles.[13] The ideal mirror-man can, and believes he *should* only react to what happens by. He should because that is his ideal, the destruction of himself as the source of all distortion, all possible interpretive creation. He must embrace fidelity and eliminate the "noise" of living. He should "adapt," which is purely a reactionary attitude. He should only react but even then, only enough to reflect.

What is this? It is the "*Ressentiment* of creatures to whom the real reaction, that of the deed, is denied and who can indemnify themselves only through an imaginary revenge."[14] And this revenge is "conscience"; loathing turned against the self. Guilt and self-hate are the sources of the ascetic ideal. The dissociated, unengaged vision forms platitudes of revengence, wasting life imagining all the bad things she would do to her enemies, especially herself if only she dared. The imaginal that forms the core of conscience, however, is a dishonest hate for it never discharges itself. It never dares to pronounce its true beliefs but instead curls itself into the obsequious smile for superordinates while displacing natural aggression onto the weak. Imagined vengeance consumes her life.

In the play *Waiting for Godot*, Vladimir and Estragon find themselves at a crossroads. To pass the time, they decide to call each other names. The game goes from bad to worse, from "Cretin" to "Abortion." But the final insult that is so heinous as to end the game is "critic." Objective analysis, the "innocent speech" of pure reflection turns out to be what Roland Barthes calls the greatest myth of all.[15] Only silence follows this utterance.

Friends in Low Places

There is something of the power of touch that is so strong that in the case of the stenciled hands painted on ancient cave walls, it is disturbing. Of course we want to lay our hands there too, to see if they "fit," to touch and identify with those Others across millennia. But in fact, we cannot escape the now ... or can we? In an eternal universe, there are an infinite number of yesterdays and an infinite number of tomorrows. Two infinities split by "me." I am not only the center of all the space I perceive but also of time. The now, which is where I always am, is a "standing streaming" moment caught between the past and the future.[16] But because we cannot escape the now the past is now too, as is the future, as such. I am touching the cave painting now. Similarly, while standing amongst the overgrown ruins of a drive-in theater, I wonder what scenes have flickered across the empty screen, what contortions of vitality have parked there in the musk of dusk, all pointing toward the secular gods of Hollywood. I cannot escape my embodied world, my unique perspective. I imagine what I know. And so, I am the center of space/time, the *axis mundi*.

Live performance is a happening. It is now. In a drive-in "theater," the real action is with the audience. Theatrical distance is so great that the open sky does not allow us to forget whom, when or where we are. The cinema, no matter the size of the screen, is overwhelmed by the "great outdoors." The darkness is neither total nor artificial. It is real. And so, when driving home after the late-night double-feature, tired, deep in mental rhythms rarely experienced, with June bugs hitting the windshield, I think I saw a Wolf Man, there, off to the side of the road, next to the railroad tracks. Didn't you see it too, bolt off into the gully? And so the local (not urban) suburban legend is suggested into my world, this local world. Maybe he was a Communist Wolf Man, or a Negro Wolf Man (aren't they all?). Or maybe his name was "Jack." Sophomoric will o' the wisps conflate with screen imagic and a whole pop industry just for teens. But then the late '60s–early '70s happened with the civil rights movement, the Vietnam War, popular pornography, environmental concerns, the Pill, and everyone "got educated." Suddenly the Wolf Man just wasn't scary any more because people started "thinking globally." Sex wasn't innocently terrifying any more; it was "safe," and "free."

Because the darkness is real night, we are not metaphysically jarred like Plato's hapless hero, "awakened" when we open the exit door at midday into the reality of the blazing sun. This is the point. Being at an "ozoner" is more than watching a movie. It was an attitude in an America before it lost its virginity and became "worldly." It was the Working Man's monumentalism to match the Soviet Sputnik that winked as it tumbled overhead. The drive-in does not constitute the best venue for appreciating filmic art. It is not so sanitary and sophisticated a sanctuary. It doesn't have such pretenses. Instead, the poor fidelity of message, the wired speaker box that garbles the sound track, the screen in need of a paint job—it all suggests the wilderness a traveler must traverse. It is the background to the real foreground. It offers the suggestion of a tale for the road, on the road worthy of a Twenty-First Century Canterbury character. What does it matter if the retelling of the filmic narrative mixes with the night's adventures and misadventures?

This is not a discourse that lends itself to referential authentification. It does not merely repeat in a disinterested manner, sheer facts (things already done). Rather the telling and retelling is created and is creative "as it goes." Stories of the drive-in theater are themselves worthy of a movie. Rudolf Otto might appreciate the mystery of the adolescent *deus machina*, the back corner, Ulysses in a deuce and a quarter with glass packs and some carefully concealed body putty for pimples and other blemishes; for the contingent is the cosmic blemish. The intrigue is not explained away, demythologized and understood by the telling and retelling. Quite the opposite, it is the telling that conjures the identification with the mysterious, the fascinating, and the scary. "How far did you go last night at the drive-in?" is the talk at the school lunch table for both girls and boys in the midst of their own sexual adventures.

The action is local. The action and the actors are in the cars, not just on the screen. The screen is an excuse and an opportunity to hide. In the dark, in the steel cocoon of the automobile, privacy is nearly complete because it is small and mobilized. It is mine! And intimately so. No others eat, sit, sleep, make love, *live*, in this seat. It's better than trying to hide in the back of a theater on a rental chair.

The drive-in is not a place for appreciating art in its most transcendent eminence. It lacks the purity of fidelity. It is grungy. It is a place of monetary economy but a surplus of passion. It is a landmark in its own right, unlike the multiplex mall cinema, which effaces itself in the process of mediating the filmic text. If you've been to one mall cinema, you've been to them all. Interaction is minimized. You can't even control the volume. And that is good because the film is the star there. But the drive-in is local. It is not universal. What happens there is utterly unpredictable, risky, daring. It is ironically, absolutely specific, always different. People plot maps of the locations of drive-ins along famous by-ways like Route 66 and visit *them* for themselves, regardless of what's showing. Afficionados form clubs and websites nostalgically noting the flimsy association between America's most famous road, Route 66 with its Beat Generation halo and the fact that last year marked the sixty-sixth anniversary of the first "official" drive-in theater at Camden, New Jersey, June 6, 1933.

The drive-in is lowly technology with lowly patrons and lowly content and lowly food. They have lowly intentions on their minds. They even deface their suspensions to lower their cars not for the sake of engineering, not for a "lower center of gravity," but for tantric purposes; the kundalini (mojo by another name) is raised when the car is lowered. It is comfortable and comforting, close to the earth and the compost heap of unofficial culture. It is for many home, the place where America, with its obsession with Hollywood and cars, can convergently go, thus answering a Nietzschean anthropologist's (Carlo Marx's) question, "Whither goest thou, America, in thy shiny car in the night?"[17] The car is the destination, it is what we aspire to and work for. Beyond that we don't know. The smoldering heap is a mobius mass with endless twists and turns, a long and winding road indeed, snaky even. Like Harry Angstrom ("Rabbit") who "wants to go south, down, down the map into orange groves and smoking rivers and barefoot women."[18] He heads desperately down. Down for the tropics, for the Gulf of Mexico only to be turned back by his domestication in the middle of the night to look for his old basketball coach in the hopes of some expert guidance, a road map of arrows and pivots to his disheveled life. But it, he, the world only unravels. The road map turns into a Kandinsky-like set of scares. And Lewis Carroll's Rabbit turns into a jabberwocky

on wheels, "whiffling through the tulgey wood."[19]

It is the acceptable risk of the automobile that soothes his dissonant mind. After all he is a used car salesman, a modern pretender to reasoning, a grungy sophist. The car has locks and windows that can be closed tight, and it can be used to flee as well as explore. When the getaway car starts, a sigh of "Praise be" involuntarily escapes from deep inside.[20] Like the man who says he drove down to the local convenience shop for cigarettes one banal evening after supper, but for some impulse lurking so deeply within that it could not come up to the threshold of rationality for a gulp of sun burnt air (a "reason"), on the way "home" he turned right instead of left and never stopped. The car is the real "American Beauty."

Drive-ins are acceptable momentary "voyages" that *others share with us*. They share everything with us. Peer pressure comes from the inside out. We are one, a gang of co-conspirators. Unlike driving alone to work or the market, the drive-in trip is a "road trip," a mobile party so that we escape together. Thus we have the best of both worlds, our "homeboys" leave home with us to make up new rules, new games. And what is home to the young wealthy American? The paternal source of domestic constraint. The road trip not only leaves place behind, but mores too. The parents' house where "my room" is, is the moral place of rules and regulations. The car is the space/time machine that can get one away from the gaze of authority to "mess around," "down in." The car, being the epitome of individualism, stands for freedom.

The drive-in is like going to the art

gallery to admire the frames. The drive-in is more real for its lack of pretense. It makes less effort at upholding the illusions that feed realism, insisting by its very structure, that realism after all is only another genre of fiction. Even the "true" drive-in movie content, like the films of Ed Wood and Roger Corman, is more approachable. They are more local ... more like "home movies." When the effort that sustains realism is abandoned, we say, "get real." There is no mythic innocence in a drive-in. There is little pretense or transcendental standards to uphold. The kids get into their pajamas and wrestle with the pillows in the back seat while the next car over steams up, and one more over exudes the combative odors of pot and pizza struggling for atmospheric supremacy.

The drive-in is the quintessential modern American answer to the Renaissance plaza. It is pseudo-public space. It is shared to be sure. Flipping on one's lights quickly draws not only moths but honking horns of irritated neighbors. But it is also private. This is my car, my steering wheel, my stuff. And you are "my girl" (or boy). We are not just going to see a movie. We are making history here, biography of the unspeakable sort. These are unforgettable moments to be cherished unto death. Everything can happen only one first time.

What is localism in an age when globalism is roaring across the planet exterminating all sense of place? Localism is the lowly, the backward, the unsophisticated. It is where things get wet and sloppy, like a swamp. It is the source of life. Localism is the sense that a thing is cheap and accessible even to the poorest of the poor. Privacy is mostly afforded to the wealthy who hide themselves in that other, "different," "gated" world, as F. Scott Fitzgerald made Ol' Sport say of Gatsby. However, privacy, access and control exist even for the lowly in the realm of the local. It is in the local that "every man is a king and every woman a queen," where everyone "counts," where community happens with all its thick molasses of relationships.

Here, genuine talk, the talk that has sustained the species for millennia, is paramount. Gossip is organic. It is relevant. It is about people I know and me. In today's world of global corporatism, where only one value, "efficiency," exists any more (and it too can be quantified)—in this world, gossip is a bane, a waste of time. Instead, the ideal is to merely download information without distortion, not to converse about "personal," relevant things. Instrumental communication has come to dominate the world of administration. Even language is drained of all inherent power and reduced to a purely arbitrary tool, a system of signals. The magic dimension of language, its "spelling," has been bled to death. Only statements that are logically coherent and/or empirically falsifiable are said to have any meaning.[21]

Under these rules, to say "I love you" is deemed to be a string of completely nonsensical noises. But a kiss is still a kiss and a sigh is still a sigh. In England dogs say "bow wow," in France "oua-oua," in Japan "wan-wan" and in Bantu "pyee" (but only after being kicked).[22] Accent is local. Interest mutates into intrigue there. By minimizing communication itself to a string of zeros and ones, the message is so simplified that fidelity is made complete. Anything that disrupts the syntax elicits an "error message." Deviance, local heterogeneity, difference is criminalized. Interpretation is outlawed verging on madness. Each message has only one possible correct meaning, and each problem has only one best solution. But in the organic world, where things are taken seriously and people "get personal," everyone rubs off on everyone else and they tend to be irrational and to stick together when an outside threat appears. This is why real communication is a form of intercourse. In a conversation that shares us, it is impossible to say where I stop and you begin. Risk is a constant and accommodation a dance.

The human mind is a geography of concentric spheres. The first sphere is the realm of the private self, which concerns itself with the embodied self, its itches, wounds, daily anomalies, changes and feels. Each day teenagers across cultures survey the map of their acne, the build of their physiques and the shape of their hair, pruning and primping, for despite the modern ideology that wants to postpone everything for work preparedness, for capitalist demands, the ancient mating call still beacons. The next circle for the adolescent/young adult is not so well defined. It is an overlap of allegiances that marks the move toward greater independence. The usually conflicting forces at this level range from the ego to the family and the sub-tribe of contemporaries made up of best friends, friends, worst enemies and the supporting cast of marginal Others who continually move in and out of focus.

The most significant is the love interest. This is as local as local gets. As personal as personal gets. As serious as serious gets. Local is where personal concern and care dwell, where identity blurs and emotions blend. The self is a consequence of group membership. Friendship and animosity are most palpable. Beyond this, for the young adult, is a vast uncharted realm "where there be dragons" and conquests, endless potential. Exploration for the young adult means doing many things for the first time, which usually makes for an especially intense and meaningful period of life. It is the time of life before "the thrill of livin' is gone," as John Mellencamp sings. This time of life is a time that is so intimate that it challenges attempts at intergenerational understanding. It is a magical time when reputation is everything and the public realm resides in the halls and bleachers of one's mind. Care, or *sorge* as Martin Heidegger would say,[23] is intense. It has not yet evaporated with the dissociation, boredom and distanciation that marks "maturity." The world of the teenager is an emotional churning. And being "in" is absolutely vital.

The local is the place where the struggle for status and control is taken seriously, where we think we can make a difference and we guard our self-interests. It is also the place where the animal needs to be able to relax, to repair to lick and share its wounds with others who are supposed to care and dress them without question. The local is thick with sympathy, hatred, joy, fear. Magic is at the surface of the skin. And by mutual implication the world and I share the same boundary, like two adjacent rooms sharing a common wall. The boundary of the world is my skin. We continually adjust to a common contour. Magic works as a fetish. Magic is not logical but powerful. It is touch, and it works best in the dark.

The Spirit in the Machine

At the drive-in, all movies have a green tint that gets stronger toward the top of the picture. The car, for an American teenager in the mid- and late twentieth century, is a magic machine that is mighty in its powers to confer status and independence. Its size is just right for the most local of stories to unfold within. Two is a crowd and three or more intimates makes a riot. It is a movable feast. The *first car* is rarely fancy, or expensive, yet never forgettable. Its power resides in its ability to whisk the child away from the nest, even if it must be borrowed from a parent or older sibling.

The fancy movies limp into the drive-in worn and tattered if at all, to be projected onto the drive-in screen, that rural spectacle arising majestically from the midst of corn, soybean and wheat fields across the land of the automobile: a North American, mostly U.S. phenomenon like no other. Drive-ins constitute the real "field of dreams." Storms rage in the cars while lightning hits the screen. As noted above, fidelity is not the goal. Rather the goal is to break new ground, to rupture limits passing into whole new worlds. Everything is a gamble and with it comes the rush of discovery.

Rain and fog may intercede between the eye and the world "out there" that comes "in here" to the intimate space of my car. The sound system may be barely audible. Mosquitoes may force a Solomon-like choice between a midsummer night's heat and open windows. Fresh air that cools with the deepening evening may turn into "country air" if the cows come home next door or a skunk happens into the theater. The steering wheel, center console, sun visors, tinting accent the information coming from the screen, fusing with it to create a unique film experience.

But the viewing experience is not evaluated by these measures of fidelity. Instead it is the infidelity that is at the core of the experience and the desire. For in my car, I am both free and encapsulated. Hidden in my metal nest where I can turn to my most intimate interests with only an occasional, semi-public and furtive glance from the car "next door" that may intrude. This is suburbia on wheels. Individualism, with all its empowering promise and all its fragmenting isolation, revels here. Perpectivism marks the landscape with crisscrossing roads, and marks the mindscape of orientation toward a fantasy world, row upon row facing the Mecca of yearning.

Lack of "class," which is a sure sign of class, and informality express the disinterest in accurate reproduction. Pickup trucks are parked backwards with folding lawn chairs in the beds. Children swarm in the twilight over teeter-totters and swing sets of dubious construction down in the pit of the screen where for other classes a symphony would accompany an opera or stage play. Because the cost may be one price per car, gangs arrive to see the double feature bargain with comrades stuffed in the trunk: local espionage and intrigue.

The machine vehicle is my very own declaration of independence, chamber of dreams and exploratory spaceship rolled into one. It is probably not fancy, but that is because it is my first car. Likewise the movies at the drive-in are not the fancy expensive ones that stay pure in the showrooms of sheltered space where proper society (a race of critics) takes its cushy seat. Instead, the drive-in weathers the storms happening in and out of the vehicles. The drive-in is intimate, local, down to earth, "Grade B." And whoever goes there is automatically transformed into a Grade B person. There are no new Mercedes-Benzes or Cadillacs here. So, while Leslie Caron, and Maurice Chevalier were singing their way through *Lili* (1953) and *Gigi* (1958), depictions of the veiled wonders of coming-of-age mixed with sanitized high class prostitution where the Parisian *bon vivant* stalks his courtesan, such movies remained the fodder for a different kind of "serious" date, a "sit up" date with a proper "sit down" dinner and an ambiance that was foreign to the real life of teen America. Throughout this era, sexuality was veiled beyond the double entendre. Was not Sheriff Matt Dillon's "lady friend" Kitty actually an aging prostitute turned pimp? And was not the patriarch on *Bonanza* a serial polygamist? In the end, the McCarthy era romantic comedies signifying the epitome of apolitical, and therefore thoroughly political cinema, starring Doris Day and that paragon of heterosexual manhood Rock Hudson, proving that he really was a good actor after all.

But the drive-in is the theater of a reversal of priorities, and an honesty that presents itself with confidence. The common discourse makes a "heavy" date the truly serious one. When a "sit down" date, though expensive, just can't compare with a "lay down" date that has a seriousness of an entirely different magnitude.

When the families disappeared, the drive-in screen was taken over by the new and cheap sex and gore. Titillating "women convicts in chains" movies and blood-spurting amputees jiggled and lumbered across our retinas. Drive-ins were like drive-through fast food. If one wanted a nice "sit down" movie or meal, one had to get out of the car. But the drive-in audience didn't particularly expect or care to see "real cinema" anyway. The lowly technology would only spoil *Lawrence of Arabia* and *Doctor Zhivago*, and dull the "full effect" of movies like *Star Wars* and *2001: A Space Odyssey*. The sound systems rendered films like *West Side Story*, *Oliver*, *My Fair Lady* and *The Sound of Music* into something like dog whistles. We suspected that there was more there but just couldn't hear it.

Many didn't need romance on the screen because the real action was in the car itself. As Freud would no doubt have predicted, the combination of screams with zippers would sell. So we had monsters with sex appeal like Christopher Lee's Dracula, and busty victims snagging their negligees on branches while running from very male fiends. Were these actually, or virtually thinly veiled rape scenes? In the drive-in, everything is reversible. No matter the metaphysical implications, such images combined into low-level S&M,

acting as detonators for the powder keg of teenage hormones. In the cars, reality and fantasy intermingled.

Postscript

As suburbia expanded and land values continued to rise, and the audience became more and more sophisticated, the drive-in passed out of vogue, replaced by the multi-screened, "surround sound" mega-movie theaters offering expensive flavored coffees in malls. Gory video games and Internet porno belie the tame nature of the wild streak of the 1950s and 1960s. The ornery grin of James Dean and the sexual power of Marilyn Monroe seem light years removed from the angst of Kurt Cobain and the Goth movement. But in fact their tragic real lives inform today's youth identity. Today, many high schoolers follow a cultural trend introduced by the stylish horror pics produced by Hammer Films. Today, high schoolers need not go to the drive-in to see a pierced vampire because "there are three in my second period English class." They have found an ersatz identification with images from the ozone, like putting one's hand up to the cave wall or peering at a Lennon cartoon. Somewhere in the immediacy of the moment, the split infinity, throbs a shared humanity, a very personal connection.

NOTES

1. See Jean Gebser's *The Ever-Present Origin*. Translation by Noel Barstad, with Alis Mickunas. Athens OH: Ohio University Press, 1985.
2. See Richiko Ikeda and Eric Kramer's "Enola Gay: The Transformation of an Airplane into an Icon and the Ownership of History." *Keio Communication Review*. Issue 20, 1998: 49–73.
3. See Eric Kramer's *Modern/Postmodern: Off the Beaten Path of Antimodernism*. Westport CT: Praeger, 1997.
4. See Gebser's *The Ever-Present Origin*; also see Lewis Mumford's *Technics and Civilization*. New York: Harcourt, Brace and World, 1934; and Paul Virilio's *Speed and Politics: An Essay on Dromology*. London: Automedia, 1986.
5. See Kramer's *Modern/Postmodern*.
6. See Book 5, Section 347 of Friedrich Nietzsche's *The Gay Science*. New York: Vintage, 1974. Also, see Eric Kramer's "Cultural Fusion and the Defense of Difference" in *Socio-Cultural Conflict Between African and Korean Americans*. Ed. by Asante and Min. Landham MD: University Press of America, 2000: 181–227.
7. Gudykunst, William and Young Yun Kim. *Communicating with Strangers*. New York: McGraw Hill, 1997: 364.
8. See Book 5, Section 359 of Nietzsche's *The Gay Science*.
9. Nietzsche, Friedrich. *Beyond Good and Evil*. New York: Penguin, 1972: Section 207.
10 See Book One, Section 48 and Book Five, Section 347 of Nietzsche's *The Gay Science*.
11 See Jean Gebser's *The Ever-Present Origin*.
12. See Nietzsche's *Preface* to *On the Genealogy of Mortals*. New York: Vintage, 1967; the first essay, Section 5 of *On the Genealogy of Mortals*; Book 2, Sections 99 and 134 of *The Gay Science*; *Postscript* to Nietzsche's *The Case of Wagner*. New York: Vintage, 1967.
13. See the Third Essay in Nietzsche's *On the Genealogy of Mortals* and Book 5, Section 347 of *The Gay Science*.
14. Nietzsche's *On the Genealogy of Mortals*, Section 10.
15. Barthes, Roland. *Mythologies*. New York: Hill and Wang, 1982.
16. Husserl, Edmund. *The Crisis of European Sciences and Transcendental Phenomenology*. Evanston IL: Northwestern University Press, 1970.
17. Kerouac, Jack. *On the Road*. New York: Penguin, 1955.
18. Updike, John. *Rabbit Run*. New York: Fawcett, 1960: 23.
19. Carroll, Lewis. *Alice's Adventures in*

Wonderland and Through the Looking Glass. Grosset and Dunlap: London, 1946.
    20. Updike, p. 21.
    21. See Karl Popper's *Popper Selections.* Princeton NJ: Princeton University Press, 1985.
    22. Hardison, Jr., O. B. *Disappearing Through the Skylight.* New York: Penguin, 1989: 164.
    23. Heidegger, Martin. *Being and Time.* London: Robinson, 1962.

2

Drive-In Horror Across the Outback: Surf, Sand and *Sisters* in 1970s Australia

Graeme Harper

Part I

Almost immediately after the Second World War, as refugees from the war in Europe flowed into Australia and the balance of Western and world power shifted away from Europe, Australians began to turn their cultural interests away from Britain and, increasingly, toward America. This is where the story of the Australian Drive-In Horror Movie begins.

The period from the late 1940s onward brought both new attitudes and new groups of immigrants to Australia, particularly those from Southern Europe and from Asia. Australia was a vast and sparsely populated country, determined to increase its small population and to find powerful Pacific allies in order to protect its borders. Though the majority of the Australian population, even today, remains British by descent, this need for growth and protection brought about one of the most significant cultural movements in Australia's history. Drive-in movie theatres found themselves caught up in this movement.

Drive-ins were extremely popular, operating everywhere from the new expanding Australian suburbias to the vast red "outback,"[1] and were vigorously fueled by the postwar birth of Australia's own Baby Boomer youth culture, a boom not unlike that in America. Yet it is easy to see why Don and Susan Sanders, writing in *The American Drive-in Movie Theatre*, suggest that the Drive-in craze in Australia "never caught on quite as it did in America."[2] Drive-ins in Australia were, much more than they were in America, symbols of a change in culture. The competition they entered, and the films that they screened, were challenges to an older, established order. In the 1960s and 1970s, these films certainly included Disney animations and bikini movies, some British films and the occasional local productions. But, without doubt, one of the most popular and influential imports onto Australian Drive-in movie screens was the American horror film.

Part II

Australian drive-in movie theatres were modelled closely on the American example, right down to the concession stands and the uniforms of the attendants. The bright bobby-soxer concession attendants were a stark reminder to Australians of how different these movie theaters were to the more British-oriented Australian indoor cinemas. Where as the indoor cinemas had "kiosks," the drive-ins had "milk-bars"; the former represented the fun pier shows of British popular entertainment, the latter the new suburban youth scene of postwar America. In the 1960s and early 1970s, the drive-ins' competition were remodelled picture palaces. Many of these had been engulfed by new suburban shopping developments and, stuck between anodized steel and red brick buildings, gave the architectural appearance of buildings taken out of their time.

The Roxy Cinema in Parramatta, a western suburb of Sydney and one of the foundation sites for European colonization in Australia, was a perfect example of this. A grand white cupolaed building, the Roxy stood on the outskirts of the main shopping precinct, slowly surrounded by Woolworths stores, new shopping malls and offices blocks. Its interiors were pure "theater classic," with its foyer dominated by sweeping stone stairs, red carpet and brass fittings, and the walls of the cinema itself (divided neatly between "Dress Circle" and "Stalls") jutting with ornate balconies, tracery, mock turrets and columns.

Around ten miles to the west of the Roxy, on the outskirts of the new estate suburb of Blacktown, the Blacktown Drive-In Theatre attracted car loads of youths or the new western Sydney suburban families out to cinema. Around the Blacktown Drive-In there were only small farms. The landscape, thick with gum trees and threaded by narrow bitumen or dirt roads, seemed to ache to be incorporated into the new suburban expansion nearby. One of the most distinct characteristics of the Australian drive-in was watching an American movie, windows open in the hot Australian summer, surrounded by the steady droning of black bush cicadas.

Australian drive-ins competed with the older, indoor venues in a similar fashion to their American counterparts—that is, by offering not only the outdoor, large-screen drive-in experience but also good value "per car" deals, of which families and teenagers took full advantage. Even today, the South Australian Wallis Cinema chain advertises "$12 per car" admission rates at its Gepps Cross Mainline and Modbury Valleyline Drive-Ins—though it does so now not only in local newspapers but also on the Internet![3]

Like the American drive In, the Australian drive-in relied on crossing bridges between youth-focussed entertainment and family fun. No surprise then that a '70s drive-in theater could be showing on a Saturday evening *The Love Bug* (1969) or *The Aristocats* (1970) while on Friday its bill included George Romero's *Night of the Living Dead* (1968) and Brian DePalma's *Sisters* (1973). The horror double-bill was a feature of many Australian drive-ins, though as the suburbs grew rapidly, more "adult" horror needed to be moved onto remoter screens. In the 1970s, for example, new homes surrounding the Bass Hill Drive-In, in the south-east of Sydney, caught surreal glimpses of those giant actors of the ozone, drifting in the sky over freshly built paling fences.[4] The penchant for what Australians have long seen as their birthright, a free-standing bungalow on a quarter acre of land, meant that the new suburbs met the drive-in when both were at full pace.

Not, of course, that all Australian drive-in theaters were suburban. The "outback" drive-in, the drive-ins that stood on the outskirts of country towns like Dalby, Queensland, a wheat and sheep town (1991 pop. 8338) around 100 miles west of Brisbane, or in Taree (1991 pop. 15,994), in the center of the mid-northern New South Wales dairy farming district, were popular entertainment venues for the youth of Australia's important rural heartlands.

This, therefore, is the beginning of the picture. The postwar Australian drive-in drew on the steady turning of the Australian population to gaze across the Pacific and on the vibrancy and changing ethnicity of a population whose ambition to grow and embrace Baby Boomer youth culture was strong. The drive-in horror film occupies a significant place in this cultural change.

It is true to say that, at a very basic level, the climate of Australia's population center—the South East Coast—and of the America's West Coast shared as much in common as the cultural climate and that this only helped to push the popularity of the drive-in. Surf, sun and the outdoors made the Australian and American ozoners close physical relatives. But it is also true to say that in the 1970s a burgeoning government commitment to expanding the Australian national film industry put some more serious weight behind Australia's interest in successful American film genres such as horror.

It was this interest in successful Hollywood genre that almost certainly helped kindled an interest in horror amongst an emerging group of Australian directors as diverse as Peter Weir, Dr. George Miller and, later, Russell Mulcahy. The films these directors first produced, Weir's *The Cars That Ate Paris* (1974), Miller's *Mad Max* (1979) and Mulcahy's *Razorback* (1984), all in the horror genre, are surely stark declarations of this influence.

Part III

To the set the scene: The Australian film industry, before the 1970s, was at a very low ebb. Both distribution and filmmaking was dominated largely by American or British films. The split between the American and British dominance can be divided, simply, between the global expansion of Hollywood, its financial power and its control of distribution in peripheral English-speaking markets like Australia, and the influence on the population of its predominant Anglo-Celtic heritage.

Only 15 features were made in Australia in the 1960s and the majority of these were financed and controlled by non–Australian interests.[5] Not to say that the situation is vastly different in the present day. As Tom O'Regan pointed out in *Australian National Cinema* (1996), only between five percent and 21 percent of the local cinema box-office as late as the 1980s was made up of local product.[6] The power of the market to define both what is seen, and how it is seen, cannot be underestimated in a exhibition environment like Australia's fed so strongly from outside.

What filmmaking did occur within Australia prior to the 1970s owed a great deal to the use of Australian settings, Australian literature or Australian myths for what were essentially British films. This worked in two ways: firstly, to engender stereotypes about the Australian character and lifestyle and, secondly, to give access for local filmmakers to modes and techniques of filmmaking not well developed in their own country. We need only look at Harry Watt's *The Overlanders* (1946), Jack Lee's *A Town Like Alice* (1956) or Michael Powell's *They're a Weird Mob* (1966); and the less naive, less romanticized pictures of the Australian environment presented in Nicolas Roeg's *Walkabout* (1970), with its often horrific images of decay and voracious animal life, and Ted Kotcheff's *Wake in Fright* (1971), with its interest in barbarism and the harshness of male society.

These stereotypes involve now internationally familiar pictures of "bush life," tales of "pioneering" and images of "sun-bronzed ockers." This, despite the fact that the majority of the Australian population have always lived in the lower south-east corner of the country, in urban areas based around Sydney and Melbourne, and under urban conditions not unlike those experienced in many American cities.

The combination of a lack of local industry, with an obvious commitment by Australian audiences to British and American films, meant that film directors who emerged in Australia in the 1970s were open to a variety of genre influences, of which horror was a significant source. As Peter Weir has said:

> There is the thrill, particularly for my generation, a pre-television generation, that the first movies you saw were American, the first ones you loved and touched were American, from the matinee B-grade movies to horror films, and including British movies too.[7]

No surprise, therefore, that Weir's first feature film was the surreal horror film *The Cars That Ate Paris* (1974). No surprise either that *Cars* features a town of car-crazy, accident-faking gore junkies who prey on their victims not only for their auto parts but for the medical experiments which likewise drive the Paris economy. Weir draws strongly on paranoia and displacement narratives found in films such as *Invasion of the Body Snatchers* (1956) and *The Stepford Wives* (1974), creating what Jonathan Rayner has rightly pointed out is a prime example of Australian Gothic. Mixing horror with fantasy, "spaghetti" Western with social satire, *Cars* clearly reveals the attempts the new Australian directors of the period were making to broaden their repertoire.

Though not commercially successful, *The Cars That Ate Paris* was one of those films, like *The Love Bug*, *Death Race 2000* and *Mad Max*, that continued to creep onto selected Australian drive-in screens long after it was released, and to feed Australia's love affair with the car.

One of the many road accidents in *Death Race 2000* (1975).

The link between American and Australian car culture is one of the primary links between the popularity of the drive-in in Australia and its counterpart across the Pacific. Unlike European drive-ins, which fell victim to the smallness of modern European cars, frequently as well as to climatic disadvantages, Australian drive-ins could draw on local production of "American-sized" cars made by Holden (a General Motors associate) and by Ford. The former was responsible for the Kingswood, a model of family car made famous in the Australian '70s TV comedy series *Kingswood Country*, while the latter manufactured the Falcon, the Kingswood's only real rival. These two cars, in a variety of configurations (sedan; wagon; utility truck, the "pick-up" in American parlance), made up the bulk of Australian-made cars in the 1970s and, together with a variety of similar models and designs in six-cylinder and eight-cylinder configurations, dominated drive-in theater crowds.

Life indeed imitated film art. In George Miller's popular drive-in horror—science-fiction hybrid *Mad Max*, it is the Ford Falcon that features, a "souped-up" version admittedly, but a familiar sight to Australian drive-in audiences, both on the screen and in drive-in rows around them. The souped up Ford Falcon, along with the Holden Kingswood and its sportier stable-mate, the Monaro, were status symbols of '70s Australian youth. Their popularity, however, paled against distinct auto craze, the panel van.

Founded partly in the surf culture, Australian '70s youth became enamoured with the panel van. Not the square GM-style vans seen in America, but sedan chassised commercial vehicles, like high-topped single-seater station wagons. At drive-ins it was not uncommon to find several dozen rows dominated by this style of van, the bulk of which were Holdens, with their rears facing the screen and their back windows and tailgates propped open for the teenagers who were stretched out inside. These were the audiences to which both *Cars* and *Mad Max* were appealing.

As it turned out, Miller's first venture into horror film was a far more successful film than Weir's had been, not least because it was more focussed on commercial genre conventions. It created one of the most enduring male leads in contemporary cinema; Mel Gibson. Gibson's American-born, Australian heritage is a useful metaphoric representation of the position of the *Mad Max* film itself and, indeed, of many of the emerging group of Australian directors who looked to horror and other popular Hollywood genre such as the thriller and, to a certain extent, urban social drama, to go beyond Australia's earlier commitment to the rural romance.

In *Mad Max*, set in the near future, the highways are ruled by gangs of lunatic speed maniacs and Gibson plays a fed-up good cop looking to leave the road and retire somewhere idyllic with his wife and child. This is not to be. A gang of "road warriors" kills Max's wife and child as revenge for an earlier killing of one of their members. With nothing left to live for, Max returns to the road to avenge their deaths. The avenger narrative, not so far removed from the evil-meets-good scenario of *A Nightmare on Elm Street* (1984), or of a classic Western, puts Max back on the road against the psychotic gangs. And it is not just any car in which the new avenging Max hits the road, it is a V–8, a symbol of power and privilege both in Max's futuristic dystopia and in the car cultures of both Australia and America. It must be noted that the director saw the film as differentiating between Australia and America in one distinctive way. Asked if he felt he was reworking a distinctively American genre Miller answered:

> The Americans have a gun culture—we have a car culture....
> Out in the suburbs it's [cars] that are a socially acceptable form of violence. That's the wellspring a film like this had.[8]

The fact that two of Australia's soon to be most successful international directors chose in their first outing to combine horror and the car was hardly coincidental. Though Australians could not take advantage of the convertible, which was not available in Australia for much of the mid-century due to safety concerns, Australian's commitment to large, big-engined cars and to using them was profound. Australia's public transport network and America's are disadvantaged similarly: Each is encumbered by distance, a pattern of intermediate size cities providing relatively low levels of passenger feed to long distance lines, the cost of maintenance and servicing on long, uneconomical routes, and a history of trade union disruption and governmental non-commitment.

Similarly, the automobile plays well to a "pioneering" ethos in both America and Australia, promoting individualism and self-reliance while allowing the "portability" of status. The drive-in was one of the few cinematic places where you could declare your individual wealth, taste and "coolness" to a captive but regularly changing audience and mix with the changing ethnic profile of Australia without ever having to leave the safety or comfort of your own personal space.

The Australian drive-in movie theatre in the 1970s equalled: youth, "new" money not old and, though it met its social obligations with Out gate reminders to "Fasten Your Seatbelt" and "Drive Safely," a vibrant amalgam of familiar personal space and the thrills and dangers inherent in car culture. This distinctive mix of speed, "personalized" cinema (cinema that could be self appropriated in ways that would not really be achieved again until the birth of video years later) and youthful American culture was a potent mix in 1970s Australia. It represented a bold break with the Old World and it happily fed the sense of "living on the border of danger" which compelled Australian drive-in horror audiences.

It is the theme of danger and personal appropriation which Peter Carey, one of Australia's most successful novelists, winner of numerous literary prizes (including the National Book Council Award for Fiction and of the prestigious British Commonwealth prize, the Booker McConnell Prize for Fiction), picks up in his drive-in story *Crabs* (1974).

Born in 1943, and of the same generation as directors Weir and Miller, Carey's oeuvre moves very distinctively between quirky and expansive historical novels which highlight Australia's traditional ties with Britain, novels such as *Oscar and Lucinda* (1988) and *Jack Maggs* (1997), and novels with contemporary settings which focus on the expansiveness and cultural complications of Australia's new economic and social relationship with America, novels such as *Bliss* (1981) and *The Tax Inspector* (1991). Once a young man in London, Carey now lives in New York.

Crabs involves a character of the same name, his friend Frank, who owns a 1956 Dodge that Crabs admires, a trip to the Star Drive-in, and the Karboys who, as in *Mad Max* and *The Cars That Ate Paris*, are a gang that roam futuristic highways in search of cars to steal and strip. The story develops along these lines:

> The official word is not to resist the Karboys, to give them all your car if you have to, but you don't see a man giving his car away that easily.... And you don't go to drive-ins. Drive-ins are bad news. You get the odd killing. The cops are there but they don't help much. Last week a cop shot another cop who was knocking off a bumper bar. He thought the cop was a Karboy but he was only supplementing his income.[9]

But Crabs, borrowing Frank's Dodge, does head to the drive-in and the result is as surreal and horrific as it is inevitable. Not only are the wheels of the Dodge stolen while Crabs is making love to his girlfriend on the car's prized "leopard skin upholstery," he is then marooned in the drive-in where similarly marooned families live out bizarre lives, raising their children on food from the concession stand and listening to the music they play through the speakers.

> The manager fills out two forms and gives them meal tickets. He is a slow fat man with a worn grey cardigan. He explains the meal ticket system — the government will supply them with ten dollars' worth of tickets each week, these tickets can be spent at the Ezy-Eatin right here on the drive-in.[10]

The story ends as Crabs returns to the drive-in. It has become his entire world. "To be," Crabs says, "you must be a motor car or vehicle in good health." And so Crabs, in this surreal world, becomes a car himself:

> He feels better, warmer already. The highway takes him towards

the lights, the only lights in the world. They are closer. They are here. He turns off the highway and finds himself separated by the lights of the high wire fence. Inside he sees people moving around, laughing, talking. Some are dancing. He drives around the perimeter of the wire, driving over unmade roads, through paddocks until, at last, he comes to a large gate. The gate is locked and reinforced with heavy duty steel.

Above the gate is a faded sign with peeling paint. It says, "Star Drive-in Theatre. Please turn off your lights."[11]

Part IV

The cultural origins of the 1970s Australian drive-in and what it represented for Australians are obvious influences in Peter Carey's story *Crabs* and reference that vein of "living on the border of danger" which at very least reflects both a newly forming sense of Australian "self," and a certain foreboding about what this movement away from a British Commonwealth focus might mean for personal and societal safety. Both *The Cars That Ate Paris* and the *Mad Max* trilogy make full use of this foreboding.

Post–1975, assisted by the creation of such bodies as the Australian Film Development Corporation (AFDC), the Experimental Film and Television Development Fund (EFTF) and the Australian Film, Television and Radio School (AFTRS), Australian domestic film production, certainly in comparison with the previous quarter of a century, took off. This government commitment initiated what has been called a "re-emergence"[12] or a "revival,"[13] effectively creating the contemporary Australian film industry. This was partly due to the fact that, as the 1969 Australian Council of the Arts reports stated, cinema was seen as important in kindling "Australia's efforts to interpret itself to the rest of the world."[14] Yet it represented also exactly the kinds of re-defining and re-aligning ideas which the early work of directors like Weir and Miller exemplifies. These were not only local ideas, but a search for successful genre formula and, as their future directions showed, a definite gaze in the direction of Hollywood.

As an icon of a new cultural vision culture, a barometer of cultural change, as well as a direct cinematic influence on the early cinema of some of Australia's most internationally recognized contemporary directors, the drive-in theatre was ideally placed to encourage an interest in, and an audience commitment to, the Hollywood horror film.

Part V

Perhaps the most distinctive starting point for any discussion of the kinds of Hollywood horror imports that graced Australian drive-in theater screens is that classic of self-referential drive in horror, Peter Bogdanovich's 1968 film *Targets*, not least of which because it so brilliantly encapsulates the distinct brand '70s horror centred around domestic psychosis.

In *Targets*, Bobby Thompson (Tim O'Kelly) is a disturbed, gun-loving young man who hides in the tower of a drive-in theater and terrorizes the audience. The film is heavily self-referential in that it opens with a film clip from Roger Corman's *The Terror* (1963) which ends to reveal a screening room in which aging horror movie star Byron Orlok (played by horror movie legend Boris Karloff) is sitting. Orlok, of course, a reference to the infamous count of F.W. Murnau's seminal vampire film *Nosferatu: Eine Symphonie des Grauns* (1922). Reality meets film fantasy here in a way which very much later films like Mark Herrier's *Popcorn* (1991) and Wes Craven's *Scream* (1996) would audaciously repeat.

Orlok informs some film executives, one of whom is Bogdanovich himself playing filmmaker Sammy Michaels, that he no longer wishes to be in horror films and intends to return to his home in England. He believes his films no longer frighten people and that the public, in fact, is more horrified by the real events they read about in newspaper headlines. He declares:

> The world belongs to the young. Make way for them. Let them have it. I am an anachronism.

But "real life" and "fiction" are about to collide. Young Bobby Thompson, across the road purchasing a high powered rifle, kills his wife and then begins to snipe at the drive-in audience during, poignantly, the drive-in premiere of the latest and, it's to be assumed, last Orlok film. The audience screams in fright not at the aging film legend but at the "real" Thompson as he shoots them one by one.

Bogdanovich's film played well on the evolution of the horror genre, moving from the scenario of the grotesque monster in the mad scientist's lair, on which Karloff himself had built his career, to the "guy next door" who crosses or perhaps cracks over from control to psychotic anarchy. *Targets* is both a simple declaration of the horrors and transformations that modern society engenders "in the heads" of ordinary people and a depiction of the new "domestication" of horror. The scene in the drive-in, which is the film's finale, incorporates exposure in the open arena of the drive-in theater with the theme of invasion of otherwise sacrosanct personal space.

The same brand of domestic upheaval finds its way into Brian DePalma's 1973 film *Sisters*. This film teamed well on a double bill with George Romero's *Night of the Living Dead* on the Blacktown Drive-In Theatre Screen, in western Sydney, in the spring of 1974, *Sisters* leading and *Night of the Living Dead* following.

In *Sisters*, Margot Kidder is the schizoid half of Siamese twins. Jennifer Salt plays a reporter who witnesses from a nearby window the murder of a game show contestant who is inadvertently paired with Kidder during a TV game show. In a close reference to Alfred Hitchcock's *Rear Window* (1954), De Palma has Salt struggling to convince Dolph Sweet of what she has seen. Though aided by a private detective (Charles Durning), Salt needs someone to see that the logic of the cozy domestic situation is merely a cover for a brand of psychological horror which threatens to undercut our ideas about the safety and integrity of the family. Both notions of benign femininity and of the integral importance of maintaining the family prevent Sweet from recognizing the inherent danger which Kidder's psychosis produces.

It is no surprise to find this kind of horror film appearing on drive-in screens in the 1970s. Not only did a new mode of family living, more open to secular "marriages," increasingly inclined to question paternal autocracy and to promote such ideals as "doing your own thing," mean a disintegration of traditional ideas about the constitution of the Western family unit, but the birth of modern feminism meant the role of women in the family was in the process of being redefined. To find a "hip young director"[15] making "trendy, youth-orientated"[16] horror films where women are focal, and their psychological states are powerful, was entirely in keeping with this.

De Palma's counter-culture hit *Greetings* (1968) features Gerrit Graham playing a paranoid character obsessed with the

Grace Colier (Jennifer Salt) visits a sanitarium and is confronted by one of its inmates in DePalma's *Sisters* (1973).

Kennedy assassination. Robert De Niro plays Jon Rubin, a character who appears to be largely a De Palma alter ego, channelling his voyeurism through a film camera. The film's sequel *Hi Mom* (1970) continued the satirical approach to the late 1960s, reprising De Niro in the role of the unwound filmmaker, making dirty movies and bombing apartment blocks. But both *Greetings* and *Hi Mom* were little more than preliminaries for *Sisters*, where the satire of the opening TV game show sequence is quickly undercut but the disorientation and brutality engendered in Kidder's unprovoked slasher attack.

It is in *Sisters* that De Palma not only shows his preoccupation with Hitchcock but firmly declares his commitment to psychological horror. Here too, women in the domestic arena are shown as powerful initiators of horrific narratives. The same occurs in De Palma's later film *Carrie* (1976). Based on the best-selling Stephen King novel, *Carrie* draws considerably on the same thematic interests in domestic upheaval that De Palma revealed as central to *Sisters*. In this case, however, rather than psychosis producing a disintegration of a safe family space, it is the cruelty and confusion of a gawky teenager's world which generates a bizarre and ultimately violent psychic reaction. That is, Carrie's telekinetic powers.

Carrie White, played by Sissy Spacek in a stunning performance which saw her Oscar nominated, is both troubled and sexually repressed. The kids at school don't seem to like her and her mother is a religious fanatic who hates men. The rage that builds inside her finally overflows when her classmates jokingly elect her prom queen, and the ensuing blood-soaking that follows sets both her repressed temper and her prom night on fire.

Carrie, unlike *Sisters*, certainly targeted a specifically teen audience. Yet, similarly, *Sisters* displays fully De Palma's strong sense of visual filmmaking. The film's climax (that is, if you don't consider the twist in the dying moments of the film's coda!) is a spectacle of color and camera movement which casts back to his earlier erotic thriller *Murder a la Mod* (1967), in which he experimented with multiple perspective, and forward to his lavish festival of violence *Scarface* (1983) in which Al Pacino, playing Cuban hood Tony Montana, is famously framed from above, soaking in a bath so obscenely lavish that it somehow manages to match the violence of the film, which De Palma makes poetic with melodramatic tone and showboat cinematic style.

Scarface, like *Carrie*, and like the TV game show so successfully satirized in the opening of *Sisters*, is essentially concerned with the domestic American dream. All of which begs the question: Would it be all that tenuous to suggest there is a relationship between the decided domestic environment of the drive-in and '70s "down home," psychological or domestic horror?

Certainly to suggest that there is a direct link between the two would be critically difficult. It is, after all, a chicken-and-egg argument. Likewise, if drive-in notables such as *The Cars That Ate Paris* and *Mad Max*, or even the teen racer flicks *Motorcycle Gang* (1957) and *Hot Rods to Hell* (1967), seemed tailor-made for both America's and Australia's auto culture, films like *Sisters* and *Carrie* were something else, a look behind the walls of postwar suburbia.

Undoubtedly, however, the drive-in's relative informality—kids in pajamas, teens making out under cover in the back seats of cars, parents more likely to have decided to go out on the spur of the moment than they could possibly in the relatively formal surroundings of the closed cinemas—combined with the wider, and often remoter, darkness of the drive-in environment did nothing to downgrade the feeling of domestic infiltration which these '70s horror films generated. This combination of "danger outside" and "tension within" forms a backdrop to the drive-in success of George Romero's *Night of the Living Dead*.

That *Targets*, *Sisters* and *Night of the Living Dead* should appeal so strongly to the Australian psyche is a reflection of the degree to which Australian postwar society saw cracks in its previous confidence in the strength of its British heritage and was aware of its geographic and cultural vulnerability as an essentially European cultural outpost, sparsely populated and surrounded by the decidedly non–European environment of the South Pacific. The failure of Britain to arrest the match southward of Japan during the Second World War had indeed made it clear where British priorities ultimately lie.

Thus the appeal of narratives of invasion, conspiracy and betrayal was strong in Australian postwar culture. This appeal shared much in common with the appeal of Cold War narratives to American cinema audiences of the period, and largely preceded a more general societal awareness of the existence and importance in both cultures of first peoples and people of non–European descent.

The combination of spreading suburbia and its new domestic paranoias and societal unease makes it clear that self-referential horror films such as *Targets* and films about societal disintegration, such as

Night of the Living Dead, were more than mere diversions for Australian drive-in audiences.

Part VI

Double-billing *Night of the Living Dead* with the newly released *Sisters* was a stroke of genius by Skyline's Blacktown Drive-In. *Sisters* opens with the closed apartment of the contemporary America city, encapsulating such relatively "tame" plot elements as the relationship and rivalries between twin sisters, the professional life of an ambitious news reporter, the overworked life of a city detective. *Night of the Living Dead*, however, sets up these kind of iconic narratives of contemporary life only to cut them away in the first 20 minutes.

If the drive-in audience, out in the half-built suburbs, on the edge of the Australian bush around the Blacktown, was lulled into thinking "Oh, that could only happen in a city, somewhere else, with *those* kinds of people," then Romero gave them something more sinister to think about. In this film, good does not necessarily triumph over evil, those who seem bound to be heroes do not live long, and the values of a patriarchal society are undercut without any alternative being offered.

Barbara (Judith O'Dea) and her brother Johnny (Russell Streiner) have reluctantly agreed to visit their father's grave, a kind of annual pilgrimage which they are only prepared to undertake at their mother's insistence. As they travel, Johnny reminisces about a game he used to play as a child in which he would frighten his sister by intoning "They're coming to get you, Barbara" in his own impersonation of Boris Karloff. Barbara is dismissive, but not entirely unaffected by Johnny's performance. Things then turn really weird when Johnny spots a man in the distance lurching from side to side and declares: "Look, there's one of them now!"

When the weirdo grabs Barbara savagely, Johnny steps in and, almost certainly about to become the hero, is knocked down by the madman, strikes his head on a tombstone and is seemingly killed. His sister flees, joins Ben (Duane Jones), a young black man, in an old farmhouse and is informed by him that the recently dead have been returning to life to eat the living. While Barbara, not unreasonably, becomes semi-catatonic for much of the rest of the film, Ben goes about fortifying the house against the roaming zombies.

That the *Night of the Living Dead* seemingly kills off one heroic plotline after another is one of Romero's distinct contributions to contemporary horror. That its real hero is black, but that this is not a point of contention or obvious note, is another. That is sets up subplots which initially offer some relief—the sick little girl who must surely get better, the couple whose love much surely keep them safe, and then abruptly overturns them—is a third. Each of these elements revealed a new mode of concern with society's direction, the effect of the Vietnam War on domestic politics and on individuals, and the mood of disintegration and dissatisfaction which had begun in the celebrated changes in social order heralded in the 1960s.

Like *The Cars That Ate Paris*, Romero's film was decidedly low budget. Made for less than $150,000, it featured relatively inexperienced actors, including both the producers and the co writer. Shot in black and white and with such a downbeat narrative, it was hardly surprising that major studios rejected it, nor that its initial distribution was haphazard.

But *Night of the Living Dead* soon found its niche and from this built up a cult following. This niche was, in part, the matinee and midnight movie circuit; but it was, importantly, also in the drive-in theater. Here, similarly "barricaded" in their cars, teenagers could themselves pit themselves against the zombies in the dark beyond, and the trip "out" to the concession stand no doubt took on new meaning! *Night of the Living Dead* went on to become one of the most successful independent films of all time.

Part VII

The relationship between the drive-in horror film, the revival of Australia's domestic film industry and the emergence in the 1970s of Australian directors now with international reputations, is not documented. Other than the casual comments by directors such as Peter Weir and Dr. George Miller, other than their interest in car culture and their watching of American horror movies, what real evidence exists that the drive-in played a role in the revival years of the Australian domestic film industry?

None. Except of course these directors' early films: the zombie-like meanderings of Weir's Paris townspeople, the psychosis of Miller's Mad Max road gangs. Except, also, the drive-ins' surreally horrific appearance in the work of a major Australian fiction writer such as Peter Carey. And, not to forget, the continued programming of the drive-ins themselves, like those of the South Australian Wallis cinema chain, the Gepps Cross Mainline and the Modbury Valleyline. Perhaps, therefore, the evidence is far stronger than it first appears.

Undoubtedly, as Australia turned its attention away from Britain and towards America, the drive-in offered a cinematic bridge between the cultural, geographic and youth orientation of a new, modern Australia. The 1970s drive-in horror film not only identified a successful film genre which directors such as Weir and Miller could initially adopt, but it offered Australians, particularly the young, a new vision of suburbia and of culture they could see emerging around them. That this culture was imbued with as much a sense of foreboding as it was a sense of youthful excitement only made the drive-in horror film an even more popular Australian entertainment.

Notes

1. "outback": 1. (sometimes caps) remote, sparsely inhabited back country.—adv 2. in or to the back country. *The Penguin Macquarie Dictionary: The International Dictionary for All Australians,* Penguin: Ringwood, 1986, p. 434.
2. Don and Susan Sanders, *American Drive-In Movie Theatre,* Motorbooks International, Oscoela, 1997, p. 104
3. See www.wallis.com.au/drive-in/drivein. asp, as accessed in the year 1999.
4. Interview with Louise Harper, local Bass Hill resident.
5. Stephen Crofts, "New Australian Cinema" in Geoffrey Nowell-Smith, ed., *The Oxford History of World Cinema,* OUP: Oxford, 1997, p.722.
6. Tom O'Regan, *Australian National Cinema,* Routledge: London, 1996, p. 47.
7. Jonathan Rayner, *The Films of Peter Weir,* Cassell: London, 1998, p. 9.
8. O'Regan, p.105.
9. Peter Carey, "Crabs" in Graeme Harper, ed, *Swallowing Film,* Quasimodo Books: London, 2000, p. 40.
10. Carey, p.42.
11. Carey, p.47–48.
12. Brian MacFarland and Geoff Mayer, *New Australian Cinema: Sources and Parallels in American and British Film,* Cambridge University Press: Cambridge, 1992, p. 53.
13. Crofts, p. 722.
14. O'Regan, p. 95.
15. Kim Newman, ed, *The BFI Companion to Horror,* Cassell: London, 1996, p. 92.
16. Newman, p. 92.

Situating the Horror

3

Naked! Screaming! Terror! The Rhetoric of Hype and Drive-In Movie Trailers

J. Rocky Colavito

"He seems to be getting stronger as he melts!"
—*the trailer for*
The Incredible Melting Man

"D*A*M: The Battle Cry that Could Save the World!"
—*the advertising for* Destroy All Monsters

I'm flashing back to a time when I was ten or eleven years old, and just starting to get intrigued by advertisements for movies at one of the five local drive-ins that dotted Rochester, New York, circa the late 1960s. One ad caught my eye; it announced in bold newsprint, "Thing-O-Rama," the title for a dusk-to-dawn movie marathon running during the week of Halloween. Four pictures were being trumpeted: *Reptilicus* (a prime piece of made-in-Denmark cheese to be discussed at length later in this essay), *Konga* (the early 60s British rip-off of *King Kong* starring a very pre–Batman Michael Gough), *Godzilla vs. the Thing* (complete with the famous covering of Big G's adversary), and, as the main feature, the newly released Toho man-in-a-suit monster battle royale *Destroy All Monsters*. All my pleas to be taken to this awe-inspiring visual feast were met with parental rolling eyes and reminders about the running time being well past bedtime. I simmered, stewed and eventually forgot my loss, until about two years later....

I'm 12, and in the process of enjoying one of the few Saturdays that I can spend watching cartoons. Right in the midst of an otherwise typical spate of *Scooby Doo*, *Johnny Quest* and my other favorites, I see flashed on the screen the answer to a closeted monster lover's prayers. The screen split into three vertical sections, each one containing, in glorious color, one of Toho's major "players" (i.e., their monsters) King Ghidorah (the tree-headed terror from space) occupied the middle, flanked by Godzilla and his brethren. The letters "D", "A" and "M" appeared on the left of the screen, going from top to bottom. After the acronym appeared the final words of the titled scrolled across the screen as if by magic. Oh joy, *Destroy All Monsters* was making a return engagement to the Coronet Theater. This time, I was able to convince my parents to let me see it, and the rest, as they say, is history.

The trailer for *Reptilicus* distills the film's highlights into a three-minute package that shows the creature's discovery, its development under the watchful eyes of scientists, and its panic-inducing destructive rampage.

Strangely, history has somehow managed to focus my interest in these movies that were staples of the drive-ins, and this focus has formed itself around marketing campaigns for these admittedly exploitative or B-type flicks. The reason for this focus revolves around wondering how the makers of these films managed to make their product all the more interesting given all too obvious shortcomings in production value, story depth or other aspects that usually shape the public's perceptions of a film's overall quality. So far I've determined the obvious: Makers of these films weren't necessarily out to make the next *Citizen Kane*, nor were they targeting the discriminating filmgoer with their product.

Their target audience represented the primary drive-in attendees: teenagers and young adults who sought thrills, chills, and titillation. As Sam Arkoff puts it, "We often said the target audience for our movies was a 19-year-old boy who made the decision on where to take his girlfriend on Saturday night ... teenage boys who might be drawn to theaters playing movies with provocative titles like *Diary of a High School Bride*, *Girls in Prison* and *Hot Rod Girl*." As such, marketing campaigns had to be designed in such a way that these desires could be addressed. Posters, as discussed by another contributor to this volume, are an obvious part of this marketing. But posters are static, and though they do well in conveying inventive taglines (e.g. the inventive "They Rise at Night for More than a Bite" from *Cemetery Girls*) and shocking visuals (e.g. the unforgettable skull-headed spider that must "eat you to live" from the Bert I. Gordon *Tarantula* homage *Earth vs the Spider*) from their respective movies, they cannot present "action." This is where trailers come into the marketing picture, and drive-in movie trailers are unique in their own right because of their ability to thrill, chill and titillate through their reliance upon time-honored rhetorical techniques centered in emotional appeal and hyperbole. In point of fact, the techniques of drive-in movie trailers are so influential, and so effective, that vestiges of these techniques can still be found in the ballyhoo of today's direct-to multiplex seasonal blockbuster or the latest in a long line of direct-to-video/premium cable cinematic Cheese Whiz.

This essay, then, will examine the rhetorical techniques of drive-in movie trailers, with special attention given to elements designed to appeal the emotions of the audience. The rhetorical technique of hyperbole also must receive attention in this mix, because it is brought to bear upon more subtle features of the trailers (e.g. individual words, writing fonts, even scenes chosen for presentation) as well as the trailer taken as a whole. By magnifying the "exploitable" qualities of individual films, the makers of drive-in films sold their wares to a public looking for (and usually finding) the action they craved at their local "ozoner."

Pathos, Hyperbole, and a Trailer's Rhetorical Template

Whether we consider emotion in advertising to be about the stimulus or the response, we generally are talking about ... "emotionality" or "mood"—the things that are happening in the stimulus to which we ask viewers to empathize or identify—the emotion that is generated or tapped as a consequence of exposure.[1]

—Stuart J. Agres,
"Emotion in Advertising:
An Agency Point of View"

The arousing of prejudice, pity, anger, and similar emotions has nothing to do with the essential facts, but is merely an appeal to the man who is judging....

—Aristotle, *On Rhetoric*[2]

Aristotle's oft-cited definition of rhetoric is still applicable even when analyzing the techniques of marketers trying to sell pictures rife with hormonal teenagers, even more hormonally charged critters from outer and inner space, stock plots padded with stock footage and all the other traits that make drive-in pictures so wonderful. Succinctly, Aristotle saw rhetoric as "the faculty of observing in any given case the available means of persuasion,"[3] and its primary means of eliciting persuasion lay in "the personal character of the speaker; ... putting the audience into a certain frame of

From the trailer for *I Bury the Living* (1958).

From the trailer for *The Blob* (1958).

rhetorical practice that primarily make their mark upon the construction of drive-in movies to see the proverbial "big stars" of the time. These "stars" usually worked in "A" films (although there were always exceptions; Ray Milland in *X—The Man with the X-Ray Eyes* and *Panic in Year Zero!* comes to mind) thus costing the drive-in film the hint of legitimacy (and, by extension, the ethos or personal character) of films starring eminent Hollywood performers. So drive-in movie marketers had some work to do.

mind; ... [and] the proof ... provided by the words of the speech itself."[4] It is these last two elements of the classical conception of

And work they did, because the trail-

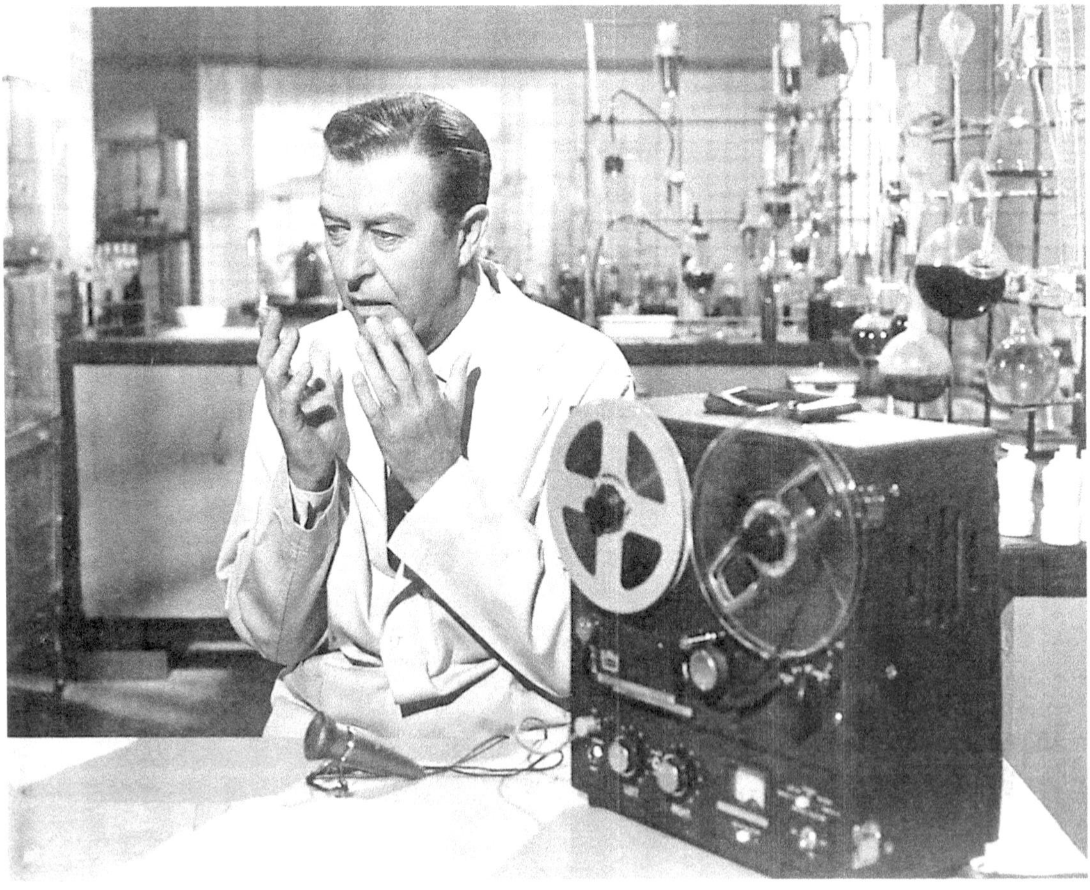

The trailer for *X: The Man with the X-Ray Eyes* mentions that the protagonist (Ray Milland) "secretly studies sexology."

ers themselves often surpass the actual films they are trying to sell. Tiuu Lukk discusses two types of movie trailers that serve as the templates for preliminary marketing of movies. "Teaser trailers run about ninety seconds and are designed to tease the audience and pique their interest ... [while] standard theatrical trailers run about two and a half minutes," and are designed around presented a "beginning, a middle, and an end ... [and] a theme."[5] According to Chris Arnold, interviewed by Lukk for *Movie Marketing: Opening the Picture and Giving It Legs*, a standard trailer also "needs to go somewhere and leave ... [the audience] on some kind of high."[6] In the case of drive-in movie trailers, it appears that elements of the tease were exploited and readily combined with the elements of standard trailers—a meshing that produced marketing devices highly dependent upon shocking scenes of mayhem (monster-generated or otherwise), fleeting glimpses of female flesh, and revealing relevant plot points of the films they represent. A drive-in movie trailer, then, embraced the principle of "hyping" the movie in question by emphasizing the most appealing elements of the films: the naked, the screaming and the terror mentioned in the title of this essay.

I mention the feature of hyperbole in the preceding sentence; for a rhetorician, hyperbole is one of the many means of promoting emotional appeal. It was "one means of amplification ... using self conscious exaggeration to emphasize feelings and intensify rhetorical effect."[7] Interestingly enough, drive-in movie trailers, in their quest for appealing via emotional and logical techniques, employ the qualities of amplification, exaggeration, emphasis and intensification as primary constructional elements. These qualities appear in individual trailers in a variety of subtle and/or overt ways, and are not limited solely to the use of scenes from individual films (through the use of significant plot-point divulging scenes does much to amplify the content of the films). Printed texts often superimposed over the scenes found in trailers. Melodramatic voiceovers, even print fonts and punctuation are other textual elements of drive-in movie trailers influenced by hyperbole.

From a purely rhetorical standpoint, drive-in movie trailers come to represent a viable crucible for the mixing of traditional rhetorical practices put to thoroughly modern ends. The available means of persuasion are strengthened by the ability to show *and* tell (and quite often it is the showing that does most of the telling). Logical and emotional appeals are given visual dimension to supplement the vocal, making for a powerful combination to assail the senses of an audience in search of a thrill fix. The audience for such trailers was arguably not all that discriminating in its selection of films; drive-ins of the time were more social gathering points rather than bastions of cinematic quality. Films tailored for such a medium did not necessarily have to measure up to Academy Award standards (which is not to say they were bad films); drive-in films sought to provide the aforementioned chills and thrills (with liberal doses of sex and violence) in the most direct fashion possible. Selling the films to the public became an endeavor rooted in packaging the most exploitable elements of such films in a two- to three-minute format that titillated the audience, told the story, and, most importantly, hyperbolized these two elements.

Naked!: Baring the Soul of Drive-In Movies

>...a collide-oscope of interfaced situations.
>
>—Marshall McLuhan, *The Medium Is the Message*[8]

> Though the objects themselves may be painful to see, we delight to view the most realistic representations of them in art, the forms for example of the lowest animals or dead bodies.
>
> —Aristotle, *Poetics*⁹

It's by now a cliché, but the timeless observation that "sex sells" had major bearing on the construction of drive-in movies and the trailers that accompany them. Whole genres of films that went directly to drive-ins (and their contemporary counterparts that go direct to video or premium cable) had nudity and sex (mostly softcore, but often colored with elements of roughness that's, usually off-limits today) as their *raison d'être*, and the trailers capitalized on the presence of this element as a means of titillating the audience and appealing to emotions. *Revenge of the Cheerleaders* (whose trailer is one of many on Something Weird Video's *Dusk to Dawn Drive-In Trash O-Rama* compilation¹⁰), for example, uses full frontal nudity as part of the trailer, showing the heroine sneaking up on members of their high school's men's basketball team (including a young David Hasselhoff) in the shower. This is coupled with scenes of rather intimate "making out" in back seats, school corridors and other available venues. I remember hearing a radio ad for this movie (I had to be about 15 when it was showing at another local drive-in that specialized in this kind of film) that proclaimed that "the best way for our team to get ahead was for them to get a little behind," so I guess the trailer went one step further in reinforcing this proclamation.

This movie, however, appears to be of the teen sex comedy genre, where the primary aim of such movies was to show as much flesh as possible without sacrificing a passable plot. In other words, the sex and nudity drive the plot and essentially become inextricable from the rest of the film's elements. Other drive-in–type movies made less use of sex, but still found ways to include it in trailers. The trailer for *X—The Man with the X-Ray Eyes* speaks of the protagonist (Ray Milland) "secretly studying sexology," and goes right to a party scene where Milland, after rubbing his eyes (which have been liberally dosed with the vision serum), is able to see the other partygoers *au naturel* (though cleverly hidden by camera angles, plants and furniture). The suggestion of nudity does the job; it emphasizes the use of the serum to see people naked, and plants the suggestion that the movie will show more (the film follows through on this promise, but in a very ironic and unsettling fashion). The trailer for *Dr. Tarr's Torture Dungeon* (a made-in-Spain film based on a Poe story) includes brief glimpses of bared breasts on three occasions, and culminates with the pursuit and suggested rape of a female character, whose screams take over the voiceover soundtrack as her top is ripped off, revealing her breasts in a prolonged shot that is altogether too much like leering.

In these cases, the presence of nudity (whether suggested or otherwise) is a primary means of getting the audience's attention and fostering interest in the picture. Nudity is an exploitable quality that appeals to many segments of the audience, and the use of bared female flesh is enough to get a primarily adolescent or newly post-adolescent audience intrigued because of the possibilities of perhaps seeing more in the course of the film. The film doesn't necessarily have to deliver the goods if the trailer does its job; the merest suggestion of nudity goes a long way toward getting the audience to the drive-in.

Nudity need also not be limited to that of the physical variety. A metaphorical form of nudity with respect to trailers laying bare the major plot elements of a drive-in film is also a play in the construction of a trailer. Many past and contemporary trailers thrive on distilling the movie's "highlights" into a three-minute package that unveils the action (some of which is disposal as trailer scenes sometimes aren't even included in a movie's final cut). The trailer for *Reptilicus* is a case in point. We are treated to the creature's discovery (pieces of its flesh are unearthed by a drill), its development under the watchful eyes of scientists, its escape and its panic-inducing destructive rampage (around and in Copenhagen). This latter scene from the trailer incorporates a "show stopper" from the film in which a fleeing crowd is chased onto a drawbridge, which is inexplicably set to raise by the fear-crazed operator. Pedestrians and bicyclists are shown tumbling off the bridge into the river below. We are also treated to a scene where the creature crushes a Jeep and its driver underfoot; the scene is shown in close up from the driver's point of view initially, and then the aftereffects are shown in longer shot. The effect is still the same; the creature and its destructive capabilities are laid bare for the viewing audience.

From the trailer for *The Astounding She-Monster* (1958).

This tactic does make sense on rhetorical grounds, particularly given the visual nature of a movie trailer and the subsequent ability of this medium to unite showing and telling. Baring the content of a movie puts facts before the audience, and by selecting key scenes of high action, the audience's interest is piqued. Partial or full physical nudity in these situations intensifies the message because the act of baring the body can be used to create interest instantaneously. Lust is a powerful magnet for audiences, and advertisers know this. And the developers of drive-in movie trailers were no different.

From the trailer for *The Hideous Sun Demon* (1959).

Screaming!: *Visual, Verbal and Vocal Hyperbole*

> If fear is associated with the expectation that something destructive will happen to us, plainly nobody will be afraid who believes nothing can happen to him.... [F]ear is felt by those who believe something is likely to happen to them, at the hands of particular persons, in a particular form, and at a particular time.... [T]he orator must make them feel that they are really in danger of something, pointing out that it has happened to others who were stronger than they are, and is happening, or has happened, to people like themselves at the hands of unexpected people, in an unexpected form, and at an unexpected time.
>
> —Aristotle, *On Rhetoric*[11]

> Suddenly the screen went black and the theater was in total darkness.
>
> —William Castle, *Step Right Up! I'm Gonna Scare the Pants Off America*[12]

Actual screams play a major role in the development of drive-in movie trailers; they can occur at almost any time and serve any number of functions. A scream at the opening of a trailer can serve to jolt the viewer, a scream placed in the context of a crucial scene's appearance in a trailer adds to the suspenseful atmosphere the movie hopes to create as a selling point. A scream at the end of a trailer, coupled with a quick dissolve to the film's title, or a fade to black, can punctuate the trailer's structure and bring it to a rousing finish.

The scream as sound effect is thus an integral part of trailers for drive-in horror films, for it is through screaming that filmmakers can convey the actors' responses to the scenes or situations. Placing these individual scenes in a trailer captures the audience's attention on a number of levels. Loud noises usually jostle the senses, and immediately get attention. Gaze is focused, and interaction with the film's wares become possible. Some trailers use a prolonged scream to build suspense; the trailer for *The Incredible Melting Man* opens with a long shot of a woman running down a long hallway, screaming all the way. She crashes through a glass door in her haste to escape whatever is chasing her, a something that is not revealed until later in the trailer. More popular is the scream immediately following an actor's shocked expression, which is then immediately followed by either a peek at the terror-inducing sight or a sudden enfolding of the screamer that snuffs out the scream. In either case, the scream has become so popular as an element of trailer construction that it is now almost a cliché.

The act of screaming, however, is most interesting when examined in the more subtle context of "visual language," the innumerable phrases and sentences that crawl, slash or bubble up on screen during a trailer. In an echo of Aristotle's notion that "elaborate diction ... is required only in places where there is no.... Character or Thought to be revealed,"[13] trailers work magic on the text, using it to echo commercial taglines, create mood or reinforce the "spectacular" nature of the film being sold. Single letters can even be given more significance; witness the exploitation of the X in the aforementioned *X—The Man with the X-Ray Eyes*. The letter always appears enlarged throughout the trailer; it is found in the word "Exciting!", in the phrase "Builds to a thrilling climaX!", and even functions as a shield, covering the whole screen so as not to reveal the aftereffects of a character's falling out of a high window. The emphasis on, and enlargement of, the letter X figuratively screams the title of the movie at the audience, and subsequently ingrains it in their minds through repetition.

Panic in Year Zero!'s trailer makes similar use of screams and visual language; in this case, the two combine to reinforce the sense of panic that drives the movie. Screams, honking horns and gunshots raise the sound quotient of this trailer markedly, while visuals of recklessly moving vehicles combine with text that appears diagonally across the screen with little regard for pattern. The text reinforces the "troubled times" that drive the movie's plot. We are told via on-screen text that the film depicts "the most shocking experience of your life" with the last three words coming out of the screen at the audience. Names of the stars are flashed across the screen diagonally, enclosed by ragged text blocks that accentuate the torn nature of society depicted in the film. The aforementioned offcamera scream is also a prominent part of this trailer. A rape is suggested: The camera cuts to one of the rapists fondling and smelling an article of the victim's clothing, and the screams rise in crescendo as the scene suddenly shifts.

In other trailers too numerous to list, the screaming nature of visual language is reinforced by the presence of exclamation points, larger-sized type and "artistic" manipulation that accompanies written and spoken text. The "linear components," i.e. words, numbers, letters—the building blocks of written text combine with these visual manipulations and verbal intrusions to "profoundly shape the texture of a page or screen."[14] Text in the trailer for *Reptilicus*, for example, informs us that "Civilization is Shocked!" What appears to be blood oozes down the background in the trailer for *The Blood Spattered Bride* while voiceover text reveals psychological data about "the Judith complex" which is then flashed on the screen as the blood trickles become larger and larger. The title of the film *Horror High* is superimposed on the screen multiple times throughout the trailer, usually accompanied by screams off-screen. Words that trumpet hyperbolic qualities of characters or creatures are uniformly larger to emphasize the heightened nature of the subject's powers. In all cases, these figurative types of screams (which are often coupled with literal soundtrack-based outcries) are one of the more obvious embodiments of hyperbole's tendency to use "exaggerated terms for the purpose of emphasis or heightened effect."[15] The terms in this case extend beyond mere words and enfold the visual dimension that we find in movie trailers. Words are supplanted and supported to a certain extend by scenes, which are in a sense of the "lexical" materials that are used create visual texts.

Screams, whether real or figurative, perform another important rhetorical function in the construction of drive-in

From the trailer for *Devil Girl from Mars* (1954).

movie trailers. Taken literally, they are a primary part of a trailer's soundtrack, and come to perform tasks ranging from getting attention all the way up to creating suspense. More subtly, screaming is embodied in the ways that words present themselves in the trailers. Words and phrases can be coupled with exclamation points, can be manipulated to appear to come flying off the screen, and can be combined with visuals to "double team" the viewing audience. It's a potent combination, and is certainly one of the more persuasive elements of drive-in movie trailers.

Terror!: Why We Need Reminding That It's Only a Movie

> Spectacle is less artistic, and requires extraneous aid.
>
> —Aristotle, *Poetics*[16]

> Rhetoric clearly does more traffic in the "excitation of emotions," as Gadamer put it. More than simply a spontaneous awareness of what is happening to an *other*, there is doubly reflexive move, from awareness of our own emotion (fear) to a recognition of what may involved when it is others who are suffering.
>
> —Thomas Farrell, *Norms of Rhetorical Culture*[17]

The now-famous tag line for *Last House on the Left* left its indelible imprint on the movie going public. Oft repeated now, but misapplied, it counseled us to "keep repeating, it's only a movie!" Those six words created an unsettling atmosphere surrounding the film, suggesting that what occurs in the film blurs the lines between film and real life and that the audience must be jolted out of this reverie.

A successful ad campaign should thus capitalize on the film's terrifying elements without revealing too much. Suspense is just as emotionally appealing as overt nudity. Ironically, it is the promise of seeing more that makes striptease so captivating for some. The suspense inherent in the slow removal of garments draws the audience in.

Strangely, however, drive-in movie trailers quite often seem to ignore this precept, choosing instead to revel in the "gory" details in an effort to attract audiences. It's an homage of sorts to Aristotle, who reminds us that "fear and pity may be aroused by the Spectacle."[18] More often that not, I found the trailers I viewed in researching this essay to be concerned with giving up the goods, essentially reducing their respective movies into three-minute packages that showed key plot points. The aforementioned *Horror High*'s trailer shows the protagonist swallowing some sort of potion that turns him into a shambling madman, a fact reinforced by seeing his transformed hand gingerly placing the beaker on a counter. We are also treated to death by immersion in a chemical vat, a teacher having her fingers graphically chopped off with a paper cutter, and the revelation of a "star attraction's" (ex–Dallas Cowboy John Niland) status as a victim of the killer. *Don't Look in the Basement* introduces us to principal characters and some shocks, but its hand is tipped by the voiceover declaring that the movie is about the day "the insane took over the asylum." *The Night Evelyn Came Out of the Grave* proves true to its title, showing us the aforementioned Evelyn, complete with a gnawed-away face and exposed teeth, in moonlight glory.

More successful are trailers that invoke terror without being a shortened version of the film. The trailer for *Dr. Tarr's Torture Dungeon* catalogues numerous visions of horror in the asylum setting (e.g. feathered dancers who threaten a character with scythes, inmates enclosed in glass boxes *et al.*), and its suspense quotient is heightened by the narrator's verbalized wondering about becoming a victim himself. The trailer for *Night of the Lepus* (the oft-maligned movie about genetically enlarged killer rabbits) shows the results of attacks, and only allow us glimpses of the creatures' eyes, leaving us to wonder what is committing these acts. The trailer for *Frogs*, after telling us that frogs have the capability of laying millions upon millions of eggs, then jolts us with a question about what would happen if they all hatched at once. After multiple scenes of multiple frogs, but never any scenes of frogs and victims, we were left with the film's tagline: "Today the pond; tomorrow, the world."

Terror, whether forthrightly or subtly presented, is a crucial component of drive-in movie trailers, for it is perhaps the transfixing of hyperbole in visual terms. Similar to nudity and screaming, terror has the effect of engaging the attention of the audience. Unlike nudity or screaming, terror has the ability to maintain this transfixion because of its ability to prolong the mood by playing out the scene. With nudity, the audience gazes or leers; with screams, the audience jumps and wonders what is going on; with terror, the audience is captured, and watches to see the event unfold. It seems a direct echo of Aristotle in the *Poetics*, for "incidents arousing pity and fear ... have the very greatest effect on the mind.[19] Terror, then, as a rhetorical device in the construction of drive-in movie trailers, is the mystical portion that completes the "hyperbolic trinity," we notice (naked); we jump (at screaming), and we watch (the terror play out).

And Now the Screaming Stops

> [Hyperbole is] the boldest figure of rhetoric ... it enables us to describe what would otherwise be beyond description.
>
> —Willard Espy, *The Garden Eloquence: A Rhetorical Bestiary*[20]

> Instant communication insures that all factors of the environment and of experience co-exist in a state of active interplay
>
> —Marshall McLuhan, *The Medium Is the Message*[21]

Drive-in movie trailers owe a good deal of their notoriety to their makers' ability to effectively present hyperbolic elements in entertaining packages. The movies provide the elements that are so "beyond description" that only the visual nature of the trailer can do them justice. The trailers thus can "instantly" communicate their messages to the audience by hyping the contests via the manipulation of scenes, sounds and script. And lest you think the techniques have been supplanted by a more market-savvy age, I submit to you a trailer for Tri-Star's 1998 remake of *Godzilla* (there were several different ones used). We are treated brief glimpses of the creature's visitations, but more important is the message of "size does matter" that leaps off the screen at the audience. With this trailer, it appears that marketing of movies has now taken up the sword of defending America. The double entendre with respect to size is readily apparent, as is the suggestion that the size of the budget improves the quality of the picture. Perhaps the marketers were seeking the titillation implicit in the double entendre; perhaps they really believed the hype surrounding their "version." Whatever the case, the hype outdistanced the quality of the movie, which was roundly derided as a pale imitation of Toho's finest. So maybe it isn't the marketing tendencies that change over time—hype is still alive and thriving in the media spotlight when it comes to movies (and other entertainment spectacles for that matter). I guess the old saw of "they don't make 'em like that any more" just isn't accurate. Today's trailers, like their predecessors, carry on the traditions of hyperbole ... all the way to the bank.

Notes

1. Agres, Stuart J. "Emotion in Advertising: An Agency Point of View." *Emotion in Advertising: Theoretical and Practical Explorations.* Stuart J. Agres, Julie A. Edell and Tony M. Bubitsky, eds. New York: Quorum, 1990. p. 3.
2. Aristotle. *On Rhetoric.* New York: Oxford, 1991. p. 20.
3. *Ibid.,* p. 24.
4. *Ibid.,* p. 24–25.
5. Lukk, Tiiu. *Movie Marketing: Opening the Picture and Giving It Legs.* Los Angeles: Silman-James Press, 1997. pp. 219–220.
6. *Ibid.,* p. 220.
7. Patnoe, Elizabeth. "Hyperbole." *Encyclopedia of Rhetoric and Composition: Communication from Ancient Times to the Information Age.* Theresa Enos, ed. New York: Garland, 1996. pp. 219–220.
8. McLuhan, Marshall. *The Medium Is the Message: An Inventory of Effects.* New York: Bantam, 1967. p. 10.
9. Aristotle, *Poetics,* Grinnell, Iowa: Peripatetic Press 1990. p. 227.
10. Something Weird Video, headed up by Mike Vraney, offers VHS and DVD copies of horror film trailer compilations, as well as all manner of bizarre exploitation and low budget films from years past.
11. Aristotle, *On Rhetoric,* p. 105
12. Castle, William. *Step Right Up! I'm Gonna Scare the Pants Off America!* New York: Pharos, 1976: 143.
13. Aristotle, *Poetics,* p. 259.
14. Kostelnick, Charles, and David D. Roberts. *Designing Visual Language: Strategies for Professional Communication.* Needham, MA: Allyn & Bacon, 1997. pp. 119–20.
15. Corbett, Edward P.J., and Robert J. Connors. *Style and Statement.* New York: Oxford University Press, 1998. p. 67.
16. Aristotle, *Poetics,* p. 240.
17. Farrell, Thomas. *Norms of Rhetorical Culture.* New Haven: Yale University Press, 1993. p. 71.
18. Aristotle, *Poetics,* p. 239.
19. *Ibid.,* p. 236.
20. Espy, William. *The Garden Eloquence: A Rhetorical Bestiary.* New York: Harper and Row, 1983. p. 98.
21. McLuhan, p. 63.

4

A Drive-In Horror by Default, or, The Premiere of *The Hideous Sun Demon*

Gary D. Rhodes

Many horror movies were not planned for the drive-in theater circuit.

Filmmakers, even horror filmmakers, generally hoped their movies would be well-received at indoor theaters. Success and money could result, and possibly, *possibly* even respect. But by the 1950s, indoor theaters—known, affectionately or not, as "hardtops"—were drawing a sharp contrast to their drive-in counterparts. And many films slated for hardtops instead found they could only exist in the "ozoners," the "passion pits." Even if not originally projected for the drive-in market, that would become some films' major site of projection.

Samuel Z. Arkoff, who became one of the best-known producers of drive-in films through spearheading American-International Pictures (AIP) with James H. Nicholson, explained:

> At that time, the running gag about drive-ins was "They play last run movies, right after drug stores." The major studios never really considered them reputable—in fact, unlike today, they nearly ignored the summer moviegoing market altogether, which was when the drive-ins drew their biggest crowds. While we found the summer a lucrative time for releasing pictures, we sometimes had to open our movies in drive-ins or, in some cities, they wouldn't play at all.[1]

Arkoff's final comment indicates that drive-ins became a major outlet for AIP films, most of which fell into the horror, science fiction, teenager-"beach" and juvenile delinquent ("J.D.") genres. In fact, AIP sometimes developed movie titles and posters to show to drive-in theater chain owners before starting production to help insure bookings. During the 1950s and 1960s, drive-ins helped AIP achieve a degree of financial stability and success.

Why *were* drive-ins the savior of low-budget horror, science-fiction, beach and J.D. genre films? For one thing, while drive-ins certainly attracted rural, urban and suburban couples and families, teenagers and young adults soon constituted perhaps the majority of audience members at some drive-ins. When traveling the country in the 1950s, producer Herman Cohen noticed this:

> I got out of Hollywood and saw what happened and what was happening, and that it was the teenagers who were buying the

records. It's the teenagers that were leaving the home, getting away from that TV box in the living room. The teenagers wanted to get away from the home. They wanted to get away from their parents, and they went to the cinema. They went to the theater, and they had fun with the horror pictures....[2]

As a result of what he saw, Cohen produced and co-wrote movies like *I Was a Teenage Werewolf* and *I Was a Teenage Frankenstein* (1957).

The success of such films can also be attributed to the lack of product available to drive-in chains. During the 1940s and beyond, the established indoor chains pressured movie studios to either avoid distribution to drive-ins or delay product rental until well after the same films had been screened at hardtops. By the end of the 1940s, the drive-ins waged a stronger war for better film rentals. Several lawsuits were filed, but—despite some successful litigation—the drive-ins continued having problems getting major films to show to their patrons.

Drive-ins garnered audiences initially due to their newness, but soon the novelty wore off and competition from other drive-ins increased. Films were needed, and new low-budget movies helped fill the need. Kerry Segrave's excellent history *Drive-In Theaters: A History from Their Inception to 1933* suggests:

> The times that a drive-in would play a first-run film from a major Hollywood studio would always remain rare. Ozoners would always feature distinctly different programming from that shown at indoor houses.[3]

Thus was born the drive-in horror: the film which may or may not have been intended for hardtops and perhaps even played some, but that was primarily seen at "ozoners." They—along with the science-fiction, beach and J.D. films—helped continue and even increase interest among potential drive-in attendees.

According to *Shared Pleasures: A History of Movie Presentation in the United States*, "[o]ne estimate had the public spending more at drive-ins, which had not existed a mere decade before, than at live theatre, opera, and professional and college football combined.... For the first time, during one week in June 1956, more people attended drive-ins than went to traditional 'hard top' theatres."[4] By 1958, there were 4,063 drive-ins as compared to only 820 in 1948. And their numbers meant good money, even if not a good reputation. Samuel Arkoff claimed, "In good weather, a drive-in could draw a gross of two to three times the average hardtop."[5]

Drive-ins were arguably at their zenith in 1958, when actor Robert Clarke was growing weary of starring in low-budget films and playing secondary roles at the major studios and on television programs. Clarke had a wife (Alyce King of the King Sisters) and family to support, and he had something else. "A really burning fever to make movies," he has called it. "Crazy, really, to want to make a film of my own independently, but that's what I wanted almost more than anything."[6]

The idea stemmed partially from his starring in three very low-budget productions produced and directed by Ronnie Ashcroft. Ashcroft, who generally worked as an editor for hire, made one of those films—*The Astounding She-Monster* (1958) for only $18,000; he then struck a distribution deal with AIP for $60,000. Clarke was of course impressed by the huge profit Ashcroft made, and also the fact that his own share of the profit at four percent resulted in more money than his $500 upfront cash salary.[7]

Though *The Astounding She-Monster* was the only one of what became three Clarke-Ashcroft film collaborations with a science-fiction–horror storyline (the other two being *Outlaw Queen* in 1956 and *Girl With an Itch* in 1959), Clarke himself was no stranger to the horror genre. He grew up watching films in Oklahoma City, admiring the work of Bela Lugosi in *Dracula* (1931) and Boris Karloff in *Frankenstein* (1931). Some of his earliest film work in the 1940s came in the Val Lewton horror films *The Body Snatcher* (1945) and *Bedlam* (1946); he later starred in Edgar G. Ulmer's low-budget classic *The Man from Planet X* (1951). Clarke recounted:

> I felt like I could make a good picture on a small budget. At least, I knew I could do better than Ashcroft had with *The Astounding She-Monster*. No offense to him, but with just a bit more money, I thought I could end up with a lot better picture. Logically, a better picture could get at least as much return as *She-Monster*. And for that picture, I knew I wanted to do a horror story. There was a growing market for them; plus, I've always enjoyed them so very much.[8]

These plans spawned *The Sun Demon*, a story which Clarke desperately wanted to translate to the screen.

The idea for the script came from combining science-fiction ingredients with one of Clarke's favorite films, *Dr. Jekyll and Mr. Hyde* (1931). The new plot featured lead character Dr. Gilbert McKenna being rushed to the hospital after exposure to a new atomic isotope in a laboratory mishap. McKenna then suffers a transformation into a mutant human, a "Sun Demon," when he contact with sunlight. Horror was thus combined with modern science–science fiction.

To prepare for production, Clarke enrolled in a screenwriting class at USC, where he met several film students who would become pivotal behind-the-scenes figures: Tom Boutross (co-director and editor), Vilis Lapenieks (one of the three cinematographers), E.S. Seeley, Jr. (who translated the story into a rough script), and others.[9] A casting call helped find both lead actresses, Patricia Manning and

Advertisement from the August 29, 1958, *Amarillo Daily News*.

Nan Peterson. And several of the other actors were Clarke's in-laws, members of the well-known King Sisters/King Family. Even Clarke's young niece was recruited to play a role in the film.

The film's budget started with only $10,000, half contributed by Clarke and half contributed by USC student Robin Kirkman. Filming got underway in late 1957. To keep costs low, Clarke shot only on weekends, enabling him to get camera, lighting and sound equipment rentals for a full two days at the cost of one. The entire production phase took only 12 weekends, with Clarke using existing locations as a way to work more quickly and economically.[10]

Editing took much longer, but finally the film was finished. What to *do* with it was the next question. Clarke noticed and clipped a series of articles on the "how and why of horror movies" that were printed in the *Los Angeles Herald and Express* in June 1958. The title of the first article—"Horror Films Lure Teeners"—stuck in Clarke's memory; the under–20 crowd was definitely the major constituency of horror. The article suggested, "Chances are that when Junior borrows the family car and he and his date will hold hands at a drive-in while the monster with three heads and a million eyes pursues a teenage movie heroine through outer space."[11] The *Herald and Express* understood what Herman Cohen had the year before.

Perusing the series of articles, Clarke also read about the specific storylines of some of the more successful films. Mention of *Invasion of the Saucer Men* and *I Married a Monster From Outer Space* helped build a case for the popularity of films involving space travel, but the *Herald and Express* journalist also noted another important theme:

> A generation schooled in the dangers of fallout, radiation, and the perils of mutations easily accepted the script writers' conceptions of monstrous humanoids and mutants roaming an atom blasted earth.[12]

Radiation and mutation were a key factor in *The Sun Demon*, further raising Clarke's hopes for successful film distribution.

Thirdly, Clarke read perhaps the most important and inspiring proclamation of all: "While most Hollywood producers are in deep mourning for the bonanza days when television was something out of science fiction and big stars meant big money, the makers of horror movies ... laugh all the way to the bank. The horror cycle is at its peak. Independent producers, geared to cheap production and fast returns, have gotten rich."[13] Clarke wanted fast returns and the chance to produce again.

But to get rich, a producer has to get his or her film shown on theater screens. And *The Sun Demon* had no pending screenings. Nothing had been booked. Nothing at all. Hopes for a big indoor theater premiere were rapidly diminishing.

Bob Clarke's brother William had an idea. Since 1952, Bill had been sales manager at KGNC-TV, Channel 4 in Amarillo, Texas. During his years at the NBC affiliate, Bill had gotten to know many people in the Texas movie and entertainment business. For example, he regularly chatted with Blue Doyle, manager of the Crossroads Company, which owned three drive-in theaters in Amarillo. They often spoke about Bob Clarke and the various movies in which he acted.[14]

"Why not premiere *The Sun Demon* in Amarillo?" Doyle proposed, and quickly Bill Clarke phoned his brother. Bob excitedly agreed to the idea; after all, an edited and completed *Sun Demon* was just sitting on a shelf waiting to see the light of a projector.

Plans solidified, with Amarillo's Tascosa Drive-In chosen as the venue. It was the largest of Doyle's theaters, featuring more parking spaces than any other, and also it was percentage-wise the best attended. Even better was the fact that it was geographically adjacent to KGNC-TV, which then acted as a kind of headquarters for publicity. "You could walk from the back door of the station straight into the concession stand of the Tascosa; they were that close together," Bill Clarke reminisced.[15]

Doyle scheduled the premiere for August 29, 1958, booking Allied Artists' *Attack of the Crab Monsters* (1957) for the bottom of what would be a double bill. He also wanted to feature Clarke in person, as well as Nan Peterson, thinking the actress's attractive appearance would help generate interest among local movie buffs. After getting their assurance of a live appearance, Doyle and Bill Clarke moved into action.

The Crossroads Company arranged for the local firm of Ray Johnson Advertising, Inc., to design two different 3 × 7 newspaper ads and one 4 × 10 newspaper ad. All proclaimed that spectators could "See the star of the picture in person. He will change from man to monster before your eyes. Never before attempted in any theatre. Don't miss it." Each ad also showed Clarke wearing the Sun Demon mask, not leaving the creature's looks to the potential audience members' imagination.[16]

Ray Johnson Advertising also designed and printed 6,000 heralds to be distributed around Amarillo. These were nearly 11 ×

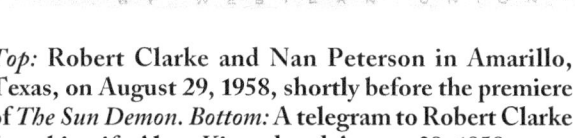

Top: Robert Clarke and Nan Peterson in Amarillo, Texas, on August 29, 1958, shortly before the premiere of *The Sun Demon*. *Bottom:* A telegram to Robert Clarke from his wife Alyce King, dated August 29, 1958.

14 in size, presumably posted in area businesses and given out to would-be patrons. The design was similar to the newspaper ads, picturing the Sun Demon, a progression of photos of Clarke undergoing the transformation to the monster, and a somewhat provocative image of Nan Peterson.[17]

The same advertising firm wrote and arranged airplay for several radio ads, which ran on various Amarillo stations. For example, KZIP ran a 30-second ad on 40 occasions, as well as a ten-second ad on 20 occasions. The half-minute ad also ran 50 times on both KGNC and KLYN. The ten-second ad also ran on other stations, specifically for ten times on KLYN and 50 times on KAMQ. All of these were aired between August 28 and September 1, 1958. A script for the ten-second commercial claimed:

A beautiful girl.... A handsome man.... A sunny beach.... Romance.... Then ... before her very eyes.... (Scream.... Snarls).... From man.... To Monster! See *The Sun Demon*.... Tonight at the Tascosa Drive-in Theatre.... North on Fillmore Street![18]

The script is none too different from ad copy for many other horror films, even of prior decades. However, the 30-second commercial allowed time to build on the modern scientific aspects of the story:

SOUND: *Bubbling* SOUND.... BG For:
ANNOUNCER: It was born in the seething cauldron of an atomic furnace ... and came to life with a roar like thunder!
SOUND: *EXPLOSION*:
ANNOUNCER: (In Echo Chamber).... The Sun Demon!

SOUND: *SCREAM AND SNARLS*....
ANNOUNCER: Never in the wildest nightmare ... was there a creature like this unbelievable product of a scientific mistake! A normal human being in the cool of night.... But in the ultra violet rays of the sun....
SOUND: *EXPLOSION*:
ANNOUNCER: (In Echo Chamber).... The Sun Demon!
ANNOUNCER: See the stark and startling story of *The Sun Demon*.... Tonight at the Tascosa Drive-in Theatre ... North on Fillmore Street! He changes from man to monster ... before your very eyes! *The Sun Demon*.... Tonight.... At the Tascosa Drive-in Theatre ... North on Fillmore Street! Also showing ... *Attack of the Crab Monsters*.[19]

Sounds of explosions and buzz words like "atomic" created a modern texture for the film; they placed it more firmly in the cross-genre of horror-science fiction, a combination that those *Los Angeles Herald and Express* newspaper articles had claimed were hits with teenagers at drive-ins.

As a further aid, Bill Clarke was able to arrange some television ads, hoping to target some of the very people who were staying at home watching television rather than making frequent visits to the drive-in. The KGNC-TV continuity for the first commercial, dated August 29, 1958, is as follows:

> "Announcing—the WORLD PREMIERE of a motion picture that will long be remembered for its terror, its fright, and shocking suspense.... The searing rays of the sun—that has been worshipped and feared by humans since the beginning of time—turns Man into Monster.
>
> Before your eyes, you will see the terror that is unleashed by *The Sun Demon*. Experience the shock

and suspense that *The Sun Demon* brings to a mighty Metropolis. Thrill to the brutal tower of strength that flows in its veins—the hypnotic spell cast by his evil face."[20]

Oddly, the TV script does not build on the science fiction elements in the story. Much like the shorter radio ads, the script is little different than horror film publicity of the prior decade.

Publicity also came from free press, much of which centered around the fact that Clarke and Peterson would attend the premiere in person. "Two actors Due for Premiere Here Friday," one article proclaimed. "The actors will appear onstage ... one time only on Friday. The stage appearance will take place between the two features and will last for approximately 10 minutes...."[21]

Interest in the premiere continued

throughout the weekend of August 29, spurred in part by Bill Clarke's friends in the local media scene. A TV interview with Bob Clarke was broadcast on KGNC, and a radio interview on KLYN caused enough advance excitement for the station to sell ad time to support it. [22]

Bill McReynolds, staff writer at the *Amarillo Daily News*, caught Clarke and Peterson shortly after their arrival in Texas, writing that they were "understandably tired, [having] left Hollywood Friday morning and land[ing] in Amarillo to the customary fanfare of television and interviews." Clarke also spoke to the newspaper about his choice of making a "monster picture" as his first film as fledgling producer:

> Well, it all goes back to why people go to see picture shows. Survey after survey indicates that our audiences of today are predominantly teenagers. At least, the teenagers are the ones that most frequently attend.... Naturally, then, I decided to tailor my film to those who would be most likely to see it.[23]

Clarke was drawing again on the very ideas he had read about in the *Herald and Express*, still hoping for the kind of box office success the newspaper had described. After all, if *The Astounding She-Monster* had made a large profit, *The Sun Demon* certainly could. All that remained was scoring a success in Amarillo. Good press and large crowds—that would be key.

When the premiere evening arrived, excitement in Amarillo grew. Bob's wife Alyce sent a telegram which arrived late that afternoon; it read, "The most of everything tonight darling, especially all my love."[24] A few hours later, at twilight, the film began, flickering onto the Tascosa screen. Crowds of cars filled the pavement, meeting and soon exceeding attendance expectations.

The Sun Demon played well, eliciting a number of audible screams and laughs from the parked cars. The people weren't disappointed. And while the film lit up the screen, Bob Clarke was sitting a few blocks away, hoping and praying it was well-received.

By the time of the film's concluding credits, a motorcade began a few blocks away. Police cars led a Cadillac convertible into the Tascosa parking lot. Clarke and Peterson waved from their open air vehicle while police sirens sounded in front of them. Searchlights began spiraling into the night air as Clarke and Peterson made their way up a makeshift flight of stairs onto the top of the Tascosa concession stand. Its roof was flat, sloping slightly towards the screen.[25] Other lights hit Clarke and Peterson, as an announcer started the live show amidst cheers from the crowds.

Details of most drive-in theater premieres are scant, lost forever to the past. But fortunately *The Sun Demon*'s remains intact, each word preserved for posterity. The following is a transcript of the premiere, which was recorded on August 29, 1958, on an audio transcription disc by Patterson Recording:

ANNOUNCER: We've got *The Sun Demon* now with Robert Clarke and Nan Peterson, escorted by the highway patrol and the sheriff's department. Here they come in the big white Cadillac. Stars of *The Sun Demon* ... [applause] ... world premiering here in Amarillo. [applause]

ROBERT CLARKE: That was some chase, wasn't it? [apparently referring to the number of police vehicles]

ANNOUNCER: Can you hear us out there, ladies and gentlemen? Can you hear? Can we get a little more volume, please? Need just a little more volume. Can you hear us all right now? Not yet? Is that all the volume we can get? Hello? Testing. Hello? Testing. Hello? Testing. [banging sound against the microphone] More volume, Mr. Projectionist. [Clarke and Peterson exchange two or three words too quietly for recording to clearly preserve] Ladies and gentlemen, we'd like to welcome our stars for the *Sun Demon*, Nan Peterson, very lovely lady that you saw in our movie, and I think we're getting a little more volume, and Mr. Robert Clarke, who flew in from Hollywood, California, early this afternoon. He left California early this morning, and we'd like to talk to him just a few minutes to find out just how he came about making this picture, *The Sun Demon*. And first of all, ordinarily it's ladies first, but Bob, we'd like you to get another fellow for us in a little bit, so we'd like to talk to you before we get Mr. Brooks.

ROBERT CLARKE: Okay Larry, just so that I don't crowd Nan here. She is so pretty, this girl.

ANNOUNCER: Oh, isn't that the truth? Can ya'll see this pretty lady? [cheers] Can ya'll? Wow-a! [cheers] Bob Clarke has been in the motion picture industry for quite some time. Bob, I wonder if you can tell us where you came from originally.

ROBERT CLARKE: Well, originally my home is right near Amarillo. Oklahoma City.

ANNOUNCER: And whatever prompted you to go out to Hollywood to become a movie star?

ROBERT CLARKE: Well, I guess, uh, crazy ambition like anybody would have who would wanna get into this crazy business.

ANNOUNCER: I see. Did you have any background before you went to Hollywood?

ROBERT CLARKE: Yeah, I was at the University of Wisconsin in theatrical school there.

ANNOUNCER: Can you give us a list of a few of the pictures you've played in in Hollywood?

ROBERT CLARKE: Well, perhaps some of you remember *The Man from Planet X*, and the picture I did with Claire Trevor *Hard, Fast and Beautiful*, and ... uh ... more recently one that was here in Amarillo, *Girl With an Itch*. 'Course, I've been on TV.

ANNOUNCER: *Benny Goodman Story*.

ROBERT CLARKE: *Benny Goodman Story*. That was....

ANNOUNCER: [interjects] Saw that one!

ROBERT CLARKE: ...Awhile back. And been on *Sea Hunt* and of course *Dragnet* and quite a number of TV things.

ANNOUNCER: Quite a lot of TV shows and we've seen you over several of the channels here in Amarillo.

ROBERT CLARKE: Thank you, Larry. Keep lookin'.

ANNOUNCER: Oh, we'll certainly do that. And Bob, how did you ever get the idea for *The Sun Demon*?

ROBERT CLARKE: Well, it came about as a result of my having a sincere interest in pictures that are full of action and science fiction type of, uh, story. I remember the picture, the original *Jekyll and Hyde*. You probably recall?

ANNOUNCER: Oh, yes. Oldtimers remember that.

ROBERT CLARKE: The old ones remember that. Well, I got a big kick out of that as a kid. Not too big a kid. And, uh, been kind of an ambition to do something along that line and bringing ... bring it up to date, with science fiction and radiation poisoning and so on.

ANNOUNCER: Where was this picture shoot? On location?

ROBERT CLARKE: Well, this picture was made in the environs of Los Angeles, principally. We ... we went on location, uh, about a hundred miles away, but mostly around Los Angeles itself.

ANNOUNCER: How long did it take to shoot the picture, *Sun Demon*?

ROBERT CLARKE: Actually, three weeks of shooting. In the entire preparation, planning, and so on, about nine months.

ANNOUNCER: I see.

ROBERT CLARKE: There's a lot of work in there.

ANNOUNCER: I imagine so.

ROBERT CLARKE: And ... and you have to pay a lot of money for a girl [Nan

Peterson] like this, you know. Her salary is at least 50 cents an hour. [laughter]

ANNOUNCER: Well, that's about a quarter more than I make. [laughter] But Bob, we sure want to thank you for coming by, and I wonder if you would be kind now to get Mr. Brooks up here.

ROBERT CLARKE: Mr. Brooks, who I think should certainly receive a wonderful hand, as well as Mr. Doyle, who made it possible for us to be here tonight. We want to thank them and all of you wonderful folks for coming. Let me get Mr. Brooks. I'll be back in just a second.

ANNOUNCER: Okay, fine. Thank you very much. While Bob is going to get Mr. Brooks, who is the executive ... uh ... [cheers].... Oh boy! This is one of the best jobs I ever had in my life, and they gave me two Cokes and a bag of popcorn for doing the job tonight. And it was well worth it. I wonder if Nan Peterson, if you could tell us a little bit about your background. How did you ever get into moving pictures?

NAN PETERSON: Well, I come originally from Minneapolis, Larry. I've been out to Hollywood about a year, and I've always wanted to be an actress.

ANNOUNCER: You've always wanted to be an actress ever since you were a little girl. What did you do to prepare for it?

NAN PETERSON: I went to the University of Minnesota and took up radio-speech, and I spent my junior year at UCLA studying theater arts and then spent a summer at Paris studying mime.

ANNOUNCER: And then you came to Hollywood. And how did you ever meet Bob and get into this movie, *Sun Demon*.

NAN PETERSON: Um ... on a regular interview. He interviewed for the part.

ANNOUNCER: Oh, I see ... interviewed for the part.

NAN PETERSON: And I was tested for the part.

ANNOUNCER: And you made good by testing for the part. And I guess you all remember this young lady. You couldn't hardly forget her. Her first appearance in a movie was as the singer in the nightclub [scene in *The Sun Demon*]. Is that right?

NAN PETERSON: Yes.

ANNOUNCER: And from there you progressed admirably well.

NAN PETERSON: To the beach! [referring to the beach scene in *The Sun Demon* where she embraces Bob Clarke]

ANNOUNCER: [laughter] Is this your first picture, Nan?

NAN PETERSON: This was my first picture, yes.

ANNOUNCER: I understand that there's something in the works for future pictures with you.

NAN PETERSON: Yes, I'm going to do one called *Bourbon St. Blues* in New Orleans.

ANNOUNCER: Oh, in New Orleans. Wonderful.

NAN PETERSON: I'll be playing a....

ANNOUNCER: Huh? You'll be playing a....

NAN PETERSON: A strip dancer.

ANNOUNCER: A strip dancer. Oh!

NAN PETERSON: I'll have a double!

ANNOUNCER: She'll have a double...! Well, Nan, we heard during the show tonight that they're never going to go out into the Sun again. [laughter] Did you have quite a thrill making this picture with Bob?

NAN PETERSON: It was a lot of fun.

ANNOUNCER: What was the....

NAN PETERSON: [interjects] The only bad part of it: We shot all of the sequences at the beach in the morning about five o'clock and....

ANNOUNCER: [interjects] Oh my gosh!

NAN PETERSON: And the times when I had to go in the water, it was always ice cold.

ANNOUNCER: Ice cold! What was the thrilling incident while you were making the picture about the car when you parked the car at the cliff with Bob after you left the nightclub.

NAN PETERSON: Well, we almost went over the cliff!

ANNOUNCER: Almost went over the cliff!

NAN PETERSON: In fact, one time I jumped out of the car. They thought I was silly.

ANNOUNCER: They thought you were silly?

NAN PETERSON: I don't believe in suffering that much for your art.

ANNOUNCER: [laughs] Wonderful! Nan, uh,

there is Mr. Brooks, the fellow who made this world premiere possible, standing back here. Wonder if you could get him up here. Mr. Hal Brooks, who is the executive, uh, executive manager. Is that right?

HAL BROOKS: Yes, that's right.

ANNOUNCER: Executive manager at the Crossroads Theater Company. Uh, how did you ever happen to arrange for this world premiere here at the Tascosa?

HAL BROOKS: Well, we've just been most fortunate that we were selected here in Amarillo to have the picture first, and most so at the Tascosa Theater.

ANNOUNCER: Wonderful! And I'll bet it's been a bigger pleasure for you meeting Nan Peterson and Bob Clarke.

HAL BROOKS: Yes.

ANNOUNCER: And it has been for me and most of us here in the industry, uh, in local places. And we want to, uh … I know the people of Amarillo have enjoyed this picture tremendously. And, uh, I think they owe you a big vote of thanks for bringing it here.

HAL BROOKS: Well, we've been very thrilled to have them and I'd like to say now that we've been successful in talking both Bob and Nan into staying another night.

ANNOUNCER: They're going to be here….

HAL BROOKS: [interjects] They're going to be here tomorrow night.

ANNOUNCER: They're going to be here tomorrow night in person?

HAL BROOKS: Uh-huh.

ANNOUNCER: Wonderful! Well, I hope some of the folks will come back and see them.

HAL BROOKS: I hope so too.

ANNOUNCER: Fine. Thank you very much, and where did Bob go, Mr. Brooks?

HAL BROOKS: I'll see if I can find him.

ANNOUNCER: Uh, bye-bye, Mr. Brooks.

ANNOUNCER: Well, Nan, we certainly enjoyed your role in the movie tonight. Uh, Bob said it took about three….

NAN PETERSON: [screams twice loudly][26]

The archival recording of the premiere concludes with a number of screams and cheers and hollers from the crowds as the Sun Demon briefly runs into the parking lot. As a result, the film—incarnated in the personage of its title character—breaks the boundary between movie and audience. The Sun Demon invades the audience's space, moving from car to car as the recording comes to a halt.

After Clarke ran behind the concession stand and took off the mask, he brushed the sweat off of his forehead. It was time to remove the scaled claws and prepare for a night of glad-handing. A cocktail party honoring him and *The Sun Demon* began at ten that night at the Tascosa Country Club.

Among those present that evening at these events was Michael F. Price, future musician, journalist, movie reviewer, and film historian. In a 2002 email, he recalled that night well. "I was 10, going on 18, at the time. The event registered as keenly on the high-society scale as with the more typical drive-in habitués. The publicity and advertising campaigns had been extraordinarily effective, appealing both to the see-and-be-seen socialite crowd (of both country clubs, the *goyishe* Amarillo Country Club and the predominantly Jewish Tascosa Country Club)."

"We left the automobile in the staff's parking area and settled into chairs on the Tascosa's patio, adjoining the concessions building, where there was a catered buffet arrayed. In any case, the occasion was a delight. I got to meet the visiting celebrities beforehand, even got to wear (however briefly) the Sun Demon's headpiece, and my first taste of after-dark country-clubbing, all on top of a perfectly okay movie."

The Sun Demon brought 1,469 attendants on opening night; 1,343 on Saturday, August 30; 1,172 on Sunday, August 31; 482 on Monday, September 1; and 244 on Tuesday, September 2, the last day of the film's run.[27] The dropoff on the last two days was not unexpected, as weekdays (especially Tuesday through Thursday) generally brought in much smaller crowds than the weekend. Instead, the surprising day for attendance was probably August 31, a day on which Clarke and Peterson were not present in person but that was almost as strong as the two days when they were.

Blue Doyle soon mailed a "Percentage Engagement Report" to Bob Clarke which included a check for $785.84, which amounted to half to the net proceeds. The gross had been $3,061.50, but authorized deductions amounted to $1,489.81. These broke down as $660.83 for newspaper ads, $214.72 for Clarke and Peterson's airline tickets, $499.26 for radio ads and ad designs and heralds, and $15.00 for the *Attack of the Crab Monsters* rental fees.[28]

The percentage Clarke received did not include a cut of the concessions, which generated a large percentage of the profits which drive-ins made. "We didn't even bother asking Doyle for a cut of those," brother Bill Clarke said. "We knew they wouldn't give a cent of that take, so we didn't even try to get them to budge."[29]

But Bob Clarke had done well, not only in attendance but in the overall deal itself. Most drive-ins of the era preferred to pay flat fees to show the films they rented, and when they did pay percentages in 1958, they weren't usually deals for 50 percent.

Doyle was impressed enough by the film's premiere that he immediately offered to fly Clarke in his Piper Cub airplane to Dallas and screen the film for the city's Universal Studios Exchange. Clarke's wife Alyce telegrammed that his "Pillsbury commercial interview postponed until Friday 10:15 A.M. if you are interested. Good luck in Dallas. Just get the money and get the heck out. The kids miss you and I need you."[30]

Getting money in Dallas was not as easy as it had been in Amarillo, however. Clarke remembered:

> It was really hot weather, and my *God* I was sweating as I carried film cans for a few blocks to get to the Universal people. When I finally got up to speak to them, they said they had been watching me trudging down the street. That must have been a sure signal to them that I was in deep and wasn't in much of a bargaining position.[31]

Once his screening began, the response was relatively warm. Talks continued, and R.N. Wilkinson of the Dallas office later penned a letter advising:

> Pursuant to our conversation of yesterday, I wish to advise that there is a possibility of our using a picture such as your *Sun Demon* which might possibly be placed as a lower half of a double bill with a suitable companion picture for the top half. It may be possible for us to use this picture with a subject currently going into production based on the *Phantom of the Opera*.
>
> As I discussed with you yesterday, after you have been able to work on the print some our [sic] people would be interested in screening this picture on the basis of a distribution deal only. We are currently not interested in buying any small pictures outright.[32]

Clarke patiently waited for a response, hoping for a distribution deal, even if it meant a delay in receiving much-needed money.

Days went by, turning into weeks. A little over a month later, Clarke quickly seized his letter opener to tear open an envelope from F. J. A. McCarthy at Universal's New York City office. After reading several kind words, Clarke saw the news: "We had our Screening Committee look at *Sun Demon*, and they were of the opinion that this picture would not fit into our schedule of releases."[33] Clarke's heart sank, bolstered only by an appointment to screen the film for the Warner Brothers staff on the West Coast. But they passed on the film too, giving an even quicker "no" than Universal had.

Possibilities of deals with the major studios had basically crumbled, and Clarke was too leery of AIP to sign a distribution deal with them. A friend pointed him to a third option: Miller Consolidated Pictures. Two business partners started the business to compete with AIP, and offered to pair *The Sun Demon* with their own first film, *A Date with Death*. Clarke agreed, and even ended up acting in the Millers' movie.

On January 27, 1959, the film—now sporting *The Hideous Sun Demon* as its title—opened at the bottom of the *Date with Death* double bill at the indoor Plains Theater in Roswell, New Mexico. Similar to his act at the Tascosa, Clarke appeared live onstage in the Sun Demon costume. Only two days later, the double feature played the indoor Lyric Theater in Odessa, Texas. The *Odessa American* reported that Clarke would once again "wear his monster suit at the personal appearance" scheduled for the January 29 screening.[34]

Thanks to Miller Consolidated's distribution, *The Hideous Sun Demon* played in many areas of the United States and England. A number of the bookings returned Clarke's film to where it had first been screened: the drive-in theater. Of those screenings, Clarke later ruminated that, "On the lower level of exploitation, 'drive-in'-style sci-fi flicks, *Hideous Sun Demon* has certainly found its place of popularity."[35] But Clarke never intended for the film to become known as merely a drive-in horror film. Even worse was the fact that Miller Consolidated went bankrupt shortly after distributing *The Hideous Sun Demon*, meaning that Clarke never got a penny for his film from the fledgling company.

Despite its lasting cult status among horror and science-fiction film fans, *The Hideous Sun Demon* may not really be a signifier of the typical drive-in horror. Certainly some films in that category made a profit, and a smaller number generated very large grosses. Many drive-in horror films also acted as opportunities for their producer-directors to move onto bigger budget projects. None of these results occurred for Robert Clarke or his film.

But the history of *The Hideous Sun Demon* illustrates the rocky path and various travails that a drive-in horror film could encounter from its origins to its destinations. And its premiere in Amarillo acts as a timepiece of an event that for most drive-in films no longer exists: a record of opening night at an "ozoner." The hollers, the laughs and the screams, all yelped out of a sea of automobiles parked in West Texas at the height of the drive-in's popularity.

NOTES

1. Arkoff, Samuel Z. *Flying Through Hollywood by the Seat of My Pants*. New York: Random House, 1994: p. 59.
2. Cohen, Herman. Quoted in *The Horror of It All*. [Documentary Film] MPI Home Video, 1991.
3. Segrave, Kerry. *Drive-in Theaters: A History from Their Inception in 1933*. Jefferson NC: McFarland, 1992: p. 59.
4. *Ibid*, p. 91-92.
5. Arkoff, p. 59
6. Clarke, Robert. Interview with Gary D. Rhodes. 15 Aug. 2000.
7. *Ibid*.
8. *Ibid*.
9. *Ibid*.
10. *Ibid*.
11. Parker, Ray. "Horror Films Lure Teeners." *Los Angeles Herald and Express*, 9 June 1958.
12. *Ibid*.
13. Parker, Ray. "Recipe—Monsters and Plenty of Gore: Horror Films Classed as Mod-

ern Type Fairy Tales." *Los Angeles Herald and Express,* 11 June 1958.

14. Clarke, William. Interview with Gary Rhodes. 23 Nov. 2000.

15. *Ibid.*

16. Undated clipping in the *Hideous Sun Demon* scrapbook kept by Robert Clarke.

17. Herald preserved in the *Hideous Sun Demon* scrapbook kept by Robert Clarke.

18. Ad copy preserved in the *Hideous Sun Demon* scrapbook kept by Robert Clarke.

19. Ad copy preserved in the *Hideous Sun Demon* scrapbook kept by Robert Clarke.

20. Ad copy preserved in the *Hideous Sun Demon* scrapbook kept by Robert Clarke.

21. Undated, unidentified press item preserved in the *Hideous Sun Demon* scrapbook kept by Robert Clarke.

22. Clarke, William. Interview with Gary Rhodes. 23 Nov. 2000.

23. McReynolds, Bill. *Amarillo Daily News*. Aug. 29, 1958.

24. Telegram preserved in the *Hideous Sun Demon* scrapbook kept by Robert Clarke.

25. Clarke, William. Interview with Gary Rhodes. 23 Nov. 2000.

26. The recording of the film's premiere is preserved in the collection of Robert Clarke.

27. "Percentage Engagement Report" preserved in the *Hideous Sun Demon* scrapbook kept by Robert Clarke.

28. *Ibid.*

29. Clarke, William. Interview with Gary Rhodes. 23 Nov. 2000.

30. Telegram preserved in the *Hideous Sun Demon* scrapbook kept by Robert Clarke.

31. Clarke, Robert. Interview with Gary D. Rhodes. 15 Aug. 2000.

32. Letter from R. N. Wilkinson to Robert Clarke. Dated September 5, 1958. Preserved in the *Hideous Sun Demon* scrapbook kept by Robert Clarke.

33. Letter from F.J.A. McCarthy to Robert Clarke. Dated October 8, 1958. Preserved in the *Hideous Sun Demon* scrapbook kept by Robert Clarke.

34. "Actors to Appear in Odessa." *The Odessa American* 29 Jan. 1958: p. 2.

35. Clarke, Robert and Tom Weaver. *To "B" or Not to "B": A Film Actor's Odyssey*. Baltimore MD: Midnight Marquee Press, 1996: p. 198.

Ideology and Style in the Double Feature *I Married a Monster from Outer Space* and *Curse of the Demon*

Michael Lee

This essay undertakes the problem of looking at two films which played at drive-in theaters and have already enjoyed a fair amount of scholarly attention, Jacques Tourneur's last horror film *Curse of the Demon* (originally released in Britain as *Night of the Demon*, 1957) and American horror maven Gene Fowler, Jr.'s, *I Married a Monster from Outer Space* (1958). These two films merited attention precisely because they both enjoyed popular and critical success at a time when many historians feel that the horror genre had entered into a fallow period. The late 1950s witnessed few filmmakers of auteur status working within the horror genre. Tourneur, by virtue of his superb work with producer Val Lewton at RKO during the previous decade on such films as *Cat People* (1942) and *I Walked with a Zombie* (1943), and Gene Fowler Jr., who had completed his influential film *I Was a Teenage Werewolf* (1957), provided fans with some of the more interesting drive-in fare of the period, and certainly rank among the closest the genre had to auteur status directors. What brings these two films together and justifies a joint critical revisiting is their appearance on double bills at drive-ins from coast to coast.[1] What this essay seeks to explore is the question of what students of the genre might learn from exploring the commonalties and dissimilarities of two radically different films which won the admiration of the same audience. Historians of the horror genre generally emphasize a periodic understanding of the genre and highlight dissimilarities between genre films of each succeeding decade. By looking at one throwback to a former style and one film which illustrates the succeeding style, we may find some grounds for caution in continually replicating periodized models of horror history rather than looking for similarities which bind dissimilar films.

Curse of the Demon marks in many ways the last gasp for the Tourneur-Lewton style of understated horror film which had enjoyed such tremendous popularity during the 1940s. More than an exemplar of the British horror renaissance which was spearheaded by Hammer Films and visionary director Terence Fisher with which it shares some stylistic territory and a certain urbane British sensibility, *Curse of the Demon* belongs to the 1940s style of RKO's Lewton unit thanks to Tourneur's decisive participation. By contrast, *I Married a Monster from Outer Space* provides a fairly typical example of the dominant style of giddy alien invasion films directed toward a youth audience and clearly marked by anxieties unique to America during the early years of the Cold War. The difference in generic priorities between the two films are many and should be discussed one by one, but here is a list of key differences: (1) *Curse of the Demon* suggests rather than depicts its central horrors, while Fowler's film offers numerous visual thrills and most certainly depicts the aliens. (2) Tourneur's film, when it failed to deliver explicit visual horrors, ran afoul of its own producer, who ordered the addition of material shot without Tourneur's participation. Fowler served as producer and director on his film and naturally had no such difficulties. (3) The protagonist in *I Married a Monster from Outer Space* is a young woman comparable in age and class to the target drive-in audience, Tourneur's protagonist is a middle-aged man and established authority figure. (4) Sex, a popular topic with drive-in audiences, is a central concern in Fowler's film. Issues of gender and sexuality lie on the extreme periphery of Tourneur's film. (5) The two films handle the re-establishment of a "normal" order, or status quo presumably operative before the films began, differently on the surface. This last dissimilarity, the essay will conclude, is misleading. Beneath the surface of the narrative, the two films share common misgivings with the youth audience of America about the power of mainstream institutions to protect society from disorder.

During the 1950s, Britain replaced the United States as the most influential nation producing horror films. Tiny Sabre Pictures' contribution to the British horror renaissance appeared in 1957 under the title *Night of the Demon*, a stylish reworking of Montague R. James' *Casting the Runes*. Jacques Tourneur, whose career during the 1950s saw him drifting from studio to studio shaping various Western and espionage projects into solid "B" pictures, agreed to direct. He found the supernatural topic of the script very much to his liking, being a believer in the supernatural himself.[2]

The story of *Curse of the Demon* involves an investigation by scientists into the activities of an English devil cult led by Julian Karswell (Niall MacGinnis). The bulk of that investigation will be conducted by Dr. John Holden (Dana Andrews), an American expert in England for an international conference on the supernatural. Initially the investigation belongs to Professor Harrington (Maurice Denham). The film opens with Harrington driving to see Karswell through a fog-shrouded woodland in rural England.

Tourneur and director of photography Tod Scaife craft a haunting and memorable sequence as every tree takes on an ominous aspect. The trees in the foreground of each shot blot out the light of Harrington's headlights as he careens past and in so doing fairly crackle with menace. A running theme in the script is the light of reason and the shadows that light can cast on truth. The headlights and shadowy silhouettes of trees provide a fine visual foreshadowing of that theme. Clifton Parker, who scored the film, presents a romanticized frenzy of subdued anxiety which lends a wonderful urgency to the film's opening. Taken as a whole, this wordless sequence stands with some of Tourneur's best work.

Arriving at Karswell's palatial estate, Harrington insists on seeing Dr. Karswell despite the protests of a domestic. Karswell leaves his game of cribbage with his dotty mother (Athene Seyler) to confer with Harrington. We learn that Harrington has led an investigation of Karswell's doings and has now come to apologize, promise to discontinue the investigation and ask for Karswell to "call it off." Karswell makes vague assurances promising only to do what he can. Harrington thanks the doctor profusely and departs. The

exchange has many cryptic elements which leave first-time viewers uncertain. For example, the "it" Harrington wants called off is not explained, but clearly has this man of science frightened in the extreme. His drive home, while less urgent than his earlier mission, still drips with foreboding thanks to more lovely photography and Parker's brooding score.

The next scene is crucial to this discussion, as it contains the first amendment to the film mandated by producer Hal E. Chester. Harrington arrives at home, parks his car in the garage, then sees an undulating patch of strangely illuminated fog high in the trees. He reacts in horror, returns to his car and hastily pulls out of the garage. Panic-stricken, he backs into a telephone pole, bringing hot electrical wires down around his wrecked vehicle. The professor exits the vehicle in terror and dies horribly on the wires while threatened by some unseen force. Unseen, that is, had Tourneur had his way. At this point, we see a huge demon reach down and claw the professor to death. Without Tourneur's cooperation, shots of a huge demon armed with a spray of talons for hands were inserted not only into the scene described above but at the film's climax as well.[3]

Tourneur must have felt a keen sense of history repeating. Back in 1942, RKO's chief of production Charles Koerner ordered Tourneur to insert footage of a black panther into *Cat People*, thus damaging that film's delicate ambiguity regarding the supernatural. Without five shots of a hideous demon which were inserted into the sequence of events described above, the viewer would have only uncertainty about the balance of power between the supernatural and reason. With them, reason's posture is drastically weakened.

While many film fans decry the damage done to Tourneur's work by producer Chester, Chris Fujiwara, in his important monograph on Tourneur, makes the best case possible for the demon's appearance in the film by pointing out the many times that Tourneur allows the camera to show the audience materials in a manner distorted by the subjective perspective of a character (or, in one interesting case, by simply showing the viewer something that could not be there by having a mysterious hand appear on a banister only to have the next shot reveal that no one could be in possession of that hand). That shot is in no way an error of continuity, but part of Tourneur's calculated effort to foster a sense of uncertainty and menace inspired by unexplainable events. Tourneur's camera is not a wholly trustworthy nor objective observer at several crucial junctions, which Fujiwara illustrates in his book.[4] This study need not linger long on purely aesthetic issues of the sort Fujiwara discusses so persuasively. The importance of the addition of visual horror merely serves to illustrate how, in the opinions of financially interested parties such as Chester and the distributors of the film who supported him, the presentation of explicit visuals of a horrific nature were necessary for the picture's success in the present commercial environment. The Tourneur-Lewton style was simply too old-fashioned for the new, teen-dominated market for horror.

I Married a Monster from Outer Space suffered from no demands for re-shooting or insertions. Within two minutes of the film's opening, a scene depicting a group of male friends drinking at a roadhouse on the eve of the nuptials of their friend Bill's (Tom Tryon), Bill heads home from the proceedings only to discover what appears to be a dead body on the road. He stops to investigate only to be attacked from behind by a glowing space alien with huge menacing hands which then takes the form of a vapor and inhabits Bill's body. The appearance of the glowing alien so early in the film served the distributor's purposes and saved director-producer Gene Fowler, Jr., considerable trouble during post-production. Moreover, similar giddy visual thrills pepper the film's entire duration and include: a streetwalker disintegrated by a laser gun, a point-of-view shot for a puppy as it is strangled by its owner, an alien squirting black liquid from a severed tube emerging from its chest, alien faces superimposed over the human faces of hosts when illuminated by lightning, and alien appendages transformed into a lumpy goo which oozes from shirt sleeves and collars.

From its opening shot, *I Married a Monster from Outer Space* reveals the extent to which Fowler understood the special needs the drive-in placed on filmmakers. After a nice credit sequence showing the words of the credits seemingly aimed at the Earth from more remote reaches of space like an invasion fleet of consonants and vowels, Fowler dissolves to a crane shot high over the woods around a sleepy California roadhouse. The camera pans left as though the area lies under some surveillance from above. The ethereal music of the credits sounds like any number of other credit cues composed for science fiction films with ominous warblings of electronic origin, in this case a theremin. This music fades into a "big band" number presumably on a juke box within the roadhouse. As the camera continues to pan left, it also starts to drop to eye level. We see a pair of men in medium shot as they emerge from a car that has just pulled up to the roadhouse. One of the men sneaks up on a convertible in which two teens are making out with enthusiasm. He slaps the front door of the convertible with the intention of startling the couple, but they don't react. Here Fowler makes his first cut of the film. In this interesting establishing shot, Fowler self-reflexively underscores the problem facing producers of entertainments configured for teens at the drive-in. How can you scare kids who have something better to do than watch your moving picture? With a shrug, Fowler's anonymous man enters the roadhouse, having failed to scare the smooching teens, and the story begins in earnest. The entire film can be seen as Fowler's effort to do better than the man in the opening at attracting the attention of his predominately teen audience.

Giddy visual effects constitute only part of Fowler's efforts, however: Fowler also employs sex to keep his youthful audience mollified. Once the alien inhabits Bill, the film Pocusses on Bill's fiancée Marge (Gloria Talbott). We first see her fretting on her wedding day. Bill is extremely late for the wedding, and Marge can't hide her exasperation. Perhaps 20 years old, Marge offers an ideal protagonist for a film aimed at teens. Madison Avenue has long known that young people prefer to watch the doings of young people slightly older than themselves. A sterling recent example of this marketing strategy can be seen in the *Barney* television show where the plush, purple dinosaur cavorts with children awkwardly too old actually to watch his show yet pretending with all their might to love him deeply. Marge, on the verge of marriage as the film begins and newlywed for most of its duration, is slightly further along life's path than the target audience of dating teens, thus lending her concerns an added urgency.

Bill proves an inattentive husband and marriage disappoints poor Marge. Bill fails, for example, to open Marge's car door after they arrive at the hotel where they'll spend their wedding night. "Bill," she calls. "I know you've been absent minded lately, but you can't have a honeymoon without a bride." The subsequent wedding night finds Bill unnaturally distant from his bride. Among the many indications that something is now wrong with Bill (such as his uncanny ability to see in the dark, the fact that dogs now hate him, and his newly acquired aversion to alcohol) his inability to impregnate Marge. Harry Benshoff, in his landmark study *Monsters in the Closet: Homosexuality and the Horror Film*, cites *I Married a Monster from Outer Space* as an example of a film which indulges in a common form of 1950s double coding. On the one hand, the film operates as an allegory on Communist infiltration, but on another level the aliens are coded as homosexual.[5] The aliens are entirely male, the females of their kind having died out along with their Sun. Moreover, they distinctly prefer male company. In a telling exchange after Bill's identity as a space monster is in the open, Marge asks Bill, "Did you love your women before they died?" Bill responds listlessly. "Love? No, we came together for breeding purposes only." For most of the film, Bill leads a double life. On the one hand, he is married and having sex with his young wife, although he presumably doesn't enjoy it much; while on the other hand he and his kind secretly pose a terrible threat to the orderly unfolding of heterosexual hegemony on Earth.

The sexual theme of the film reaches fever pitch when Marge seeks the advice of Dr. Wayne. He reassures her that there's nothing wrong with her and no reason why she can't give birth to a dozen children. Suddenly the subject moves to Bill: Dr. Wayne suggests that Bill come see him. In a scene that draws Bill's sexual potency into question, Marge delivers the doctor's message to Bill, who tries to appear calm but reveals his true feelings by

inadvertently smashing a metal cigarette lighter in his hand. Just then, Sam, one of Bill's old drinking buddies, comes to the door. Sam has recently been inhabited by an alien too, and has dropped by to deliver the message that he's "one of them." The two men share a few grins as Marge heads to bed alone. Instead of joining his wife, Bill heads back to the spaceship in what Benshoff hints might be seen as a sequence coded to resemble homosexuals cruising a park after dark.

Marge follows Bill and has her worst fears about him confirmed. Terrified, she rushes into town. She first finds herself in a bar which Bill and his friends used to frequent before they became alien hosts. Among the patrons present that night, we meet a women of ill repute. This minor character, who will be disintegrated by the aliens later—their way of dealing with a human female interested in sex rather than breeding, one might suppose—serves to clarify for the viewer what Marge is not. Marge's conventional sexual conduct is both demarcated and sanctioned through the introduction of her fallen opposite. For much of its middle, the film fixates on the formation of both attractive and unattractive male and female identities, rendering it ideally suited for a teen audience similarly preoccupied with forming their own sexual identities in a confusingly repressive society.

Fowler's film pleased both audiences and critics and proved a modest hit. Its brisk pace, visual thrills, reasonably strong performances, and appealing theme (marrying sexual preoccupations with a Communist infiltration allegory) account for

both its enduring popularity and consistent three-star ratings from journalistic critics. While much of the plot is a rehash of territory previously covered in *Invasion of the Body Snatchers* (1956), the film's sexual concerns and—rare for the genre—female protagonist bring a degree of vitality to the somewhat generic story line.

Curse of the Demon also enjoyed considerable popularity, but clearly for different reasons, reasons which may expand our understanding of what teen audiences craved in a horror picture. Dana Andrews as Holden leers at the extraordinarily beautiful Peggy Cummins in her role as Joanna Harrington, the deceased professor's niece, and makes wolfish cracks to her even minutes after learning of the tragedy of her uncle's death; but overall, the film is old-fashioned in its general lack of sexual content. Interestingly, the film supports Benshoff's theory that many horror films rely on queer signifiers to differentiate the monstrous from the normal. MacGinnis' mincingly eccentric performance as Karswell, coupled with the middle-aged, unmarried character living with his mother, could all be read as coded queer. Karswell's mother at one point informs Joanna that her son "really ought to be married but he's so fussy." Beyond this reference to Karswell's lack of amorous initiative and Holden's wolfishness, the film navigates well clear of sexual issues.

The protagonist here, unlike Marge, is considerably older than the target audience and more importantly an authority figure. The moment when we first see Holden works extremely well. Trying to catch some sleep on a transatlantic flight, Holden covers his face with a newspaper. A picture of Holden appears on the newspaper with the headline "Prominent Psychologist Flies to London for International Convention." While this gesture serves to introduce us to the principle character, it also serves to critique our protagonist. Holden at that moment is no more detailed than his photograph. A two-dimensional man inhabiting a three-dimensional world, handicapped by his title "prominent psychologist."

Dr. Holden's smug confidence in his scientific expertise finds a lovely illustration in a scene shared with Joanna early in the film. Prof. Harrington is dead, and while the official cause of death names an automobile accident involving power lines, his niece is unconvinced and feels Karswell may be involved. "His body was mutilated horribly as though by wild animals," she reports to Holden. She reads to the doctor from her uncle's diary a gripping tale of his mounting suspicion that he has been cursed. Holden should be interested, as Karswell has previously placed him under the same curse. Instead, Holden doesn't so much as allow Joanna to finish reading her uncle's chronicle before punctuating her reading dismissively with psychological jargon. At one point he interrupts her, saying, "As a doctor, I can assure you, you're wrong. It's a pure case of auto-suggestion." His certainty seems wholly unjustified, partly because the audience has seen for ourselves that he's wrong, but more importantly he has no more first-hand experience with the case than Joanna—in fact *less*, as at least she read her uncle's first-hand account of events.

Put off by Holden's condescension, Joanna finally protests, pointing out that she too majored in psychology. She then states one of the important themes of the film, pointing out that her contact with children through her work as a kindergarten teacher has exposed her to the childlike capacity for simple belief and the honesty with which children fear the dark. She conjectures that adult efforts to soothe their childish fears may amount to fooling them. Through his extensive use of darkness and shadow to generate menace, Tourneur provides an artful visual demonstration of her position throughout the film as the audience is encouraged to relive childhood fears of the dark. Tourneur's camera serves Joanna, not Holden.

The insufferably self-assured Holden engages in similar exchanges with other characters. His colleague at the international conference, Mark O'Brien (Liam Redmond), responds to a telling question posed by Holden.

Holden: "skepticism—that's the proper position for the scientist, isn't it, O'Brien?"

"Sometimes," O'Brien responds simply and succinctly. O'Brien serves as the balanced figure between the credulity of Kumar, an expert in the occult from India who reports that he absolutely believes in demons, and Holden, who believes in nothing which he has not sensed for himself.

O'Brien points out to Holden the striking similarities between a drawing of a demon by the illiterate farmer Rand Hobart, one of Karswell's followers who survived Karswell's curse by passing it on to a brother cultist, and those of similar demons depicted in the lore of various ancient civilizations. Holden's thoughtless response to O'Brien's iconographic evidence takes the form of a single word: "Bunk." O'Brien continues, "I know the value of the cold light of reason. I also know the deep shadows that light can cast." In the end, O'Brien is the perfect foil for Holden. He neither believes nor disbelieves Karswell's power barring definitive evidence one way or the other. Holden's mind is made up before the evidence comes in. At one point, the affable

Karswell says to Holden, "But perhaps I could persuade you?" Holden answers bluntly, "I'm not open to persuasion." Karswell persists, "But a scientist *should* have an open mind." Close-mindedness serves as the *bête noir* in Tourneur's horror pictures.

Interestingly that's the problem Holden shares with many of the ill-fated characters throughout the Lewton cycle. Whether certain of the supernatural (like Irena in *Cat People*, or Wesley Rand in *I Walked with a Zombie*—two characters effectively doomed by their belief in the supernatural) or certain of the daylight world of appearances (like Oliver in *Cat People*, or Paul Holland in *I Walked with a Zombie*—two characters who suffer and inadvertently facilitate tragedy through the confidence in reason), certainties in any form surely lead to suffering within the twilight world Lewton and Tourneur sought to craft in those earlier films. And just like the flexible characters whose minds remain open in those earlier films, the open-minded O'Brien steers well clear of mishap in *Curse of the Demon*.

While an old-fashioned horror film in many ways, *Curse of the Demon* disrupts one convention of the classic horror model. Ordinarily, figures of authority often drawn from the ranks of scientists help the forces of order gather expertise sufficient to destroy the film's force of disorder, most usually a monster.[6] In *Curse of the Demon*, the chief authority figure of the film does everything in his power not to gather information needed in restoring order. In the process, his identity as an authority trickles to nothing as the curse begins to erode his confidence and convince him of his imminent doom. In the end, Karswell's curse works at cross purposes with his ambition and acts to break up Holden's steadfast unwillingness to investigate the curse with seriousness, although most of the credit for progress toward thwarting Karswell goes to O'Brien and Ms. Harrington rather than Holden himself who merely follows leads reluctantly and at the prodding of his allies.

At the film's close, Holden gives himself over to uncertainty. Minutes before the appointed time when Karswell's demon should kill him, Holden manages to pass the curse back to Karswell. Karswell then pursues a parchment containing runic symbols onto railroad tracks (an action mandated by the curse itself). He looks in the direction of an oncoming train, and a strangely illuminated swirl of mist akin to the one Harrington saw earlier mingles with the smoke from the locomotive. Karswell dies on the tracks. Of course, Chester insisted on showing us the demon kill Karswell, although the film proceeds as though observers present at the railway station did not see the huge creature ripping at the hapless cult leader.[7] The official cause of death, we can rest assured, will mention only that Karswell was struck by a train and dragged. Holden considers walking over and investigating for himself, but he balks. Joanna opines, "Perhaps it's better not to know." Seemingly in agreement with her, Holden walks away from the scene, unsure of Karswell's fate and perhaps unsure in a more global sense as well. For the first time in the film, Holden keeps his opinion to himself and leaves us unsure at least about his acceptance or refusal of Joanna's preference for uncertainty.

The appeal for the youthful audience in this film surely doesn't stem from the clunky demon's manifestations or any other visual thrills. The appeal flows from the film's systematic destruction of certitude rooted in conventional authority. Holden serves not merely to represent himself, a man confident in his senses and their ability to grasp the real. He serves as an emblem for all adults who place faith in their adult credentials and lay claim to certainty, all "grown-ups" who assure children that the darkness holds no danger without actually investigating open-mindedly the space that holds the threatening dark. The pleasure for rebellious teens lies in the film's confirmation of their suspicion that adults with fancy degrees and elaborate theories are full of beans.

Disabling the value of authority also serves as an important concern in *I Married a Monster from Outer Space* and offers the most important link between these two films. Marge, like Holden, lives out a terrible nightmare. Her first move to deal with her situation once she has taken hold of her instinct to panic sees her turning to authority figures. After the jolt of seeing Bill's husk emptied of its alien occupant standing motionless and lifeless outside an alien spacecraft, Marge rushes into town. There she first meets the occupants of the barroom, including her fallen opposite. When this band of derelicts fails to help her, she turns to her godfather, who happens to be the sheriff of Norrisville, the town where the story is set. He wavers between gentle support and condescension. His promise of assistance culminates in his instruction that she return home to Bill. When Marge protests, he insists by gently pointing out how dangerous it might be to arouse Bill's suspicions. After Marge leaves, lightning reflecting on the sheriff's face reveals that Marge's kindly godfather also serves as host to an alien.

The figures and institutions of authority in Norrisville either fail Marge, or actively work to undermine her efforts on behalf of imperiled humanity. The Western Union man tears up her telegram to the FBI as soon as she leaves the office. The telephone company is compromised as Marge repeatedly learns that all lines to Washington are busy (an obvious echo of a similar event in *Invasion of the Body Snatchers*). When they're not committing murder, the police force of Norrisville block Marge's effort to drive to a neighboring town to seek help. As a last resort, Marge returns to Dr. Wayne's office and confides her suspicions. He both believes her and isn't an alien. He marshals a small army of men rounded up in the maternity ward. These potent men who have recently sired children are clearly not like Bill and the other alien hosts. Yet Dr. Wayne's plan fails in all of its details. The aliens are immune to bullets, and the men are otherwise unarmed. Only the surprising intervention of a German Shepherd, who courageously slinks up to one of the aliens and bites a valve on its chest, prompting a spew of black fluid, saves the day. This hitherto unknown weakness, discovered by complete happenstance, and seemingly a trope on a Rin Tin Tin film, brings *I Married a Monster from Outer Space* to an unlikely climax that leaves the film with no human to admire except the youthful Marge. Unlike so many films dealing with alien invasions made during the 1950s where the forces of the government solve the crisis, *I Married a Monster from Outer Space* sees this invasion thwarted by a resolute young woman perhaps in her late teens or early twenties and a lucky dog which chances upon the aliens' weakness. Not even the outstandingly paranoid *Invasion of the Body Snatchers* can boast a bleaker depiction of conventional authority and its complete inability to deal with crises.

The success of this strange double feature comprised of two seemingly dissimilar films teaches us that while the classic archetype of Val Lewton's era comprised of suggested horror may be dead as of 1958, the sense of paranoia concerning established authority would maintain its appeal for a significant number of teens. Both films enjoy minor classic status because they delegitimize the normative forces of order in society. For American youth on the verge of social upheaval and prepared to question the legitimacy of conventional authority on a previously unheard-of scale, these two texts resonate with one another interestingly. They could hardly be more different in tone, but both succeed precisely because they demonstrate the failure of adult society with its certainties to contain real threats. Marge, the unlikely heroine, blocks an alien invasion despite the meddlings and many failings of adult society. Holden, the embodiment of a calcified view that authority figures know all, plays out the unraveling of his position. Visual thrills were a preoccupation for the teen-centered genre of drive-in horror films. However, the success of this twin bill may prompt students of the genre's history to privilege ideological consistencies which remain important over a period of many decades rather than looking toward purely stylistic understandings of the horror genre.

NOTES

1. Regional distributors were entitled to pair films as they saw fit. This author has identified at least two other second features which ran with *I Married a Monster from Outer Space*. One common pairing was with *The Blob*. Another common pairing, perhaps even more common than the pairing under discussion here, was with Hammer's *The Curse of Frankenstein*.

2. Jacques Tourneur, "Propos" *Positif* (November, 1971) p. 15.

3. Chris Fujiwara, *The Cinema of Nightfall* (Jefferson, NC: McFarland, 1998) p. 246.

4. Ibid, 245–55.

5. Harry Benshoff, *Monsters in the Closet: Homosexuality and the Horror Film*. (Manchester: Manchester University Press, 1997) 130–32.

6. For a superb discussion of classic horror narrative patterns, see Andrew Tudor, *Monsters and Mad Scientists: A Cultural History of the Horror Movie* (Oxford: Basil Blackwell, 1989).

7. In an interview with Joel Siegel, Tourneur claimed that he wanted to insert only four frames of the demon ripping at Karswell: "Boom, boom—did I see it or didn't I? People would have to sit through it a second time to be sure of what they saw." Joel Siegel, "Tourneur Remembers," *Cinefantastique* 2, (1973) p. 24–25.

6

The Legacy of *Last House on the Left*

Steven Jay Schneider

> In *Last House*, we set out to show violence the way we thought it really was, and to show the dark underbelly of the Hollywood genre. We consciously took all the B movie conventions and stood them on their heads ... so that just when you thought the shot would cut away, it didn't. Someone gets stabbed, but then they get back up and start crawling ... death becomes much more protracted and sexual. That was all a breaking of convention.
>
> —Wes Craven[1]

> My feeling about *Last House on the Left* is that it was a stroke of genius. It was a defining moment in film history, and Wes and Sean had the creative foresight that it takes to break ground. When you talk about breaking ground, you talk about Picasso, or about certain musicians who led the way, who broke with tradition and began a new form of the arts. I put *Last House on the Left* in the same category.... It almost took hindsight to be able to appreciate the vision, the ground-breaking genius behind the concept.
>
> —Lucy Grantham[2]

I. Introduction

In the fall of 1971, a 32-year-old ex–English Lit professor with a Masters degree in Philosophy by the name of Wes Craven directed his first feature film, a low-budget drive-in horror production called, by turns, *Sex Crime of the Century*, *Night of Vengeance*, *The Men's Room*, *Krug & Company* and finally *Last House on the Left*. Craven and the producer of the film, Sean S. Cunningham (who would go on to direct *Friday the 13th*), had previously collaborated on a soft-core pseudo-documentary porn flick, *Together* (a.k.a. *Sensual Paradise*, 1971; now believed to be lost), starring a pre–Ivory Snow Girl, pre–*Behind the Green Door* Marilyn Chambers. *Together* did surprisingly well at the box office, and the financiers backing the project, Hallmark Releasing Corporation, rewarded the pair with an informal offer to make "some drive-in fodder, a no-holds-barred horror movie."[3]

Though he never envisioned himself a horror director, Craven jumped at the hard-to-come-by opportunity. He began writing almost immediately, and completed

"To Avoid Fainting Keep Repeating, It's Only a Movie ... Only a Movie ... Only a Movie ... Only a Movie"—advertising for *Last House on the Left*.

his 60-page script in less than two weeks. *Last House* was shot mostly in Westport, Connecticut (a number of scenes were actually filmed at Cunningham's mother's home), with largely unknown actors, almost no money and an inexperienced crew (including a young production assistant by the name of Steve Miner, future director of *Friday the 13th* Parts *Two* and *Three* and *Halloween H20*). After four arduous weeks of shooting, Craven spent approximately five months editing the film, trying desperately to compensate for numerous gaps in the master shots. Finally, on July 11, 1972, *Last House on the Left* made its debut at a pair of Hallmark-owned drive-ins in rural Massachusetts. The horror film genre would never be the same.

Before the "mock-doc" pretensions of *The Texas Chain Saw Massacre*, *Snuff* and *The Blair Witch Project*, before the codified stalker rites of *Halloween*, *Prom Night* and *Scream*, before the mainstream splatter of *Evil Dead*, *The Re-Animator*, and *Dead Alive*, *Last House on the Left* bombarded audiences with a volatile mixture of sadistic sex, realistic violence and misplaced humor. In no small part due to a brilliantly conceived exploitation ad campaign, the film attracted large crowds at drive-ins and cinemas across the United States, and later Europe. But response to the film was by no means universally positive; quite the contrary. Unsuspecting middle-class moviegoers in particular were furious, often demanding that *Last House* be removed from theaters and their owners subjected to prosecution. Aside from a couple of important defenses by reviewer Roger Ebert and cineaste Robin Wood, critics generally excoriated *Last House*. Everyone from the Motion Picture Association of America to community censorship boards to individual projectionists had a hand in cutting down the film, deleting entire scenes and severely editing others to the point where nobody knows for certain whether a wholly intact print even exists. Today, *Last House* has a kind of mythical status among horror fans, its infamy attested to by the fact that, despite its popularity, it has never been shown on television ... network *or* cable. In the United Kingdom, *Last House* remains banned on video, following a 1974 ruling by the British Board of Film Censorship. With all of the controversy surrounding the film, it comes as something of a surprise to learn that a definitive investigation of *Last House*'s place in the history of the horror genre has yet to appear. What follows is as an initial attempt to correct that deficiency by examining the legacy of *Last House on the Left*—a drive-in feature that made horror movie history.

Before going any further, it would benefit us to summarize briefly the plot of *Last House*, which Craven based (rather loosely, even he admits) on Ingmar Bergman's Academy Award–winning film, *The Virgin Spring* (*Jungfrukällan*, 1960). (We shall have more to say about the nature of the relationship between these two pictures below.) Bergman's film which the opening credits explain is itself "based on a fourteenth century Swedish legend," tells the tale of Karin (Birgitta Pettersson), the naïve, virginal daughter of a prosperous farm family who, accompanied by a pregnant servant girl, sets off through the forest on a religious pilgrimage. En route, the pair get separated, and Karin is ensnared by a trio of goatherds. While the youngest of the trio, an innocent boy, watches in disgust, the other two rape and then kill her. In an ironic twist of fate, the herdsmen later seek refuge from the cold at the girl's parents' home, and are suspected of murder when one of them attempts to sell back a distinctive item of Karin's clothing.

After the father (Max von Sydow) has his fears confirmed by the servant girl, who bore witness to the crime and has finally made her way back to the farm, he exacts a murderous revenge on his three lodgers, only to plead to God for forgiveness. These pleas occasion the eponymous "virgin spring" to miraculously burst forth from the spot where his daughter was killed.

In *Last House on the Left*, Mari Collingwood (Sandra Cassell), the virginal—though perhaps not wholly innocent—daughter of a bourgeois Connecticut family, takes off with her rebellious friend Phyllis Stone (Lucy Grantham) to see a rock concert by a violent group called Bloodlust. Looking to score some pot before the show, they are lured to the hideout of four dangerous criminals: the leader, Krug Stillo (David Hess), his junkie son Junior (Marc Scheffler), his buddy Fred "Weasel" Padowski (played by prolific porn actor, director and producer Fred Lincoln) and his bisexual, proto-feminist girlfriend Sadie (Jeramie Rain). Stuffing the young ladies into the trunk of their car, the gang take off the next morning, but are forced to pull over when the vehicle breaks down, ironically and unbeknownst to them right across the street from Mari's parents' house. The criminals drag their terrified prisoners into the woods nearby, where they are, in the words of David Szulkin, "subject[ed] ... to a harrowing ordeal of sexual torture and humiliation. Krug leads the vicious game, which includes forced urination and sadomasochism, while Weasel and Sadie hoot and cheer him on."[4] Junior is the only one who refuses to join in, and pleads with his father to desist when things turn violent. Phyllis eventually breaks free, but is stabbed in the lower back by Weasel just as she reaches the end of the woods. Together with Krug and Sadie, Weasel savagely attacks Phyllis as she tries in vain to crawl away. Stabbing her repeatedly while she lies helpless on the ground, the three eventually (in some deleted but famous footage) disembowel her.

Meanwhile, Mari has talked Junior into helping her escape, giving him a peace-symbol necklace she only just received from her parents for her seventeenth birthday. As the pair make their way through the forest, they run into a bloody Krug and company by the edge of a pond. In a terrifying series of events, Krug carves his name into Mari's chest with a switchblade, rapes her and then shoots her as she walks, traumatized, into the water. A short while later, the murderers (and Junior) turn up at the front door of the Collingwood residence, hoping to use the phone to call a mechanic. Mr. and Mrs. Collingwood (soap opera regulars Gaylord St. James and Cynthia Carr) invite the gang to stay overnight, only to become suspicious when they notice their daughter's necklace hanging from Junior's neck. Overhearing a conversation between Krug and Junior, the Collingwoods' worst fears are realized. Unable to save Mari, whose body they find by the edge of the pond, they embark on a gruesome course of revenge.

Weasel is first, the victim of an oral "Bobbitt"-ing: Estelle Collingwood bites off his member during a session of fellatio. Junior winds up committing suicide after Krug orders him to shoot himself in the mouth with the gun he originally had aimed in the other direction. And Sadie accidentally falls into the backyard swimming pool while engaged in a struggle with Estelle, who proceeds to slash her throat at the same time John Collingwood decapitates Krug with a chainsaw. Finally, at the film's end, "Mr. and Mrs. Collingwood are left bloodied and dazed, exhausted and seemingly debased by their own violence."[5] These same words—"exhausted and seemingly debased"—describe pretty accurately how most viewers feel after watching *Last House on the Left*. As we shall see, this is no accident. Rather, it is an intended effect of the director, which begs the question how and why such a film could possibly have succeeded at the box office. And *Last House did* succeed, making it all the way to #3 on *Variety*'s list of top-grossing movies in December 1973, almost a year and a half after its initial release!

II. Production History

Last House certainly wasn't the first horror film to be made on the cheap by an independent studio, a green director and a cast of mostly unknowns. Nor was it the first horror film to showcase rape, gore and bloody revenge. Heck, it wasn't even the first horror film (and we're talking pre–*Texas Chain Saw Massacre* here) to feature a death by chainsaw; that prize most likely goes to Herschell Gordon Lewis' *The Wizard of Gore* (1969). In fact, it is to Lewis' notorious splatter fests of the 1960s—including *Blood Feast*, *2000 Maniacs* and *Color Me Blood Red*—that *Last House* must defer when it comes to manufacturing high gore on a low budget. What really distinguishes *Last House* from a production standpoint is the fact that it was the first B-grade, realist horror film to attract great numbers of mainstream, middle-class viewers. Four years earlier, George Romero's independently financed *Night of the Living Dead* took America by storm, but the film's supernatural plot enabled audiences to distance themselves from the terrible events that take place in a way that *Last House* makes all but impossible. Distributed to its own outdoor theaters by the same company (Hallmark Releasing) that produced it, and expertly marketed by savvy ad executives, *Last House* was released with an R rating despite its volatile, graphic content. (A lot of rumors have circulated as to just how this favorable rating was obtained. Craven

According to film archivist David Beach, "Going to see films like *Last House on the Left* ... at the drive-in was like a rite of passage for a whole generation of teenagers in New England."

himself has stated that Cunningham simply snipped the R rating tag off the negative of another film, and pasted it to the front of *Last House*!) Wherever the film played, drive-in or theater, city or suburb, storms of controversy followed, which in turn led to even higher receipts.

Today, more than 25 years after its initial release, it is easy to forget that *Last House* was a huge draw at the box office before it became a cult film. Or if it *was* a cult film back then, it was a cult film with the same drawing power as a *Rocky Horror Picture Show*. According to Szulkin:

> Hallmark Releasing believed in milking its product to the limit. With no cable television or home video to cut into cinema attendance, *Last House on the Left* enjoyed a lengthy and lucrative run on the big screen. The movie was continually revived at drive-ins, college campuses, and second-run houses throughout the 1970s, and even into the following decade. Even after its U.S. home video release in 1985.... *Last House* was still being exhibited on big screens in Hallmark's home base of New England.[6]

It is safe to say that *Last House* set a new standard for the horror genre, by making a certain type of horror film not just possible to produce, but desirable. This fact is amply attested to by the numerous take-offs, spin-offs and outright rip offs which have followed in its wake. Below is a list, in no particular order, of some of the production elements that contributed to the unique film that is *Last House on the Left*. It is not so much that any *one* of these elements played an essential role in the film's success; it is rather that their specific conjunction resulted in a winner, to the complete surprise of everyone involved.

1. A low, low budget: The people at Hallmark who commissioned a horror script from Craven on the basis of his previous work with Cunningham were supposedly quite impressed with what he wrote. If so, they certainly didn't back up their enthusiasm with cash. According to Cunningham, the original budget for *Last House* was a mere $45,000, chump change even by '70s standards. (By way of comparison, John Carpenter's *Halloween*, made in 1978, cost $320,000 to make.) Although Hallmark eventually had to kick in another $50,000 or so for post-production work, most of those on the set of *Last House* agreed, "It was Craven's professional editing skills that saved the film from disaster."[7] The bottom line here is that operating under such severe financial constraints forced Craven and company to make some tough decisions about the style, and therefore the spirit, of the film. In this case, necessity was definitely the mother of invention: an industrious crewman named Vic Hurwitz actually built his own Super 16mm camera, which recorded an image approximately 40 percent larger than that of a standard 16mm camera. Using the Super 16mm format gave *Last House* a look that was considerably more polished than that of the typical drive-in horror feature. In a recent interview, sound man Jim Hubbard recalled that upon viewing some of the early rushes, Cunningham felt the footage "looked much more professional than he had expected ... that this could actually be a good, solid low-budget production. I think he realized that he could be a little more pretentious with it, that a better film was going to come out of it than just exploitation."[8] It is this so-called pretentiousness, this dramatic—one might even say artistic—sensibility filtered through the rules of low-budget, exploitation filmmaking, that paved the way for such (still under-appreciated) '70s horror classics as *God Told Me To*, *It's Alive* (both written and directed by Larry Cohen), Bob Clark's *Deathdream* and David Cronenberg's *They Came from Within* (a.k.a. *Shivers*).

2. Documentary style: When Craven first left the academic world for New York City in the hopes of becoming a director, he learned the ropes of documentary filmmaking through his association with Harry Chapin, Academy Award–winning documentarist and singer–songwriter of such '70s hits as "Taxi" and "Cat's in the Cradle." Craven's interest in and familiarity with the *cinema verité*, hand-held camera style was brought to bear on the shooting of *Last House of the Left*. Hurwitz was a documentary filmmaker in his own right, and together with Craven and Cunningham, the group decided on the following strategy for their picture:

> We set about making the film by staging scenes, beginning to end, and filming them from three or four different angles, figuring that we'd cut it together just like a documentary. We decided to use hand-held camera for all of the action sequences, and a tripod for anything with a dialogue scene. That was the essential style of the film ... to try to capture a very reality-based situation.[9]

Adding to *Last House*'s "reality-based" feel is the following blurb appended to the beginning of the film in place of opening credits: "THE EVENTS YOU ARE ABOUT TO WITNESS ARE TRUE. NAMES AND LOCATIONS HAVE BEEN CHANGED TO PROTECT THOSE INDIVIDUALS STILL

LIVING" (compare this with the *Virgin Spring* blurb quoted earlier); similar plot devices would be employed by Tobe Hooper in *The Texas Chain Saw Massacre* (1976) and by Daniel Myrick and Eduardo Sánchez in *The Blair Witch Project* (1999). In interviews, Craven has called his work on *Last House* "guerrilla filmmaking," since all of the shooting was done without permits in off-limit locales. Elsewhere, Craven has acknowledged being "very impressed by some of the footage coming out of Vietnam; that seemed to have a lot more immediacy and truth to it than anything else I was aware of, so that was the style that I adopted."[10] As we shall see, the shadow of Vietnam lingers over *Last House* in more ways than just this (stylistic) one.

3. Inexperienced actors: Partly because of budgetary constraints, partly because of the nature of the material, the actors who played in *Last House* were, with the exceptions of St. James and Carr, relative neophytes, unsure of just what they were getting themselves into. But the rawness of Hess (an aspiring musician who also co-wrote the film's soundtrack), Cassell, Grantham, Scheffler (a future children's television producer), Lincoln and Rain turned out to be one of *Last House's* best assets, contributing to the movie's documentary feel. As Phil Hardy writes in *The Overlook Encyclopedia of Horror*, "The unmannered acting, the lack of posturing, the attentive ear for dialogue and nuance ... all help to explain the film's peculiarly upsetting ambience."[11] There is a freshness and vitality to their performances, a complete lack of self-consciousness, that makes it difficult for the viewer to remember that they are just acting. Hess and Lincoln in particular took their Method acting ways to the extreme, remaining in character all during shooting, and actually frightening the rest of the cast and crew. Hess was so convincing as sadistic murderer Krug Stillo that he got "rewarded" with an offer to reprise his role in the Italian *Last House* spin-off *House on the Edge of the Park* (*La Casa sperduta nel Parco*, 1979). As for Lincoln, "He made such a good psychopath ... I honestly didn't know how much of his performance was acting," remarked production Steve Dwork in an interview. "Either he got into the role prior to appearing and didn't leave it until departing, or he wasn't playing a role at all. I don't remember him *not* acting like that character."[12]

The first and third of the production elements described above were typical of drive-in horror features generally, and *proto*typical of drive-in horror features of the '70s. That is to say, shooting on a very tight budget with inexperienced actors became the norm once "first run" Hollywood product was restricted for use by indoor theatres. As drive-in movie expert Kerry Segrave explains:

> [Drive-in theaters] almost never got first run at major Hollywood product during the 60s and 70s. As always they remained stuck with second-and third-run or with B or worse films.... So cut off from mainstream films were the drive-ins that a production industry developed especially to service them.[13]

What Craven and his crew managed to do was use the "B or worse"-grade restrictions placed upon them to their advantage. Rather than produce something of a markedly inferior, or at best a kind of "campy" quality (*à la* Herschell Gordon Lewis), they made a film that eschews gloss for grit in order to disturb viewers, provoke them, force them to question their own motives in going to see such a violent tale. In a brief but positive review of *Last House* written six years after its release, Roger Ebert makes a similar claim: "As a plastic Hollywood movie, the remake [of *The Virgin Spring*] would almost certainly have failed. But its very artlessness, its blunt force, makes it work."[14] And although Canadian film scholar Robin Wood has criticized Ebert and his ilk for the condescending terms in which independent productions such as *Last House* typically get characterized in print, on this point he and Ebert seem to agree: "The exploitation format and the request from the producer to 'do a really violent film for $50,000' seem to have led [Craven] to discover things in himself he scarcely knew were there."[15]

We shall now turn to the commercial and critical reception of *Last House on the Left* in order to determine just what those "things" were that Craven apparently discovered in himself ... and in society at large.

III. Audience Response

No discussion of *Last House* would be complete without mention of the innovative and highly successful marketing campaign put together by the publicists at Hallmark. In order to drum up interest and (later) to fan the flames of controversy generated by the film, three basic strategies were employed. The first was to revive the catchy, hyperbolic tagline first used in slightly different form to promote William Castle's *Strait-Jacket* (1964) and Lewis' *Color Me Blood Red* (1964): "TO AVOID FAINTING KEEP REPEATING, IT'S ONLY A MOVIE... ONLY A MOVIE ... ONLY A MOVIE ... ONLY A MOVIE...." Cunningham and others, including David Whitten, one of the Hallmark ad execs assigned to *Last House*, have dismissed the notion that this tagline is at all sophisticated in its message. But the fact is, advice on how to prevent what one might call "snuff film anxiety" by way of a catchy epistemological mantra ("It's only a movie ... only a movie ... only a movie...." = "It's not real ... not real ... not real....") actually serves to *reinforce* (by calling attention to) *Last House*'s documentary (cl)aims.

The second strategy employed was a turning of all the negative response to the movie on its head by publicizing it—in severely truncated form, of course—along with fabricated retorts by the producers. The following disclaimer, for example, appeared atop some of the advertisements for the film:

> LAST HOUSE ON THE LEFT: CAN A MOVIE GO TOO FAR?
> Many people who have gone to see the movie LAST HOUSE ON THE LEFT and many public officials contacted by outraged moviegoers believe the answer is YES! WHY...? LAST HOUSE ON THE LEFT relates to a problem and a situation that practically every teenage girl is vulnerable to and every parent lives in dread of.... A young girl savagely brutalized, killed by a wanton band of degenerates. Revenge of the most horrible kind exacted by the parents of the dead girl—the killers are themselves killed.
> Yes, you will hate the people who perpetrate these outrages—you should! But, if a movie—and it is *only* a movie—can arouse you to such extreme emotion then the film director has succeeded.
> Violence and bestiality are not condoned in LAST HOUSE ON THE LEFT—far from it! The movie makes a plea for an end to all the senseless violence and inhuman cruelty that has become so much a part of the times in which we live. WE DON'T THINK ANY MOVIE CAN GO TOO FAR IN MAKING THIS MESSAGE HEARD AND FELT!

Among the many things worth calling attention to here is the fact that no effort is made whatsoever to keep the storyline a secret. People weren't lining up to see *Last House* in order to be surprised by the narrative, and the publicists at Hallmark knew it.

The third strategy used to promote *Last House* was the targeting of a particular demographic, namely those adolescents and young adults primed to identify with the film's teenage victims. According to Whitten, "We wanted to tell the public at large, particularly young people, that 'This is your kind of movie.'"[16] One advertising slogan for the film read, "NOT RECOMMENDED FOR PERSONS OVER 30!" The beauty of such a slogan is that it indirectly but effectively attracts one demographic by directly (but only half-seriously) dismissing another. In general, this third strategy is notable in that it elides two important facts about the film: (1) Krug, Weasel and Sadie are *also* victims, if not of the Collingwoods' fury, then certainly of socioeconomic circumstance, and they are not youths at all; and (2) after the murders of Phyllis and Mari, the film shifts gears and becomes in effect a wish-fulfilling revenge fantasy on behalf of Mari's grieving parents. What all this means is that the identificatory processes set up in *Last House* are by no means straightforward and unambiguous: contrary to the message sent by the folks at Hallmark, Craven simply wasn't interested in effecting an unproblematic identification between adolescent viewers and "the film's teenage victims."

Since there is no such thing as *the* (one and only) audience for a movie, there is no such thing as *the* (one, homogeneous) audience response to a film. If we are to say anything of interest about the latter, however, some degree of generalization seems appropriate, even desirable. In the case of *Last House on the Left*, two basic types or patterns of response can be distinguished; the amazing thing is that, contrary to what one would expect from such a profitable and long-running film, neither of these response types involve declarations of pleasure.

On the one hand, adult viewers, especially those of the middle-class and from suburban locales, were furious after watching *Last House*. At a theater in Hartford, Connecticut, patrons protested almost immediately after the film opened. According to an editorial in the September 3, 1973, edition of the *Hartford Courant* (p. 129), "[The audience] began gathering in the parking lot petition-bound to stop the manager from showing the movie.... Apparently, some people thought it should have had an 'X.'" Szulkin is of the view that "the patrons' outrage ... stemmed from the fact that they had expected a more polished, palatable 'mainstream' film for their price of admission," and that "a crowd at a rural drive-in or an urban grindhouse might not have been fazed by the shocking elements of *Last House on the Left*." This talk of subverted audience expectations goes some way towards explaining why middle-class suburbanites went to see *Last House*, at least in the first place, but considering how well the film did at the box office, it doesn't go all the way. After the first wave of surprise and shock ran its course, these same people *still* went to see the film, and they *still* reacted with anger. The question is why.

We find a clue to the answer in something Craven tells Szulkin in an interview:

> A lot of people really hated us vociferously for [*Last House*] ... especially among the culture we lived in, middle-class people with kids. When they saw that film, people literally wouldn't leave their children alone with me.... They would get up and walk away from the table when I went out to have dinner. There was this powerful feeling that we had done something unspeakable.[17]

From these remarks, it looks as if it was not simply adults who despised the film, but *parents* who worried that their own children would be the ones eager to see it at the local drive-in. That their own children would identify, and therefore suffer, with Mari and Phyllis. And worst of all, that their own children would get influenced by watching all of the film's gratuitous acts of violence. Of course, this way of thinking takes no account of those subtle shifts in identification effected by Craven during the course of the movie. Nor does it take account of the wholly unromanticized manner in which violence is depicted in the film. But that is clearly beside the point. What matters is that a great many parents *believed* these things would happen, and wanted to see for themselves what all the fuss was about, wanted to determine whether or not they really *did* have cause for concern. Hallmark's publicists were well aware of all the parental interest in *Last House*. They even tried to capitalize on it, as is testified to by the "Open Letter to Our Critics" hastily prepared by Whitten and appearing in the *Hartford Courant* on September 8, 1972: "[*Last House*] relates to a problem that practically every teenage girl and parent can identify with, yet does not pander to the subject matter.... This fact is already being borne out by the number of parents who have recently been taking their daughters to see the film. These parents regard this film as a perfect deterrent to this type of behavior." Yeah, right! But regardless of the letter's insincerity, it helped keep *Last House* in the news, and on parents' minds.

It is not surprising to learn that middle-class adults, parents especially, were upset, even angered, by *Last House*. A little harder to make sense of is the fact that most of the young people who lined up to see the film, many of them more than once, didn't "like it" in the traditional sense all that much either. That is not to say the reason for their dislike was the same as their parents'; nor is it to say that their dislike took the same form as their parents'. So how did the responses of these two audience types differ? Whereas parents tended to find the movie senseless and without any redeeming qualities, their kids tended to find it disturbing but highly entertaining. According to film archivist David Beach, "Going to see films like *Last House on the Left* ... at the drive-in was like a rite of passage for a whole generation of teenagers in New England.... *Last House* was the horror movie to see back in the '70s; if you didn't see it one summer, it came back the next summer."[18]

The phrase "rite of passage," especially when understood in reference to the drive-in phenomenon, is illuminating here. Early in the twentieth century, French anthropologist Arnold Van Gennep concluded from his studies of primitive communities that "the life of an individual in any society is a series of passages from one age to another and from one occupation to another.... For every one of these events there are ceremonies whose essential purpose is to enable the individual to pass from one defined position to another which is equally defined."[19] Post-Freudian cultural theorists characterized these "defined positions" in sexual, rather than chronological or vocational, terms. This alternative model gets taken up by James B. Twitchell, who argues in a 1985 book that horror films are secular rites of passage for youths desiring initiation into the secret world of reproductive sexuality. As he puts it:

> [T]hese rites of passage are occurring every day (or every weekend).... [T]he adolescent crowd assembled at the theatre on Friday night is up to something important—something both they and we don't understand.... [T]he stuff of sexual initiation inheres in

all the major horror myths and informs the audience of important knowledge....[20]

Though Twitchell doesn't say so, drive-in theaters would have been especially conducive locales for such initiation rites, since (1) they provided greater freedom for viewers to engage in sexual relations while watching the film, (2) the content of B-grade drive-in features tended to be a great deal more explicit than their Hollywood competitors, and (3) the teen audience at drive-ins was even higher, percentage-wise, than at in-house theaters.

If drive-ins were excellent places for adolescents to learn the ropes of reproductive sexuality, *Last House on the Left*, surprisingly enough, was an excellent film to do the teaching. Without ever resorting to the kind of dull didacticism guaranteed to drive young viewers away (literally!), *Last House* provides brief introductions to such adult themes as harassment, molestation, promiscuity, polygamy, bisexuality, degeneracy, sadism, casual sex, marital infidelity and, of course, rape. Contrary to what many parents believed, and in line with the film's documentary pretensions, *Last House* neither condones nor glorifies sexual misconduct. By refusing to cut away when things get uglier than the audience can stand, it actually serves to deromanticize such activity (one memorable shot has Krug pulling away from Marie after raping her, a thin line of drool connecting his mouth to her cheek). This goes some way towards explaining the "exhausted and seemingly debased" feeling many viewers are left with upon watching the film. It is often pointed out that rites of passage (e.g. ceremonial piercings, ritual scarring, etc.) don't have to

Many critics believed *Last House on the Left* featured excessive, gratuitous, senseless and tasteless violence.

be enjoyable to be efficacious. Often enough, as in the case of *Last House*, they fulfill their function by other, far less pleasurable means.

IV. Critical Response

If audiences were fundamentally split in their feelings towards *Last House*, older crowds disliking it intensely, younger ones conferring upon it "must see" status, critics were almost uniformly against the film. Surprisingly enough, those working for small press horror–sci-fi publications, usually generous to a fault when it came to reviewing B-grade drive-in fare, also ripped *Last House*. For example, Danny Peary, author of a popular book on cult movies, declared the film "absolute trash ... [an] incitement to violence" that "deserves to be banned."[21] As was mentioned above, the two critics who did the most to support *Last House* were Roger Ebert and Robin Wood, and even between them there was substantial disagreement, Wood accusing Ebert among other things of setting "a new record in critical inaccuracy (combined with characteristic critic-as-superstar complacency)."[22]

Why did *Last House* push such incredibly negative buttons for critics and reviewers, who, much more than other parents and adults, were used to seeing all different sorts of films, and often enough found reasons to champion seemingly unworthy ones? The main criticism of *Last House* had to do with its presentation of violence. Excessive, gratuitous, senseless, tasteless—all were terms frequently employed by reviewers to describe the film's violent content. As Wood observed, the critique of violence in *Last House* served to situate the film firmly on one side of the Art vs. Exploitation dichotomy. "The *Virgin Spring* is Art; *Last House* is Exploitation," Wood wrote. "One must return to that dichotomy because the difference between the two films in terms of the relationship set up between audience and action is inevitably bound up with it."[23] Lest one conclude from this that Wood holds Art films to be "better" or more valuable than Exploitation films, he continues:

> I use the terms Art and Exploitation here not evaluatively, but to indicate two sets of signifiers—operating both within the films as "style" and outside them as publicity, distribution, etc.—that defined the audience-film relationship in general terms.[24]

This paper will end with a closer look at the violence in *Last House*, in an attempt at dispelling some of the myths that have proliferated about the film.

MYTH #1: *The violence in* Last House *is gratuitous, and possesses no redeeming value.* In interviews, Craven has stressed the fact that the ongoing war in Vietnam was on his mind while he wrote and directed *Last House*. Of course, Craven would have had a hard time ignoring the war even if he wanted to; as Robb notes, "the newsreel footage of the American carnage in Vietnam playing on television every night provided a running commentary as [Craven] and Cunningham planned and executed ... their film."[25] How might the war, or rather, *newsreel footage* of the war have exerted an influence on *Last House*? According to Craven:

> *Last House* did not play by the rules that had been established for handling violence, where the people who did violence were always bad, and if a good guy did it to the bad guy it was very clean and quick. That was the sort of attitude that America had gone into

Vietnam with ... that they were the bad guys and we'd go in like *Gunsmoke*, face 'em down, and bang, they'd be dead. The fact of the matter was that the war involved horrendous killings piled upon killings.[26]

Elsewhere, Craven states that *Last House* is "in a way ... a protest film. It was made during a time of protest, the early seventies. It had, among other things ... been an attempt to show violence the way I and the producer thought it really was, rather than the way it was typically depicted in films. In that sense, it had a real purpose to it and I think it has a legitimate artistic power."[27] Examples of protracted, messy, hyper-realistic violence abound in the film: When Junior shoots himself in the mouth, we see the bloody remnants of his skull splattered on the wall; just before raping Mari, Krug carves the letters of his name into the horrified girl's chest; after Weasel stabs Phyllis, the killers disembowel her as she lies helpless on the ground. This last sequence is so disturbingly believable that Atlantis International, the distribution company that released *Last House* in Germany, used segments from it in a pseudo-documentary snuff film called *Confessions of a Blue Movie Star: The Evolution of Snuff* (1976). Scenes such as these are only gratuitous if one misses or denies Craven's point that they are there (at least in part) to send a socio-aesthetic message, or if one holds the dubious view that critique and exploitation are mutually incompatible cinematic effects.

It should also be noted that Krug Stillo's perverse charisma and utter disregard for human welfare is highly reminiscent of real-life psychopath and cult leader Charles Manson, on trial for murder at the time *Last House* was being shot. Szulkin notes that the character name "Sadie" is the same as the nickname of Manson Family murderess Susan Atkins. Of course, "Sadie" could simply be short for "sadistic," just as "Krug" anticipates the surname of Craven's most famous monster, Freddy Krueger. Regardless, it would be difficult to deny that Krug and company represent, in much the same way as Manson's cult did, family values gone completely awry.

MYTH #2: *The violence in* Last House, *because of its purported realism, is wholly lacking in artistic value.* There are a couple of problems here. For one thing, just because a film is, or attempts to be, realistic, this does not mean it lacks style (assuming for the sake of argument that "style" is a necessary condition of artistic value in cinematic texts). After all, none of the violent sequences in *Last House* really occurred, and Craven's crew must be given credit for manufacturing such convincing illusions, especially given the fact that they were working on an extremely low budget. For another thing, although *Last House* may give the impression of falling squarely in the *cinema vérité*, "style of no style" category, upon closer examination this impression looks to be misleading. As Stephen Prince writes in another context, during a debate concerning the depiction of violence in the films of Sam Peckinpah, "Insisting on *realism* can be a trap for the unwary, and stylization need not impede a filmmaker's efforts to find truth."[28]

Far more than in *The Virgin Spring*, and in sharp contrast to its own pseudo-documentary pretensions, *Last House* evinces a pattern of juxtaposing opposites by means of both parallel editing and *mise en scene*. At the level of narrative, Craven's film in effect weaves together a number of distinct stories, all of which take place simultaneously. In the first half of the film, scenes of Mari and Phyllis on their way to the Bloodlust concert are interspersed with scenes of Krug and company making their way to a hideout in the city. These two stories come together when Junior lures the naïve girls up to the gang's apartment with the promise of some good pot. In the second half of the film, scenes of (A) Krug's gang torturing, then killing, Mari and Phyllis in the woods outside the Collingwood home are interspersed with (B) scenes of Mari's parents making preparations for their daughter's birthday, and worrying when she fails to return home that night, as well as (C) scenes of the bumbling town sheriffs (played by Marshall Anker and Martin Kove) trying unsuccessfully to get their act together. (A) and (B) come together when Krug, Weasel, Sadie and Junior show up at the Collingwood home looking for help with their car. Finally, (C) gets resolved when the sheriffs arrive at the end of the movie, just in time to witness Mari's father murder Krug with a chainsaw. Bergman's film, for all of its technical accomplishment and gorgeous black-and-white cinematography, is far less complex than *Last House* when it comes to narrative and editorial sophistication.

At the level of *mise en scene*, Michael Brashinsky writes that "the black-and-white *Virgin Spring* is ruled by dichotomy. It juxtaposes the virgin, Catholic, and blonde Karin ... with the pregnant, pagan, and brunette Ingeri."[29] Brashinsky implies that this is one way in which Bergman's film differs from *Last House on the Left*. But *Last House* is similarly "ruled by dichotomy": The shot of Krug on top of Mari, their faces pressed together as he brutally rapes her, is extremely powerful in large part because of the profound incongruity of their expressions and mannerisms. Just as effective, and even more self-consciously constructed, is the scene in which Krug, Sadie and Weasel eat dinner with Mr. and Mrs. Collingwood, the gap in their relative socioeconomic status dramatized and thereby enhanced through the difference in table manners and conversation topics. Craven shoots this scene against an all black background, removing all extraneous reference points in order to charge the event with symbolic import. Narrative cinema doesn't get much more anti-realistic than this.

If the critique of violence in *Last House* is as off the mark as the discussion above indicates (which is not at all to say that the depiction of violence in *Last House* is beyond criticism), what should we make of the film's status as a paradigmatic example of exploitation moviemaking, as mere "drive-in fodder," to quote Craven once again? The best option seems to be to admit that, in a number of key respects (e.g. its marketing campaign, its stilted dialogue, its sexualized violence), *Last House is* an exploitation film, but to deny the further claim that exploitation films are necessarily lacking in artistic value. *Last House* proves that exploitation can also be art, that these terms are *not* mutually exclusive—a finding with important implications when it comes to understanding and evaluating the work of such B-movie, drive-in directors as Russ Meyer and John Waters.

V. Conclusion

With *Last House*, Wes Craven showed himself to be not only "a pioneer of rediscovery," to quote Brashinsky,[30] but a master of cinematic innovation. The film is at once proto-stalker, revenge drama and (in its uncensored form) uncompromising gorefest. Its legacy to the horror genre includes the depiction of "creative" killings (*Friday the 13th*; *A Nightmare on Elm Street*), multi-dimensional—even (dare we say it?) likable—psychopaths (*Henry: Portrait of a Serial Killer*; *Natural Born Killers*) and disquieting humor (*Texas Chain Saw Massacre*;

The People Under the Stairs). That some of Craven's later movies figure prominently on this list is no accident: *Last House* was just the start of this former teacher's reign as the premier horror director in America.

As was noted earlier, in the years following its release, dozens of *Last House* take-offs, rip offs and so-called "sequels" popped up in the U.S. and abroad. Italian cheapies such as *House on the Edge of the Park*, *Last House on the Beach* and *L'Ultimo Treno della Notte* (*The Last Train of the Night*, a.k.a. *The New House on the Left*) sought to capitalize on the original's catchy title. In the States, *Last House* was regularly teamed at drive-ins with *House by the Lake* (a.k.a. *Death Weekend*, 1976) and *The House That Dripped Blood* (1970). And at least three different films have at one time or another during their theatrical runs been advertised as *Last House on the Left II*. But it is the film's less immediate, more pervasive influence on the horror genre which undoubtedly stands as its greatest accomplishment. We end with a quote from Szulkin, whose book on the making of *Last House* combines the researcher's thoroughness and respect for fact with the fan's love of an underappreciated cult classic:

> Even Craven himself, whose directorial skills have since developed light years beyond the crude level exhibited in *Last House*, has rarely duplicated the simple, savage impact of his debut.[31]

Notes

1. Quoted in Szulkin, David. *Wes Craven's Last House on the Left: The Making of a Cult Classic*. London: FAB Press, 1997, p. 15–16.
2. Quoted in Szulkin, p. 183.
3. Wes Craven, quoted in Robb, Brian J. *Screams & Nightmares: The Films of Wes Craven*. New York: Overlook Press, 1998 p. 21.
4. Szulkin, p. 12.
5. *Ibid*, p. 15.
6. *Ibid*, p. 150.
7. Robb, p. 30.
8. Szulkin, p. 48.
9. Wes Craven, quoted in Szulkin, p. 48.
10. *Ibid*, p. 48.
11. Hardy, Phil, ed. *The Overlook Film Encyclopedia: Horror*. New York: Overlook Press, 1993, p. 257.
12. Szulkin, p. 53.
13. Segrave, Kerry. *Drive-In Theatres: A History from Their Inception in 1933*. Jefferson NC: McFarland, 1992, p. 174.
14. Ebert, Roger. "Guilty Pleasures." *Film Comment* 14.4 (July–August 1978), p. 51.
15. Wood, Robin. *Hollywood from Vietnam to Reagan*. New York: Columbia University Press, 1986 p. 125.
16. Whitten, quoted in Szulkin, p. 126.
17. Craven, quoted in Szulkin, p. 136.
18. Beach, quoted in Szulkin, p. 151.
19. Van Gennep, Arnold. *The Rites of Passage*. 1909; reprint. Chicago: University of Chicago Press, 1960, p. 3.
20. Twitchell, James B. *Dreadful Pleasures: An Anatomy of Modern Horror*. New York: Oxford UP, 1985, p. 89.
21. Peary, Danny. *Cult Movies: the Classics, the Sleepers, the Weird, and the Wonderful*. New York: Dell, 1981, p. 146.
22. Wood, p. 123.
23. *Ibid*, p. 124.
24. *Ibid*, p. 124.
25. Robb, p. 24.
26. Craven, quoted in Szulkin, p. 16.
27. Craven, quoted in Robb, p. 25.
28. Prince, Stephen. "Reply to Schneider." *Film-Philosophy* 3.19 (April 1999): 2. Available http://www.mailbase.ac.uk/lists/film-philosophy/files/prince.html
29. Brashinsky, Michael. "The Spring, Defiled: Ingmar Bergman's *Virgin Spring* and Wes Craven's *Last House on the Left*." In *Play It Again, Sam: Retakes on Remakes*, eds. Andrew Horton and Stuart Y. McDougal. Berkeley: UC Press, 1998, p. 164.
30. Brashinsky, p. 165.
31. Szulkin, p. 17.

Boiling Hot and Cold: The Pressures of War

7

Apocalypse Here and Now: Making Sense of *The Texas Chain Saw Massacre*

Mark Bould

Robin Wood considers the "the impingement of Vietnam on the national consciousness/unconscious, and the astonishing evolution of the horror film" to be the "keys to understanding the development of the Hollywood cinema in the 'seventies." In exploring some elements of the complex relationship between these phenomena, it is not the intention of this chapter to ignore his accompanying advice to "avoid any simple suggestion of cause-and-effect,"[1] but as the historical moment of the release of *The Texas Chain Saw Massacre* (Hooper, 1974) recedes, Wood's caution jeopardizes his critique of the movie. By revisiting early criticism of the movie, this chapter will establish, with a degree of explicitness avoided by Wood, a number of critical and historical contexts in order to recover and expand upon his analysis, to inquire how one can make sense of such a challenging movie and what sense one can make of it. Central to this discussion is a sense of *Chain Saw Massacre*'s intra- and inter-generic play.[2]

Chain Saw Massacre as Gothic Fantasy and Horror Movie

Gothic fantasy is commonly divided into two varieties. Supernatural fantasy, usually dated from *The Castle of Otranto* (1756), and typified by the pulp magazine *Weird Tales* (1923–54), ascribes a supernatural origin to all its spooky goings-on. In contrast, rational fantasy—beginning with *The Mysteries of Udolpho* (1794) and *Wieland* (1798), and exemplified by the pulp *Unknown* (1939–43) and, of course, *Scooby Doo Where Are You!* (1969–70) and its sequels—establishes rational, material explanations for seemingly paranormal shenanigans. Some gothic fantasies—*The Scarlet Letter* (1850), "The Turn of the Screw" (1898)—make a virtue of suspending the reader between these alternatives.

For all its economic rationale, verité camerawork, location shooting and "realistic" disruptions of Hollywood conventions, *Chain Saw Massacre* hints at several supernatural explanations for the unfolding horror, including solar flare activity, astrology, lunar madness and powers invoked by the blood hex, fetishes and "ritual" burning of the photograph of Franklin (Paul G. Partain). But if the terrible events the movie depicts derive from economic conditions, what is to be made of the foregrounded suggestions that they are the result of malefic Saturn being in the ascendant, or of solar activity?

The tendency to reinforce and universalize the apocalyptic sense created by these superstitious propositions through radio reports of death and disaster and the sequence of shots of sick cattle is disturbed by a shot, filmed from a camera placed among the livestock, of the protagonists' van as it passes. This foreshadowing suggests their status as raw materials or commodities, but despite the potency of this connotation, the rational, material framework it implies does not supersede the paranormal possibilities. In fact, it is repeatedly undone by further references to the heat and to astrology, and by the invocation of a lunar influence through images and visual echoes of the full moon which only appear later in the movie. The supernatural explanation is never clearly established as the opposite of the mundane framework, and it could be seen to be the root of the economic and social causes of the horror rather than its proximate cause. Alternatively, the characters' dependence on or tolerance of superstition can be seen as a symptom of a secular apocalypse. In weighing these possibilities, infinite regress threatens because the fragmented presentation of both rationales does not suspend the viewer between options, as in Hawthorne and James, but undermines their coherence. Frustrating as it might be, this incoherence is, I contend, essential to the senses we can make of the movie.

Christopher Sharrett's anthropological reading of *Chain Saw Massacre* focuses

In *Chain Saw Massacre*, the protagonists are stalled by the energy crisis and terrible things befall them, but at the drive-in, the audience *chooses* to abandon motion, just as many chose to abandon the Movement.

on its "denial of causality and emphasis on ritual structures." He rejects the suggestion that cannibalism is "a logical extension and a proper metaphor for consumerism in capitalist society," and argues that Wood's "rigid" Marxism:

> ...projects an ideological view onto the film that is not wholly justified by the evidence. It is reasonable to assume that the situation in the world of the film has economic/ideological origins to an extent, but to suggest Marxism as an ameliorating force has little relevance here.[3]

Indeed, Wood *does* write of "the extension into relationships of the property-principle"[4] *and* suggest that "[c]annibalism represents the ultimate in possessiveness, hence the logical end of human relations under capitalism"[5] *and* that Leatherface's "family, after all, only carries to its logical conclusion the basic (though unstated) tenet of capitalism, that people have the right to live off other people."[6] However, the 1986 republication of Wood's essay as a chapter of *Hollywood from Vietnam from Reagan* demonstrates the extent to which Sharret's own rigidity caused him to misread Wood. Considering the incoherence of "the most interesting 70s films,"[7] Wood indicates the limits to his interpretation by arguing:

> [T]he "thinking" of the films can lead logically only in one direction, toward a radical and revolutionary position in relation to the dominant ideological norms and the institutions that embody them, and such a position is incompatible with any definable position within mainstream cinema (or even on its exploitation fringes); it is also incompatible with any degree of comfort or security within the dominant culture.[8]

It is precisely because *Chain Saw Massacre* does suggest an economic motivation, however contested, for the murders and cannibalism that it can be read as satire on and indictment of capitalism in general, and of its American manifestation in particular. But in any text there is an excess of signification, signification which is often ambiguous, and in *Chain Saw Massacre* such material is too often foregrounded to be ignored. A short inventory of that which would seem to exceed or problematize Wood's analysis would have to include not only the supernatural elements detailed above but also a number of puzzling images (a pocket watch with a nail driven through it, a fatted chicken in a canary cage, a human skull with a horn thrust through its mouth), and such features as the circular narrative, time distortions, fragmented editing, bizarre percussive soundtrack, disruptions of classical Hollywood narrative, space, and conventions of characterization, and confusions of genre and tone.

Wood characterizes the basic formula of horror movies as normality, generally represented by "the heterosexual monogamous couple, the family, and the social institutions ... that support and defend them," being threatened by the monster, a figure who signifies all that is excluded by "conformity to dominant social norms."[9] Inasmuch as the five young "quasi-liberated, permissive"[10] travellers represent normality, and the slaughterhouse family represent the threatening Monster, he considers *Chain Saw Massacre* a partial reversal of his formula. However, Franklin, whose family relationship with Sally (Marilyn Burns) disrupts the neat pairing-off of the travellers, constitutes a surplus unrecuperable to heterosexual monogamy. On the other hand, the cannibals are depicted as a family, and as such they belong to the comic-horror tradition of the family of monsters, which includes

The Old Dark House (Whale, 1932), *Arsenic and Old Lace* (Capra, 1944), *The Comedy of Terrors* (Tourneur, 1963), *Carry on Screaming* (Thomas, 1966), *The Addams Family* (1964–66), and *The Munsters* (1964–66). These last three are particularly instructive. As the Universal horror cycle collapsed into a series of encounters with Abbott and Costello, the icons it celebrated fell from grace, only to re-emerge in such spoofs and gentle sitcoms. Recognizing the irrelevance of Eurocentric gothic monsters,[11] *Chain Saw Massacre* returned to the model of criminal monstrosity with hints at supernatural menace. Simultaneously, the camp demeanor of the aproned Leatherface (Gunnar Hansen) and the irascibility of Old Man (Jim Stedow) on his return home from work recall the husband-wife relationship central to the classic American sitcom, with Hitchhiker (Edwin Neal) as the child who gets into scrapes. Despite the absence of a wife-mother, the slaughterhouse family is a family, and this suggests that Wood's formula is not reversed at all. Remaining intact, it is instead subjected to a significant shift in values. *Chain Saw Massacre* is a story told from a perspective sympathetic to the Monster (the young travellers) caught in the grinding wheels of Normality (the slaughterhouse family and the bourgeois capitalist order they represent).

Elsewhere, Wood makes a clear distinction between the domestic comedy and the domestic melodrama-tragedy. The former, which "depends for its very existence on the repression of any sense that the wife/mother could be other than blissfully content, completely fulfilled by her role,"[12] is "built on the entrapment of the male,"[13] and the latter "on that of the female."[14] Situated between these genres, the comic-horror tone peculiar to *Chain Saw Massacre*, and the "sadistic torments visited upon Sally [which] go far beyond what is necessary to the narrative"[15] can be seen, at least in part, as a product of the generic relocation of the family in American film from comedy to horror, the genre in which "it ha[s] always rightly belonged."[16] Leatherface, feminized (by his clothing, appearance and mannerisms) and emasculated (his chainsaw a mere kitchen implement), seems contented within an undisturbed domestic setting, but Sally's presence in and return to the house disrupts this arrangement. Sliding from comedy to tragedy, "tension and catastrophe" erupt from the "recognition of female entrapment,"[17] and the diegetic and cinematic excesses of Sally's torture are essential if the movie is to express the tyranny of the family as an institution.

In the 1950s, Herbert Marcuse drew an important distinction between basic repression, "the 'modification' of the instincts necessary for the perpetuation of the human race in civilization," and surplus-repression, "the restrictions necessitated by social domination."[18] The slaughterhouse family wish to incorporate Sally both literally, by ingestion, and metaphorically, by offering her the seat at table belonging to the missing wife-mother. It is, then, precisely the prolonged and hyperbolic ordeal to which she and the viewer are subjected, including its discomfiting moments of comedy, that generate the movie's indictment of the surplus-repression necessary for the perpetuation of the bourgeois capitalist order and embodied in institutions like the family. The threat to Sally is that of being restricted to, and consumed by, the roles of wife and mother. Her suffering is an expression of the curtailment and containment to which we are all, like the fatted chicken in the canary cage, subject. Her desperate determination to escape constitutes a refusal on behalf of the Monster to be suppressed. However, as the final image of Sally indicates, just because

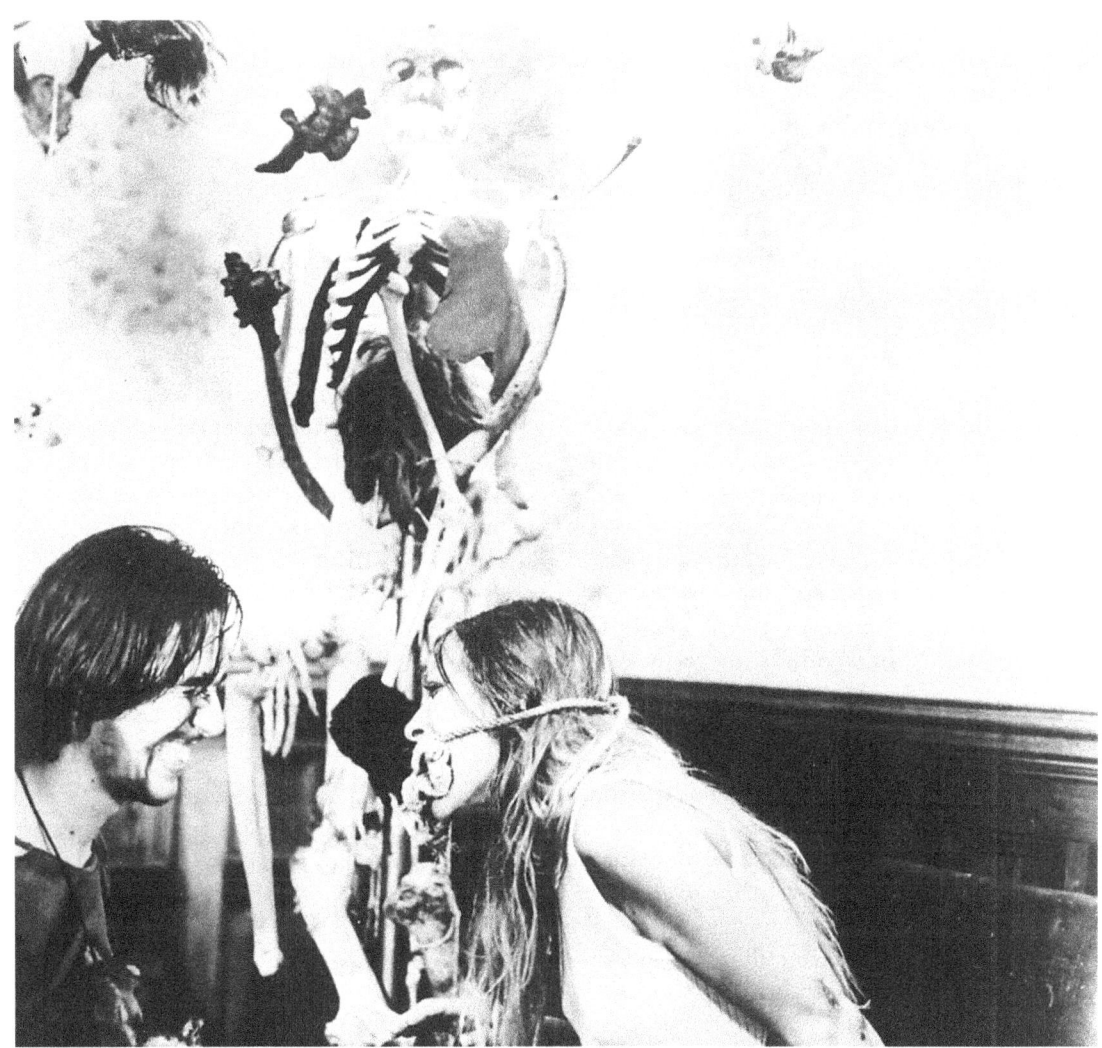

In discussing *Chain Saw Massacre*, it is imperative to bear in mind this historical moment, to treat the U.S. invasion of Vietnam, domestic repression, economic recession, and the kind of brutality depicted in the movie, as specific manifestations of a more deeply-rooted, more general phenomenon.

she has escaped is no guarantee that she has survived. It is the end of the road, and not just for her.

Chain Saw Massacre as Road Movie

Although it is important to recognize *Chain Saw Massacre* as a gothic fantasy and horror movie, its relationship to the road movie provides the main impetus for this chapter's reconsideration and expansion of Wood's work. A genre of special significance to the counterculture, the road movie resonated strongly with its desires and aspirations, as well as its critical perspective on contemporary America. For example, *Bonnie and Clyde* "muted" the Depression-era context of the protagonists' crime spree in favor of foregrounding "*will*, the will to be young and free and potent: will as excitement, the drive to overcome impotence in a flat world"[19]; and *Easy Rider* (1968) "juxtaposed" 'America the beautiful' with 'Amerika the ugly': the pristine wilderness of the landscape, representing the great potential of the country's historical past, with the profane sentiments of its fascistic and bigoted inhabitants, threatening the very foundations of democracy in the present."[20]

Recent critical discussions are divided as to whether the road movie, despite numerous prototypes, is a strictly postwar phenomenon "rooted in the institutional turbulence that describes the cinema [of the period], with its foundation in the fifties and its maturity in the sixties and seventies,"[21] or whether, as a result of the changes wrought on the American landscape by interstate highway developments and a growing car- and leisure-oriented culture,[22] it is a genre divided into distinct prewar and postwar phases. However, there is a consensus that the roots of the genre are to be found in the *Bildungsroman*, the narrative arc of which sees the protagonist depart from the familiar world on a journey across space, time and social class, encountering obstacles and ultimately confronting himself or herself so as to become "wiser" and, usually, comfortably bourgeois. Postwar road narratives like *On the Road* (1957), *In Cold Blood* (1965), and *Fear and Loathing in Las Vegas* (1971) reject this arc, resembling postwar road movies in their concentration on interstitial places and in their refusal of "abstract freedom in favor of generally open-ended passages through a series of concrete experiences"[23] in "familiar land that has somehow become unfamiliar."[24] As with these literary texts, the postwar road movie tends to focus on the homosocial possibilities offered by the liminal space of the road, excluding women in a self-conscious display of gender and sexual anxieties arising from "historically recent proliferations of the threat of male hysteria."[25]

Corrigan suggests three other important characteristics of the postwar road movie: the dissolution of the family, "preserved only as a memory or desire with less and less substance"; the relative passivity of characters who do not do things but have things done to them; and, the mechanization of the quest motif as the "protagonist's identity is almost fully displaced onto [his] vehicle" and the "perspective of the film as relayed through the central characters becomes a function of those vehicles."[26] Importantly, as the genre develops,

> ...[e]nergy becomes the key metaphor but that energy ... has nothing spiritual or intellectual about it: energy is gasoline; energy is material, and to have it concretized in the form of a car is the surest sign that the past is disappearing in your rearview mirror.[27]

However, "[b]ehind every billboard a highway patrolman potentially lurks, [lying] in wait for any expression beyond the boundaries of the law."[28] The in-between setting of the road movie licenses numerous articulations of the central tension in American ideology between "consumption and renunciation," but as Schaber notes, the freedom imagined by the postwar road movie is, ultimately, "only the freedom guaranteed by the highway lobby and the gas companies, the freedom to drive,"[29] and when the gasoline begins to dry up in the seventies the vehicles it propelled become scrap by the road.[30]

The relationship of *Chain Saw Massacre* to the road movie is clear. It is not a tale of embourgeoisification. The "road and the country may be known" to Sally and Franklin, but the social, cultural and psychological impact of economic recession and changes in the ownership and practices of local industry have "made it foreign."[31] Although structured around a heterosexual axis, with a woman as the main character, the movie is deeply concerned with male hysteria in the absence (memory of family) and presence (desire for family) of women; indeed, it is this hysteria which affords Sally her centrality. The travellers are victims rather than initiators of actions, and the identities of both Franklin and Leatherface are displaced onto mechanical devices. The physical difficulties of maneuvering Franklin's wheelchair presages *Chain Saw Massacre*'s subversion of the road movie's material-energy metaphor. If the road movie considers cars and motorbikes as prostheses which enable the body to "move farther and faster than ever before and quite literally evade the trajectory of classical narrative and twentieth-century history,"[32] then a lack of fuel embeds the same body in the Oedipal torments central to such narrative and in the anarchic social and economic conditions of the capitalist present. If the road movie "comes closest of any genre to the mechanical unrolling images that define"[33] cinema, then Leatherface's whirring chainsaw, which fragments bodies and edits lives, captures the brutality of the industrial production process itself.

Despite their countercultural dress and accoutrements, the "on-the-road" protagonists of *Chain Saw Massacre* have nothing of Kerouac and Cassady about them. Theirs is not a Magic Bus carrying Merry Pranksters. Their story does not celebrate marginal culture—although it does extend *Easy Rider*'s recognition of the "searing sacrificial of the social itself"[34]—and they exhibit little of the exuberant will of Penn's *Bonnie and Clyde*. Their daytrip into the rural wasteland, visiting a desecrated cemetery before being stalled by a fuel shortage, reveals only the ugliness and savage heart of the American Dream. The single idyllic moment in the movie—Kirk (William Vail) and Pam (Teri Minn) laughing and playing as they run through the high grass—is cut short by a swimming hole as dry as the gas station, and then the sound of a generator lures them to the house where they will be murdered.

If *Bonnie and Clyde* and *Easy Rider* are the counterculture's road movies, then *Chain Saw Massacre*—made after the collapse of the Movement, and after McGovern's New Politics and almost-daily Watergate revelations somehow failed to prevent Nixon's second term—must be its end-of-the-road movie.

The Movement, the Counterculture and the Invasion of Vietnam

In his speech following the April 17, 1965, March on Washington to End the War in Vietnam, Paul Potter, the President of Students for a Democratic Society (SDS), argued that because the invasion of Vietnam "implicated the entire American social order ... the whole system had to be uprooted"[35]:

> We must name that system. We must name it, describe it, analyze it, understand and change it. For it is only when that system is changed and brought under control that there can be any hope for stopping the forces that create a war in Vietnam or a murder in the South tomorrow.[36]

The antiwar position articulated by Potter insisted on its interconnectedness with other issues with which SDS was concerned, including civil rights, urban poverty and education, university

For all its economic rationale, verite camerawork, location shooting and "realistic" disruptions of Hollywood conventions, *The Texas Chain Saw Massacre* hints at numerous supernatural explanations for the unfolding horror.

reform and the development of participatory democracy.³⁷ SDS's refusal to just treat one issue in isolation can be seen as a stance against surplus-repression, and therein lies the central connection between the Movement and the counterculture³⁸ as well as one of the main causes of their demise.

Marcuse argues that throughout history, "the instinctual constraint enforced by scarcity" which makes civilization possible "has been intensified by the hierarchical distribution of scarcity and labor," that it is the "interest of domination [which has] added surplus-repression to the organization of the instincts under the reality principle."³⁹ His analysis of the escalation of domination in postwar culture identifies the administrative apparatus which perpetuates the capitalist state with a Father who cannot be overcome:

> [T]here is no freedom from administration and its laws because they appear as the ultimate guarantors of liberty. The revolt against them would be the supreme crime ... against the wise order which secures the goods and services for the progressive satisfaction of human needs. Rebellion now appears as the crime against the whole of human society and therefore as beyond reward and beyond redemption.⁴⁰

In a passage proleptic of the collapse of the Movement and the counterculture, he contends that, in response to the threat of liberation from surplus-repression found in the radicalism espoused by the groups within the Movement, society would strengthen its "controls not so much over the instincts as over consciousness, which, if left free, might recognize the work of repression in the bigger and better satisfaction of needs."⁴¹ The mechanisms by which this would be achieved were the "promotion of thoughtless leisure activities, the triumph of anti-intellectual ideologies" and the "relaxation of sexual taboos" even as "sexual relations themselves ... become much more closely assimilated with social conformity."⁴² Most obvious in the antiwar protests, the overlap between radical projects and other countercultural revolts more concerned with sex, drugs and rock 'n' roll resulted in the marginalization and decline of radicalism. In conjunction with the assimilation of elements of the counterculture into mainstream culture, the failure of the antiwar movement and the extensive, often brutal suppression of moderates as well as radicals effectively terminated any large scale radicalism. Losing their sense of the interconnectedness of these surplus-repressions, "[t]he children of the new consciousness were substituting pot for politics and rock for revolt."⁴³ The consequences of this are clear. By 1970, for example, many women were rejecting further involvement in the often misogynistic New Left, and what was left of SDS was splintering into factions, including the Weathermen. Testimony to the declining image of the Movement can be found in John Carpenter's abandonment of the spaced-out surfer space hippies of *Dark Star* (1973) in favor of Street Thunder in *Assault on Precinct 13* (Carpenter, 1976) who, despite the Black Panther styling of their Guevaran leader, are nothing more than a violent criminal gang. The strength of the growing division between political radicalism and the counterculture can be seen in the fact that while the IRS harassed antiwar organizations, COINTELPRO infiltrated *agents provocateurs* into antiwar Black and Brown Power groups, the White House ordered the CIA's illegal Operation Chaos and the FBI continued to wage a covert war on the Black Panther Party and the American Indian Movement.⁴⁴ Timothy Leary, who in 1969 was fined $630,000 and sentenced to 30 years in jail for possession of a single joint, was released, following his escape and recapture, by 1975, just in time to remake himself as a respectable media guru for the information age.

In discussing *Chain Saw Massacre*, it is imperative to bear in mind this historical moment, to treat the U.S. invasion of Vietnam, domestic repression, economic recession and the kind of brutality depicted in the movie as specific manifestations of a more deeply rooted, more general phenomenon. With this in mind, *Chain Saw Massacre* invites a further contextualization, positioned somewhere between Martha Rosler's series of photo collages *Bringing the War Home (House Beautiful)* (1967–72/90), Mailer's *Why Are We in Vietnam?* (1967) and Lansdale's "Night They Missed the Horrorshow" (1988).[45]

Rosler's collages reassembled images from *Life* magazine and similar sources, joining together "two sites of human experience" typically and falsely separated in mainstream media, thus requiring her viewer "to consider the real social and economic connections between our comfortable sofas and someone else's dead body."[46] In one of the collages, two elegant chairs face a patio window overlooking a well-kept garden. The garden gives way to a scene of devastation in which U.S. tanks and infantry advance down a Vietnamese street. Bodies of dead Vietnamese are strewn against the bullet-pocked walls of their homes. This image breaks down the spatial distance between the American home and the invasion of Vietnam by removing it from the TV screen and placing it in the back garden. However, as the action is moving away into the background, there is no real sense of threat to those who might command this vantage point. Absent from the frame, the homeowners are able to consume, or not consume, images of death and destruction just as they might consume, or not, the view of their garden.

Another of Rosler's collages displays the immaculate interior of a middle-class suburban kitchen. In the background, visible through twin doorways, are U.S. soldiers in tropical kit. By importing their scorn for (the myth of) private property and systematic violations of the "sanctity" of the home into a U.S. setting, Rosler attempts to communicate not only the day-to-day indignities suffered by Vietnamese, Cambodians and Laotians but also something of the hypocrisy in pro-invasion rhetoric which sought to conceal or justify the trampling of values in order, supposedly, to preserve them.

Mailer's short novel is a manic, improvisatory account of a crazed, helicopter-assisted Alaskan hunting trip undertaken by one High-Grade Asshole, two Medium Assholes and 2 Tough Adolescents-Tested for whom this is a rite of passage. Although it does not mention Vietnam until the final page—"tomorrow Tex and me, we're off to see the wizard in Vietnam … Vietnam, hot damn"[47]—it does capture the profane, arrogant, brutal nature of the particular white bourgeois American machismo into which DJ and Tex are initiated, implying that the answer to the question posed in its title is that the war stemmed from, was fuelled by, and appealed to such macho assholery. Mailer problematizes the identity of the narrating persona (does it belong to DJ, one of the tough, white Texan adolescents? or is DJ the creation of a Harlem-based African-American narrator? or is he the creation of DJ? or are both the creations of another persona?) so as to strengthen his analysis by transforming the narrative into one which fluctuates between confession and indictment.

"Night They Missed the Horrorshow" is set, it seems, in 1968, a year in which most of Lyndon Johnson's Wise

Men (the Senior Advisory Group on Vietnam) became convinced "that American policy [concerning Vietnam] had reached a dead end"[48]; a year in which Martin Luther King and Robert Kennedy were assassinated, the Chicago police rioted, U.S. troops murdered the inhabitants of My Lai, protestors against a segregated bowling alley at South Carolina State University were shot and killed, and President Nixon was elected. Lansdale's story mentions none of these events, and makes no reference at all to Vietnam. Instead, it tells of what happens when his protagonists do not go to the drive-in to see *Night of the Living Dead* (1968) but instead encounter snuff-porn-watching, racist rednecks who torture and kill them. Rather than pursue the metaphorical possibilities offered by Romero's undead apocalypse or make explicit comment on the invasion of Vietnam, Lansdale favors the everyday atrocities which occur without the benefit of carpet bombing, defoliants, napalm, zippos, government sanction, etc. By establishing a context of racial hatred, local conflicts and disregard for human life, by pursuing the terrible logic built on these premises, and by omitting reference to the real-world crimes and atrocities which characterize 1968 in popular consciousness, "Night They Missed the Horrorshow" implies that the brutal events it depicts are symptoms rather than aberrations. Sharrett argues that it is because crimes such as those which inspired *Chain Saw Massacre* "are seen as remarkable that the reason for aberration remains enigmatic"[49] For example, the My Lai massacre registered in this way because it was presented as an anomaly, rather than as part of the same fabric as the pacification programme, the My Khe massacre, the ninth Division's slaughter of civilians in Kien Hoa province, the destruction of subsistence agriculture and the creation of a massive refugee population, and so on.

Lansdale's failure to mention Vietnam—or any domestic events—generalizes the possibility of atrocity.

Chain Saw fits somewhere in this cluster of texts. Like Mailer's novel and Lansdale's short story, it brings the atrocities home, indicating how deeply entangled they are in U.S. culture and society; through its references to unemployment, the oil crisis and the cost of living, it establishes, like Rosler's collages, a broader context, linked to industrial capitalism and global politics, within which its everyday atrocities occur. In the words of Ursula Le Guin, the "ethic which approved the defoliation of forests and grainlands and the murder of non-combatants in the name of "peace" [is] only a corollary of the ethic which permits the despoliation of natural resources for private profit or the GNP."[50]

Conclusion: Making Sense of Chain Saw Massacre

Although Sharrett's reading of *Chain Saw Massacre* as a contribution to the tradition of the secular apocalypse is, like any reading, inevitably selective in its emphases, marginalizations and suppressions, he rejects Wood's reading because of those elements of the movie which do not fit easily into it. Despite this, he does open up the central problem in Wood's argument: In interpreting a movie, is it reasonable—plausible, even—to conclude that, despite its overall incoherence, certain elements reveal its "true thinking"?

This question returns us to Marcuse, who argued that although advanced industrial society as a "whole appears to be the very embodiment of Reason," it is nonetheless "irrational as a whole."[51] One of the most vexing aspects of advanced industrial civilization" is the "rational character of its irrationality"[52]; for example, the nuclear arms race, in which "the deterrent also serves to deter efforts to eliminate the *need* for the deterrent,"[53] and in which "the insanity of the whole absolves the particular insanities and turns the crimes against humanity into a rational enterprise."[54] He also notes that:

> [T]orture has been reintroduced as a normal affair, but in a colonial war which takes place at the margin of the civilized world. And there it is practiced in good conscience for war is war. And this war, too, is at the margin—it ravages only the "underdeveloped" countries. Otherwise, peace reigns.[55]

In a footnote which helps to connect these global events to the fictional atrocities of *Chain Saw Massacre*, Marcuse refers to a suggestion by Herman Kahn, recorded in the 1959 RAND report RM-2206-RC, that the experiences of con-centration camp survivors might be transformed into guiding principles for nuclear shelter design.[56] Redolent of the strategic hamlets policy pursued in southern Vietnam, the "rational" spirit of this appalling proposal, recommending the continued industrial processing of Jewish and other peoples persecuted and murdered by the Nazi regime, is also recognizable in the behavior of the slaughterhouse family, especially as revealed in the difference between their house and the old Franklin house. The latter is derelict, possibly gutted, its desuetude signalled by peeling wallpaper and paint, missing walls and door panels, and most emphatically by an infestation of spiders, the sound of whose movements are distorted and amplified. In contrast, the other house appears to be immaculate. Closer inspection, however, reveals that, in addition to their anthropophagic antics, the slaughterhouse family hoard everything, from the cars of previous victims (their source of gasoline?) to the inedible remains of animals, birds and humans which, as well as meeting material needs, provide a medium for cultural expression (furniture made of bones and, echoing concentration camp tales, a lampshade made of human flesh).

This drive to maximize the potential of raw materials is signalled by the strange image of the fatted chicken, stuffed into a cage like a ship in a bottle; appropriately, Pam, who finds it, is crammed—still alive—into a freezer. Furthermore, this rational spirit produces two of the movie's most striking and confounding image, both of which link it to irrationality. In the same room as the fatted chicken, amid all the sculptures, ornaments, articles of furniture and decorations made of human and animal remains, Pam discovers, hanging from the ceiling, an inverted skull with an animal's horn thrust through its mouth, connoting oral rape and an assault on the seat of reason. Earlier, as she and Kirk approach the house, we see a watch with a nail driven through it hanging from a bush. Reminiscent of the self-consciously irrational decision of the anarchists to blow up the Greenwich Observatory in *The Secret Agent* (1907), this image also hints at the modernist thematics of time, temporality, *duree* and memory evoked by the Dali's soft clocks,[57] suggesting the extent to which the slaughterhouse family are determined to halt the passage of time, to resist history, and maintain the normality of the bourgeois capitalist order.

Although it is possible to construct meanings for these images, they do nonetheless demonstrate the central dilemma of interpretation. In constructing these meanings, the critic is reducing them, implying that they are coherent instances within a text which is itself coherent. By first suggesting that these images are representative of the movie's significatory excess but then constructing meanings for them which support a particular reading, the critic is guilty of a logic in which the proposed meaning of the movie and its supporting evidence produce each other. This is unsurprising as critical exegesis is subject to, and a product of, the same irrational reason at the heart of the Enlightenment project and its bourgeois, capitalist offspring.

How, then, to conclude?

In a certain sense, *Chain Saw Massacre*, like Lansdale's "Night They Missed the Horrorshow," is not about the U.S. invasion of Vietnam. Rather, although their diagnoses might differ, it is, like Mailer's *Why Are We in Vietnam?*, about a general condition, of which the invasion is symptomatic and constitutive. Moreover, it does offer the kind of critique of capitalism that Sharrett insists is merely a product of Wood's Marxism, and it is not necessary to obscure the movie's incoherence to arrive at this conclusion; in fact, its incoherence must be insisted upon as that is what gives the movie's critique its strength and clarity of perception. *Chain Saw Massacre* is incoherent because so is the normality promulgated by bourgeois capitalist ideology; or, as Marcuse might put it, there is irrationality at the core of capitalism's reason, and capitalism's unreason is rationally pursued.

Coda

Writing about *Chain Saw Massacre* in Britain is a peculiar experience. One of a number of movies dubbed "video nasties," it endured a 15 year ban, during which it could only be seen at specially licensed screenings, or on foreign, pre–1984 domestic, or pirated video cassettes. Under such conditions, the identity of the movie became fixed in popular consciousness as a spectacularly gory splatter movie so depraved and depraving that audiences needed to be protected from it. Such descriptions are, to say the least, inaccurate.

The ban itself is indicative of the extent to which the tension between "consumption and renunciation," which Schaber describes as "the pervasive, even if contradictory logic of American ideology,"[58] came to dominate British culture during the 1980s, a decade that witnessed an emphasis on consumerism and the individual at the expense of public spending on welfare, health, education and other social services. This redistribution of wealth away from the impoverished, and the accompanying ideological blitz—from the myth of the Thatcherite economic miracle[59] and the ugly nationalism surrounding the Falklands conflict to racist immigration policies and homophobic constraints on education and public culture—promoted the twisted ethics of the "right" to consume. Having learned a lesson from the suppression of the countercultural protests of earlier decades, the massive civil unrest which accompanied these changes was misdescribed as a law-and-order issue[60] engineered by a few fanatics, and quashed, often brutally. Simultaneously, the market for consumer durables expanded, and the new-fangled technology of the domestic VCR provided a more conducive explanation for the apparent increase in youth crime than having to acknowledge complicity in Thatcherism's systematic extension and expansion of impoverishment, its assaults on working class and other marginalized cultures, and is rejection of any concept of community more complex or deeply rooted than a Neighborhood Watch Scheme. In the contexts in which this chapter has discussed *Chain Saw Massacre*, it is, I suppose, appropriate that it became a victim of this renunciation.

It is also appropriate to consider it as a drive-in movie. Corrigan argues that, in the road movie, the

...rearview mirror ... along with the window frames of a car, ... assures a kind of perceptual self-consciousness that identifies a generation whose present, past, and future is more and more mediated by the images of visual technology and whose ultimate aim is to possess those images within the frame of a moving body. For the children of the fifties and sixties, the world viewed is always and anxiously viewed as image, distanced, disenfranchised, and eventually possessible.[61]

In addition to describing the exchange of being on the road for road movies, of participation (in the social) for consumption (of the mediated) which ruptured the Movement and the counterculture, the tension between consumption and renunciation mapped by Corrigan is also present in the drive-in's modes of exhibition and spectatorship: to drive to a venue to sit in a car to watch pictures of motion; to invest in the automobile's concretization of energy but to then use it to sit still. In *Chain Saw Massacre*, the protagonists are stalled by the energy crisis and terrible things befall them, but at the drive-in, the audience *chooses* to abandon motion, just as many chose to abandon the Movement. We are living in the consequences of such decisions, in the here-and-now apocalypse of *Chain Saw Massacre*.

NOTES

1. Wood, Robin. "The Incoherent Text: Narrative in the '70s," *Movie* 1987. 27/28: 25.
2. Although restricted in this chapter to a consideration of its relationship to varieties of Gothic fantasy, horror, the road movie and, tangentially, the family comedy and family melodrama, it is also important to note *Chain Saw Massacre*'s relationship to the Western, yuppie nightmare movie and SF. The key yuppie nightmare movies are *After Hours* (Scorsese, 1985), *Into the Night* (Landis, 1985) and *Something Wild* (Demme, 1986); important precursors include the Western-derived redneck/heart-of-darkness narratives found in *Deliverance* (Boorman, 1972), *The Last House on the Left* (Craven, 1972), *I Spit on Your Grave* (Zarchi, 1980) and *Southern Comfort* (Hill, 1981). *Chain Saw Massacre*'s relationship with SF is harder to define, but the tension invoked between supernatural and material explanatory frameworks (discussed below) is a major dynamic of SF film, ranging from the quasi-religious aura surrounding the destruction of the Martians by disease in *The War of the Worlds* (Haskin, 1953) and the slippage between Creation myth and science in the opening narration of *Creature from the Black Lagoon* (Arnold, 1954) to the incessant Christ imagery in *The Terminator* (Cameron, 1984) and the loopy material basis of the Force explicated in *Star Wars: Episode 1—The Phantom Menace* (Lucas, 1999).
3. Sharrett, Christopher. "The Idea of the Apocalypse in *The Texas Chain Saw Massacre*." Barry Keith Grant, editor. *Planks of Reason: Essays on the Horror Film*. Metuchen, NJ: The Scarecrow Press, 1984, p. 262.
4. Wood, Robin. "Introduction." Robin Wood and Richard Lippe, editors. *The American Nightmare: Essays on the Horror Film*. Toronto: Festival of Festivals, 1979, p. 9.
5. *Ibid*, p. 21.
6. *Ibid*, p. 22.
7. This category includes Larry Cohen movies, *Taxi Driver* (Scorsese, 1976), *Looking for Mr. Goodbar* (Brooks, 1977) and *Cruising* (Friedkin, 1980). That *Chain Saw Massacre* belongs to this grouping would not necessarily become clear until Wood's Introduction to *The American Nightmare* was republished in his *Hollywood from Vietnam to Reagan* between a revised version of "The Incoherent Text: Narrative in the '70s" and expanded versions of two essays ("World of God and Monsters: The Films of Larry Cohen" and "Apocalypse Now: Notes on the Living Dead') from *The American Nightmare*.
8. Wood, Robin. *Hollywood from Vietnam to Reagan*. New York: Columbia University Press, 1986, p. 101–02.
9. Wood, "Introduction," p. 14.

10. *Ibid*, p. 20.
11. Although their revival by Hammer lasted from 1958 until 1973, it rapidly became both tired and tiresome.
12. Wood, Robin. "The American Family Comedy: from *Meet Me in St. Louis* to *The Texas Chain Saw Massacre*." *Wide Angle*, 1979. 3 (2) p. 9.
13. *Ibid*, p. 8.
14. *Ibid*, p. 8.
15. Wood, "Introduction," p. 21.
16. Wood, "The American Family Comedy," p. 11.
17. *Ibid*, p. 9.
18. Marcuse, Herbert. *Eros and Civilization: A Philosophical Inquiry into Freud*, London: Abacus, 1972, p. 42.
19. Gitlin, Todd. *The Whole World Is Watching: Mass Media in the Making and Unmaking of the New Left*. Berkeley CA: University of California Press, 1980, p. 197–8.
20. Klinger, Barbara. "The Road to Dystopia: Landscaping the Nation in *Easy Rider*." Steven Cohan and Ina Rae Hark, editors. *The Road Movie Book*, London: Routledge, 1997, p. 181.
21. Corrigan, p. 143.
22. Schaber, passim.
23. *Ibid*, p. 34–35.
24. Corrigan, p. 147.
25. *Ibid*, p. 143.
26. *Ibid*, p. 146.
27. *Ibid*, p. 147.
28. Schaber, p. 34.
29. Ibid, p. 34.
30. Corrigan, p. 153.
31. *Ibid*, p. 147.
32. Corrigan, p. 146.
33. *Ibid*, p. 146.
34. Schaber, p. 36.
35. Gitlin, p. 56.
36. Potter, Paul, quoted in Gitlin, p. 56.
37. SDS was not alone in perceiving this interconnectedness: The Vietnam Day Committee argued that "Vietnam, like Mississippi, is not an aberration, it is a mirror of America" (quoted in Anderson, 1996: 146); a 1967 Black United Action Front poster argued that drafting blacks "is a part of the Anti-Poverty Program! The way to solve the poverty of the black people is to get them killed in foreign wars!" (quoted in Anderson, 1996: 158); Stokely Carmichael contended that Selective Service was just "white people sending black people to make war on yellow people in order to defend the land they stole from red people" (quoted in Anderson, 1996: 158–59); and in 1967, Martin Luther King described the invasion of Vietnam as "a symptom of a far deeper malady' in American democracy, adding, "I could never again raise my voice against the violence of the oppressed in the ghettos without having first spoken clearly to the greatest purveyor of violence in the world today—my own country" (quoted in Anderson, 1996: 160). A mirror image of the SDS platform can be found in Rusty's 17-point foaming-at-the-mouth bigoted rant on all that is wrong with and ruining America in *Why Are We in Vietnam?* (Mailer, 1988: 110–11).
38. Although there is some debate about this nomenclature, by the Movement I intend the loose coalition between (coincidence of?) various political groupings (including movements for civil rights, women's rights, gay rights, Black Power, Brown Power and the New Left), and by the counterculture I intend a much wider but often politically unfocused subcultural phenomenon centering on music, drugs and dropping out (or at least dressing and behaving like one might).
39. Marcuse, p. 42.
40. Marcuse, Herbert. *One-Dimensional Man: Studies in the Ideology of Advanced Industrial Society*. Boston MA: Beacon Press, 1966, p. 74.
41. Marcuse, *Eros and Civilization*, p. 77.
42. *Ibid*, p. 77.
43. Blum, John Morton. *Years of Discord: American Politics and Society, 1961-1974*. New York: W.W. Norton, 1999, p. 364.
44. Churchill, Ward and Jim Vander Wall. *Agents of Repression: The FBI's Secret Wars Against the Black Panther Party and the American Indian Movement* (corrected edition). Boston MA: South End Press, 1990: passim.
45. Lansdale, Joe R. "Night They Missed the Horrorshow." Paul M. Sammon, editor. *Splatterpunks: Extreme Horror*. London: Xanadu, 1990, p. 1-17.
46. Cottingham, quoted. in Williams, Val. *Warworks: Women, Photography and the Iconography of War*. London: Virago, 1994, p. 54. [Something of this effect is achieved in countercultural favorite *Fear and Loathing in Las Vegas*, when Hunter S. Thompson, loitering

outside a hotel, scans the front page of the Las Vegas *Sun* rearranging fragmented stories: a young woman's heroin overdose; a report to the House Committee on drug-related deaths among GIs serving in Vietnam; police suppression of an antiwar protest in Washington; a report to a congressional panel on torture techniques used by the U.S. Army in Vietnam; an unidentified gunmen opening fire on passersby in New York; a Las Vegas pharmacist arrested over 100,000 missing pills; and, on the sports page, news of Muhammad Ali's final appeal to the Supreme Court over his refusal of the draft. Thompson's respatialisation of these stories into a linear narrative more strongly evokes the possible connections between such events than their arrangement on newspaper pages might.]

47. Mailer, Norman. *Why Are We in Vietnam?* Oxford: Oxford University Press 1988, p. 208.

48. Blum, p. 297.

49. Sharrett, Christopher. "The Idea of Apocalypse in *The Texas Chain Saw Massacre.*" Barry Keith Grant, editor. *Planks of Reason: Essays on the Horror Film.* Metuchen, NJ: Scarecrow Press, p. 260.

50. Le Guin, Ursula. *The Language of Night* (revised edition). London: The Women's Press, 1989, p. 127.

51. Marcuse, *One-Dimensional Man*, p. ix.

52. *Ibid*, p. 9.

53. *Ibid*, p. 53.

54. *Ibid*, p. 52.

55. *Ibid*, p. 84.

56. *Ibid*, p. 80.

57. Dali develops this image in *Premature Ossification of a Station* (1930), *The Persistence of Memory (The Soft Watches)* (1931) and *Disintegration of the Persistence of Memory* (1952-54).

58. Schaber, p. 34.

59. Johnson, Christopher. *The Economy Under Mrs. Thatcher, 1979-1990.* London: Penguin, 1991: passim.

60. After the failure to indict the police officer who killed the Mexican American rights activist Ruben Salazar in 1970, Charles Chavez of the League of United Latin American Citizens (LULAC) wisely observed that "law and order is not synonymous with justice but merely represents the violence required to uphold the interests of the establishment" (quoted in Anderson 1996: 365).

61. Corrigan, p. 147.

8

In the Science Fiction Name of National Security: *Cat Women of the Moon*

Tony Williams

Cat Women of the Moon (1953) is a forgotten science fiction film of the early '50s in comparison to more well-known works such as *Destination Moon* (1950), *The Day the Earth Stood Still* (1951) and *The War of the Worlds* (1953). Also known as *Rocket to the Moon*, the film's limited references in most works on American science fiction cinema usually involves dismissive comments concerning its acting, low budget and poor lunar sets left over from a Marco Polo film. Judged in terms of acceptable definitions of art and production values, *Cat Women of the Moon* certainly cannot escape criticism. Although featuring accomplished character actors such as Victor Jory, Marie Windsor and Douglas Fowley, the film has no claim to being regarded as an unjustly neglected science fiction generic classic but appears to be a typical disposable drive-in movie. Low-budget values appear to hinder any serious attempts to reevaluate its current "disreputable" status. Actors Douglas Fowley and Betty Arlen do double-duty work as dialogue and dance director respectively as well as playing engineer and Cat Woman. Furthermore, the twice-repeated explicit appearance of a ludicrous giant spider threatening the heroine and her male companions evokes laughter rather than terror. Unlike most of its '50s contemporaries, the film has no scary monster and the attempt to supply one is more inept and humorous than anything else.

However, the significance of *Cat Women of the Moon* may lie in other directions than mere suspense and science fiction situations. With Sonny Tufts (formerly Bostonian-bred Bowen Charlton Tufts III) cast in the leading role of Commander Laird Grainger, both the film's title and star appear to support readings legitimizing its current status as a neglected "camp" classic. After a brief period as a legitimate Hollywood star, Tufts' career had declined by the end of the '40s. He soon became reduced to secondary roles like his lightweight performance in Billy Wilder's *The Seven Year Itch* (1955), his weatherbeaten rube in *Come Next Spring* (1956) and leading roles in Poverty Row productions such as *Cat Women of the Moon*. Having never recovered from Joseph Cotten's sarcastic '40s radio outburst concerning his screen name, which continued for years in nightclub and TV talk show jokes, Tufts had become an alcoholic. During the 1950s, he was more celebrated for being sued by several showgirls for allegedly biting them in the thigh than for any acting achievements. Tufts ended his film career by appearing in the appropriately titled camp film *Cotton-pickin' Chickenpickers* (1967).

Both leading man and title appear to legitimate dominant readings of the film as a mere "camp" product. But, as Susan Sontag has shown in "Notes on Camp," the very term may involve a means of aesthetizing an oppositional discourse such as homosexuality and enabling it to enter the public sphere, thus making it an object of admiration and respect.[1] It is impossible to verify whether such an intention occupied the minds of director and actors at the time of production. But both the script and low-budget associations must have been rendered the film as something less than serious by a group of actors who had done better work either in big-budget movies or more accomplished low-budget ones.

Cat Women of the Moon is certainly a camp film, whether deliberate or not. Its raw aesthetic features, limited acting, hilarious screenplay lines and direction qualifies it for inclusion into that category whether viewed from a contemporary or retrospective position. Although *Cat Women* lacks the stylistic pleasures associated with more privileged high-budget camp products such as melodramas and musicals in the Cold War era, the film does privilege a particular style over content.[2] Jack Babuscio describes the gay cinematic attributes of camp as "an emphasis on sensuous surfaces, textures, imagery, and the evocation of mood as stylistic devices—not simply because they are appropriate to the plot but as fascinating in themselves."[3] Babuscio's definition fits many features of *Cat Women of the Moon* in more than one sense. The film often lavishes particular attention to stylistic details which often appear redundant to the plot. For example, a slow dance sequence featuring the Cat Women in black leotards occupies an over-proportionate part of the narrative's brief running time of 64 minutes. It parallels those dance sequences in '50s musicals often beloved by gay male spectators for displaying a particular type of spectator pleasure. While the rest of the film positions its solitary Earth female amidst either her male colleagues or as an object of competitive exchange for the two leading men, the dance sequence depicts an all-female group engaging in an activity pleasurable only to themselves and not for others. Secondly, the film also contains three eerie shadow images of a murderous Cat Woman's head when one would easily have sufficed. But these images do not have the redundant associations they would have had they occurred within any major studio production. They function as ominous signifiers of female power often operating as a silently subversive presence undermining male control. The last shadow image occurs immediately before Cat Woman Zeta kills engineer Walt with a knife.

Both these examples breach classical Hollywood narrative conventions of tight construction and editing[4] but are easily explained by Babuscio's definition. Dealing with an Amazonian colony of women on the Moon who threaten American patriarchal values and attempt trapping an earthly sister within their sinister scheme, *Cat Women of the Moon* contains a lesbian camp sensibility despite the presence of males occupying the positions of director, editor, photographer and art director. As will be shown, it is not just a drive-in film. It contains subversive features absent from most contemporary Cold War big budget features as well as having several historical associations to its own era.

Since the film is not as well-known as most of its contemporary science fiction companions, a brief plot summary is necessary here. Moon Rocket Four takes off as Earth's first exploration of its lunar neighbor. Comprising a mixed gender

crew of four males and one female, the rocket already contains enough ingredients for the typical sexual tensions governing any exploration narrative involving disparate elements. Commander Laird Grainger (Sonny Tufts), co-pilot Kip Reissner (Victor Jory), engineer Walt Walters (Douglas Fowley), and young assistant crewman Douglas Smith (William Phipps) are temperamentally different characters who certainly do not foreshadow the bland organization man team characterizing the three males who made the actual historical Moon landing several years later. As if this situation was not problematic enough, a woman is on board performing the male role of navigator. But Helen Salinger (Marie Windsor) is not only romantically involved with Laird but has had a previous relationship with Kip, who still carries a torch. American security has obviously not done a very good job in selecting individuals for this flight. However, the film does not operate on common sense levels of rationalism and reality but moves in other directions.

Of all the crew members, Helen has some secret affinity with the actual mission. Looking out at the stars, she comments, "I have the strangest feeling as if all this has happened before" and then mysteriously adds, "Alpha. We're on our way." Helen not only accurately charts a safe landing for the rocket but discovers the presence of a hidden cave near a crater. Helen plots a landing in an area bordering on the dark side of the moon. She affirms her abilities in the challenging enterprise of navigator, normally confined to males in '50s movies. "I know it for sure." However, Kip becomes suspicious when he informs Laird that the angle of the ship would make it impossible for any navigator to discern the presence of a cave on the lunar surface from inside the ship.

Helen becomes more self-assured, her voice losing her sultry deep intonations and becoming more high-pitched as she leads the men further into the cave. "I know where I'm going and I'll go there." She takes over the leadership role from the mission's ostensible commander, Laird. Inside the cave, the group remove their spacesuits when they discover the presence of oxygen. Helen leads them to a hidden city beneath the moon's surface as if she already knows of its existence. She affirms that her knowledge resembles a dream and lays claim to a form of feminine intuition absent from her male crew members. However, the film soon informs viewers as to the nature of this intuition and where it originated.

Taking advantage of a diversion when several Cat Women attack Doug in the deserted city, Helen reports to Alpha (Carol Brewster), the leader of the moon colony, who introduces her to Zeta (Suzanne Alexander) and Lambda (Susan Morrow). After telepathically contacting Helen from the moon, Alpha has taught her the requisite navigation skills so she can be the only qualified female to participate on Earth's first expedition to the moon. Zeta has already "brainwashed" Helen in the cave, after she recovered from an attack by a giant black widow spider, by touching her hand and implanting a control beam there. Alpha plans to use Helen to take her and three Cat Women back to earth by using spacesuits captured from the crew and gaining information about the ship's technology from Laird, Walt and Doug. Since Laird's knowledge is crucial, Alpha has programmed Helen to become romantically involved with him. Alpha's eventual aim is to colonize the earth by turning Earth women against men and using the survivors to breed a future generation of artificially inseminated Cat Women. Since the oxygen level beneath the moon is decreasing quickly, Alpha's plan must be carried out as soon as possible. The moon's inhabitants now comprise only females since the last male died a generation ago. Since the oxygen supply was already limited, Roy Hamilton's screenplay suggests that the colony drastically reduced its numbers in the past to ensure that the survivors had enough oxygen.

Alpha now officially designates Helen as "one of us." Since Helen's name parallels Homer's infamous heroine who caused chaos and the downfall of many heroic males during the Trojan War, the Greek associations of female names in the film is far from accidental. Alpha's community represents a science fiction version of Sappho's lesbian colony existing beneath the moon rather than a Greek Island. Also, since the Greek number "lambda" later became one of the prominent identifying marks of the gay community from the '60s onwards, it is tempting to suggest that Lambda's very name in the film may represent the same type of underground coding as Cary Grant's line "Because I've gone gay all of a sudden" does in Howard Hawks' *Bringing Up Baby* (1938).

However, attracted by young Doug's youthful all–American sincerity and descriptions of home-town Saturday night activities, Lambda eventually reveals her cat sisters' scheme and heroically dies when later trying to prevent Alpha, Zeta and Helen from reaching the spaceship to inspire Earth women into beginning a feminist revolt. The alert and suspicious Kip, who has moodily refused to join the celebrations organized by the Cat Women, finally overpowers Helen by his masculine assertiveness, and gains access to the real woman behind the brainwashed earthly Cat Woman persona. He then reveals the plot to the uncomprehending Laird and eventually shoots Alpha and Zeta off-screen. The survivors are all reunited in the rocket and return to earth.

Several features in *Cat Women of the Moon* have certain visual links to *film noir*. After the high-key lighting characterizing the interior of Moon Rocket Four, the landscape of the moon and the dark cave are filmed in unmistakable *film noir* lighting. This change in illumination also parallels Helen's desire to land the rocket in an area bordering on the dark side of the moon, a location not generally accessible to earthly eyes who see only the bright side. The area thus anticipates earthly movement from the high-key lighting of the rocket's interior towards the dark *film noir* world represented by the cave and the shadowy presence of Cat Woman Zeta, who stalks her prey inside its dark domains. Though formally a science fiction film, *Cat Women of the Moon* also belongs to that rich diffuse vein of Hollywood genres which often fuse with each other to express dangerous issues existing within the heart of American society not usually given full expression or allowed liberating solutions in most big-budget mainstream productions. As Robin Wood has pointed out, it is a mistake to regard genres as isolated entities since "they represent different strategies for dealing with the same ideological tensions."[5] *Cat Women* contains not just visual features resembling *film noir* but thematic ones as well, particularly those involving male fears of the independent woman.

Although Arthur Hilton's director credits are minimal, he had worked as a film editor since 1928. In the mid–'40s, he collaborated with émigré director Robert Siodmak on three classic *films noirs*, significantly dealing with issues of male crisis and fear of the independent female, *Phantom Lady* (1944), *The Suspect* (1944), and *The Killers* (1946). Hilton also worked as editor on Fritz Lang's *Scarlet Street* (1945), *Secret Beyond the Door* (1948) and *The House By The River* (1950). Before he resumed his profession as an editor in film and television, Hilton directed two other low-budget films. His first film as director was *The Return of Jesse James* (1950) starring John Ireland as an outlaw bearing a light resemblance to the famous outlaw and who decides to "pass" as him. As we will see, "passing" forms a significant narrative movement in *Cat Women*. Hilton's last film as director was the crime movie *The Big Chase* (1954). Despite the fact that Hilton's talents never seriously challenged those of his more eminent contemporaries Fritz Lang or Robert Siodmak, *Cat Women* does reveal faint traces of a *film noir* sensibility in its visual style, chosen themes and casting strategies. For example, Marie Windsor had previously appeared in *Song of the Thin Man* (1947), *Force of Evil* (1948) and *The Narrow Margin* (1952) and was usually typecast as a *femme fatale* in most of her films. William Phipps had played the vulnerable "hick" Leroy in Edward Dmytryk's *Crossfire* (1947). Although not associated with *film noir*, both Victor Jory and Douglas Fowley made a career of playing villainous roles. However, the casting of Marie Windsor as an Earth woman susceptible to brainwashing by her Amazonian sisters and capable of destroying the moon mission from within makes her *Cat Women* role another addition to her accomplished gallery of *femmes fatales*. Although Alpha has programmed her to seduce Laird to get information concerning the rocket from him, Helen seems to willingly agree with Cat Women desires to dispose of the male crew members after they have served their purpose.

Cat Women's "noir" features also involve acting characterizations as well as lighting techniques in the films. Virtually all the characters represent types from the gallery of *film noir*. Although Victor Jory was never associated with this particular aspect of Hollywood film style during his long career, his role as Kip typifies the hard-boiled detective persona characteristic of the genre. Like Philip Marlowe and Mickey Spillane's Mike Hammer, Kip will not allow himself to be fooled by any "broad." Of all the male crew members, he is the only one who takes a gun with him on the moon expedition and moodily removes himself from the banquet prepared by the Cat Women for their earthly guests. While Laird, Doug and Walt prove easy victims for Cat Women charms, Kip seats himself away from temptation, holding his gun like a protective talisman in very much the same way as R.G. Armstrong's Deputy Ollinger does in Sam Peckinpah's *Pat Garrett and Billy the Kid* (1973). Also, his perspective of the Cat Women becomes represented in a traditional male point of view shot not associated with any of the other crew members in the film. A cat female displays herself before him as a spectacular object in imagery identical with Laura Mulvey's observations concerning female representation and male observation in her classic essay "Visual Pleasure and Narrative Cinema." Both the audience and Kip see her in a shot which begins by showing her feet. The camera then tilts up to reveal a smiling face offering the "party pooper" a tray of goodies. This Cat Woman's exhibitionistic display is obviously meant to satisfy two types of appetites. She also clearly offers herself as a sexual commodity for the man. Kip's gaze represents Mulvey's definition of the sadistic voyeurism conditioning male objectification of the female body.[6] But it also represents a female knowingly employing the male gaze's inherent pleasure in the feminine body in order to trap him. However, it does not work. Kip is a tough guy who will not allow any dame to fool him and thus avoids the fate of engineer Walt. Walt allows Zeta to engage his interests seductively by playing on his desires for moon gold as well as her body. After gaining engineering information from him, she murders him in the cave in very much the same way Mary Astor's *femme fatale* does to Sam Spade's partner in *The Maltese Falcon* (1941). Furthermore, as an engineer, Walt parallels Alan Curtis' similar character in *Phantom Lady*. His male occupation does not prevent him eventually losing masculine supremacy over a member of the supposed "weaker sex" who causes his downfall. Kip survives because, like Humphrey Bogart's Sam Spade, he objectively views what goes on around him and makes the correct judgment concerning character. Like Spade, Kip also applies physical pressure on Helen to make her tell the truth. Although Zeta plants a spherical device on Helen's hand which Alpha later touches to recruit her into the Cat Women, ("You are one of us"), Kip more forcibly squeezes her body to learn the truth. Young, inexperienced Doug parallels both William Phipps' Leroy character in *Crossfire* as well as his fellow G.I. Mitchell who feels equally vulnerable in a confusing situation. But while Alpha schemes to get Helen to betray her men and planet, Doug's sincerity concerning the American way of life touches Lambda and eventually makes her a traitor to the cause of the Cat Women. Finally, Laird's character of a dumb, undiscerning male fooled by a manipulative woman parallels those male naive *noir* characters played by Robert Mitchum in *Out of the Past* (1947) and Burt Lancaster in *The Killers* (1946).

The *film noir* associations are thus not accidental but an integral part of the film. As a product of Cold War America belonging to a genre which often articulated

The landscape of the Moon is filmed in an unmistakable *film noir* lighting style.

contemporary concerns better than big-budget productions, *Cat Women* not only participates in its own version of a crisis in masculinity which many critics regard as a fundamental part of *film noir* but also responds to a particular set of social fears current in the postwar era concerning gender.

According to Robert Corber, the postwar Cold War crisis concerned not just the presence of Communists infiltrating American society but a gender crisis affecting the very foundations of acceptable definitions of heterosexuality. In *In the Name of National Security: Hitchcock, Homophobia, and the Political Construction of Gender in Postwar America*, Corber reads Hitchcock's films against their historical background. Although several of his observations conflict with what actually occurs in the text, the value of his work is that it provides a significant contextual background for reading not just the films of Hitchcock but also several other neglected works of popular culture such as *Cat Women*. As a low-budget example of a prolific contemporary cinematic genre, the film provides an interesting example of revealing the very same tensions Corber finds in Hitchcock's '50s cinema.

According to Corber, the Cold War era exhibited a climate of fear in more senses than one. Not only did the post war era reveal features such as the emergence of McCarthyism, the demonization of the Soviet Union, the undermining of the

New Deal and the enforced return of working women to the home but also ideological tendencies comparing Communism to gayness. Prominent liberals such as Arthur Schlesinger, Jr., eager to reclaim liberalism from the historical legacies of radical '30s Popular Front movements and American Communist movements, often criticized Communism in homophobic terms.[7] This led to gays and lesbians being often targeted as threats to national security as much as supposed Communist sympathizers. During this hostile era, the rights of independent working women and minorities also suffered major setbacks resulting in their discursive invisibility from the national scene for over a generation.[8] Since the Kinsey Report undermined rigid stereotyping principles governing the identification of gays and lesbians, a paranoid government employed the FBI to detect suspected "perverts" regarded as threats to national security. As D'Emilio notes, "Regional FBI offices gathered data on gay bars, compiled lists of other places frequented by homosexuals, and clipped press articles that provided information about the gay world. Friendship with a known homosexual or lesbian subjected anyone to investigation."[9]

Cat Women is a text combining these two Cold War phobias. While most contemporary texts either deal with one issue (politics) or another (gender issues), the film unites both these concerns under the combined generic and stylistic worlds of science fiction and *film noir*. While most critics have long defined '50s science fiction films as allegories for contemporary fears of the Red Menace, very few have noted the socially relevant gender issues accompanying this particular cinematic discourse.[10]

Like Patricia Laffan's character in *Devil Girl from Mars* (1954), whose feminist alien threatens British patriarchal institutions by virtue of her commanding presence and dominant sexuality, the Cat Women also have a wider agenda. In the opening part of the film, Helen intuitively knows what will happen on the mission. The audience later learns that she has received transmissions across space, allowing her to transcend her historically bound '50s gender role and travel with the men in the capacity of a navigator. In most of the film, she acts like a brainwashed female little better than a disposable "Commie dupe" in contemporary films such as *I Was a Communist for the FBI* (1951), *My Son John* (1952) and the various stooges seen later in the 1953–56 syndicated television series *I Led Three Lives*. However, Alpha's scheme implicitly aims at the eventual elimination of virtually all remaining males on earth once the Cat Women gain control. Little is said about why all the Cat Women's men have died except for Lambda's reference that she remembers them living when she was a little girl. However, Alpha's dialogue suggests that the lack of oxygen resulted in the purging of all males over the generations in much the same way as Stalin's Russia eliminated potential threats from the 1930s onwards. We must remember that *Cat Women of the Moon* appeared a year after Stalin's death when knowledge of the purges and gulags became more common than a decade before. In Hilton's film, the female-bonded Cat Women colony are not only future threats to Earth's national security but represent contemporary images of a perverse sexuality which will adopt Stalinist methods to ensure its control unless stopped in time. Lesbianism in *Cat Women* becomes not only a perverse erotic threat but also an "exterminating angel" for all males and their institutional patriarchal values.

The film adopts strategies to deal with this menace privileging the hard-boiled tactics of Kip over the "by the book" mundane attitudes of the mission's actual leader commander Laird. Although Laird adopts the tough persona of the wartime leader in criticizing his crew for exhibiting too much "infantile romanticism" before they begin exploring the moon's surface, this criticism applies more to him than anyone else. Despite his assumed leadership qualities, he allows himself to be seduced by a brainwashed Helen, who plays on his own infantile romantic qualities before they set off on the journey. Later, Kip discovers Laird with Helen about to reveal the rocketship's operational secrets to the Cat Women's agents. A fight briefly occurs between the two men before Laird shrugs his shoulders like the archetypal Hollywood leading man who realizes he has lost his girl to another man, grins and finally realizes his error. Quite obviously, the film contrasts two forms of male leadership. Laird represents an idealistic FDR type of wartime leadership which is now both anachronistic in a new era and susceptible to manipulation as the conviction of New Deal politician Alger Hiss had recently revealed to the American public. The film's narrative privileges the more cynically paranoid, suspicious, tough-guy qualities of Kip. He is not only a cinematic descendant of the detective from hard-boiled fiction such as Sam Spade but also embodies many of the qualities of Mike Hammer. Mickey Spillane's Cold War hero who carried on a crusade against gangsters, Communists and sexual perverts alike throughout his popular series of novels during the '40s and '50s. Although Kip does not ruthlessly shoot Helen like the unfortunate heroine of the novel *I, the Jury* (1947), he does eventually kill off-screen the fleeing figures of Alpha and Zeta, who are both unarmed and unable to fight back. The women are threats to national security and perverse in terms of their unnatural female bonding. Kip eventually rescues Helen from contamination as Mike Hammer often rescues Velda from various threats to her body and mind in the novels. Victor Jory's clipped delivery resembles the hard-boiled tone of the private eye. He eventually achieves his mission by restoring Helen to her rightful place as navigator and her future domestic role when they safely return to Earth. Although Laird comforts the bereaved Doug, who has lost Lambda, in the final scene of the film, his leadership position has been undermined since he allowed himself to become the romantic dupe of a brainwashed Helen who had as much use for him as the Cat Women had for men. Ironically, he also acts self-importantly adopting a superior role to someone who also exhibited the same romantic infatuation as himself. However, Lambda's feelings for Doug were more genuine than Helen's for him. There is a special reason for Lambda's change of mind and gender orientation.

Attracted by Doug's idealistic descriptions of the American way of life, Lambda undergoes a similar transformation as those female Russian Bolsheviks played by Greta Garbo in *Ninotchka* (1939) and Cyd Charisse in *Silk Stockings* (1957). Unlike Alpha, Beta and Helen, who all express their contempt for the male of the species, Lambda represents that younger component of a political and sexual system who may achieve salvation under the right circumstances. However, although she helps Doug and the others to escape by "naming names," she eventually dies by Beta's hand when she attempts to prevent Alpha, Beta and Helen escaping to the ship.

Like science fiction Cold War visions of the "Red Menace," the Cat Women plan to take over the Earth and regard the male explorers as necessary evils to fulfill their future plans. The Cat Women are the last survivors of a once populous race now diminished due to lack of oxygen. They have obviously disposed of their own men in much the same way as Stalin disposed of those he regarded as threats to his leadership. Although Lambda finally sees the light, she dies in very much the same manner as the saloon girl in the traditional Western who stops a bullet meant for the hero. Like her generic counterpart, she is already contaminated not only by her former association with the Cat Women ("Once a Cat Woman, Always a Cat Woman") but also by the perverse nature of her past practical involvement which renders her easy transition into normative American heterosexuality highly suspect.

"Passsing" and performative masquerades also form significant features of the film. Influenced by her lunar sisters, Helen drops Kip and "passes" as Laird's lover. Alpha's Cat Women "pass" as friendly aliens, inviting the men to engage in a banquet and enjoy their feminine company despite the fact that they despise the male species. They fool Laird, Doug and Walt in the process. The fear of "passing" was not only a phenomenon confined to gays in this period but also involved other minorities as well such as Afro-Americans as films such as *Pinky* (1949), *Imitation of Life* (1959) and *I Passed for White* (1960) all show. However, despite her Cat Woman status, Lambda feels sympathy for Doug, falls in love with him and warns him about the danger he faces. While Alpha and Zeta remain constant in characterization, Helen and Lambda's feelings fluctuate during the course of the film. This is not just a contradiction in the screenplay but a key feature related to the social and historical factors influencing the construction of *Cat Women*.

As well as exhibiting Cold War Red paranoia and homophobia, *Cat Women* also cinematically contributes to the debate following the publication of the Kinsey Reports on male and female sexuality in 1948 and 1953. The last report appeared in the actual year *Cat Women* appeared. Rather than confirming traditional stereotyping images of homosexuals and lesbians, the Kinsey Reports revealed that Americans not only engaged in a diverse number of sexual practices but that gays were not emotionally maladjusted individuals but productive members of society little different from their heterosexual counterparts. As Robert J. Corber shows, far from resulting in a more tolerant America, the Reports actually contributed to the Cold War crisis by not only showing that gays could "pass" as heterosexuals but also in calling attention to the fact that sexual identities "were fluid and unstable rather than exclusively and permanently heterosexual and homosexual. Following the publication of the Kinsey reports, homosexuals and lesbians were thought to threaten national security not only because they were emotionally unstable and susceptible to blackmail but also because they might convert heterosexuals to their 'perverted' practices by seducing them."[11]

This is very much what happens to Helen in *Cat Women*. Also, Laird, Doug and Walt allow themselves to become "feminized" by their passive submissions to Cat Women charms. However, while Zeta murders Walt and Helen nearly causes Laird's death after he has served his purpose, young Doug finds Lambda less dangerous than her female companions. She changes after "passing" as a friendly Cat Woman by showing Doug the dangerous side of her Cat Woman association in suddenly becoming touched by him. She thus reverses Helen's direction; Helen moves from a genuine attraction to Kit to "passing" as Laird's love by being manipulated by the Cat Women's scheme. But rather than regarding Lambda's sudden change as a discordant element in the script, it is important to see it within its particular social context. According to the findings of the Kinsey Reports, many

Americans had engaged in same-sex practices as adolescents before becoming exclusively heterosexuals as adults. Others had married and borne children while still engaging in same sex practices.[12] The film sees Lambda change her sexual orientation while Helen is quite prepared to engage in heterosexual practices with Laird to aid the cause of her lunar sisters who will eventually free all Earth women and kill off the men except those needed to breed females.

Kip remains apart from all this. He preserves his separate identity and remains constant in maintaining masculine control throughout the entire film. Another historical factor also explains his role. During the Cold War era, male identity underwent a series of challenges typified by the rise of an "organization man" discourse now defining male success less in terms of former qualities involving personal ambition and individual initiative but rather by the more "feminine" traits of respect for authority, loyalty to one's superiors and an ability to get along with others.[13] Laird typifies these qualities. Young Doug is still wet behind the ears. Walt obviously resents these new American corporate forms of behavior by dreaming of striking it rich by finding gold on the moon like a nineteenth century pioneer. However, his dreams of "striking it rich" lead to his vulnerability and eventual death at the hands of Zeta. Kip remains outside this discourse for certain historical reasons. As Corber shows, "*film noir*" offered one of the areas of popular resistance to this domestication of masculinity by providing not only visually subversive styles and themes, but also supplying another male role representing a fantasy return to another masculine model now redundant in the post war era. While Walt fantasizes a return to the old, outmoded, individual entrepreneur model of the forty-niner, Kip embodies the return of the '30s proletarian gangster hero in the form of hard-boiled detective. As Corber points out, "The American people identified with the hard-boiled detective, despite his involvement in the criminal underworld, because his defiant behavior expressed their own anger and frustration. In the hard-boiled detective, the American people saw reflected their own needs and aspirations. For them, he represented 'the individual seeking individuality in a mechanized, socialized society, where his life is ordered and restricted at every turn, where there is no certainty of employment, far less of being able to rise by energy and ability or going West as in the old days.'"[14] If no private eye refusing to participate in female spheres of domesticity and consumption by preferring to associate "with unkempt offices and seedy boardinghouses."[15] Kip moodily seats himself away from his male colleagues by enjoying scopophiliac pleasures in eyeing the Cat Woman who offers herself to him. But he remains apart like a male cinema spectator refusing to participate actively and instead viewing his antagonist with a sardonic hard-boiled male gaze. But, despite Kip's male veneer of social control and his tough-guy methods in making Helen "name names," his eventual victory in alerting dumb organization man Laird to the dangers they face relies less on his abilities and more on the co-operation of Lambda. She not only reveals the plot to Doug but actively participates in returning the spacesuits, and trying to prevent Alpha from gaining access to the rocket. The film never displays Kip shooting Alpha and Zeta. Instead, it gives more screen time to Lambda's attempt to stop her former female compatriots as well as the poignant final scene of Doug mourning her dead body. Despite her Cat Woman status, the film actually privileges Lamdba's sacrificial action rather than Kip's elimination of Alpha and Zeta.

If not an artistic or generic achievement worthy of inclusion within any great tradition film canon, *Cat Women of the Moon* is nevertheless a culturally rich film by reflecting certain contemporary contradictions and tensions. Despite the final "happy ending" scene where Laird acts out the role of hearty leader disavowing everything which has happened before, the film's strongest images still remain those of a threatening lesbian community who have the power to sway a female heterosexual into their domain and nearly decimate her male companions. The Cat Women are not only external threats to national security but also embody alternative forms of behavior which Cold War discursive patterns attempted to render invisible. However, they remain highly visible within a low-budget, generic product which destabilizes rigid forms of categorization in more than one sense.

NOTES

1. Susan Sontag, "Notes on Camp," *Against Interpretation* (New York: Farrar, Straus, & Giroux, 1966), p. 277–93.

2. For camp's role as an oppositional spectacle and its presence in the Hollywood musicals and melodramas of Vincente Minnelli and Douglas Sirk, see Robert Corber, *Homosexuality in Cold War America: Resistance and the Crisis of Masculinity* (Durham, Duke University Press, 1997), p. 58–59.

3. Jack Babuscio, "Camp and the Gay Sensibility," Gays and Films, revised edition Ed. Richard Dyer (New York: New York Zoetrope, 1984), p. 43. Considerable debate exists as to whether camp provides a viable oppositional spectatorial strategy for a marginalized group. See the different arguments presented by Andrew Ross, *No Respect: Intellectuals and Popular Culture* (New York: Routledge, 1989), 135–70, and David Bergman, *Gaiety Transfigured: Gay Self-Representation in American Literature* (Madison: University of Wisconsin Press, 1991), p. 103–21.

4. See David Bordwell, Janet Staiger and Kristin Thompson, *The Classical Hollywood Cinema: Film Style and Mode of Production to 1960* (New York: Columbia University Press, 1985).

5. Robin Wood, "Ideology, Genre, Auteur," *Film Genre Reader*, Ed. Barry K. Grant (Austin, University of Texas Press, 1986), p. 62.

6. Laura Mulvey, "Visual Pleasure and Narrative Cinema," *Screen* 16.3 (1975), p. 6–18.

7. See Arthur Schlesinger, Jr., *The Vital Center: The Politics of Freedom* (Boston, Houghton Miflin Co, 1949), 126–27; Robert J. Corber, *In the Name of National Security: Hitchcock, Homophobia, and the Political Construction of Gender in Postwar America* (Durham: Duke University Press, 1993), p. 19–26.

8. See Lois W. Banner, *Women in Modern America: A Brief History* (New York: Harcourt, Brace, Jovanovich, 1974), 211–228; Barbara Eherenreich and Deidre English, *For Her Own Good: 150 Years of the Experts' Advice to Women* (New York: Anchor Press, 1984), 226–33; Mary Frank Fox and Sharlene Hesse-Biber, *Women at Work* (New York: Mayfield Publishing Company, 1984), 29–31; Lynn Y. Weiner, *From Working Girl to Working Mother: The Female Labor Force in the United States, 1820–1980* (Chapel Hill: University of North Carolina Press, 1985); Shema Berger Gluck, *Rosie the Riveter Revisited: Women, The War and Social Change* (Boston, Twayne, 1987), 259–270; Corber, 61–69; John D'Emilio, *Sexual Politics, Sexual Communities: The Making of a Homosexual Minority in the United States 1940–1970* (Chicago: The University of Chicago Press, 1983), 40–53; *Intimate Matters: A History of Sexuality in America* (New York: Harper, 1988), 288–95; Allan Berube, *Coming Out Under Fire: The History of Gay Men and Women in World War Two* (New York: Free Press, 1990), p. 176–201, 255–70.

9. D'Emilio, *Sexual Politics, Sexual Communities*, 46–47; see also *The Employment of Homosexuals and Other Sex Perverts in Government* (Washington: Government Printing Office, 1950).

10. See Ehrenreich and English, 227–28; Brian Murphy, "Monster Movies: They Came from Beneath the Fifties," *Journal of Popular Film* 1.1 (1972): 31–44; Andrew Dowdy, *The Films of the Fifties: The American State of Mind*

(New York: Morrow, 1975); S. Samuel, "The Age of Conspiracy and Conformity," *American History/American Film*, Eds. John O'Connor and M. Jackson (New York: Ungar, 1979), 203–17; and Peter Biskind, *Seeing Is Believing* (London: Pluto Press, 1984), p. 101–59.

11. Corber, *In the Name of National Security*, p. 8–9; John D. Emilio, *Intimate Matters*, p. 239–300.

12. Corber, p. 9.

13. See especially the classical study by William H. Whyte, Jr., *The Organization Man* (New York: Anchor Books, 1957). Based upon the observance of a decade of change in postwar American society, his findings are still relevant today—particularly to the world of higher education and its conformist tendencies! See also Corber, *Homosexuality in Cold War America*, p. 23–54.

14. Corber, 27–28. He quotes from 50s Marxist sociologist C.L. R. James, *American Civilization*, Ed. Anna Grimshaw and Keith Hart (Cambridge, Massachusetts: Blackwell, 1993), p. 127.

15. Corber, p. 53.

Interpreting Gender and Sexualized Identities

9

"Horror Has Its Ultimate, and I Am That": Severing the Bonds of Identity in *The Head* and *The Brain That Wouldn't Die*

David Annandale

The living severed head does not have the most distinguished pedigree in the field of recurring motifs in SF-horror films. There is no severed head film that stands as a classic—there is no *Bride of Frankenstein* (1935) of severed head stories. That said, 1959 saw the production of not one but two severed head films. One has become the schlock masterpiece of the genre, and the epitome of cut-rate drive-in sleaze. The other, while now considerably more obscure, displays a level of artistry not usually associated with head tales. These two films are *The Brain That Wouldn't Die* (released in 1962) and *The Head* (*Die Nackte und der Satan*, which arrived on American screens in 1961). I propose to examine how these films present a critique of the imposition of a male-defined identity on women, and how the women in these films subvert this imposition. Now, I do not pretend that either of these films has a firm feminist (or even proto-feminist) agenda, but there is much of interest nonetheless. Exploitative as these films might be (particularly *The Brain That Wouldn't Die*), they still lay bare the mechanisms of exploitation. This is a case, if you will, of sleaze hoisted by its own petard.

The two films have a number of plot points in common, beyond the obvious one of the severed heads. *The Brain That Wouldn't Die* tells the tale of Bill Cortner (Herb Evers), a brilliant but unscrupulous transplant surgeon. His reckless driving results in the decapitation of his fiancée Jan (Virginia Leith). In the basement of his country house, Bill keeps Jan's head alive in a photo developing tray. He then sets out to find a new body for her, prowling strip clubs and beauty contests before finally settling on Doris Powell (Adele Lamont), a photography model whose face has been scarred. Bill lures Doris back to the mansion with the promise of corrective plastic surgery. Meanwhile, Jan has entered into telepathic contact with a monster (whose face looks like melted putty) locked in a basement closet. This cone-headed giant is the sum total of Bill's unsuccessful transplant experiments. Obeying Jan's commands, it disposes of Bill's assistant, breaks out, sets the lab on fire, kills Bill in a surprisingly gruesome scene for the time and carries the unconscious Doris off to safety. The film ends with Jan's head laughing maniacally as flames consume the laboratory.

In *The Head*, we have the sinister Dr.

Ood (Horst Frank), who is obsessed with finding a new body for the hunchbacked nurse Irene (Karin Kernke). Ood is initially hired by Dr. Abel (Michel Simon). Abel, who has a weak heart, wants to have the healthy heart of a recent accident victim transplanted into his body. The operation goes awry, however, and Abel regains consciousness in much the same circumstances as Jan. Abel's head plays a much less active role than Jan's, however, and is largely reduced to impotently railing against Ood. Ood promises Irene he will operate to cure her deformity. Ood makes good on his promise, but what he doesn't tell her is that he succeeds where Bill failed: He transplants Irene's head onto the body of stripper Lilly (Christiane Maybach), a former criminal associate of his. Irene gradually suspects that her body is not really hers. She flees the besotted Ood, and takes up with Lilly's artist boyfriend Paul (Dieter Eppler). Ood tracks her down and kidnaps her. Paul leads the police to the lab, which Ood has set on fire. Paul rescues Irene, Abel's head is unplugged and Ood falls to his death.

At base both films are about demented surgeons willing to murder in order to provide beautiful bodies to match the beautiful heads of the women they love. In execution, the films are worlds apart. *The Brain That Wouldn't Die* is hugely enjoyable, but (to give the critics their due) this is undeniably in large part because it is such deliriously incompetent sleaze. The cinematography is drab. The sets are so featureless they are almost blank slates. (This is especially the case during the beauty pageant scene, where the contestants appear to be parading before an absolute black void.) The make up is primitive. The acting is atrocious. The dialogue is risibly over-the-top. (Jan, for example, who showed no tendencies toward portentous overstatement prior to her decapitation, subsequently announces, "Like all quantities, horror has its ultimate, and I am that.") The soundtrack is equally lacking in restraint: When Bill visits the Moulin Rouge strip club, the music is so overheated that *Mystery Science Threatre 3000* lampooned it as being broadcast by "KPORN." Finally, there is no getting away from the fact that the film is aimed squarely at the exploitation market. Bill's search for a body for Jan serves as an excuse for director-scenarist Joseph Green to linger over scene after scene of scantily dressed women. A nadir of sorts (or acme, depending on your point of view) is reached when two strippers get into a fight over Bill. The camera pans up from where they are wrestling on the floor to come to rest on a cat-shaped clock on the wall. Just in case we missed the point, "Meow," says a voice-over.

The Head, by contrast, is an exercise in gothic atmosphere, aided in no small measure by art direction by Hermann Warm of *The Cabinet of Dr. Caligari* (1919). Dark clouds scud across the moon during the opening credits, establishing a scene that takes place in perpetual night. Dr. Abel's home is bright pseudo–Bauhaus on the inside, but it is forbiddingly dark on the outside, almost completely obscured by a tangle of leafless tree branches. The time spent in the Tam Tam club (the hostess–strip bar where Lily works) is devoted primarily to plot development—Lily's performance is treated in cursory fashion. Some care has gone into the characterization as well. Irene, post-operation, is tormented by a sense of fragmenting identity as her body appears to have memories that her mind does not—her movements are not her own, but Irene's. Even Dr. Ood, while undoubtedly a traditional Mad Genius, is not without his tragic elements: Both his genius and his madness are due to the fact that he is a medical experiment himself.

I find that the real interest of both

these films, however, lies not their relative qualities but in what they say, consciously or not, about what drives their male characters to such extreme acts, and in the way they are illustrations of the social mechanism that not only allows such actions, but encourages them. This mechanism is "faciality."

In *A Thousand Plateaus*, Gilles Deleuze and Felix Guattari use the term "faciality" to describe the mechanism that assigns individuals their identity and their place in society based on their faces. The face is "less a particular body part than the abstract outline of a libidinally invested categorical grid applied to bodies."[1] In other words, the face itself is the metonymic representation of the mechanism of faciality. This mechanism operates on principles of binary logic and opposition. It constructs a grid, and then submits everyone to "either/or" tests. Faciality performs this operation in two principal ways. Deleuze and Guattari describe the first in the following manner:

> [T]he machine constitutes a facial unit, an elementary face in biunivocal relation with another: it is a man or a woman, a rich person or a poor one, an adult or a child, a leader or a subject, "an x or a y...." The face of a teacher and a student, father and son, worker and boss, cop and citizen, accused and judge...: concrete individualized faces are produced and transformed on the basis of these units, these combinations of units—like the face of a rich child in which a military calling is already discernible, that West Point chin. You don't so much have a face as slide into one.[2]

And you slide into one because something (faciality) forces you in. In this binary logic grid, everything is something precise, and each precise something has its place. The slots come in pairs, since each defined face comes with another face upon which it must function, or which must work upon it: the cop must police the citizens, the worker must submit to the boss, and so on. Of course, an individual is not limited to being one and only one of these faces, but at any given time, no matter what slot they find themselves in, they cannot occupy both halves of the pair at once. Hence the emphasis on the "or" above; there is no room for an "and."

So faciality's first way of imposing binaries is through the creation of categories. The second tactic sets up a form of hierarchy, and completes the grid. If the first case consists of "an x or a y" choice, the second is "yes-no." The machine examines each face to see if it fits into a category, and if it fits into none (if, for instance, the face is androgynous, neither clearly male nor female), it is rejected:

> At every moment, the machine rejects faces that do not conform, or seem suspicious. But only at a given level of choice. For it is necessary to produce successive divergence-types of deviance for everything that eludes biunivocal relationships, and to establish binary relations between what is accepted on first choice and what is only tolerated on second, third choice, etc.... A ha! It's not a man and it's not a woman, so it must be a transvestite: The binary relation is between the "no" of the first category and the "yes" of the following category, which under certain conditions may just as easily mark a tolerance as indicate an enemy to be mowed down at all costs. At any rate, you've been recognized, the abstract machine has you inscribed in its overall grid.[3]

The Brain That Wouldn't Die (1962), the schlock masterpiece of severed head films and an epitome of drive-in sleaze.

The deviances begin right away, since everything that is not the White Man receives a first-level rejection. The White Man face is the face that sits at the center of the grid, and is the standard by which all faces are measured and found wanting. The White Man face "with his broad white cheeks and the black hole of his eyes"[4] is the European face. It is the ideal representation of the dominant force in society. A hierarchy sets in, as the further you are from conforming to the White Man face, the further out on the grid you are. The decisions and divisions are racial; they are sexual; they are along age lines (children on the margins); they are whatever is necessary to define that which will not conform at the current level. The fact that a possible categorization is that of "an enemy to be mowed down at all costs" indicates the incredible strength of the facializing grid. Destruction is a category in itself, still part of the grid, simply indicating that we have arrived in a region beyond the bounds of tolerance, but where everything is still recognizable. You are recognized as belonging to the category of faces to be stamped out.

This is the mechanism which produces racism (and homophobia, and sexism, and all other such attacks), and so racism "never detects the particles of the other; it propagates waves of sameness until those who resist identification have been wiped out."⁵ Similarly, in the case of sexism, the existence of woman as being with her own trajectory, her own way of being, is not recognized. She is simply allocated a function that is defined entirely by its relationship to the White Man face.

Bill and Dr. Ood act in perfect accord with the mechanism of faciality. True, Ood is offering Irene something that she wants: an end to deformity (which, of course, would move her closer to the center of the grid). But Irene has worries and doubts about the procedure (and initially turns it down). Ood never does. It is coincidence that Irene's desires happen to coincide with Ood's at this point. Ood would have made her undergo the operation even if she had objected. And this is, of course, the situation with Bill and Jan. Jan pleads with Bill to let her die, but her desires have no bearing on the matter as far as he is concerned. Ood and Bill are interested in Irene and Jan only insofar as the women's lives have some relevance to their own.

Bill and Ood declare that the heads (and most particularly the faces) define the identities of the women, and set about rigorously enforcing this system. From the perspective of the men, there is a problem to be fixed when the rest of the female body does not conform to the beauty of the face. Both women must be altered because they deviate too far from the norm to be acceptable objects of love. (Jan initially conforms, but is of course completely unacceptable once she is reduced to a mere head.) The films thus play out the logic of faciality to its most grotesque, but inevitable, conclusions. True, both Bill and Dr. Ood are clearly psychotics, and neither film pretends their actions are anything but appalling and illegal. And yet, it is curious how impotent the forces of law and order are in these two tales. In *The Head*, the police do close in on Dr. Ood, but it is the sound of the wind and the sight of the moon that drive him to suicide. In *The Brain That Wouldn't Die*, the police are completely absent. Jan and the monster—Bill's most thoroughly violated victims—are the only ones who do anything to stop him. The social system is so helpless because it is so completely permeated by faciality. Bill and Ood do not challenge this order. They simply push it a little further. While the police might have a word or two to say about Bill and Ood's methods, they would not challenge the diagnoses the two men make regarding the women.

I would now like to consider the films in turn to show how faciality plays out in each, and how each provides us with different insights into the evils of this system, and finally see what each has to say about resistance.

Of the two, *The Head* is arguably the more depressing in the conclusions that we can draw from it, even though it does end ostensibly happily with the mad doctor dead and a young couple united. The problem is that, though Ood is dead, the systemic problems that he represented are still very much in force—now incarnated in the apparently (but only apparently) benign figure of Paul.

Though antagonists, Ood and Paul have more in common than either would likely be willing to admit. Both men have had a relationship with Lilly: Ood as her accomplice in murder, Paul as a boyfriend. Both have little patience for her now, treating her with a contempt that is either thinly veiled (Ood) or blatant (Paul). Both are only interested in her now for her body: Paul sketches her absently while she changes, and Ood examines her while she has her dress over her head (thus obscuring the disposable portion of her being). For Paul, she is an increasingly boring raw material for his drawings. When asked if he ever loved her, he says, "Oh, I don't know. To say I loved her is maybe going too far. It could have been that I loved her as an artist may have: as a beautiful form." For Ood, she is the attractive raw material for his surgery that will create a new, improved Irene. Unlike Irene, Lilly cannot be improved. She can only be discarded. The reason for this is that, beautiful though she may be, she is also aggressive and independent. She has her own agenda, one that involves only strategic, rather than subservient, relationships with men. This is unacceptable for both Paul and Ood. The fact that Lilly is also a murderess suggests that her forcefulness is also unacceptable from the point of view of the film. Certainly we are not encouraged to shed too many tears over her demise. At any rate, Lilly's "imperfection" cannot be solved (except with finality) through anything as simple as surgery. Her rebellion—her refusal to conform to the role alloted to her as woman—means she must be eliminated. This is what Deleuze and Guattari mean when they say that faciality never detects the particles of the other: The grid through which the men organize their existence cannot accommodate a program that is different, that is at odds with theirs. Lilly must conform or be wiped out. She resists identification (literally, since she has changed her name and appearance to escape the law). So she is wiped out.

Ood and Paul also have identical reactions to Irene. From Ood's perspective, Irene may be hunchbacked, but she can be improved. All she needs is an entirely new body. Her personality is exactly as it should be: respectful, passive, subservient. The fact that she is a nurse (draped in a uniform more than suggestive of a nun's habit) while Lilly is a stripper makes even more explicit the madonna/whore contrast between the two women. That Paul and Ood dally with Lilly only to reject her for Irene thus seems all the more inevitable. Paul only encounters Irene after the operation, but he soon discovers the truth. The first time he sees Irene, he initially thinks she is Lilly—their very movements are identical. When he finally realizes what has happened, he is not unduly disturbed. Irene is agonized: "Which is my past? Which is it?" she asks him. "The past of Lilly's body or the past of my head, Paul? Paul I'm scared." Paul's response is meant to be comforting, but is in fact rather sinister: "Don't be afraid. Now you have a normal body. You can fall in love. You'll be like everyone else. You've no need to feel ashamed. Don't fight against it. Your face is so lovely." Paul does not see Irene and Lilly, two victims in one body. He sees a "fixed" Irene, and sets about convincing Irene of the correctness of his point of view. He, like Ood, sees the face as that which defines the individual. He is, after all, an artist, one specializing in sculptures of the female form. Ood, the surgeon-artist, tells Irene, "You are my creation," and Paul makes Irene sit as his model. He sculpts her head, idealizing her. His gaze is just as controlling as Ood's. It is simply less nakedly so.

Irene's torment, however, contradicts the principle by which both Ood and Paul act. Lilly's body, as mentioned previously, has its own memories. Identity, the film suggests, is not contained entirely within the face, despite what Ood might believe. The result is torture for Irene, as she finds herself torn between what she has always known as her self, and the vestigial but still powerful remnants of Lilly's personality. Irene finds that she has Lilly's cigarette habit, for instance, and that she can dance superbly though she has never danced a step before in her life. When she examines herself before a mirror, her movements recall Lilly's strip tease. The other characters notice the contagion of personality, and Ood speculates: "She's still ruled by her head. I'm wondering, though, if that lovely body will end up by demanding entirely too much of her spirit." In other words, Irene is being defined by more than her face. If this keeps up, she too might wind up trying to shift out of her place in the faciality grid.

After being recaptured by Ood, Irene lapses into a semi-catatonic state from which she never emerges. She shows no reaction when Paul sets her free. Her comment here—her last words in the film—is: "It's no use. I'll never get away from him." At the literal level, she is immediately proven false: Ood falls to his death moments later. But where it counts, she is absolutely correct. Nothing has changed in the system that permitted Ood to act as he did, Paul is merely a less overtly violent version of Ood, and the mental agony caused by the confusion of identities is not going to go away. The surgery cannot be undone. Irene cannot escape facialization.

Paul has the last line in the film. As Irene crouches over the body of Ood, Paul stands over her and says, "Come, Irene. Now you're free. Come." The emphasis here is on the imperative ("Come"). Paul makes her stand and walk with him off into the dark woods. Paul may think things have ended happily for Irene. The film begs to differ. The music is an eerie, funereal drone not unlike the wind that has driven Ood mad. Paul is leading Irene deeper into the gothic woods, not out of them. And Irene has a shell-shocked, vacant look to her. Her gaze is unseeing. Her movements are stiff, unsteady. She has, in fact, been almost completely indifferent to the rest of the action in the film since her recapture broke her spirit. The men can play out their conflict, but it has no more relevance for her. The only options open to her are surrender to faciality or complete withdrawal, and she has chosen withdrawal. The conclusion we are left with is that Irene has, finally, defeated Ood and Paul's intentions. She no longer conforms. She might physically be what they want, but her personality is now as flawed as Lilly's—it is completely absent. She is nothing more than a robot. She escapes the tyranny of the face, but at a terrible cost to herself, and without exacting any real price from faciality itself.

The Head, then, does not appear to offer, in its story at any rate, much by way of means of resistance against faciality. The film's attitude is itself problematic since, as we have seen, the only forceful woman in the plot is a murderess. But there is value in showing us the all-pervasiveness of faciality. Viewing *The Head*, we become aware of the problem. That is a necessary first step. Further steps are taken in *The Brain That Wouldn't Die*.

I have said that *The Brain That Wouldn't Die* is much more blatantly exploitative than is *The Head*. The fact that it is so blatant, however, coupled with both the role that the male gaze plays in the plot and the tawdry, down-at-heels nature of the exploitation, starts to transform the film into something very like an exposé of the mechanism behind exploitation.

The male gaze in the film itself belongs to Bill. We see most of the story through his eyes. The audience's perception of, and relationship to, Bill is therefore crucial. Bill Warren writes that this part is so confused and confusing that [Herb] Evers, generally an okay actor, can make nothing of it. He seems to be a standard mad-scientist type, with his experiments, dedication, and monster in the closet, but the role isn't played that way. Evers plays Bill as if no one told him this guy were was written not as the hero but as the villain.[6]

This very confusion is what makes Bill so interesting and, for my purposes here, so useful. If Bill were played as a mad scientist, a certain degree of dissociation between him and the audience would be possible. In *The Head*, Dr. Ood is so bizarre, so thoroughly a mad genius that, under normal conditions, it would be entirely possible for (male) viewers to regard him as virtually an alien species, one that has very little to do with them. The conditions are not normal because the character who is presented as the identification figure for male viewers, Paul, has so much in common with Ood. In *The Brain That Wouldn't Die*, Bill functions as both Ood and Paul. His acts are monstrous, but he is handsome, charming, loves his fiancée, and is supremely confident. There is no other male character in the film who presents an alternative to Bill as hero. The other men are either overbearing authority figures (Bill's father, who vanishes from the story after the opening scene), snivelling, spineless grotesques (Kurt [Leslie Daniel], Bill's lab assistant, whose right/left arm is another of Bill's less successful transplant experiments) or drooling voyeurs (other spectators at the Moulin Rouge and at the Body Beautiful contest, and the photographers, all of whom should be wearing raincoats, who surround Doris). In fact, the male character with whom the film ultimately wants us to side is not human at all: It is the monster in the closet who kills the villains and rescues Doris.

The contradictions that make up Bill's character are not, when we consider them in the light of faciality, contradictions at all. Bill is rich, white and handsome. He is at the very center of the faciality grid; he is both the norm and an agent for it. He behaves like the hero because he believes he is the hero. The goal of his experiments, after all, is to save lives by perfecting absolute transplantation, replacing the defective parts of one body with normal ones from another. (In fact, Bill's goals are alarmingly like the current controversy over the concept of growing clones for spare parts.) In the case at hand, Doris' face is ruined (by faciality's standards), and Jan needs a body. The solution is as obvious as in *The Head*, where Irene needed a new body and Lilly needed a new personality. But this atrocity aside, even if Bill's broader goals weren't ostensibly for the good of humanity, it wouldn't matter. Membership has its privileges, and there is no reason for him to think that what he is doing is wrong because his position in the grid means that whatever he does is, by definition, right.

Evers' performance, then, presents the insane as sane. The film, however, clearly marks Bill as the villain. Even if we didn't get this idea from the horror of his actions, the other characters denounce his evil, and there is the nicely retributive justice at the end when the monster kills him (going so far as to bite off chunk of his throat). The audience is left with a central male figure who is simultaneously the embodiment of evil and of normality. It becomes difficult not to infer that the darkness Bill represents extends far beyond himself and into the social fabric itself.

The film drives this point home in Bill's first scene with Doris. He arrives in her tiny studio apartment, where she is just finishing posing for a group of photographers (one of whom suggests she have a private sitting with him). Initially, Doris does not recognize Bill as a high school acquaintance, and is as hostile toward him as she is to the photographers. Her hostility is understandable: The last photographer's proposition indicates that he and his cohorts view her as little more than a prostitute, and she resents having to be ogled in order to make a living. The roots of her hostility go deeper than this, however. "I trusted a man once," she says, "all the way. What did it get me? He gets his head full of jealous lies, and I get…." She pulls back her hair to reveal the scar on the side of her face. Doris, as a model, is ostensibly the physical perfection of woman, as defined by faciality. Her scar is hardly a massive disfigurement, but by the terms of faciality, it is crippling. Just as the beauty of Irene's face dictated that a corresponding body must be found, so Doris' scar somehow renders her grotesque. Because she at first appears "perfect," the presence of a flaw is a violation, and so the scar's importance is hugely magnified. Because her face is marred, Doris herself is critically imperfect. Her hatred of men is now all the more understandable: they are responsible for the scar, and (even more damagingly) it is the power of their gaze that gives the scar its importance and makes it such a torment.

Bill, in his most persuasive mode, convinces Doris that not all men are responsible for her pain: "Because you've been battered around, don't go sour. You shouldn't lose your trust in people. Not all of us." Bill is quiet, understanding, tender and supportive. If we were to see this moment out of context, we would assume that Bill wore the white hat in this film. The irony, of course, is that he does not, and his speech that convinces Doris she is wrong paradoxically convinces us that she is right. Her paranoia and misandry are entirely justified. Bill is only interested in her for her body.

Doris' face is flawed, and so she becomes disposable in toto. Jan's face, on the other hand, is unharmed by the accident, and so she is salvageable. The appearance of her head, as it sits in its tray, is significant: With white cloth bandages covering her dark hair, the only thing we can see of Jan now is her face. By being reduced to her face, Jan has been reduced to what is, in this system, the most fundamental element of her identity. But then something curious happens: Jan's personality undergoes a complete transformation. There is no longer any trace of Bill's fiancée in this maddened, vengeful being. Even her speech patterns change: Gone are contractions, and Jan now speaks in the elaborate, portentous manner one usually associates with Dark Lords of one sort or another. It is in one of these speeches that she utters the "horror has its ultimate, and I am that" line. When I mentioned this line earlier, it was as an example of bad writing, which it is. But as an illustration of just how powerful faciality is, it is superb.

Here is how Deleuze and Guattari describe the face. The language is that of the horror tale: *"The face, what a horror.* It is naturally a lunar landscape, with its pores, planes, matts, bright colors, whiteness, and holes: there is no need for a close-up to make it inhuman; it is naturally in close-up, and naturally inhuman, a monstrous hood."[7] The italicized opening sentence is an exclamation of horror, a recoil like that of Christine's before the unmasked Phantom of the Opera. The ensuing description is that of a monster. With its evocation of the cold, bleak alienness of the moon and its piling on of inhuman detail (details that are nonetheless vague — we do not get the delineation of a specific face), the description could almost come from Lovecraft. The use of the words "horror," "inhuman" (twice) and "monstrous" emphasize the terrible distance this monster has from us, as well as its malevolence. But the eerie thing is that this monster is the face, the human face one normally does not think twice about. To drive home their point about (among other things) the tyranny of the normal, Deleuze and Guattari need to separate us, their readers, from the unthought norms of the face. They are rendering the face alien to us, making it as monstrous to us as Jan's new being is to her. The result is that we recoil. We realize what a horror faciality is. Jan, then, is right to describe herself as horror's ultimate. But the apotheosis of horror is not because she is a living head, but because she has become the literal representation of faciality. She isn't just a face: she is the Face.

After presenting the face to us as a horror, Deleuze and Guattari appear to find hope in modes of existence that move to escape faciality's grasp:

> Beyond the face lies an altogether different inhumanity: no longer that of the primitive head, but "probe-heads"; here, cutting edges of deterritorialization become operative and lines of deterritorialization positive and absolute, forming strange new becomings. Become clandestine ... for the wonder of a nonhuman life to be created. Face, my love, you have finally become a probe-head....[8]

If the face and its normality that we once took for granted are monstrous, if the face is in fact inhuman, then once we realize this and escape, we are free to construct new representations of ourselves, and to become something new. This new construction is "nonhuman," which is not the same thing at all as "inhuman." "Inhuman" is that which hurts, that which is malefic. It is evil. And it is inhuman because it is unattainable, even while presenting an enforced norm. "Nonhuman" is that which is free of the inhumanity of the face. "Nonhuman" is linked with "Face, my love," the negative image of "The face, what a horror" (which was inhuman). The multiple use of the word "face" might be confusing, but it would appear that the new face is a face that, by virtue of being nonhuman, is free of all the strictures and oppressive impositions that the paradoxical inhuman human face imposes. This is the "postive and absolute deterritorialization": a total escape from the grid. The liberated face is no longer both means and representative of faciality's tyranny. Instead, it has become a probe with which to undermine the system and jab at its weaknesses. This is what happens with Jan. On the one hand, she has become the inhuman representation of faciality, and in the process acquires new powers—she has mental command of the monster in the closet. She does not, however, act as the agent of faciality. She uses her power to cause the death of Bill and destruction of the lab.

In the final moments of the film, Jan laughs maniacally as the flames lick towards her. We would be forgiven for wondering if she is not now completely insane. "Dismantling the face is no mean affair. Madness is a definite danger.... The organization of the face is a strong one."[9] So Deleuze and Guattari warn us. But the dismantling is necessary, for all its risks. Jan may have lost her mind, but she does put a stop to the intolerable cruelty of her fiancé, a cruelty made all the worse by his unshakable conviction that no matter how much pain he has caused, he is in the right. Jan's reactions to her circumstances, and her actions to correct it are, arguably, the only truly sane path open to her.

The Head and *The Brain That Wouldn't Die* both show the oppressive workings of faciality, showing the face for what it is, demonstrating the need for resistance. Already, this exposure of the face is a necessary step toward combatting it: "know your faces; it is the only way you will be able to dismantle them and draw your lines of flight."[10] Know the enemy. Jan finally does, coming to a consciousness and acceptance of her specific circumstances. She realizes that she is horror's ultimate. She is the face now, and this liberation gives her power. Her decapitation has severed the bonds of her identity (defined as an attractive nurse subservient to doctors, and as an attractive fiancée subservient to Bill). Bill wants to re-create the bonds by assigning Jan a new body. The body Jan chooses, however, the body that moves to her brain's commands, is the monstrous one. She turns faciality against itself, wielding its own power to free herself from the grid.

The Head and *The Brain That Wouldn't Die* provide us, then, with a twofold approach to combat faciality. Firstly, the face is made strange. Abel's hugely fat head, Jan's stark whiteness broken only by mouth and eyes, and the monster's elongated head with misaligned eyes force our attention onto the face, and prevent us from taking it for granted. We become conscious of the tyranny of faciality. With that consciousness, the next step becomes possible: knowing the precise nature of our face, knowing how and where we are being slotted in the faciality grid. The dismantling of our face is risky, difficult and frightening. To conform is to embrace comfort. We must become nonhuman.

Otherwise, we capitulate to horror's ultimate.

NOTES

1. Massumi, Brian. *A User's Guide to Capitalism and Schizophrenia: Deviations from Deleuze and Guattari*. Cambridge MA: Swerve, 1992, p. 172.
2. Deleuze, Gilles and Felix Guattari. *A Thousand Plateaus: Capitalism and Schizophrenia*. Trans. Brian Massumi. Minneapolis: University of Minnesota Press, 1987, p. 177.
3. Deleuze and Guattari, p. 177.
4. *Ibid*, p. 176.
5. *Ibid*, p. 178.
6. Warren, Bill. *Keep Watching the Skies: American Science Fiction Movies of the Fifties*. Volume II. Jefferson NC: McFarland, 1986, p. 609.
7. Deleuze and Guattari, p. 190.
8. *Ibid*, p. 190–91.
9. *Ibid*, p. 188.
10. *Ibid*, p. 188.

10

Ed Wood, *Glen or Glenda* and the Limits of Foucauldian Discourse

Chris Cooling

Although he is currently a cherished and beloved cult icon, Edward D. Wood, Jr., remains a distressingly under-appreciated director; largely auteurist approaches to his work tend to emphasize his incompetence, or what is often called his lack of talent. As a result, his films are for the most part reduced to communicating little beyond their own extreme, and admittedly hilarious "badness." This paper, then, has been inspired by a simple question: What is to be gained from the close textual analysis of Wood's work?

As any writer knows, however, a seemingly simple question can quickly inspire several others, each one more complicated than the first. Can a mere formal analysis ever truly exist outside of any historicity, whether it be the historical context of the text in question, or that of the analysis itself? What issues are at stake in attempting to read a film such as *Plan Nine from Outer Space* (1959) or *Glen or Glenda* (1953) at the level of pure content, if indeed such a purity can be said to exist? More importantly, perhaps, what is at stake in deliberately opting not to consider said works in this manner, by classifying them as films without sufficient value to merit such an approach? In short, why have *Glen or Glenda* and its kin not been more thoroughly read, and what is to be gained from attempting to do so now?

In a sense, this paper is driven by a dual pull: It proposes a more rigorous exploration of Wood's *oeuvre* while simultaneously attempting a reinvestigation, and an expansion, of the concept of formal analysis itself. Each direction potentially represents a substantial amount of work; for the purposes of the task at hand, I will thus offer Wood's *Glen or Glenda* as an initial case study, while drawing upon the writing of Michel Foucault to establish a useful reading protocol for the film. Foucault's work is particularly relevant here, perhaps surprisingly so; indeed, when presenting a shorter version of this paper at a recent conference, I was struck by the number of respondents who were interested less in my contribution to the "reclamation" of the 1950s trash-horror director than they were in that of the celebrated French philosopher.

Ideally, by considering Wood and Foucault in the same breath, as it were, I am not simply presenting an eyebrow-raising intermingling of high and low discourses; rather, it is partly my aim to blur further the distinction between that which is the text and that which is the methodology. Like much of Foucault's writing, for example, *Glen or Glenda* offers us both virtuosic textual pleasures as well as ample opportunity to re-theorize the interpretive practices that allowed us to enjoy those pleasures in the first place.

This dual pull, then, can be usefully translated into two further, clearer questions. Firstly, what would Foucault do with *Glen or Glenda*? How might he read it? Secondly, for all of his brilliance as a writer, what do we do with Foucault? Is he providing us with a critical methodology for the critical and/or cultural analysis of texts? Ultimately, of course, these are the same question. Similarly, just as Ed Wood is a figure who must be rescued from his own perceived "badness" before he can be meaningfully discussed, so too is Michel Foucault in need of a certain amount of demystification—one must, paradoxically, ignore his genius in order to profit most fully from it.

My conclusions herein are largely optimistic; I think it is easy to conceive of Foucault celebrating a film such as *Glen or Glenda* (insert your own joke about his sex life here), for reasons that will soon be apparent. Moreover, I believe that he does provide us with a useful model of critical methodology. As I see it, our tendency is to resist interpreting his work in this manner because it seems somehow reductive to do so; it is as if the work we might produce that is inspired by his writing should necessarily be as intricate, difficult or as comprehensive as that of Foucault himself.

It would be presumptuous of me to claim that I'm the first to whom it has occurred to read Wood's work in terms of Foucault's. When *Glen or Glenda* was briefly re-released by Paramount in the early 1980s—a re-release about which I'll say more later—J. Hoberman described it in this way for the *Village Voice*: "Eons ahead of its time, the film is a passionate defense of transvestism—and thus free expression—cast in the mode of a half-heartedly 'scientific' exploitation flick. Wood's narrative is based on two case histories, which are recounted (with Foucaultian aptness) by a shrink to a cop."[1]

Indeed, a testament to *Glen or Glenda*'s richness as a text is the sheer number of Foucault's books that might productively be applied to it.

One sheet movie poster for *Glen or Glenda*.

This paper, for example, is influenced primarily by *The History of Sexuality—Volume One* (to consider the film's discursive depiction of sex), as well as by *The Archaeology of Knowledge* (through which I'll attempt to articulate the film's discursive depiction of discourse itself). Alongside these texts, one could feasibly add such other titles as *Madness and Civilization: A History of Insanity*, *Discipline and Punish: The Birth of the Prison* and *The Birth of the Clinic: An Archaeology of Medical Perception* in attempting to reap more from the film. One's plot summary need only be slightly more detailed than Hoberman's in order to suggest how each of these works, respectfully, is relevant. The aforementioned psychiatrist does spend a majority of the film describing the eponymous subject's mental illness to a police officer; however, "the shrink" also spends time emphasizing, for the benefit of "the cop," strictly medical details of another patient's sex change operation.

Part of Foucault's use value, throughout his writing, is what might be called a profound ambivalence toward his own historical claims, necessarily drawn from his continued investigation of power's role in the communication of authorized "knowledge." That is, despite the fact that most of his books are meticulously detailed and researched—thus, seemingly authoritative—they are also, with varying degrees of intensity, about the self-valorizing nature of historical writing itself. Indeed, George Lipsitz has suggested that all great histories are also enlightening on the subject of historiography; in Foucault's case, however, the latter field is often granted equal or greater weight than that which is suggested by a given book's title. In effect, his works achieve a degree of fluctuating sexuality; Foucault repeatedly demonstrates an admirable ability to make enlightening claims, for example, about the nature of incarceration, while simultaneously interrogating his own ability to do so from a remove of several centuries.

Consider the ambiguity of this passage: "I would like to write the history of this prison, with all the political investments of the body that it gathers together in its closed architecture. Why? Simply because I am interested in the past? No, if one means by that writing a history of the past in terms of the present. Yes, if one means writing the history of the present."[2] So concludes the introductory chapter of *Discipline and Punish*, leaving readers to ponder the subtlety of this distinction while also reckoning with Foucault's account of the Panopticon's development: We must consider the significance of this past phenomenon while asking ourselves whether such prison architecture can ever merely "be" an isolated object to be historically analyzed, or instead must always represent an element of the present moment's history. So too with *Glen or Glenda*: In attempting to read the film nearly a half-century after its production, one is forced to confront both issues held *within* the text as well as those *of* the text; that is, its multiple significances as an object of film history, as well as a recurring historical marker in and of itself.

I will proceed, then, by describing in detail a segment of the film, slightly more than three minutes in length, that manages to embrace a majority of the thematic issues and formal properties to which this paper will repeatedly return. It is my assumption that the average reader of this collection does not need to be told who Ed Wood is, or what *Glen or Glenda* is about. Those who desire entertaining accounts of a lingerie-clad future film maker storming Polynesian beaches during the Second World War would be far better off viewing Tim Burton's 1994 biopic, or reading Rudolph Grey's *Nightmare of Ecstasy: The Life and Art of Edward*

Director Edward D. Wood, actor Bela Lugosi and producer George Weiss (left to right) on the set of *Glen or Glenda* (1953).

D. Wood, Jr.[3] Indeed, the very fact that I can easily make such an assumption merits its own consideration. We must investigate the matter-of-fact appearance of such commonly held "Ed Wood knowledge." What is this knowledge, exactly? Who has the power to communicate it, and to what end? Most importantly, what alternate ways of understanding Wood and his films are being obscured by the complacent popular acceptance of such knowledge as truth?

The sequence in question, occurring approximately 11 minutes into the film, begins as Hoberman's shrink and cop discuss the case of a recent suicide, a man found wearing high heels, makeup, wig and a dress. Dr. Alton (Timothy Farrell) explains to Police Inspector Warren (Lyle Talbot) that the transvestite's death might best be understood by considering the narrative of another, similar subject. "I'd like to hear the story to the fullest," says Warren, to which Alton tellingly replies, "Only the infinity of the depths of a man's mind can *really* tell the story...." On this, the film presents an ominous lightning bolt transition to Bela Lugosi's unnamed character, a narrating figure seated in a strange laboratory whose walls are lined with shelves displaying bizarre occult objects: skeletons, items in jars, taxidermized animals, etc. Lugosi concurs with Dr. Alton: "No one can really tell the story.... Mistakes are made. But ... a story is begun!"

Another lightning bolt transition takes us to location-shot footage of Glen (Wood himself), dressed in the now infamous angora sweater that signifies Glenda, window shopping longingly at a ladies' boutique. The film cuts to extreme close-ups of two newspaper headlines, "World Shocked by Sex Change" and "Man Nabbed Dressed as Girl." The latter can easily be seen to have been pasted over the newspaper's original headline; those who watch *Glen or Glenda* on the big screen are thus also able to read the original copy and confirm that the story is in fact about taxes. "Why is the modern world shocked by this headline?" asks Alton in voice over.

He goes on to liken such gender instability to other noteworthy examples of human invention, previously thought to be immoral, or at least inappropriate. As the film cuts to stock footage of an American bomber dropping its payload, a hypothetical female's ignorant drawl can be heard on the soundtrack: "Airplanes? Hah! Why, it's against the Creator's will. If the Creator wanted us to fly, He'd have given us wings." Similarly, a stereotypical "rube," complete with a piece of hay clenched in his jaw, is next seen leaning on his hoe in front of a crudely painted "tree" backdrop, as a male voiceover complains dully, "Automobiles? Bah! They'd scare the horses."

The "silly" nature, retroactively, of these comments is then underscored by stock footage of the freeways lining Los Angeles, whose iconic city hall appears in the background. "We have corrected that which nature has not given us," intones Alton on the soundtrack as the montage progresses, emphasizing the impressive modernity of the city's skyscrapers. "We just had to learn how to put nature's elements together for our use, that's all," he explains helpfully.

After a brief cut back to the first newspaper headline, the sequence in question ends with a montage comprising only five shots and lasting just under 30 seconds. The shots consist of extreme close-ups: two pairs of eyes, then two single ears, and finally a return to the first set of eyes. Each of the five shots corresponds discretely to a piece of dialogue uttered by five different voices; the sequence is edited so that the cuts match the sentences.

The first two shots begin with a recap

of the voiceovers previously described here, regarding airplanes and automobiles. The two subsequent close-ups of ears correspond to new female and male voices, declaring respectively, "If the Creator had meant us to be boys, we certainly would have been born boys," and "If the Creator had meant us to be girls, we certainly would have been born girls." The film's previously unobtrusive score quickly becomes somber on the last shot of eyes, over which Dr. Alton ominously asks, "Are we sure?"

One of *Glen or Glenda*'s most compelling qualities, then, is a consistent and seemingly unique sense in which its form transcends, and ultimately becomes its content. This is worth considering alongside Foucault's *Archaeology of Knowledge*, in which it is suggested throughout that we should no longer conventionally interpret messages (books, films, texts, etc.) through established semiotic or structuralist approaches. Instead, Foucault proposes that we read each individual statement as communicating on some level the larger discursive practices that allowed it to come into being at a given moment in history. It is not difficult to conceive of thorough Foucault readers finding fault with this paper's basic project—the use of his writing in an interpretive analysis of a film—particularly when confronted with such passages as this: "The analysis of statements, then, is a historical analysis, but one that avoids all interpretation: it does not question things said as to what they are hiding, what they were 'really' saying, in spite of themselves ... on the contrary, it questions them as to their mode of existence, what it means to them to have come into existence, to have left traces."[4]

It is my contention, however, that Foucault is too quick to set such concepts in opposition to one another; it seems to me that they are not necessarily "contrary."

Much in the same way that *Glen or Glenda* is able to hybridize form and content, so too does it destabilize a viewer's ability to distinguish between the two reading positions described in the previous passage. It is only through detailed formal analysis that one is fully able to discern the complexity of discourses that contributed to the film's particular mode of existence. My position is that *Glen or Glenda* interrogates the nature of the cinematic statement much in the same way that Foucault himself does regarding language.

The Archaeology of Knowledge presents a discernible move away from a structural linguistics approach to analysis and towards one that is somewhat closer to that of cultural studies. Foucault shuns direct consideration of an author's intent and calls instead for a more rigorously historical analysis of statements. As he puts it, "to describe ... a statement does not consist in analyzing ... the author and what he says (or wanted to say) ... but in determining what position can and must be occupied by any individual if he is to be the subject of it."[5]

From this perspective, *Glen or Glenda* becomes a tribute to low-budget, B-level exploitation filmmaking in 1950s America, portraying its own context as a very fertile enunciative field indeed. Though it may fail as art, education, or even compelling narrative, *Glen or Glenda* nevertheless has a material existence that requires us to read what Foucault calls "the element of possibility" that allowed it to be made. Ironically, the extremely low-budget nature of its material existence is a crucial determinant of the film's considerable ability to push the discursive limits of its own particular context.

It is worth delaying upon Foucault's emphasis on the materiality of statements for a moment. Asking the question, "Does every reprinting, even every re-reading of a book comprise a different statement?"

Foucault answers by stressing instead the importance of "Repeatable Materiality." A true statement, he suggests, should be able to maintain its content across a potentially infinite number of iterations; however, it seems self-evident that one's ability to be subject to a given statement (that which Foucault compels us to read in place of the statement itself) is very much a historically contingent variable. I mentioned earlier a re-release of the film in the 1980s: Did *Glen or Glenda* at that time convey the same statement that it did in 1953, or that it would go on to convey when the film *Ed Wood* won two Academy Awards in 1995?

Faced with these questions, perhaps it is most productive to argue that Foucault's work, particularly that of *The Archaeology of Knowledge*, does not cleanly theorize a means of easily accessing textual meaning; instead, it problematizes the seemingly simple categorization of texts as texts by introducing the concept of the statement in the first place. For example, Foucault raises the possibility of that which is ostensibly the object of research also being used as an instrument, or a tool of that research; he repeatedly refers to his own work as having "themes," implicating it as a text to be studied as well as a means to studying texts; and finally, his conclusion is itself a kind of script, a literal dialogue in which Foucault writes as both "himself" and a potential critic of the book's arguments. Thus it might be more useful to present the work of Wood and Foucault as engaged themselves in a meaningful dialogue with one another; each text enriches our understanding of the other across a continuum of knowledge, rather than one decoding the other via a straightforward interpretive exchange. As Foucault puts it himself, "I am not proceeding by linear deduction, but rather by concentric circles."[6]

Specific details are in order at this point. A fruitful entry point regarding *Glen or Glenda* is the mere fact of Bela Lugosi's presence in the film. It is difficult to determine if he was cast in an attempt to give the film "star power" or simply because of his own friendship with its director. This is a surprisingly potent

Bela Lugosi in *Glen or Glenda*. The actor's status as inescapably an icon of horror raises the question of he film's generic classification.

debate that continues to rage on between Wood and Lugosi devotees; I have neither the courage nor the stamina required to enter it. The casting of an aging horror icon, however, is in itself a surprisingly useful means by which a film is able to simultaneously co-exist as individual text and theorizing of the historically contingent meanings of texts. Think of how often this occurs. For example, many critics felt Tim Burton connected with this material by equating his own friendship with Vincent Price, who appears briefly in *Edward Scissorhands* (1990), to the Lugosi-Wood relationship. Most notable, perhaps, is Peter Bogdanovich's use of Boris Karloff in *Targets* (1968), which famously contrasts the star's quaint-seeming gothic horror films with the random, senseless violence of the Vietnam war, as well as a Charles Whitman–inspired sniper. Similarly, the occult collection that sits behind Lugosi throughout *Glen or Glenda* is evocative of the Museum of Jurassic Technology in Los Angeles (well-chronicled by Lawrence Weschler), in which bizarre objects both entertain visitors and, through incomprehensible ("bad"?) juxtaposition, require them to question the discursive authority of the Museum as an institution.

Nevertheless, Lugosi's status as inescapably an icon of horror raises the question of *Glen or Glenda*'s generic classification. Typical sex education films stress their medical and/or scientific nature, as is done here through the figure of Dr. Alton; Lugosi's character, however, is also an important narrating presence throughout the film. *The Archaeology of Knowledge* frees us, mercifully, from having to interpret this narrational conflict—yet it is significant as precisely the sort of juxtaposition that fascinates intellectuals when on display in the aforementioned museum, but is a detail that has enabled so many to dismiss *Glen or Glenda* as filmically incoherent. Lugosi's character is alternately referred to, within the film's own credits and publicity, as "The Scientist" or "The Spirit." Some reviews of *Glen or Glenda* confidently refer to him as "God"; is Wood thus saying something about the relationship of Church and State? Particularly in the case of Ed Wood, it seems crucial to erect a methodology in which we strictly avoid attempts to understand "what the author meant." Such an approach invariably leads to one struggling with the humorous details of the man's increasingly desperate career; how are we to read his films, for example, in light of his repeated use of the unlikely writing pseudonym "Akdov Telmig"? (Spell it backwards.)

If the Lugosi-Alton narrational conflict is one that cannot be decisively or productively resolved, then it is at least worth noting that *Glen or Glenda* primarily combines two distinct discursive modes: that of the sex education film and that of the 1950s horror-propaganda film. This latter group is perhaps best exemplified by films such as *Red Planet Mars* (1952), today seen as displaying their anti–Communism to an absurd, hysteric degree. Lugosi's performance helps to evoke this group of films most efficiently through the repeated intonation of a single word; the actor's inimitable delivery of "Beware!", primarily spoken directly to the camera, conveys a paranoid tone that seems to interfere with the film's attempts to build genuine tolerance and trust. By combining such a discourse with the comparative sobriety of sex education, *Glen or Glenda* challenges, or at least extends, the accepted cultural meanings of both.

The film is comprised of far more, however, than two discourses alone. A recurring formal element of the film's "hodgepodge structure"—a term Eric Schaeffer uses to describe many of the exploitation films considered in his definitive study of the field, *Bold! Daring! Shocking! True!*—is cross-cutting between grainy, location-shot or stock footage and the immediately apparent artifice of painted backdrops or sparsely decorated sets.[7] Often, characters call direct attention to the limited ability of (the) film to effectively convey the nature of its subject. As Foucault says, a statement must have material existence in order to be a statement. This contrasts sharply, however, with Dr. Alton's assertion cited earlier: "Only the infinity of the depths of a man's mind can really tell the story." It is a sentiment compounded by Lugosi's mantra, "Mistakes are made." According to the film's line of argument, the statement most able to convey "truth" is the one least likely to be uttered, as it simply cannot be produced by the available channels of discourse.

This dilemma further emphasizes the textual instability suggested by *The Archaeology of Knowledge*, in which the distinction between a theory and its object is gradually erased. There are several moments at which *Glen or Glenda* is not so much a successful statement as it is a compelling theory about the "knowing" or understanding of statements. A phrase heard repeatedly throughout the film, typically from Lugosi's character (although echoed in essence by others), is "a story must be told," evoking a sense of the statement's inevitability, regardless of an institution's attempts to contain it. Here, we find that one is undeniably uttered, not through the sanctioned discourse of an author's agency, but rather despite the institutional technology of cinema itself.

Indeed, by emphasizing its own limited enunciative ability, or by guiding us to read the film not from an auteurist perspective but instead as explicitly about the act of writing and/or authorship, *Glen or Glenda* is able to use its own Poverty Row means of production as a metaphor for the restrictive social arena that prevents its characters from fully expressing themselves—or by coming out, one might say, of the discursive closet. Words uttered by Dr. Alton later in the film are worth considering here: "Thus Glen, and the character he created, 'Glenda,' much as an author creates a character in a book ... finds that the character dies only when the author wants the character to die."

The film's elaborate portrayal of writing, authorship and story-telling is thus worth exploring in some detail. As the excerpt described earlier at length suggested, the film is structured in part by the movement of a newspaper, later seen circulating amongst its characters. Despite its commonly held status as one of the "worst" pictures ever made, the film is not devoid of narrative structure; rather, it has many competing structures. As mentioned, Lugosi and Dr. Alton are both narrators; however, various peripheral characters are also granted access to voiceover status throughout the film. Moreover, the inspector's own story, of his attempt to understand the transvestite's death, provides *Glen or Glenda* with a definitive bookend. Its title notwithstanding, the film offers two emphasized narratives, of "Glen-who-was-Glenda" and "Ann-who-was-Andy," each incorporating many smaller embedded tales.

Indeed, the film's very name, alongside this complexity of structure, suggests not the communication of a static statement ("Glen"/"Glenda") but rather that of a potential message's permanent co-existence alongside an array of alternatives ("or"). Again, Foucault puts it best: "There is no ... free, neutral independent statement ... a statement always belongs to a series or a whole ... it is always part of a network of statements ... there is no statement that does not presuppose others."[8]

A line occurring often throughout Dr. Alton's narration, "I'll get to that in a moment," has actually been singled out by Schaeffer as a classic "evasive action" maneuver for exploitation films that want to seem scientific without actually having any such content. An astute observation, to be sure, but one that is not entirely appropriate in the case of this film. Instead, the line here is once more an index of the film's intricate narrative. Dr. Alton notably utters the phrase because he must defer the closure of the first story, that of Glen, until he can tell Inspector Warren a second story, that of Ann's sex change operation, as the first story's climax occurs when Alton tells the second story, of Ann, to Glen. (Got it?)

Thus, in the case of *Glen or Glenda*, an element which might facilitate its classification, or place it within a single specific discourse (for Schaeffer, it is clearly exploitation), is in fact part of the film's strategy for complicating what should be a basic discursive practice—the dissemination of statements. This complexity of dissemination is neatly echoed by the circuitous route the aforementioned paper takes amongst the film's many characters, finally to be discarded in a garbage can once its incapacity for truth-telling has been made apparent.

Glen or Glenda displays an impressively sustained ambivalence for the powers of the mass media in this regard. As the film opens, the suicide victim laments in voiceover that "the papers will tell my story for me"; later, however, Dr. Alton notes more positively about one of his narrative threads, "If the papers hadn't got a hold of it, the story would have gone untold." I call this ambivalence "impressive" because it seems to represent a measure of canniness on the part of the film. Clearly, if it is at all interested in educational status, it is compelled to suggest that a certain amount of information dissemination is good. Yet, it is also consistently passionate about the absolute subjectivity of a statement's enunciation "Glen is the author" "only the infinite depths," etc.)

I delay on these details, and stress one of Foucault's books more than the other, because I feel that *Glen or Glenda* has more to say about the discursive practices that allow its characters—and by extension, us—to speak about sex than it does about its ostensible subject, "abnormal" gender and sexual identity. Instead of actually teaching viewers anything about sex—or rather, the already false construct we call "sex"—Wood's film exposes the artificial, codified nature of the filmic discourses that attempt to convey valid information about it. Indeed, the film's literal content is often strikingly conservative, a quality that Schaeffer, amongst others, has noted often to be the case when a film, exploitative or otherwise, is heavily promoted for its "forbidden," "transgressive" qualities. Despite his "radical" sexuality, for example, Glen is repeatedly, emphatically confirmed by Dr. Alton to be "*not* a homosexual. Glen is a transvestite, but he is *not* a homosexual." Elsewhere in certain prints of the film, it is proposed that those such as Glen must fear for falling prey to homosexuals; specifically, they (and an implied 'we') must learn to defend themselves in advance by being able to spot such a predator by the distinctive manner in which he coyly holds his cigarettes. It seems easy to suggest that the Foucault of *History of Sexuality* would find the film's depiction of sex well within traditional discursive boundaries. The two troubled main characters, Glen and Ann, are both required, for example, to submit a confession of sorts to the clinical, medical gaze of Dr. Alton before they can enjoy (his institutionalized, official conception of) happy, healthy sexuality.

What the Foucault of *History of Sexuality* would find in *Glen or Glenda*, I suggest, is a film that consistently exceeds its own discursive context; as the book demonstrates, "a veritable discursive explosion" results from the repressive (or what has been seen to be repressive) post–Victorian perspective. The context of sex education is simply not sufficiently empowered to contain *Glen or Glenda*. Similarly, Foucault's post-structural approach to power allows it to appear in many forms, at varying intensities, and to move in many directions. Indeed, as *History of Sexuality* reminds us, "discourse produces power, but discourse can also undermine it, render it fragile and potentially thwart it."[9] Though the content of *Glen or Glenda*, then, seems to suggest it is unable to escape power's grasp by relying on confessional and disciplinary procedures, its formal properties redeem the film, in my view, by consistently undermining those very procedures.

Part of the reason the film can so easily be read as a unique statement in the Foucauldian sense, rather than a text in which an author successfully gets his point across, is because of the specific enunciative field, or mix of discourses, that produced it. Consider that *Glen or Glenda* simultaneously exists within the following discursive categories:

One: The Horror Film. Though Lugosi's presence in the film is somewhat unsettling at best, a devil-figure appears later, during a surreal nightmare sequence, to torment Glen.

Two: Autobiography. Despite the fact that Ed Wood performs in the film under the pseudonym of "Daniel Davis," he did little else to hide the fact that much of *Glen or Glenda* is about his own desires.

Three: Documentary. Initiating the project, producer George Weiss originally attempted to hire actual sex change recipient Christine Jorgensen as the lead; nevertheless implicitly capitalizing on her notoriety upon her refusal to appear.

Four: Sex Education. This is a film that, on some level, does seek to spread information in order to generate understanding, tolerance and health.

Five: Exploitation. A number of the pleasures to be had from *Glen or Glenda* are without a doubt guilty ones, derived mostly from its low-budget production values. A notable example, added to some versions of the film, is a long sequence in which burlesque footage of voluptuous women, literally ripping the clothes from their bodies, is edited together with reaction shots from both Wood and Lugosi's characters, resulting in what might be called a "Fellini-Kuleshov" effect.

Six: Avant-Garde. The brief montage at the end of the sequence described earlier is a good example; close-ups of eyes and ears effect a stylized image-sound rupture when applied to incongruous voice-over dialogue.

It is not without precedent to argue for the film's avant-garde status; in a set of "Cinema Texas" program notes for *Glen or Glenda*, Louis Black suggests that such "bad-films" "confront their audiences with many of the same questions and ruminations about standards and assumptions of filmic story-telling as, for example, *Last Year at Marienbad*."[10] A useful point, to be sure, yet Black pointedly does not go on in the notes to then interpret Wood's film as an avant-garde text, or demonstrate the use value of designating it as such. His comments resultantly seem to be part of a trend in which so-called bad films are considered avant-garde, yet somehow are such without requiring the hard work of an attempt to read them.

A seventh discourse, then, that could easily have been added to the previous list is Trash. By allowing the film to transcend this category, in which so many have quickly and decisively placed it, one can see that *Glen or Glenda* ultimately presents a dialectic between the (typically opposed) aesthetic implications of empty "trash," and avant-garde "art." That is, each method presents a measure of implied attempt to convey the "truth" of its subject matter. Again, *Glen or Glenda* interrogates and theorizes each mode of film making (as opposed to neatly embodying either), questioning the distinction between one mode's enlightened attempt to achieve a higher understanding of its subject's truth through novel aesthetic means, and the other's crude denial, effectively, of any truth's accessibility through aesthetic expression alone. Thus, even though, as Foucault says, every discursive practice has its own set of historically determined rules, because of the complexity of the discourse that produced *Glen or Glenda*, it is able to exceed those rules, and as a result it is able to reveal the sex discourse's inability to convey the truth of its subject.

So, even though it is a cliché, one is left to admit that, ultimately, the film is "so bad that it is good"; it is certainly not my desire here to deny the film its legitimate badness. In attempting to juggle so many balls at once, the film can be said to, yes, drop a few on occasion. Such statements, however, remain historically significant ones. *Glen or Glenda*'s formal "badness" succeeds in opposing the institutional processes to be found within both reigning forms of Hollywood quality, and the context of sex education as well. And yet, the film's full significance must also be attributed to its ability to stand outside of history: why is this the film that defines the concept of cinematic aesthetic bankruptcy for so many? Why is it somehow the most visible of any number of other exploitation films, each of which arguably energizes many, if not all, of the various discourses evoked in this paper?

These questions reflect the approach found in an article by Robert Birchard entitled "Edward D. Wood Jr.—Some Notes on a Subject For Further Research."[11] Written for the journal *Film History*, the paper is devoted to exploring our recent fascination with Ed Wood; its publication coincided with the acclaim generated for Tim Burton's eponymous film. Birchard structures the article around a number of popular beliefs about Wood he feels compelled to disprove. To wit:

One: Ed Wood was not unique.
Two: Ed Wood did not bring a personal vision to his projects.
Three: Ed Wood was not exploited by the system.
Four: Ed Wood's films did not find a wide audience.

As Birchard puts it, "that Ed Wood has become something of a folk hero among students of film simply ignores the real man and his work and contributes to the general suspicion and lack of regard for the discipline known as 'critical studies.'"[12] Birchard is indirectly arguing that the film's meaning has been substantially altered in the decades following its release; rather than examine those new meanings, however, he is content to present what might be called a knee-jerk desire to return the film to its original context—much as an average museum typically presents its materials in an ordered, rational display, and a "good" film commits to a specific aesthetic discourse.

It is unfortunate, then, that Birchard does not consider the example, alluded to throughout this paper, of the film's brief re-release in the spring of 1981. Nearly forgotten today, it was promoted with large advertisements in major New York newspapers that displayed the following copy:

> In the vast parade of motion pictures
> there are a few that marched to a
> different drummer.
> Some were one-of-a-kind originals.
> Like 'Citizen Kane.'

> Some told their story on a wide
> emotional canvas.
> Like 'The Godfather.'
> Some were provocatively bold, thumbing
> their noses at convention.
> Like 'Freaks.'
> Some were lost. Like 'Napoleon.'
> They all had one thing in common.
> They were different, more special than
> the other movies around them.
> Beginning on April 1st at 8:00P.M.
> The Sutton Theater
> Paramount Pictures Presents
> Edward D. Wood Jr.'s
> *Glen or Glenda*

The screening never occurred; officially, the studio's position was that it pulled the film as a result of the attempt on President Reagan's life on March 30. Why it might choose to do this was never clearly specified.

In any case, this seems an intriguing example of that which Birchard is trying so valiantly to criticize as inappropriate: the deliberate mishandling, and rewriting, of the "truth" of a given film's history. Indeed, not only is it a blatant example of such, it is one that, moreover, provides historians with an easily hissable "villain": the money-grubbing Hollywood studio, knowingly misleading the public through deceptive advertising, willing "unique" status upon the film (paradoxically, by likening it to other, equally "unique" films) simply through its own massive power as an institution of discourse.

This is not the full story of *Glen or Glenda*'s re-release, however (which did occur briefly that May, perhaps once Reagan had sufficiently recovered); what is most compelling about this occurrence is the extent to which the studio's handling of the film became somehow more intriguing a media text than the film itself. Why had they deliberately chosen to re-release the film on April Fool's Day? Was Paramount serious? Did they want audiences to prepare for an indisputable masterpiece, or were they expecting savvy New Yorkers to get the joke and applaud them for their high-profile, John Waters–esque irony? A number of newspaper columnists and cultural commentators grappled notably with these very questions at the time, in some cases going so far as to evaluate each other's commentary as part of the mystery. Stuart Byron noted in *The Village Voice*, for example, that a rival publication had potentially smeared Paramount's then-chairman in its coverage by captioning its photograph of the executive, "Barry Diller: Camp Project."

At stake for Byron throughout this matter was the media's collective maturity and sensitivity towards an increasingly "out" queer culture in the early 1980s: "If Hollywood studios cannot produce or distribute gay-themed movies without sexual aspersions being cast on their executives, Tinseltown homophobia will continue."[13] In Birchard's hands, such material would be sadly irrelevant, despite the fact that it could be argued that *Glen or Glenda* had finally provoked high-profile media debate about the acceptance of alternate sexualities nearly three decades after its original release. Considered, however, from a Foucauldian perspective, this *Glen or Glenda* becomes both a representative text of the 1980s' hesitantly shifting attitudes towards sexuality (think of the numerous cross-dressing comedies of the era, alongside which it could be listed: *Tootsie, La Cage aux Folles, Victor/Victoria*, etc.) as well as a means to understanding, to theorizing yet another of many historical specificities.

There are certain thoughts, then, that I find to be inescapable at this point. One is quite simply that, if *Glen or Glenda* is "bad," then, as they say, I don't want to be "good." This statement is not meant to be as flippant as it undoubtedly sounds. Put another way, if the nature of critical studies itself is that which is truly at stake, as Birchard suggests, then perhaps the consideration of the film presented here should not, cannot leave its readers with a more traditional paper's conclusion. You have likely read phrases of the following character before: "We are thus at a crossroads from which we should strive to ensure our endeavors will become better." Instead, it is my hope that one must now reflect upon the ways in which academic work must in fact become worse, and proceed accordingly. If by "better" is meant more disciplined, more rigorous, in stricter allegiance to established theories and accepted paradigms, increasingly driven towards the proof of a claim through the development of a linear argument, then instead I, inspired equally by Ed Wood and Michel Foucault, encourage a tendency toward indulgence. Admittedly, this is a rather romantic indulgence: an emphasis on the subjective, the digressive, and ramblings that serve as calculated demystification of the academic act. In short, a necessary and corrective emphasis of its always performative, textual nature.

Clearly, these are meant to be deliberately provocative statements, perhaps absurdly so. Like Birchard, I think there is more to do with a film such as *Glen or Glenda* or a figure such as Ed Wood, than blind celebration without actual critical engagement. I am equally uncomfortable, however, with the concept of assigning the film a generic, perhaps even regressive place within a category entitled "Sex Exploitation, USA, circa 1950s." We must do more with *Glen or Glenda* than bask in its badness: We must consider the implications the film has—and, to a lesser degree, all films have—for our own ongoing work as self-aware writers of film history.

NOTES

1. Hoberman, J. "Who Was That Masked Person?" *Village Voice*. May 20-26, 1981, p. 55.
2. Foucault, Michel. *Discipline and Punish: The Birth of the Prison*. New York: Vintage Books, 1995: 31.
3. Grey, Rudolph. *Nightmare of Ecstasy: The Life and Art of Edward D. Wood Jr.* Portland: Feral House, 1994.
4. Foucault, Michel. *The Archaeology of Knowledge and the Discourse on Language*. New York: Pantheon Books, 1972, p. 109.
5. *Ibid*, p. 95-96.
6. *Ibid*, p. 114.
7. Schaefer, Eric. *Bold! Daring! Shocking! True! A History of Exploitation Films, 1919-1959*. Durham: Duke University Press, 1999.
8. Foucault, p. *The Archaeology of Knowledge and the Discourse on Language*, p. 99.
9. Foucault, Michel. *The History of Sexuality—Volume I: An Introduction*. New York: Vintage Books, 1978, p. 101.
10. Black, Louis. Program Notes. *Cinema Texas*. October 28, 1981. Volume 21, #2. 1.
11. Birchard, Robert. "Edward D. Wood Jr.—Some Notes on a Subject for Further Research." *Film History*. Volume 7, 1995, p. 450-55.
12. *Ibid*, p. 455.
13. Byron, Stuart. "Rules of the Game." *Village Voice*. April 15-21, 1981, p. 58.

11

Daughter of Horror: Low-Budget Filmmaking, Generic Instability and Sexual Politics

John Parris Springer

Daughter of Horror, a nearly forgotten example of 1950s independent filmmaking, is a work of terrible insight and truths "more terrifying than fiction"—as the film's narration puts it—packaged as a low-budget horror movie. The only film ever made by independent producer John J. Parker, *Daughter of Horror* was apparently based upon a dream related to Parker by his secretary—a woman named Adrienne Barrett. The film was made in bits and pieces under a loose division of labor, with directorial responsibilities being shared by both Parker and his leading man, 1950s B-movie villain Bruno VeSota, who claimed to have improvised many of the scenes during production. No director's name appears in the film's credits, nor is the cast identified.[1] Parker's secretary Barrett starred—in her one and only screen performance—as the central character in her own nightmare as the unnamed "daughter of horror." Character actor Ben Roseman, who played dual roles as both the menacing police Detective and the violent alcoholic Father, was also the co-producer and set designer for the film. Parker began the project as a ten-minute short, but working with VeSota he decided to expand it into a feature-length film that was initially released in 1953 under the title *Dementia*. Shot entirely at night in the back streets and alleys of Los Angeles and Venice, California, the first version of the film contained no dialogue. *Dementia* embroiled Parker in a two-year battle with the New York State Censor Board which banned the film, condemning it in unequivocal terms as "inhuman, indecent, and the quintessence of gruesomeness."[2] After only a few New York City screenings, Parker pulled *Dementia* out of theaters. Securing a distribution deal with the low-budget Exploitation Pictures in 1955, Parker wrote and recorded a voice-over narration (spoken by Ed McMahon) that was added to the film when it was re-released as *Daughter of Horror* in 1956.[3] This second version of the film, running only 55 minutes in length, got a somewhat larger distribution on the drive-in theater circuit but the film soon disappeared in the tidal wave of low-budget horror and science-fiction movies of the 1950s.

In spite of its relative obscurity, however, *Daughter of Horror* is still a work of rare visual impact and thematic daring. It is indicative of the contingencies that governed low-budget, independent filmmaking in this period, that the film's complicated production/post-production history makes it difficult to establish a definitive version of the film today. But, the fact that at the time of its release the film was treated like any other product off the low-budget horror-genre assembly line, and was consigned to the "dream dump" of midnight movies and drive-in theaters (now specialist video catalogues), is a telling commentary on how the mechanisms of film marketing function to limit and contain certain ideologically explosive texts. Essentially an experiment in cinematic expressionism, *Daughter of Horror* was carefully orchestrated to evoke the alienated and disturbed subjectivity of its central character.

Daughter of Horror is a low-budget horror film, clearly designed to appeal to the youthful, late-night audiences who would have first encountered it at the bottom of a double or triple bill. But what is the "horror" which this film evokes? *Daughter of Horror* generates an unusual dramatic intensity as well as visual interest through its use of a nightmarish urban iconography and its relentless depiction of sexual aggression and violence against women which are presented in the film as pervasive, virtually inescapable facts of life within the threatening urban milieu in which the film is set. The sinister urban landscape depicted in *Daughter of Horror* possesses the drab anonymity of any typical American city. It is a newspaper headline appearing in the *Hollywood Tribune* that establishes the setting as that most atypical though intensely familiar of cultural settings: Hollywood. Here the themes of sexual danger and violence against women played out within a kind of nightmarish cityscape have a mythic resonance evocative of the larger sociocultural arguments that have surrounded the "Film Capital."

Shot MOS (without sound), *Daughter of Horror* was overdubbed with a hypnotic musical score written by the American modernist composer George Antheil and featuring the other-worldly vocalizing of singer Marni Nixon, supplemented late in the film by an onscreen performance by jazz musician Shorty Rogers. McMahon's voiceover narration was laid over this musical track when the film was re-released as *Daughter of Horror* in 1956. In its visual style the film exemplifies what Alfred Hitchcock called the "pure cinema" of wordless images joined to music, evoking the visual rhetoric of the silent cinema in its reliance on *mise en scene* and pantomime. No doubt this stylistic nod to the film aesthetics of a bygone era was responsible for making the film seem even more anomalous at the time of its release and contributed to its blatantly "low-budget" production values by 1950s standards.

Though nominally a horror film, *Daughter of Horror* actually operates in several different generic registers. The most important of these is *film noir* and the crime drama, but the film also refers to such experimental works as Luis Bunuel's *Un Chien Andalou* and Hollywood sub genres like the "psycho-dramas" of Alfred Hitchcock's *Spellbound* (1945) and Anatole Litvak's *The Snake Pit* (1948), most evident in its interest in the subjective mental state of the main character. *Film noir*, as well, displays an interest (inherited from German Expressionism) in representing the world through the tortured subjectivity of a central character. And it is to *film noir* that *Daughter of Horror* owes its greatest stylistic debt. Practically every shot in the film is composed within the characteristic chiaroscuro style of organizing the image through the arrangement of shadow and light in ways that create visually interesting and often menacing visual patterns. In his essay on the film, Jim Morton aptly described the dark, shadowy streets of *Daughter of Horror* as resembling the work of the Spanish surrealist DeChirico, and British film critic Nigel Andrews compared it favorably to the work of Orson Welles in such

Parker (at right) poses with members of his cast on the set of *Daughter of Horror*.

noir classics as *The Lady from Shanghai* (1948) and *Touch of Evil* (1958).[4] Shot by cinematographer William Thompson, the film is a veritable encyclopedia of *film noir* visual and thematic references, so much so that the music and images alone (as in the original *Dementia*) would support a reading of the film as belonging more to the psychologically inflected social world of *film noir* than the horror genre. Indeed the narration, added by Parker to get wider distribution, seems intended to specify the film generically by emphasizing the "horror" interpretation of events over either the psychological or the sociological, despite the fact that the film offers explicitly psychological and sociological explanations of the "horror" referred to in the title. What seems apparent (though such a view is certainly the product of my reading of the film), is that *Daughter of Horror* utilizes the trapping of the horror genre—mainly through the film's altered title and the added narration—in order to smuggle into theaters a film that was something more than a typical horror movie and, in fact, offered audiences a critical view of social/sexual relations of power among men and women, circa 1950s America.

Exemplifying the film's radically unstable generic identity is the central character, the unnamed "Daughter of Horror" (Barrett). In the horror genre of the 1950s, women were almost always consigned to playing the role of screaming victim while women in *film noir*, in contrast, were often more complex and more deadly, with the *femme fatale* being the quintessential female *noir* character. The unnamed character in *Daughter of Horror* does not fit neatly into either one of these categories simply because she is shown to be both the victim and the killer. In the course of the film, her violent behavior is accounted for and explained according to clear psychological and sociological scenarios that ultimately make her less an object of horror than of sympathy and indignation. The generic discourses of horror and *film noir* compete to define the unnamed Woman in the film, yet she continually eludes their stock characterizations and emerges (in a performance of surprising power by the non-professional Barrett) as a figure of profound alienation made up of equal parts cynical despair and resistance to her fate.

The film begins with a dark screen and the sepulchral voice of the narrator:

> You! You out there! Do you know what horror is? Smug, confident, secure because you're sane. Do you know what madness is or how it strikes? Have you seen the demons that surge through the corridors of the crazed mind. Do you know that in the world of the insane you will find a kind of truth more terrifying than fiction. A truth that will shock you! Come with me into the tormented, haunted, half-lit night of the insane. This Is my world—let me lead you into it. Let me take you into the mind of a woman who is mad. You may not recognize some things in this world and the faces will look strange to you, for this is a place where there is no love, no hope, in the pulsing throbbing world of the insane mind where nightmares are real. Nightmares of the daughter of horror!

We are introduced to the Woman as the camera enters through a window of her bedroom in a seedy, downtown hotel, a large neon sign flashing incessantly outside. The desolate city street, the cheap hotel room, the flashing neon light—these are all icons of the fallen modern world of *film noir*, a world of urban isolation and social fragmentation in which the individual is fundamentally alone. Though we first see the Woman lying in bed restlessly clutching the sheets, it is unclear whether we are observing her from outside her subjectivity or are already swept up in her hallucinatory mental state. Images of a desolate beach appear superimposed over the Woman lying in bed. In the distance the Woman appears walking slowly towards the ocean. As she approaches the shore, a huge wave rises up and crashes over her, and she disappears in the surf. Then the film cuts back to the Woman back in bed who suddenly sits up, her face strained and anxious, illuminated by the intermittent flashing of the neon sign.

Clearly, on one level the "horror" evoked by the Woman is founded upon her transgressive and somewhat ambiguous sexual identity, which is constituted as markedly "male" in several ways. First, Barrett has several masculine physical characteristics: she lights a cigarette and holds it between her lips in a tough male pose; she projects an aggressive male energy evident in her gait and bearing, and her plain features and overall manner make her appear to be a person hardened by experience and possessed by a smoldering rage at some unknown injury. She is also coded as masculine by her possession of the phallic knife, which she brandishes in such a way as to indicate that she has used it to kill in the past and may again in the future.

Leaving her room, the Woman has a series of encounters that, within the dream logic of the film's narrative, take on an allegorical significance. These encounters structure our response to the Woman and to the social world she moves through.

First she encounters a small child playing alone in a dark stairway. The child holds out a toy, but the Woman does not take it and moves away. Is this a refusal of "parental" love on the part of the Woman? Or perhaps (an even more subversive possibility) there is a critique of the family in that lonely gesture towards play and companionship that the child makes and the Woman refuses. At the very least, the woman's indifference to the child suggests an unwillingness to occupy the role of "mother" and nurturer that our culture imposes on women generally.

Moving through the dark hallways and stairwells of the building, the Woman next encounters a scene of domestic abuse. A policeman questions a disheveled husband and his wife, who lowers her robe to reveal large bruises across her back and arms. As the man is led away by the policeman, the wife breaks into tears. The Woman, peering at the scene from the shadows, bears silent witness to this scene of domestic violence and familial disintegration, the first in a series of episodes in the film that point to the social fact of violence against women and to the family as the context for that violence.

Leaving the hotel, the Woman encounters a dwarf selling newspapers (Angelo Rossitto), an emblem of the grotesque social world she inhabits. He holds out a newspaper (the *Hollywood Tribune*) which bears the headline "Mysterious Stabbing!" The Woman smiles knowingly—an expression that clearly implicates her in the crime—and begins to slowly walk down the street. With stark visual economy, these opening images in the film introduce us to a sordid urban milieu populated by monstrous and tragic characters whose lives imply an underlying psychosocial pathology. Violence against women is explicitly depicted but we are also prepared to expect violence *from* the Woman, who we now realize may be behind a series of violent crimes.

Distorted, expressionistic shadows follow the Woman as she moves through the streets, continuously peering over her shoulder, creating a mood of expectation and unease. She hurries by a pair of drunks sharing a bottle, and they stare after her menacingly. Another drunk accosts her and tries to force her to drink—the first of several metaphorical rapes in the film which she resists. The scene is witnessed by a police Detective sitting in a squad car, who rushes over to assist her. But his aid swiftly turns into brutality as he savagely beats the drunk, the violent attack revealed in elongated shadows. A close-up of the Woman's face shows her laughing, clearly enjoying the Detective's unprovoked violence. All of these preliminary encounters suggest a definite generic ambiguity at work in the film. Nothing to this point has clearly linked the film to the horror genre. Instead, there are many direct references to *film noir* and the conventions of the crime drama such as the urban setting, the atmosphere of general menace and corruption, and the attention to the subjectivity of the central character and her potential for violence that links her to the *femme fatale*. The *noir* interpretation is furthered through the Woman's next series of encounters, which propel her into the central events of the narrative.

Moving away from the scene of violence, the Woman is approached by a dapper-looking gentleman with a pencil moustache who looks her up and down lasciviously. Assuming she is a prostitute, he adopts an easy familiarity towards her, taking her by the arm and steering her towards the end of the block. When they pass a Flower Girl, the Dapper Gentlemen selects a flower from her basket, but rather than presenting it to the Woman he places it in the lapel of his own jacket. While they stand on the street corner, a sudden wind whips a copy of the newspa-

per down the street and against the Woman's legs, with the headline "Mysterious Stabbing" prominently visible. The Woman looks down at the headline and kicks the paper away before the Dapper Gentleman notices it. The paper floats into the street where it is pinned beneath the tires of a black limousine that has pulled up to the curb. The Dapper Gentleman, evidently, is a procurer, and after a brief conversation with the Fat Man in the back seat of the car—observed with cold, vacant eyes by the Woman—the Dapper Gentleman slides out of the car and the Woman climbs in next to the Fat Man (Bruno VeSota). The whole episode, which revolves around a business transaction with the Woman as sexual commodity, is presented as a degradation for the Woman, but one that she appears willing to tolerate perhaps in order to exact her own form of retribution for such treatment.

As they drive away in the car, the Fat Man seems indifferent to her. They visit a series of bars and nightclubs, finally arriving at "Club Pronto" where he orders champagne but completely ignores the Woman, instead staring provocatively at a dancer who raises her skirt, flashing her legs at the crowd. At a nearby table, a young woman has to fight off the unwanted advances of a drunk. The Detective also appears at the club, though it's unclear whether this is coincidence or part of an ongoing surveillance of the Woman. The entire scene in Club Pronto dramatizes male contempt for women, who are reduced to nothing more than sexualized objects to be voyeuristically consumed or physically mauled. By this point in the film, it is evident that sexual politics—the representation of socio-sexual relationships of power between men and women—are a central thematic concern within *Daughter of Horror*.

Leaving the nightclub, the Woman and the Fat Man ride silently through the city, lights playing across their faces. At this point the narration resumes:

The pulse of the neon lights like a hammer on your brain, tormenting you, haunting you, forcing you to think, forcing you to remember your guilt! Your horror! Forcing you to go back, back into the terror that you are trying to forget. Back through the mists of time into the graveyard where your secret lies buried from the world.

Here begins the flashback in the graveyard, one of the most famous scenes in *Daughter of Horror* because it can be glimpsed in the more well-known *The Blob* (1958), where it appears on the screen at the midnight movie just before the Blob oozes from the projection booth in one of the seminal images of 1950s science fiction film.

The scene in the graveyard, along with the narration from this point on, seems specifically designed by Parker to emphasize and presumably secure for audiences the "horror" interpretation of events in the film, though even here such a reading of the film is undercut by a psycho-social explanation. Increasingly, it is the narration that bears the burden of securing the proper generic tone for a product marketing itself as a horror film to audiences in the 1950s. Specifically, the narration introduces a persona ("The Demon") who speaks to the Woman and claims to possess her soul. It is a creaky narrative device that no doubt struck the film's original audiences, no less than viewers today, as artificial and contrived.

Responding to complaints that the original film *Dementia* was confusing and hard to follow (read: generically ambiguous for audiences), Parker went out of his way in the narration to make sure that viewers would read *Daughter of Horror* as a *horror film*. Yet the rhetorical effect of the narration is contradictory: it articulates the horror interpretation of events as a supplement to, rather than a substitute for, the *film noir* and psycho-sexual aspects of the film, thus creating a generic hybrid which combines *film noir* and horror: Two film genres that were never very far apart to begin with.

The narration continues:

Yes, I am here. The Demon who possesses your soul. Wait a bit. I am coming for you. I have so much to show you ... so much that you are afraid to see. Come, let me take you by the arm and show you the bed of evil you sprang from. Let me take you back to when you were a little girl. Let me show you your father....

The flashback provides a psychological explanation for the Woman's behavior in such a way that her violence seems justified.

We see the Woman standing alone in a graveyard. Entering the frame in a sharp left to right diagonal strides a hooded male figure holding a lantern—the Demon—who approaches the woman and leads her to a gravestone which reads simply "FATHER." Dissolve to an image of the Father, sprawled drunkenly in bed. The furniture of the room is arranged in the graveyard itself, surrounded by headstones and gnarled trees. As the Woman approaches, her Father staggers upright, grabbing her by the arm and slapping her across the face. Here the film explicitly links the Woman's mental state to childhood abuse recovered in this hallucinatory flashback.

The narration resumes: "Let me show you your Mother." Another gravestone appears, this time with the inscription "MOTHER." The Mother is depicted as a blonde "floozy" with too much makeup, dressed provocatively with the straps of her dress sliding off her shoulders. She lounges seductively, reading a Romance magazine and eating chocolates, the very image of feminine indulgence. The Father walks into the frame and drops into a chair, staring at his wife with a palpable sexual hunger. When the Mother rejects his clumsy advances, he notices a half-smoked cigar butt smoldering in an ash tray, a phallic sign of the Mother's sexual infidelity. The Mother begins to laugh at Father and she turns her back on him while languorously combing out her hair in a mirror. Appearing behind her with a gun, Father shoots and kills Mother (represented by the shattering of her image in the mirror), and he stands over her body with a cruel smile. The Woman—the daughter of this ill-fated union—now appears behind her Father, a knife raised in her hand, and she stabs him in the back in retribution for his own violence. With an eloquent and economical visual shorthand, this scene depicts a family narrative dominated by alcoholism, child abuse, adultery and murder leading to the act of patricide which the narration would have us believe is the ultimate "horror." "Marked! Marked forever, Daughter of Horror," the narrator concludes as the flashback ends. Again, generic pressures at work in the scene attempt to displace guilt from Father to Daughter, but it is evident that the real horror lies in this marriage (perhaps, in the institution of marriage itself) and in the familial roles these characters enact.

Back in the car, the Fat Man observes the Woman's agitation as she recalls herself from the hellish vision of her family history we have just witnessed. They arrive at the Fat Man's luxurious apartment building. As they cross the vast lobby, the Fat Man drops his cigar on the floor in front of a washerwoman crouched on her hands and knees, who glares after him with undisguised hatred. VeSota's performance here deserves much of the credit for establishing his character as a figure of male arrogance and sexual appetite. The police Detective is also present in the shadows, observing her and the Fat Man with a knowing smile as he lights a cigar. And for the first time it becomes apparent to the viewer that the Detective resembles her Father. Is this a coincidence we are supposed to ignore—another one of those unavoidable short cuts made by low-budget filmmakers? Or is there significance to this similarity between the Father and the Law? It is clear that the filmmakers intended to highlight and draw attention to this resemblance, because it is mentioned in the narration later in the film. And of course such a resemblance also serves the film thematically by making the Woman's acts of violence crimes not just against individuals but against patriarchal society as a whole and the entire apparatus of male-authored laws and institutions that underwrite its authority. Such a threat to the dominant social and sexual order as is suggested by the act of patricide must be compulsively reenacted by the Woman, who is depicted as being trapped within a cycle of violence clearly engendered by patriarchy itself. Yet within the cultural logic of both the horror and *film noir* genres, such violence must be punished, its motivating circumstances denied and suppressed by the visceral spectacle of its representation in the film.

The scene in the Fat Man's apartment constitutes the second symbolic rape, with the Woman again revealing that capacity which defines "horror" in the film: the woman's willingness to respond to male violence with violence. But first the Woman must be thoroughly defined and contained with-in the stereotypes of femininity that prevailed in 1950s American culture. Specifically evoked here is the connection between women and consumption, as dramatized by the moment when the Woman pauses in front of a shop window in the lobby of the building, caressing the glass as she gazes longingly at a mink coat on display. The Fat Man waits impatiently while she performs the consumer ritual of "window shopping," and he lights a cigar, a reoccurring motif in the film used to suggest male arrogance and sexual power.

The scene in the Fat Man's apartment implies a conflict of class values underlying the sexual tension between the two. They are waited upon by a liveried servant, and the Fat Man plays classical-sounding music (part of Antheil's score) at a baby grand piano apparently to impress the Woman. She ignores his music and mixes a drink, which he refuses. The Woman clearly seems uncomfortable in such surroundings while the Fat Man treats her with nothing more than cold curiosity. The Servant brings in a tray of food and, without offering any to the Woman, the Fat Man sits down and begins to devour the meal. For sheer gustatory grossness, the shots of the Fat Man eating his meal of fried chicken have few equals in American films of this period. In one deep focus shot, the Fat Man dominates the foreground of the image shoving food into his mouth while the Woman sits behind him in the background, watching with undisguised loathing.

His uninhibited and messy consumption of the food displayed for the Woman seems an unambiguous metaphor for his sexual appetite, which he immediately moves to satisfy after finishing his meal and lighting another cigar. Getting up from the table, the Fat Man grabs the Woman by the shoulders and attempts to force a kiss. She breaks free of him and he throws down his cigar in anger. He then holds out a handful of money, at which the Woman smiles. Again, heterosexual relations are reduced to the level of commercial transaction and exchange. But as he pulls her toward him by the pendant that hangs around her neck, she responds by pulling out the switchblade knife and stabbing him in the chest. As he falls backwards and out an open window, the Fat Man clutches at her pendant, yanking it from her neck and carrying it with him to the street below. Turning away from the window with an ambiguous smile, the Woman is handed a cocktail by the servant, who is suddenly transformed into the Fat Man through a stop-motion cut. The Woman recoils in shock and, as she runs from the room, we see the servant grinning mysteriously. He calmly walks to the door and closes it in a strange coda to the scene.

From this point on, the style of the film becomes even more expressionistically stylized, emphasizing the Woman's subjective perspective. Fleeing into the street the Woman is pursued by the narration: "Guilty! Guilty! Guilty! Mad with guilt and the devils that have taken possession." She stops when she sees the body of the Fat Man, surrounded by a crowd of people whose faces are obscured by shadow. "There, there it is ... the body of your latest victim. And around it the ghouls of insanity, imaginary figures real only to you." Once again the narration appears to insist upon a "horror" interpretation ("the ghouls...") side by side with the psychological reading of events ("...of insanity"). And the narration takes on an expository function when it informs the Woman that the Fat Man clutches an obvious sign linking her to his death: "The pendant—the clue to your guilt!" Again, the narration specifically foregrounds the Woman's guilt:

> The Ghouls know, they know you did it! But they can't hurt you. You've got to get it. You've got to take it out of his hand. Go ahead! The Ghouls won't hurt you!

The faceless "Ghouls" that surround the body seem more fitting as symbols of a widespread public indifference to violence than the flesh-eating monsters evoked by the narration. They watch passively as the Woman approaches the body and attempts to remove the evidence of her crime. But when the fingers won't release the pendant, the Woman uses the knife to saw off the entire hand. This symbolic castration of the corpse represents a final act of transgressive violence against patriarchal society for which the Woman must be punished. Fleeing the scene, the Woman is pursued by the Detective down shadowed streets and alleys that become a visual correlative for "the twisted corridors" of her mind referred to by the narration:

> Run daughter of horror! Run from your crime! But behind you the policeman with the face of your father—the face of your first victim! Pursuing you relentlessly in your haunted brain. Hunting you through the twisted corridors of your tortured mind. The horror that can track you down! The horror that can destroy you."

The images of the Woman's flight through the dark streets of the city and her pursuit by the Detective with the face of her father is a perfect visual representation of both the character's paranoia and the threat of patriarchal retribution which is sure to come. She is followed by the Detective in a squad car, who aims the beam of his searchlight at her, placing her on display as she flees. Still carrying the severed hand—the physical sign of her transgressive sexuality—she drops it in the basket of flowers held by the Flower Girl, who stares after her silently. The narration builds to a crescendo:

> Run! Run! Guilty! Guilty! Guilty! But there is nowhere to run, nowhere to hide. If you could only wipe out the curse of your guilty past. If you could only become somebody else before it's too late. Escape into a world of your own kind of people.

Suddenly the Detective appears, blocking the Woman's escape at the end of an alley. Pulling out her knife, the Woman fumbles and drops it, and in desperation she begins to pound on a side door in the alley. As if by magic the door swings open, and the Dapper Gentleman pulls the Woman into the building. Significantly, this temporary haven turns out to be a jazz club housed in the building's basement, filled with would-be beatniks and white hipsters trying to look cool and clearly representing an alternative to the dominant sexual and social values of mainstream society. In this environment the Woman is accepted, not isolated and alone as she is outside. Yet the narration suggests underlying danger: "Safe, safe at last. Yes, you are safe in another hallucination of your crazed mind. Safe in a drugged dream." She joins a group of musicians (Shorty Rogers and his Jazz Giants) in rehearsal and seems to be welcomed with casual familiarity by them. The Dapper Gentleman shows her some sheet music and mixes her a drink, and the Woman smiles and relaxes, seemingly at ease. In another moment of magical transformation, the Dapper Gentleman presents the Woman with an evening gown which he tosses over her and instantly she is dressed as a nightclub chanteuse, complete with coifed hair and jewels. She is obviously being prepared for a performance. Another woman, also

Scenes in *Daughter of Horror* like this one exemplify the film's radically unstable generic identity, wavering as it does between the worlds of horror and *film noir*.

well-dressed and beautiful, appears in the room and tugs jealously at the Dapper Gentleman's arm while he suggestively rubs the Woman's shoulders. In the bohemian world of the jazz club—the film's symbol of counter cultural "otherness"—conventional sexual codes and inhibitions are loosened in an atmosphere that fosters libidinal energy and experimentation.

Stepping from behind a curtain, the Woman enters the jazz club, which is depicted in a carefully composed series of images. Beatniks and swingers jive and snap their fingers to the music; laughing faces are distorted by grotesque shadows; men clutch at women's bodies and couples dance in ecstatic physical abandon. One woman in the club, presumably a prostitute, has a conspicuous black eye, yet she still manages to smile invitingly at a patron. Another hipster, carried away by the music, beats out the rhythm on the floor while a young woman struggles to pull him to his feet. Amid the hectic sexual energy and kinetic movement, a sullen, morose drunk stares into an empty glass. The jazz club is a sign of sexual license and social transgression, and though it seems at first to offer the Woman a place of refuge, it soon becomes a psycho-social stage for her ritual humiliation and punishment.

As the Woman joins the musicians on stage, a policeman with a crowd of people are glimpsed through the basement window, a sign of the status quo surrounding and containing the underground, alternative community of the jazz club. Once again the Detective suddenly appears; throughout the film he repeatedly makes unexpected and unaccounted-for entrances, creating a sense of the uncanny around the character appropriate to his psychological role as the Father/Law. The Dapper Gentleman now appears seated at a table with two beautiful women, presumably prostitutes, kissing both of them full on the lips and flaunting his sexual power over them. He surveys the scene in the club, embodying in his pose and expression the essence of masculine arrogance and contempt for women. The Detective circulates through the club questioning patrons before approaching the Dapper Gentleman, who hands him an envelope—obviously a pay-off. Throughout *Daughter of Horror*, images of police corruption and violence function to convey a sense of official sanction to the fallen moral universe distilled within its sinister, urban dreamscape. The Woman watches from the stage, horrified by this transaction between the two men that signals her betrayal. The Detective turns and smiles at the Woman, dangling a pair of handcuffs in front of him. The narration resumes: "Yes, he has seen you, and you're trapped. The handcuffs are waiting for your wrists."

The Detective points to the basement window and immediately all action in the club stops and everyone points to the window, where the Woman sees a policeman holding the corpse of the Fat Man. Even more disconcerting, the Fat Man is conscious and smiling at the Woman. Laughing, the policeman holds up the empty sleeve of the Fat Man's coat and everyone in the jazz club begins to laugh and point at the Woman. "Look! Look! It's your latest victim. Now everyone knows. There is no escape. Look around your neck ... the pendant for everybody to see!" Suddenly she is dressed in her own clothes again, with the pendant around her neck. Everyone in the club turns and points accusing fingers at her, while the editing accelerates into a dizzying montage of characters and scenes from the film, superimposed with images of the waves crashing over the Woman from her dream. Rapid cuts show us the newspaper with its sinister headline, the Woman's pendant spinning wildly, the knife, the Fat Man eating, the Woman cutting off the hand and the Club Pronto dancer. Writhing, grasping hands converge around the Woman on the stage and clutch at her throat—the third implied rape in the film, this time a gang assault. The narration continues: "Now all the images of horror, the demons of your mind, crowd in on you. Guilty! Guilty! Guilty! Guilty! Guilty!" The image of the swinging pendant is juxtaposed with the swinging handcuffs and shots of the Woman running down dark, empty streets are intercut with the laughing faces of the Fat Man and the Detective in successive closeups. The montage recapitulates all of the psychological and sexual violence of the film into a stream of images which, together with Antheil's musical score, builds to a crescendo.

An abrupt cut halts this hallucinatory montage sequence and we are returned to the seedy hotel room where we see the Woman awake suddenly from what we now understand to be a dream. No doubt most viewers of *Daughter of Horror*, both in the 1950s and today, groan at this narrative contrivance of making the action of the film a dream; it is the easiest way to provide an imaginary resolution to the very real contradictions and conflicts opened up by the narrative. As such, however, it secures only a tenuous narrative closure for the text and, in fact, points out the inadequacies of such an artificial and highly conventionalized ending for the film.

Rising from the bed, the Woman's eyes go to a chest, out of which dangles the chain to the pendant. Approaching the chest, she hesitates before opening it to reveal the severed hand of the Fat Man, still holding the pendant. As she reaches for the pendant, the hand tightens its grip, and the Woman backs away, screaming in horror. The final shots of the film parallel the opening shots by tracking backwards through the open window of the hotel room to reveal the flashing neon sign and deserted street before panning up into the darkness of the night sky. The narration concludes on an uncertain note:

Only a dream. A dream of madness on a dark night. Or was it? Was it only a dream?

"Only a Dream.... Or was it?" Horror films are often built upon such subjective ambiguities, usually as a way of ultimately disavowing a supernatural explanation of events and restoring a sense of normalcy and social stability to the narrative. But in *Daughter of Horror*, this ending attempts to distance the viewer from a more terrifyingly plausible interpretation of the narrative, an interpretation which would require a reading of the film as something slightly different than a horror film: a psycho-social critique of the violence against women endemic to patriarchal society. Within the dark, urban milieu of the film—an obvious metaphor for the mind—resides an equally dark social fact: that the lives of women are often defined ("marked") by abuse, objectification, sexual threat and violence.

What makes the "daughter of horror" horrifying is her willingness to strike back at men for their treatment of her and, by extension, to strike back at the social institutions and sexual values that defined femininity in the 1950s (the family, marriage, domesticity, motherhood). The act of patricide which she commits and that transforms her into the "Horror" of the title is also an attack upon the Law, as embodied by the Detective who has the face of her Father; a figure who haunts her through the film and continually threatens punishment. Appearing in the early 1950s, such a depiction of woman's capacity for violence against men had to be displaced and contained within the imaginary realm of the Horror genre, a calculated move by Parker to enhance the film's commercial prospects. The whole purpose of juxtaposing the narrative and the narration as I have done here is to suggest that the function of the narration was to "fix" the generic identity of the film in order to secure a certain reading which could dismiss the implications of the sexual violence as the product of a genre which is wholly given over to the fantastic and the unreal, and within which women are conventionally victimized. Yet such bracketing of the film's putative content by the generic iconography and rhetoric of the horror film was only partial and incomplete. Moreover, the sexual violence in the film is also explained by making recourse to the language and imagery of mental illness—hence the original title of the film, *Dementia*. This serves a similar purpose: It renders the film ideologically "safe" by presenting the violence in the film as aberrant, an expression of a single individual's psychopathology. However, putting aside the fact of the Woman's violence (which is always retributive and defensive), the accumulation of scenes and episodes in which women are attacked in varying ways supports the conclusion that such violence is not aberrant but rather widespread and authorized both by institutions and social practice. The real horror in *Daughter of Horror* is the threat of women's resistance to their own objectification and abuse. Such resistance could be figured for audiences in the 1950s perhaps most vividly within the generic space of the horror film and encoded in the language of mental disease because these provided conceptual frameworks that could limit and contain the implications of the film, which are nothing less than to show that the real horror faced by all daughters resides within patriarchal society and the manner in which it organizes relations between women and men. *Daughter of Horror* is obviously not a sociological document, even less a feminist treatise, but I would argue that it is a work of art engaged in addressing truths "more terrifying" than the generic fictions of low-budget horror to which it was consigned by both its producers and the exhibitors who marketed the film in the 1950s.

NOTES

1. Apparently the cast and director credits were cut from the film in its transformation from *Dementia* to *Daughter of Horror*. Both versions of the film are now available from Kino Video.

2. Quoted in Michael Weldon, *The Psychotronic Encyclopedia of Film*, New York: Ballantine Books, 1983: 174.

3. What little information there is about the production of this film can be found in Paul Parla and Charles Mitchell's article "The Ghouls Know: The Untold Story of Ed MacMahon and *Daughter of Horror*," in *Scary Monsters Magazine* #25) December 1997, p. 121–122.

4. Jim Morton, "*Daughter of Horror*," in *Re/Search #10: Incredibly Strange Films*, San Francisco, 1986: 179. Nigel Andrews is quoted in Parla and Mitchell, p. 122.

12

"Evil, Beautiful, Deadly": Publicity Posters of Drive-in Horror's Monstrous Women[1]

Chrystine Berzsenyi

In the 1950s and early 1960s, drive-in theaters in the United States promised good fun for families and teenagers alike. While families gravitated to wholesome films, teenagers chose the low-budget, quickly produced B-grade horror films featured at drive-in theaters.[2] Despite the common attitude that "the film on the screen was largely irrelevant,"[3] publicity posters were distributed to drive-in theaters. Owner of Rodeo Tri Drive-in in Port Orchard, Washington, Jack Ondracek, verifies the early presence of publicity posters in his drive-in theater: "Studio-provided visuals were definitely used by this drive-in, going back to the late '40s (when the place was built)."[4] Further, Gary King, long-time projectionist of the 27 Twin Drive-in Theater in Somerset, Kentucky, remarks:

> Some posters were sent as much as 1 to 2 months in advance to use as advertisement in the lobbies or concession areas. Some were sent just a week or so before the movies were released. Posters were displayed in frames to increase interest in the coming attractions. The closer the attraction was to actually playing usually meant the poster was moved to a more prominent frame where it could be viewed more readily. They were strictly advertisements to give a scene from the movie and a brief scenario to let people see if it was something they wanted to see.[5]

King indicates that film companies took the effort and expense to provide publicity posters for the drive-ins. The fact that drive-in theater owners considered visibility of the lobby posters as well as the aesthetics of displaying them suggest that they felt these posters made an impact on ticket sales and film choices. While there were undoubtedly those viewers who came to the drive-in for reasons other than to see the film, publicity posters were targeting those spectators who made choices about the films they viewed. These posters varied in sizes from one-sheets, which are the standard at 27 × 41 inches; half-sheets at 22 × 28 inches; inserts, which are a tall, narrow poster at 14 × 36 inches; window cards at 14 × 22 inches; and lobby cards at 11 × 14 inches, which came in two types as title cards and scene cards.[6] As Wright puts it, "a poster is a tangible expression of a movie."[7] While the posters were works of art created by accomplished illustrators, they typically repeated images and slogans, which became the conventions of horror film posters of the time. While this paper is not an homage to these artists and their works, I think that it's an important reminder of the various ways art is produced by and for our media-focused culture.

Another forum for the publication of publicity posters is the newspaper advertisements of drive-in theaters' feature films. Gary King goes on to explain the role of newspaper ads in featuring the upcoming and current films at the 27 Twin Drive-In Theater:

> Our regular ad ran weekly the day before the movie was to begin showing, and continued to run through the weekend. We usually ran a small section with our regular advertisement about what was coming the following week. It was never more than 8 days, because there were times we didn't know what we were playing till just a day or two before the movie was to start playing.

Through newspaper advertisements, audience members could make choices about films they would view or even decide whether the film that was showing was worth viewing. While reduced in size, publicity photos provided that glimpse of the film, provided by studio publicists who marketed particular images of the film. According to King, audiences had up to eight days exposure to the advertisements, which offered ample opportunity for viewing the photos.

However, these publicity images, which are now highly collectible, present what many have called misrepresentations of the films they advertised.[8] In fact, Wright points out that these graphics were "often cheats, calculated to lure unwary viewers to movies that had little or nothing to do with the lurid and exciting images depicted in the poster."[9] However, what is important is the purpose of these images, which was to publicize the release of a film for profit by capturing an essence in the image.[10] They invited viewers to the theaters or back to theaters to see their favorite actors and actresses, induced curiosity about the film's plot and characters, established expectations about the film's content and style, and encouraged particular spectator relationships. What is particularly telling about these posters is how they represent the films' villains, which are the key source of thrills for horror fans. They are projections of what film publicists think fascinates, thrills and frightens horror film fans—whether they accurately portray the films or not. They depict villains in rampage, terror and destruction, typically involving women as the victims, with promises of fright.

After viewing hundreds of horror film posters, what struck me was the presence of female monsters. I say with some reservation that I am thrilled to see female villains. I tire of seeing women repeatedly occupying the damsel in distress role. As a feminist, viewing women in villain roles is a complicated experience. On the one hand, it's great to see powerful women as agents in whatever capacity. On the other hand, the monstrous women are portrayed as simply behaving in ways that male monsters do, dominating and destroying. However, female monsters certainly were not equivalent to the male versions of the same type of monster, particularly in appearance.

With her close analysis of publicity campaigns, censorship files and reviews in *Attack of the Leading Ladies: Gender, Sexuality, and Spectatorship in Classic Horror Cinema*, Rhona Berenstein provides one of the rare analyses of marketing strategies of horror films. Her work illuminates the various ways that gender issues are implicit in studios' efforts to publicize 1930s films in order to "heighten the emotional upheaval that awaits viewers."[11] Berenstein's work addresses classical film publicity and gendered spectator relations that define men's roles as the brave protectors and women's roles as the frightened viewer who needs protection and comfort. My study supplements both Berenstein's work in its focus on women as monsters in publicity posters during the '50s and '60s and in its methodology. I perform a triangulated method of rhetorical, psychoanalytic and semiotic analyses of the posters as advertisement texts. I address how they sell concepts of female and male monsters that are markedly distinct in terms of gender and monstrosity. Other works that discuss publicity posters are generally just published collections of the posters to be appreciated by the enthusiast. Some collections discuss posters' resale values and collectability.[12] Others serve to illustrate a film by accompanying a poster with a film's plot summary, which means that the focus of the work is really on the film and not the poster art.[13] Still other books present collections of the poster art for their aesthetic, historical and cultural value.[14] However, little attention is given to films with female monsters. In this essay, I will analyze horror film posters with monsters that have male and female equivalents, which were published within the same historical context. Further, I will compare and contrast images of the male and female monsters along with the posters' captions in order to establish how gender is promoted in horror film posters. More specifically, I will consider gender representations of

Publicity posters for *Devil Girl from Mars* (1955) prominently display the female villian.

monstrosity in terms of femininity/masculinity, malice, potency of threat, physical attractiveness and sexuality. My purpose is to reveal some cultural implications of how we perceive monstrosity in males and females differently in drive-in horror films of the 1950s and 1960s.

The scope of this study is further limited by my exclusion of films that feature female villains as servants to another threat such as with Dracula and his brides. Also, I'm not including films that may feature a group of villains with mixed gender. Further, I'm not including film posters of the late '60s or early '70s because of the sharp decline in the number of U.S. drive-in theaters and the fact that few posters of this later period feature female villains as the primary source of threat. The ones that do are very limited in scope, primarily portraying hyper-sexualized vampires or witches often in service of another: *Countess Dracula* (1970), *The Vampire Lovers* (1970), *Daughters of Darkness* (1971), *The Devil's Nightmare* (1971), *The Devil's Wedding Night* (1973), *Blood Orgy of the She-Devils* (1973). Finally, I will not include pure revenge films because the avenger is perceived to be justified for her violence, which means that the avenger occupies roles of victim and hero, not of villain; rather the villain is the original wrongdoer and recipient of the avenger's retribution. This study focuses on female characters that are clearly positioned in the monster role in contrast with the male equivalent of that monster type.

Female Villains and Sexuality: A Brief Historical Perspective

Prior to the 1950s, the role of a female monster in horror had been scarce. From the beginning of horror film, the few female monsters there were both threatening and irresistible perhaps owing to the femme fatale, or "the woman with a gun," which emerged in the genre of film noir in the '40s.[15] During the classical period in horror, a handful of exceptional examples of dangerous females existed. They were mostly animal-like creatures and varied from being almost impotent to quite deadly: *Bride of Frankenstein* (1936), *She* (1935), *Dracula's Daughter* (1935), *Cat People* (1942), *Captive Wild Woman* (1943), *The Curse of the Cat People* (1944), *Jungle Woman* (1944), *Cobra Woman* (1944), *Weird Woman* (1944), *Devil Bat's Daughter* (1946), *She-Wolf of London* (1946) and *The Spider Woman Strikes Back* (1946). This incomplete list shows a concentration of films with female villains during the "war years" of 1942-46, which calls for critical attention. However, the number of female villain films rises dramatically in the '50s and '60s, which elicits questions regarding what constitutes horror and monstrosity in a way that appealed to fans of the drive-in cinema. Despite this increase, not much has been written about female fiends during the 1950s and early 1960s, which has been called a horror film boom.[16] As Barbara Creed argues in *Monstrous-Feminine*, much has been written on male monsters of the classic horror and the "golden years" periods in drive-in horror film history, but relatively little has been written about female monsters, in terms of spectator relationships, image representation and cultural significance. Instead, many scholars (such as Andrew Tudor and Harvey Roy Greenberg) gloss over the absence of female villains: "...most female monster movies to date have portrayed what men find fearful about the feminine (like the eponymous Fifty-Foot Woman, archetype of the castrating harpy who stomps through the dreams of impotent male movie maniacs)."[17] One collection addresses women's representation in horror films in the roles of "bitches," "bimbos" and "virgins," which is a combination of a few serious research essays and generally unscholarly treatments of a spectrum of representations of women across the history of horror film.[18] Most scholars, including Judith Halberstam and Carol Clover, focus on women's roles as the victim because of the predominance of that representation of women in horror film; however, Clover's work addresses the turn that female victims take in the slasher film as the lone survivors, who occupy the protagonist role at the end of the film.[19] Other studies focus on post-modern horror films that postdate the '60s.[20] Still other studies address more generally the cultural theories of aggression in women characters, which have been identified as asserting lesbian politics.[21] The work that has addressed female villains most notably and extensively is Barbara Creed's *The Monstrous-Feminine*. Creed provides an in depth psychoanalytic study of female villains in film who necessarily exemplify the sense of the monstrous-feminine, a term that refers to societies' conception of "what it is about women that is shocking, terrifying, horrific, abject."[22] While her study produces valuable insights regarding the application of Kristeva's theory of abjection and psychoanalytic theories of woman as castrator or phallic mother, her primary focus is on post women's movement films beyond the '60s. Therefore, this essay serves to fill in some historical gaps regarding the interpretation of female monstrosity in film prior to the women's movement and after the classical horror period.

Gender and Monsters

The posters' images and captions do fall into gender patterns. In the edited collection *The Dread of Difference: Gender and the Horror Film*, Barry Keith Grant addresses the horror film industry's preoccupation with sexual difference. He identifies the film titles as an immediate signal of gender and asserts, "Think of *He Knows You're Alone* (1980) with a feminine pronoun instead of the masculine, and the importance of gender to the genre becomes clear."[23] Accordingly, during the '50s and '60s, most films featuring female monsters indicate the female sex in the title such as *Astounding She-Monster* (1958), *Fire Maidens from Outer Space* (1956), *Voodoo Woman* (1957) and *Queen of Outer Space* (1958), to name just a few. These titles indicate the importance of conveying the gender of the monster right up front, perhaps emphasizing when it is female since that's a deviation from the stereotype of the male monster. Further, Carol J. Clover explains how the roles of monster, hero, and victim are gendered:

> The functions of monster and hero are far more frequently represented by males and the function of victim far more garishly by females. The fact that female monsters and female heroes, when they do appear, are masculine in dress and behavior (and often even name), and that male victims are shown in feminine postures at the moment of their extremity, would seem to suggest that gender inheres in the function itself — that there is something about the victim function that wants manifestation in a female, and something about the monster and hero functions that wants expression in a male.[24]

It is important to remember that Clover is referring to films and not advertisements for films and also that she examines films of the '70s and '80s, during which some slasher films with female antagonists were released. While that period is beyond the scope of this essay, what I do find useful here is Clover's reading of the cultural sense of maleness about being a villain and a hero and femaleness about being a victim. These cultural expectations are perhaps one of the reasons that, in text, there are significantly more male villains than female villains. During the '50s and first half of the '60s, B-movie horror pictures featured an increase in female monsters. While highly conventional in terms of exhibiting femininity of body and glamorous attractiveness, these monstrous women posed a threat to the world within the film. However, during the '70s, there was a sharp decline in films featuring female villains. Andrew Tudor accounts for this phenomenon as a backlash against the women's movement, which worked toward increasing women's freedom, rights and power in American society. In effect, the majority of these films portrayed women back in their "proper" social roles, being in service to men or being preyed upon by men. As another turn, during the '80s, the film industry once again featured more monstrous women. In addition to the increase in monster roles, Clover claims that females were placed in hero roles more as well. With women no longer relegated to the victim role, female characters are able to express a greater degree of agency, power and opposition than ever before in film. With this very brief and simplistic overview of a context for representing women in horror films, I turn my attention to the '50s and '60s.

In constructing female monsters, Lynda Hart explains that the woman is more like a man than a woman while retaining her sex as a woman and that she admonishes cultural concepts of femininity, passivity, and nurturing for tyranny, selfishness and egotism.[25] Traditional ideologies that served to control women espoused that female natures are essentially "non-violent, peaceful, and unaggressive."[26] Perhaps then, what is monstrous about women is the possibility that they would demand autonomy, act independently, reject men's sexual attention, express anger, act on their own behalf, dominate through possession and control over men, live isolated from men, force their wills unto others, and so forth—patriarchy. Women with power are terribly threatening, perhaps because we aren't used to their having power in our male-dominated culture. Nothing is more terrifying than the overthrow of life, as we know it, particularly for those in charge. If a women has power, is unnatural or from outer space, and is consumed with evil and anger, you have a villainess who has tapped into fears of takeover.

Within the context of psychoanalysis, in her essay "Womanliness as a Masquerade," Joan Riviere argues that "women who wish for masculinity may put on a mask of womanliness to avert anxiety and the retribution feared from men."[27] In other words, Riviere points out that masculine women, who also want to succeed in male-dominated arenas such as work environments, may affect womanliness in order to ensure that men will not feel threatened by their success and assertiveness. In doing so, men are reassured that she is not competing with them on their terms, like a man, but rather in an unthreatening, womanly way that is charming, feminine, accommodating and attractive. If we were to apply this notion to horror film depictions of a "predatory woman, dark seductress,"[28] it makes more sense why female villains' powers of threat and terror were undermined or complicated by her sexual appeal. If 1950s audiences, particularly young males, would find a truly threatening and hideous female villain to be totally unacceptable, then the characterization of the villain had to be tempered for audiences' satisfaction. She couldn't appear to be a threat immediately or else the young males would not view the film. Rather, she had to affect sexuality in order to assuage her victim's and her spectators' suspicions with exaggerated femininity. While hideousness was acceptable for male villains, sexual attractiveness was part of the formula for creating female monsters. The few actually hideous female monsters I found presented the attractive woman in the poster before she transforms into a beast so that both the beauty and the beast parts of her character are shown. In doing so, publicists were still relying on the element of beauty in the construction of the film's female creature. Other examples include *The She-Creature* (1956) that was a beautiful woman "reincarnated as a monster from hell"; *Cult of the Cobra* (1955), which asks the rhetorical question, "Can a woman's beauty be changed to a thing of terror?"[29]; and the "half beast" "half human" women who change "from beauty to beast!" in the *She Demons* (1958). In each of these publicity photos, a young, beautiful version of the woman is shown alongside the monstrous version of her.

Even when the female creature is described in the poster as being "a hideous she-thing," as with the *Terror from the Year 5,000* (1958), the villainess has an attractive and glamorized face and a fit and feminine body that is displayed in a tight jumpsuit. As impossible as it might seem to make a female insect beautiful, B-movie filmmakers did it. In fact, there

She Demons **(1958) incorporates the tension between materialism and theism as a fear based on the hubris of scientists.**

The aggressive, dominant position of the wasp woman over her immoble victim is reminiscent of the vulnerability of a rapist and victim.

is a clear discrepancy between the emphasis placed on physical attractiveness between the male and female counterparts of the insect creatures. For example, the publicity posters for *The Fly* (1958) promote the grotesque nature of the creature that Vincent Price portrays. We don't actually get a shot of "the fly with the head of a man."[30] Instead, we are asked to imagine the disgusting fly creature with captions such as "If she looked upon the horror her husband had become, she would scream for the rest of her life!"[31] and "She had to kill the thing her husband had become—but could she?"[32] Also, the posters warn us, "For your own good we urge you not to see it alone!"[33] Clearly, the frightening and repulsive appearance of the fly-creature is emphasized. In contrast, the female human-wasp creature of *The Wasp Woman* (1959) is shown to have a beautiful and glamorous woman's head with the wasp body. The caption reads, "A beautiful woman by day—a lusting queen wasp by night,"[34] which highlights the vixen's attractiveness. I will return to a discussion of her nymphomaniac's sexual appetite.

While both males and females are clearly distinguished by features of sexual difference, there is unequal emphasis on characteristics of sexuality in the construction of male and female villains that is consistently observable, particularly during the 1950s and early 1960s, when women's roles were being re-established post World War II.[35] In horror film photos of the 1950s and early 1960s, the "golden years of drive-in horror," males were almost never sexualized as villains; rather photos and captions emphasized their terrifying power of death and destruction as well as their sexual threat to female victims.[36] More specifically, men as villains tend to be depicted as masculine, aggressive, threatening, powerful, frightening and often hideous. On the other hand, female villains were almost always depicted as very feminine, curvaceous, animalistic, sexual and beautiful, but in a threatening way. Conventional gender representations are quite obvious when comparing poster depictions of the male and female counterparts to the film roles of the gigantic human monster: *The Amazing Colossal Man* (1957) and *Attack of the 50 Foot Woman* (1958). Both posters present huge humans devastating a city with their maleness and femaleness graphically distinguished. The 50-Foot Woman has hyperbolic features that indicate her sex: obviously displayed cleavage, legs spread with a short skirt, and lots of leg in the foreground of the shot. In the poster of *The Amazing Colossal Man*, the male villain wears only a loincloth and is depicted bald, very muscular and powerful with a beautiful damsel in his clutches.

More than just being sexually attractive, female monsters are typically sexually aggressive as well. Moreover, this sexually assertiveness is portrayed as abnormal or perverse. For example, the Wasp Woman's transformation at night suggests an alternate, dark self that is not part of our social world. The night brings out her dangerous sexual power as the "lusting queen wasp" that is presented on the photo with a helpless male victim held between her front insect legs. She illustrates what psychoanalytic critics such as Barbara Creed have called the phallic woman. Creed explains that the phallic woman "either has a phallus or phallic attribute or she has retained the male's phallus inside herself,"[37] which is said by Freudian thinkers to account for her masculine character traits. As exhibited by the wasp woman, the phallic woman threatens to "penetrate and split open, explode, tear apart"[38] in what can be a physical and/or emotional act that is symbolic of rape. For example, along the bottom border of one poster for *The Wasp Woman*, the caption reads, "strong men forced to satisfy a passion no human knows."[39] Her aggressive, dominant position over her immobile victim is reminiscent of the vulnerability of a rapist and victim. Moreover, the two figures are positioned over a pile of human skeletal fragments, signifying certain death. Of course, in this photo, gender roles have been reversed, placing the female in the role of rapist and the male in the victim role. The "force" exerted by the "lusting queen wasp" overtly constructs a scene of rape. In terms of conveying threat, the description of "strong men" as the victims emphasizes the wasp woman's tremendous power over men. However, the "passion no human knows" situates the wasp woman's sexuality as excessive, incomprehensible, abnormal and inhuman. Here, the villainess' source of threat resides in her supposedly aberrant sexuality, which is symptomatic of the phallic woman as monster. Here, sex and death are brought together, constructing the most explicit and graphic example of the phallic woman in b-horror posters of the '50s and early '60s.[40] Other examples of the phallic woman in publicity posters of the period include: the predatory creature in *Terror from the Year 5,000* (1958), *The Snake Woman* (1961) who "spreads horror with fang and forked tongue" and the knife-wielding murderess from *The Ghost* (1963).[41]

Another dimension of the combination of sex and death in female villains is the second category of what Creed calls the monstrous-feminine: the castrating woman, who "threatens to devour, to castrate via incorporation."[42] Castrating women seek to disempower, consume and subsume their victims. In her essay "The Monster as Woman: Two Generations of

The female of *Black Sunday* (1960) is depicted as an attractive but terrifying and powerful woman.

Cat People," Karen Hollinger addresses various manifestations of castration anxiety played out in horror films with female monsters, articulating reasons for the destruction of the dangerous women's sexual threats. In particular, she cites *Bride of Frankenstein* (1935) as symbolic of the female monster's sexual threat in her "capacity to reject her mate"[43], which is frightening because the male creature lacks sexual control over the female creature he desires. Hollinger goes on with a close examination of Jacques Tourneur's *Cat People* (1942) in terms of the ineffectualness of traditional male efforts to control the horror of the female monster. The presentation of sexual beauty that is untouchable, unattainable is illustrative of the woman as castrator because of the control and power she denies the man. In other words, the fact that she rejects him makes her monstrous. Such a rejection of men's attention and interest most typically results in death and destruction of the female villain in horror films and their posters.

Perhaps one of the most obvious examples of the castrating woman in B-movie horror posters during the 50s and early 60s is the "she-ghost" of *Tormented* (1960). The two posters I examined incorporate many aspects of the castrating woman as monster: dangerous sexuality, a devouring nature, possession, revenge, beauty and inhuman qualities. However, these qualities come into conflict as a construction of monstrosity. First of all, in the poster, the caption states that the woman has "a vengeance that haunted him to death." While the film is a revenge story, I found to make the exception to include it because of the way the poster vilifies her as the monster, as if she were never victimized. In the film, the "she-ghost" is murdered by the man she is now haunting. By portraying the ghost as gigantic and wild-eyed with sharp claws that reach out for her victim, the poster presents a domineering and willful character. In turn, the poster projects a blameworthy creature in the monster role rather than a victim of murder with legitimate feelings of anger and vengeance. Consequently, the photo and captions disallow her seeking revenge by making the act of revenge through haunting seem monstrous. Further, the poster's center is the ghost's large and partially bare bosom. In tongue-in-cheek manner, one caption describes her as "the sexiest phantom that ever haunted a man to death," which identifies her sexuality with her monstrosity as it trivializes the fatal effects of the ghost's position as avenger. The ironic tone and the emphasis on the ghost's sexual attractiveness undermine her credibility as a formidable monster. Instead of creating

Posters for *Tormented* (1960) incorporate many aspects of the castrating woman as monster: dangerous sexuality, a devouring nature, possession, revenge, beauty and inhuman qualities. However, these qualities come into conflict as a construction of monstrosity.

fear, the caption suggests that we view her as a sexual object. While her sexual appeal may reduce her threat to spectators, a lethal possessiveness is conveyed in the tagline, "A ghost-woman owned him body and soul!" Possession is indicative of the castrating woman because of her power over her victim, controlling his very being. Other aspects that reinforce her overwhelming power is illustrated by how disproportionately large the "she-ghost" is, looming over a small, frightened man (murderer nonetheless) who is attempting to escape from her.

Other examples of the castrating woman as monster in '50s and '60s B-movie horror films include: the female phantom who "lived to destroy" in *Back from the Dead* (1957); *The Leech Woman* (1960), who "drained men of their loves and lives"; the "fiery ... fearless ... ferocious" and "love-starved" women of *Cat Women of the Moon* (1953); the "beautiful temptress from the sea, intent upon loving, consuming and killing" in *Night Tide* (1963); the mouth of sharp teeth that are ready to demolish its victims in *Voodoo Woman* (1957); the "evil ... beautiful ... deadly" woman of *The Astounding She-Monster* (1958); "the female monster ... who destroyed everything she touched" in *She Devil* (1957); the alien women who have, "in their eyes desire in their veins the blood of monsters" in *Invasion of the Star Creatures* (1962); the devouring females of *Fire Maidens from Outer Space* (1956); the "super women ... who kissed and killed" in *Mesa of Lost Women* (1952); and the seductive, gun-toting colony of females on Venus in *Queen of Outer Space* (1958).[44]

In contrast, the male villain of *The Headless Ghost* (1959), which was released one year before *Tormented*, is also a ghost creature. The characters are comparable in terms of their supernatural natures, their gigantic stature in the posters, and their presence in secluded locations; however, they vary in how their threatening power is portrayed. On the one hand, the "headless ghost" appears with a sneer on his face, holding his head in his right hand, as if threatening to hurl it at the "teenagers" who run for their lives after being "lost in the haunted castle."[45] Also, the male ghost is completely human in appearance, fully clothed in historical royal court attire, and situated behind a castle. What these elements of the scene suggest is the headless ghost's privileged background as a nobleman with social respectability. On the other hand, the "she-ghost" is portrayed as animal-like with claws, on her hands and knees resembling animal posture. In addition, the island setting reinforces her wild nature akin with non-human animals. Further, with a piercing stare at the man, she appears more determined to get her man than to be angry with him. Both posters for *Tormented* emphasize her excessive, "supernatural passion," rather than malice. Rather, they acknowledge her relentless stalking, haunting him to death. Consequently, the effect is that the "she-ghost" vilified by presenting her with a monstrous, all-consuming desire. In contrast, the male ghost is not sexualized nor is his attractiveness or sexual interest represented at all.

The most important distinction here is the potency of threat that these two ghosts present. For the "she-ghost," threat involves her persistent and wanted pursuit of one particular man and her wild and intense emotions toward him. For the headless ghost, the source of threat is with the exertion of his physical power and indiscriminate violence toward any who enter the castle. Therefore, all viewers should fear the headless ghost, but viewers need not fear the "she-ghost" because she targets only one man. Moreover, the poster's emphasis on the "she-ghost" being the "sexiest phantom that ever haunted a man to death" serves to undermine the potency of her threat because viewers are called to appreciate and enjoy her sexual attractiveness. This combination of attraction and repulsion poses a conflict of interpretation for the viewer who must negotiate responses of fear and sexual interest. In contrast, this conflict is nonexistent toward the headless ghost, who is not promoted as attractive, but only frightening.

Conclusion

The representation of female monsters as very beautiful and highly sexual are symptomatic of conventional gender attitudes of the period which were based upon the assumption that women's value in society relied heavily upon her attractiveness. During a sexually repressed cultural period, whether a female character was presented as sexually experienced or innocent determined in large part whether she was the victim or the monster. The expression of sexual interest was a monstrosity, even if the image attracted viewer's attention. While the notion that spectators may be more attracted to the "bad girl" than the "good girl" is not a new concept, it does pose require that spectators to negotiate their feelings of attraction and threat. In an effort to account for this conflict of representation and gender difference of female monsters in the '50s and early '60s, I considered Clover's claims that women's roles in film changed after the women's movement:

In its presentation of power, *The Headless Ghost* **(1959) differs from its female ghost counterpart of** *Tormented* **(1960).**

The women's movement has given many things to popular culture, some more savory than others. One of its main donations to horror, I think, is the image of an angry woman—a woman so angry that she can be imagined as a credible perpetrator (I stress "credible") of the kind of violence on which, in the low-mythic universe, the status of full protagonist rests.[46]

In other words, few hero roles, or monster roles for that matter, had been created for women because spectators wouldn't believe that women were capable of violence or even of successfully defending themselves from violence. Culturally, women have been defined as the helpless damsel in distress, needing to be saved by a male hero. Indeed, women's social roles prohibit the expression of anger because it is seen as unfeminine or counter to women's passive natures. However, as Clover points out, with the women's movement came greater empowerment for women in the roles of hero.

Given that prior to the women's movement, horror films did not produce or could not produce a culturally credible angry woman, what do we make of the female villains of the '50s and early '60s? How is it that, in response to my question, "What do you think about female villains in '50s and '60s horror films," a male colleague of mine responded, "Female monsters aren't very scary"? If female monsters aren't very scary, then how did viewers relate and respond to them? What kind of spectator relationships did the lobby posters encourage between viewers and these female antagonists? At first, I felt that my colleague was overly secure and complaisant to say that he wasn't scared of a powerful woman in a film narrative. After a great deal of consideration of his perception that female monsters exhibit little threat, some quick answers came to mind that relate to the fact that women in "real life" generally do not behave violently. Women's social roles involve patience, nurturing, care-giving, physical passivity, sexual repression and compliance with others, particularly men. This pattern of behaviors among women as feminine has been argued to be a part of women's natures as biological females as well as a result of cultural conditioning. Furthermore, women generally do not possess a great deal of political, economic or social power in our male-dominated society; therefore, this suggests that women's lack of violence can be attributed to fewer opportunities to exercise power, whether it is benevolent or malevolent. Consequently, film spectators do not expect women to be dangerous or threatening. Accordingly, the publicists' attempts to appeal to the sexual and horror interests of the teenage spectators at drive-in theaters manifests in the creation of a female monster who is more odd, curious, intriguing, and spectacular than horrifying. This point is illustrated in the poster for *Tormented*: "the sexiest phantom that ever haunted a man to death."

Since our culture associates malevolence with deformity, sneers, bad teeth and a generally poor appearance (part of the vampire tradition excluded), beauty serves to camouflage depravity. This masquerade of normalcy for a female villain can produce the effect of paranoia in viewers who can no longer identify who is good or evil based on appearance. Such as disruption of the stereotype of the female as victim can relegate the image to pure fantasy. Accordingly, the effect may be suspicion and suspense on the audience's part rather than horror. The logic here is that we generally are not frightened of what we find pleasing. On other hand, a monstrous female can suggest that the woman or girl is "simply, and perhaps more horrifyingly and realistically a rotten person."[47] While it is outside of the scope of this study to answer this dilemma, what I've shown is that there is a conflict of response between aesthetic appreciation of the woman's beauty, conventional spectator roles with female characters, and repulsion toward what is monstrous about the woman. The conflict lies in the response between attraction to and aversion from the villainess so those viewers are divided between the two emotional states of fright and arousal. Further, this conflict must be negotiated with how we typically relate to female characters, which traditionally occupy victim roles. More specifically, female villains are generally characterized as "love-starved" nymphomaniacs with a suppressed sexual drive that, when released, is dangerous if not deadly. Transgressing the puritanical model of female sexuality perpetuated in popular media, these villains offer a free and aggressive concept of women's sexual feelings and expression, one that contradicts the "good girl" model. With the descriptions of these monstrous women, viewers are called to experience what they've never seen, dared to face these sexual anomalies, and titillated into viewing the film by the combination of beauty and deadliness in an overt way.

While others have made the argument that female monstrosity is clearly linked to and even defined by her sexuality, what remains unclear is whether sexuality completely undermines the female villain's power as a threat. Does irresistibility give female monsters more power because spectators lack fear and caution initially? On the contrary, do spectators perceive a sexually attractive female monster as unthreatening because they aren't necessarily scared, only intrigued and captivated? While answers to this question are outside the scope of this essay, what has been shown here is that female monsters do transgress social roles by asserting anger, revenge, a point of view, power over others, and sexuality. The subversiveness of characters as displayed in the posters provides viewers with a glimpse of females with power and agency. What is great about the lobby poster is that scenes of monstrous women's power are captured as a still image. In opposition, films portray these same women being destroyed in spirit and/or body by the end of the film.[48] Whether it's a feminist response to take pleasure in seeing women wreak havoc, enact revenge, misbehave and display sexuality depends on cultural notions of monstrosity and feminisms in horror fantasy. Similarly, Vendelin describes a spectator relationship with a villainous female to be "a kind of identification with the underdog who prevails."[49] In effect, Vendelin expresses a qualified celebration of the autonomous, active and capable female antagonist as role model to young girls, as opposed to the dependent and passive female victim.[50] It's interesting to see how the "she-ghost" of *Tormented* is a villain while the avengers of revenge films of the late '70s and the '80s are the victim-heroes. This shift in perception of the role of the avenging woman is suggestive of the historical and social constructions of monstrosity in women. I suppose society has made some degree of progress, thanks to the efforts of the women's movement, if women characters are no longer automatically vilified if they fight back against injustice and violence or if they express their sexuality, not unlike how men do.

Notes

1. This quote is found on the publicity poster for *The Astounding She-Monster* (1958).
2. See Kerry Segrave (*Drive-in Theaters: A History From Their Inception in 1933*. Jefferson NC: McFarland, 1992), Don and Susan Sanders (*The American Drive-In Movie Theater*. Osceola WI: Motorbooks, 1997). Chrystine Berzsenyi, Elizabeth McKeon and Linda Everett (*Cinema Under the Stars: America's Love Affair with the Drive-In Movie Theater*. Nashville TN: Cumberland House, 1998) for accessible historical treatments of American drive-in theaters.
3. Segrave, viii.
4. Ondracek, Jack. E-mail to author. Rodeo

Tri Drive-In. Port Orchard WA, Sept. 8, 1999.

5. King, Gary. E-mail to author. 27 Twin Drive-In Theater. Somerset KY, Sept. 10,

6. Although Bruce Lanier Wright's book *Yesterday's Tomorrow's: The Golden Age of Science Fiction Movie Posters* is primarily focused on the films and not on the posters, Wright briefly conveys collectability, artist and plot information about a selection of science fiction movie posters from 1950–64; some of these films can also be classified as horror such as *The Wasp Woman, Tarantula, Attack of the Crab Monsters* and others.

7. Wright, Bruce Lanier. *Yesterday's Tomorrows: The Golden Age of Science Fiction Movie Posters.* Dallas, TX: Taylor Publishing Company, 1993, p. vi.

8. See Elizabeth McKeon and Linda Everett's *Cinema Under the Stars: America's Love Affair with the Drive-In Movie Theater*; Bruce Lanier Wright's *Yesterday's Tomorrow's: The Golden Age of Science Fiction Movie Posters*, Tony Nourmand and Graham Marsh's edited *Film Posters of the 60s: The Essential Movies of the Decade* (Woodstock NY: The Overlook Press, 1998); Ronald V. Borst, Keith Burns and Leith Adams, edited *Graven Images: The Best of Horror, Fantasy, and Science Fiction Film Art from the Collection of Ronald V. Borst* (Compiled by Ronald V. Borst and Margaret A. Borst. New York NY: Grove Press, 1992) and Robert Brosch's *Horror, Science Fiction, Fantasy Movie Posters and Lobby Cards, Volume I* (Allen Park MI: Archival Photography, Winter 1990) *and Volume II* (Allen Park, MI: Archival Photography, January 1993).

9. Wright, p. vi.

10. Carol J. Clover's "Her Body, Himself: Gender in the Slasher Film." *Dread of Difference: Gender and the Horror Film.* Ed. Barry Keith Grant. Austin, TX: University of Texas Press, 1996, p. 80.

11. Berenstein, "It Will Thrill You, It May Shock You, It Might Even Horrify You": Gender, Reception, and Classic Horror Cinema." *Dread of Difference: Gender and the Horror Film.* Ed. Barry Keith Grant. Austin TX: University of Texas Press, 1996, p. 117–42: 118.

12. See Brosch, Volumes I and II.

13. See Wright, as well as Welch Everman's *Cult Science Fiction Films: From the Amazing Colossal Man to Yog—Monster from Space.* New York: Carol Publishing Group, 1995.

14. See Borst and Normand & Graham.

15. See Virginia M. Allen's book *The Femme Fatale: Erotic Icon* (Troy NY: The Whitston Publishing Company, 1983: 12–13) for an analysis of the iconography of the femme fatale through verbal and visual representation and its gradual accumulation of evil traits (12–13).

16. See Andrew Tudor's *Monsters and Mad Scientists: A Cultural History of the Horror Movie* (Cambridge MA: Basil Blackwell Ltd., 1989) for a historical examination of horror film genres from the 1930s through the 1980s.

17. Greenberg, Harvey Roy. "King Kong: The Beast in the Boudoir—or, 'You Can't Marry the Girl, You're a Gorilla!'" *Dread of Difference: Gender and the Horror Film.* Ed. Barry Keith Grant. Austin TX: University of Texas Press, 1996: 338.

18. Svehla, Gary and Sue, ed. *Bitches, Bimbos, and Virgins: Women in the Horror Film.* Baltimore MD: Midnight Marquee, 1996.

19. See Judith Halberstam's *Skin Shows: Gothic Horror and the Technology of Monsters.* NC: Duke University, 1995; and Carol Clover's *Men, Women, and Chainsaws: Gender in the Modern Horror Film.* Princeton NJ: Princeton University, 1992.

20. See Lianne McLarty's "'Beyond the Veil of the Flesh': Cronenberg and the Disembodiment of Horror," *Dread of Difference: Gender and the Horror Film.* Ed. Barry Keith Grant. Austin TX: University of Texas, 1996: 231–52. Also see Isabel Cristina Pinedo's *Recreational Terror: Women and the Pleasure of Horror Film Viewing.* Albany NY: State University of New York, 1997. And see Linda Bradley's *Film, Horror, and the Body Fantastic.* Westport CT: Greenwood, 1995.

21. See Hart.

22. Creed, Barbara. *The Monstrous-Feminine: Film, Feminism, Psychoanalysis.* New York: Routledge, 1993: 1.

23. Grant, Barry Keith. Introduction. *Dread of Difference: Gender and the Horror Film.* Ed. Barry Keith Grant. Austin TX: University of Texas, 1996.

24. Clover, p. 12–13.

25. Hart, p. 13.

26. Creed, p. 156.

27. Riviere, Joan. "Womanliness as a Mas-

querade." *Psychoanalysis and Female Sexuality*. Ed. Hendrik M. Ruitenbeek. New Haven CT: College & University Press, 1966, p. 210.

28. See David J. Hogan's *Dark Romance: Sexuality in the Horror Film* for a narrative of Barbara Steele's career as a cult horror film actress in roles that are excellent examples of the blend of death and sex of a female villain.

29. Brosch, vol II, p. 29.
30. Brosch, vol. I, p. 11.
31. Brosch, vol. II, p. 37.
32. Brosch, vol. I, p. 63.
33. Brosch, vol I, p. 63.
34. Brosch, vol II, p. 37.
35. See Segrave for a historical and analytical discussion of the rise and decline of drive-in theaters in the United States.
36. Segrave refers to the mid 1950s as the "golden years of drive-in horror."
37. Creed, p. 156.
38. Creed, p. 157.
39. Brosch, vol. II, p. 37.
40. Another example of threat that associates death with sex are Barbara Steele's acting roles. In *Dark Romance: Sexuality in the Horror Film*, David J. Hogan discusses the actress' type cast roles as the dark seductress. His sense of how the combination of sex and death manifests in her characters during the 1960s and 1970s has been useful in examining cinema's culmination of the sexualized female demon.

41. The captions are taken from Robert Brosch's section d volume of publicity posters and lobvy cards.
42. Creed, p. 157.
43. Hollinger, Karen. "The Monster as Woman: Two Generations of Cat People." *Dread of Difference: Gender and the Horror Film*. Ed. Barry Keith Grant. Austin TX: 1996: 301.
44. Captions and photos can be found in Robert Brosch's volumes one and two of the *Movie Posters and Lobby Cards*.
45. Brosch, vol. I, p. 31.
46. Clover, p. 17.
47. Vendelin, Carmen. "Sugar and Spice and Everything Nice—Is That What Little Girls Are Made Of?: Girls and the Macabre in Hollywood Cinema." *New Art Examiner*. Volume 25, Issue 9. June 1998, p. 35.
48. Like the femme fatale in *film noir*, the strong woman is controlled, according to Janey Place (in the essay "Women in *Film Noir*." *Women in Film Noir*. Ed. E. Ann Kaplan. London: BFI, 1980), by "first demonstrating her dangerous power and its frightening results, then destroying it" (45).
49. Vendelin, p. 35.
50. Vendelin, p. 34.

13

Unmasking Patriarchy's Savior: Gender Politics in *Samson versus the Vampire Women*

Michael Lee

For filmgoers of a scholarly bent, the most influential figure in Mexican cinema was surely Luis Buñuel, the expatriate Spaniard who moved to Mexico from the United States in 1948. Buñuel made 20 films in Mexico including several indispensable contributions to world cinema: *Los olvidados* (1950), *Viridiana* (1961), *El ángel exterminador* (1962) and *Simón del desierto* (1965). The success of these films, especially *Viridiana*, led Buñuel back to Europe with its more robust economies where he added substantially to his lustrous credentials as a filmmaker. Buñuel's departure from Mexico during the 1960s coincided with the rise of a lengthy period in Mexican cinema (roughly 1960-80) which historians of Mexican film such as Carl Mora and Paulo Antonio Paranaguá lament.[1] This period, which saw stock plots and crass commercialism replace the poetry and social conscience which distinguished not only the creations of Buñuel but also Mexican directors such as Alejandro Galindo, also saw the rise of a figure from Mexican cinema whom movie fans not given to attending art cinemas or college film courses recognize far more readily than Luis Buñuel: El Santo.

El Santo's fame stems primarily from his sensational career as a professional wrestler, or luchador. Wearing a silver mask, El Santo racked up an astonishing undefeated record spanning the better part of four decades. He also appeared in more than 50 movies between 1961 and 1982. His first film, *Santo contra el cerebro diobólico* (*Santo versus the Diabolic Brain*, 1961) cleared 125,000 pesos at its premier, a most impressive figure at that time.[2]

Mexico's large and important film industry grew tremendously during the 1950s and 1960s, reaching a high-water mark of 138 productions in 1958.[3] Apart from Buñuel's last Mexican films, the most readily exportable Mexican movies oddly enough stem from the wrestler-versus-monster subgenre, which enjoys no equivalent in the English-speaking world. On the surface, this subgenre seems unpromising for foreign consumption given its uniquely Mexican flavor. Perhaps the use of tropes on classic monsters coupled with America's ready acceptance of north-of-the-border superheroes such as Superman might explain their crossover appeal.

Universal Pictures' horror classics won broad favor in Mexican cinemas, even prompting simultaneous shooting of Spanish-language, alternate versions for certain films and dubbing into Spanish the remainder. Mexico's appetite for films utilizing the classic monsters did not wane during the 1950s. When the supply of

A tense moment in an El Santo horror film, this one from *Santo contra el asesino de la T.V.*

horror films from America dwindled to a trickle of generally weak pictures, the indigenous cinema industry took up the cudgels and produced relatively inexpensive, but often striking horror films. The year 1957 saw the release of *La Momia Azteca*, the first Mexican horror picture to win broad release in the United States, and its two sequels along with the superb *El Vampiro* and its less successful but still worthy sequel *El Ataud del Vampiro*. These latter two films, directed by Fernando Mendez and starring Germán Robles as the Hungarian count Lavud, deserve to be seen.

As interest in the classic monsters waned in Mexico during the early 1960s, filmmakers spiced their offerings with popular luchadors as foils for Mexican variants on the tiring classic monsters.

While professional wrestling has enjoyed only on-and-off success in this country with the 1950s and 1990s providing the pseudo-sport with its greatest notoriety, Mexico has witnessed sustained interest for professional wrestling, especially among the working classes. The combination of monsters and wrestlers caught fire and prompted the production of dozens such films. Interestingly, this fusion prompted wrestling promoters to introduce monstrous wrestlers, indicating that the unlikely exchange between wrestling and horror movies was not a one-way street. Mexican wrestling fans from the 1970s are sure to recall El Santo's difficult matches with a villainous wrestler named La Momia (The Mummy), while the Masked Cadavers provided fans with a decade of matches between living and undead foes.

In 1965, when American distributor and producer Gordon K. Murray brought *Santo contra las mujeres vampiro* (1962) to the U.S. in his Americanized version, one in four movie theaters in this country was a drive-in.[4] Drive-in theater owners have long surmised that the quality of films shown was not a significant determinant in attendance, especially among regular drive-in customers. John Durant wrote for *The Saturday Evening Post* that according to drive-in owners "it doesn't seem to make much of a difference what kind of pictures are shown, because drive-in fans are far less choosy than the indoor variety."[5] Locating inexpensive films to feed the less discriminating appetites of drive-in goers partly prompted distributors such as Murray to look at foreign genre films as serviceable products for American consumption which could be obtained on the cheap.

Indebted as North American film fans may be to Murray for drawing our collective attention to Mexican horror movies, his efforts have their dark side. Murray's versions notoriously weaken the original Mexican pictures through the omission of crucial scenes, use of stilted English-language scripts and unfortunate additions of superfluous material. *Samson versus the Vampire Women* affords the viewer mild examples of all these failings. Moreover, Murray unfortunately elected to change the name of legendary wrestler Santo to Samson. No doubt Murray hoped for some crossover viewers enthusiastic about Italian "sword and sandal" melodramas who might wrongly assume that the titular Samson resembled Italian

A fight scene from *Santo y Blue Demon vs. el Dr. Frankenstein.*

beefcake heroes then making the rounds of American drive-ins in vehicles such as *Goliath against the Vampires* (1961), a violent Italian effort fusing a "sword and sandal" picture with horror elements and starring American hunk Gordon Scott as Maciste, dubbed as "Goliath" for American audiences. The name Santo—like Maciste—did not then enjoy much cachet in this country, hence Murray's change. Viewers of Murray's altered version will note the sloppy transformation of Santo into Samson. In one scene, the soundtrack clearly reveals a well-dressed man leading a crowd of wrestling fans in a chant of "Santo, Santo, Santo."

The original Mexican film, *Santo contre las mujeres vampiro*, marked the silver-masked hero's earliest cinematic encounter with a classic monster. He would later be featured in dozens of films involving horror and science fiction foes and would see his films released in America with his proper name in the title. Murray hired Manuel San Fernando to direct a few scenes not present in director Alfonso Corona Blake's original film and to coach the English-speaking actors for their dubbing sessions. Differences between the Americanized version and the original film are few. The plot and weird narrative organization of the film stand intact. This essay, by virtue of the collection's concern with the American drive-in as a venue for horror films, concerns itself exclusively with the Americanized *Samson versus the Vampire Women*.

Alfonso Corona Blake along with director of photography Jose Ortiz Ramos wove a visually and narratively striking film full of daffy pleasures. Some might be tempted to call this film "so bad it's good."[6] Personally, I find it much more interesting than most films which find themselves in that cultish category. Notoriously sloppy journalistic critics such as Michael Medved have codified a false notion of what constitutes a bad film. Such judgments should surely take into consideration budgets, pretenses and potential to say nothing of entertainment value before swinging such a moralizing terms as "bad" around. For my money, *Samson versus the Vampire Women* affords far more pleasure than the huge number of forgettable Hollywood efforts that sleepwalk through neighborhood multiplexes without drawing much ire from ripped-off filmgoers. One could easily forget seeing an action sequel or a film based on another John Grisham novel during the car ride home from the theater, yet these films rarely make lists of worst films. Medved and his ilk seemingly use the term "bad" as code for "nonconformist" in their ongoing effort to preserve the status quo at all costs.

The film unfolds with the sort of considerable leisure many Mexican horror films enjoy. Blake took pains to draw the viewer into the world of classic horror. The lengthy opening sequence, wordless for nearly five minutes as the camera pans about a creepy old castle replete with spiders, rats, bats and an owl; allows the viewer space to set aside mundane concerns and enter the film's horrific space. In addition to establishing a sense of place, this opening sequence halts importantly on a portrait of a beautiful young women. A plaque informs us that her name is Rebeca and the portrait dates from 1761. Soon we will learn that Rebeca was chosen to become the successor to Sorina (evil leader of the vampire women), but Rebeca's virtue and beauty coupled with the exploits of a courageous young man saved her from that hideous fate. Now, 200 years later, Rebeca's virtue and beauty have been passed down to a descendant named Diana. The vampire women must capture Diana, transform her into one of them and allow Sorina to join her impatient Lord of Dark Dominions as soon as possible. We learn all this in a lengthy expository speech delivered by Tondra, the vampire women's principal agent in their dealings with the world of mortals.

We first see Tondra as she emerges from a coffin propped up against the rough-hewn rock walls of a secret vault below the castle. Her clothing consists of threadbare rags. Her long stringy hair is matted with spider's webs, her complexion is marred by strange decay, and hideous fangs crowd her mouth. Even the most unsympathetic viewer should admit that the makeup for the vampire women distinguishes this film from the many thoughtless efforts which crowd the horror genre.

During the course of her rambling exposition, Tondra introduces some interesting gender-related themes into the film as a war of the sexes lurks just beneath the surface of *Samson versus the Vampire Women*. Naturally this depiction of gender war is a purely male fantasy, but even so, it reveals some interesting facets of male anxieties about patriarchy and its defense. Tondra makes her case against men, saying, "All men are addicted to corruption and dedicated to self destruction." These weaknesses, Tondra reasons, allow monsters such as herself to exist. Scenarist Blake here taps into one of the great arguments of the left, the roots of transgressive forces lie in the actions of normative forces. More interestingly, most of Tondra's words pass without refutation in the text of the film. Only the word "all" in Tondra's charge finds contradiction in the person of Santo. The failings of men hang over the film and provide the main concern for this analysis.

For their part, the vampire women illustrate a genuine threat to male dominance. A group of organized women, they disdain the usual trappings of femininity. Near the end of her speech, Tondra calls on the forces of evil to transform her from the hideous monster she is into a sexy Latin bombshell. She cries, "I must have beauty to fulfill my mission." With those words, amid a flash of smoke and sparks, Tondra is suddenly transformed into a gorgeous beauty in a revealing evening gown. Physical beauty, the property in women most prized by men addicted to corruption, possesses no intrinsic merit for the vampire women. Tondra views her new looks merely as a tool to achieve more important ambitions. Interestingly, the vampire women do value physical beauty in their female victims. In reference to Diana, the target of their nefarity, Tondra points out to Sorina that "Diana possesses great beauty." Excited, the usually sedentary Sorina insists on seeing Diana at once. The vampire women's premium on physical beauty in their victims coupled with their indifference to it in themselves gestures toward their transgressive potential as possibly lesbian, or more precisely, lesbian in that way that male fantasies of lesbianism unfold. This potential is more fully realized during a later sequence described below.

Next we meet the slaves of the vampire women. Three men in wrestling tights and black capes recline on rock slabs, chained hand and foot in a vulnerable, spread-eagle position. These men serve not only as agents of the vampire women's will but as illustrations of the debilitated role men play in the world of these female monsters. Obedient and submissive, especially when chastened by Tondra for past failures, these three figures appear in virtually every scene of the film but never speak except on one occasion and then only to apologize to Tondra for their ineptitude.

Only one powerful male figure exists for the vampire women. Three times during the film, a shadow appears on the wall of their vault. That shadow belongs to the "Dark Master," presumably Satan. Illustrating negation offers a difficult problem for filmmakers whose art emphasizes depiction. Here Blake handles the problem beautifully. The one man in the lives of the vampire women appears only as an absence. Satan does not speak, nor even appear in the film. Blake's non-depiction of the "Dark Master" underscores the extent to which the vampire women are unbridled by male power.

All horror films entail a transgressive force which crosses boundaries normally left uncrossed. A classic illustration appears in *Night of the Living Dead* (1968). In that excellent film, the ghouls spend much of the film trying to cross the boundary erected by the humans in the form of the barricaded farmhouse. More importantly in terms of cultural concerns, the ghouls cross the boundary separating the living and the dead—two realms our culture prefers to see as distinct yet one other cultures, say for example societies which place a premium on the individual's relationship with ancestors, see as more mutable. Perhaps the most interesting transgression of boundaries for horror fans crossed in *Night of the Living Dead* sees the ghouls cross the boundary of the body by penetrating flesh with teeth. In that way, they also cross the cultural boundary which forbids cannibalism. All monsters cross or blur cultural boundaries. The wolfman crosses the boundary dividing man and animal. Beyond crossing life with death, Frankenstein's Monster poignantly crosses childlike vulnerability with super-powerful physical capability. Horrific transgressions of cultural boundaries form the centrifugal force which holds the genre together. As social women working within a context where masculine power exists only through its negation and toward ends outside the boundaries of society as conventionally conceived throughout the Americas, the vampire women transgress important cultural boundaries as well.

Since *Dracula's Daughter* (1936), films concerning female vampires have raised issues of lesbianism. In that earlier film, Countess Zaleska's seductive murder of Lilly, the young model Zaleska induces to pull down the straps of her slip, serves as the paradigmatic moment for female vampires. Later films would more graphically depict vampiresses as lesbians. While great strides have been made in recent decades toward our culture providing a safe space for lesbians to enjoy all the freedoms our society offers, in 1962 when *Samson versus the Vampire Women* was made, lesbianism posed a grave symbolic threat to patriarchal order in the imagination of the majority. When Tondra first sets out to stalk Diana, the film attaches a vaguely lesbian coding to Tondra's actions. This situation should surprise no one, after all the vampire women are trying to abduct a straight woman for the purpose of making her "one of them."

We first meet Diana as she performs Beethoven's "Moonlight" sonata in the upper-class home of her father, Prof. Orloff. Her audience is initially comprised of two men, her father and George, her fiancé. The men gaze upon the lovely Diana approvingly as she plays. Then her audience expands unexpectedly as Tondra appears at the window and begins gazing on Diana approvingly as well. Just as when she and Sorina discuss Diana's physical beauty with excited admiration, Tondra crosses cultural boundaries and joins Orloff and George by taking the masculine position of observer to Diana's feminized position of observed. Next Tondra hypnotizes Diana and draws her toward the window in a symbolic act of seduction. The film brilliantly links George's desires closely to Tondra's, as both seek control over Diana.

After Tondra departs, George reminds Diana that they're supposed to go to a nightclub that evening. Prof. Orloff, aware of the threat Diana faces, protests. This prompts George to relinquish his claim on Diana's time, saying "Okay, but pretty soon you'll be using my name, and I'll be giving the orders around the house. Isn't that right, Professor?" The professor replies with a triple affirmation of George's claim: "Oh yes, certainly, of course." Diana remains silent and on the periphery of the shot throughout this exchange.

While Tondra and George vie for control over the objectified Diana, her father enjoys initial control. To say that Prof. Orloff patronizes his daughter is to understate the situation badly. He hides the truth from her about her dire peril, condescendingly assuming her incapable of effectively acting out of simple self-preservation. At one telling point, Diana begs her father to explain the source of his worries. In response, he brazenly tells her naked lies.

In addition to placing a premium on themes of transgression against cultural boundaries, the horror genre usually reveals a tripartite structure. The first phase sees order depicted. Horror films usually begin by introducing the "normal" characters. Even if the monster is seen briefly at the beginning of the film, some measure of a horror film's opening moments will be allotted toward the depiction of an everyday world of normative conduct free from any awareness of the supernatural on the part of the normal characters. The second phase, usually by far the longest, witnesses the unleashing of disorder. During this phase, the monster fells victims or at least lurks menacingly, while normalcy stands threatened. The remainder of this disordered phase of horror films sees some normative force gather power—usually in the form of knowledge—necessary to restore normalcy. These normative forces are usually represented in the 1930s by aristocrats, in the 1940s by journalists or sympathetic psychologists, and in the 1950s often by military men. The final phase, usually brief—sometimes as short as a single embrace as in *Bride of Frankenstein* (1935)—depicts order restored and a world free from the transgressive force.[7] How filmmakers go about restoring order often speaks volumes about their own ideological relationship with the dominant order. In some films, these restorations come at a tremendous price for normalcy. In naming that price, the filmmakers reveal their take on the genre as subversive or conservative. *The Mummy* (1932) asks the survivors to live in a world where the ancient Egyptian gods (or at least the goddess Isis) still hold the power of life and death, thus leaving the order of things badly shaken. While *The Thing* (1951) names the price normalcy must pay through the words of journalist Scotty at the end of the film as vigilance, thus allowing the status quo to protect itself one presumes through even more dedicated acts of global surveillance.

In *Samson versus the Vampire Women*, that basic structure is present but in a discombobulated form. The opening of the film lingers over the monsters for a solid ten minutes before embarking on a very brief opening phase. By letting Tondra outline her entire exposition of the history and present ambitions of the vampire women, scenarist Blake allows the monsters to get the first word and establish a network of expectations against which subsequent events must be judged. Considerable time passes before the normative expectations of Orloff, Diana, and George find voice. To be sure, the forces of normalcy will outline a counter set of ambitions—that George and Diana will be happily married—which constitutes the opening phase of the structure. The initial ordered phase is tardy rather than absent and posed as an alternative to Tondra's expectations rather than the base reality against which all subsequent events are judged.

Not only does the second phase of the structure get a premature start in this film with the lengthy opening sequence devoted to Tondra's speech, but this middle period of the film sees little in the way of gathering expertise sufficient to deal with the threat posed by the vampire women. Here an almost post-modern indifference to Cartesian logic or the hegemony of reason finds voice.

The activities of the normative forces require examination. Prof. Orloff has devoted much time to translating parchments containing both the history of the vampire women and prophecies concerning Diana's future. She has a peculiar black birthmark shaped precisely like a vampire bat. The parchments tell Orloff that the mark makes Diana the likely successor to Sorina. Orloff turns first to his old friend and favorite chess opponent, Inspector Charles Andrews (a name configured for the English-language version as though Anglo audiences could best identify with characters with Anglo names). Andrews listens to Orloff outline not his fears—the old professor knows Charley will never believe in vampires without proof—but his expectations for the police in protecting Diana during her twenty-first birthday party where she and George plan to announce their engagement. Orloff only confides that his daughter faces a threat far worse than kidnapping or even death itself. Orloff states unequivocally his belief that the police cannot really help his doomed daughter. He continues by revealing that he feels obliged to go through the motions of enlisting their aid. Like the architectural references to past styles such as columns or gargoyles found in the work of seminal post-modernist Charles Moore, Orloff turns to the police as a matter of form rather than function. This sensibility of doom for the conventional trappings of order marks Prof. Orloff as a unique figure within the genre. His immediate and unequivocal recognition that summoning the police constitutes nothing more than an empty ritual marks a striking moment in the history of the genre.

Just as the police find themselves reduced to window dressing in this picture (true to Orloff's expectations, they fail completely and repeatedly), Orloff himself provides a weak advocate for academic disciplines. Orloff can translate ancient parchments (that the parchments are invariably called "ancient" when they refer to events precisely 200 years ago stands as a fun example of the film's imprecise language) but in doing so immediately declares himself "at a complete loss as to what to do to save my poor daughter." The professor can accumulate some fancy knowledge, but is impotent to put that knowledge in the service of his ambitions. Like the power associated with the police, Orloff's scholarly knowledge constitutes an empty form without a function.

The only other scientifically trained character in the film, the coroner, also demonstrates a peculiar lack of faith in scientific expertise. After examining two blue marks on the throat of the corpse of a beautiful young woman found completely drained of blood outside a nightclub, the coroner opines, "I can tell you one thing, and there's no mistake about it, my friend. I attribute these two marks on her neck to an animal whose species is totally unknown, and there's no way that I can determine it." That confession warrants some interrogation. Not only does the coroner not know the species of animal which caused the wounds, but he also knows that his science is totally insufficient to ever know. While one could readily attribute this weak dialogue to a collapse in the art of writing, we must recall that this dialogue reinforces a running theme in the film of skepticism regarding the traditional institutions of modern society. The coroner is an expert who understands the futility of expertise. His title and authority, like those of the police, are an empty form. Although his authoritative statement on the limitation of his authority is based on his authority so the entire scene transforms into a crazy hall of mirrors, each mirror an evocation of authority impugning authority and reflecting an evocation of authority until the image of authority diminishes in stature to the vanishing point.

Understanding the everyday world of scientific, legal and academic authority as little more than empty forms; Orloff does the one thing he can as a father to save his daughter: He calls supreme luchador, Samson. Samson isn't in, but fortunately his secret headquarters houses a science-fiction device which records incoming messages from callers while he's out. We first see Samson doing what he does best, wrestling. One of the excellent qualities of *Samson versus the Vampire Women* lies in the variety of lively entertainments interposed into the story. Not only does the film feature two excellent wrestling matches (both of them best-two-of-three-falls affairs) shown in their entirety (in keeping with the leisurely pace of the film as a whole), but also a fine nightclub act featuring Fabian Gray crooning "Love's Sonata" (which Murray left in its original Spanish).

What should the viewer make of Santo in cultural terms? All superheroes have some interesting meaning for the culture that produces and embraces them. Describing El Santo, leading Mexican film commentator Jorge Carrasco offered this:

> Symbol of justice, tireless collaborator with the well-meaning but inept metropolitan police, Interpol's agent in Mexico, sometime inventor of simple but effective crime-fighting devices, virtuous sportsman (he doesn't drink or smoke), a gentleman admired by the so-called weaker sex to whom he never submits, Santo is all that and much more.[8]

The "much more" Carrasco refers to might entail Samson's symbolic position as the embodiment of masculine power. By concealing his identity, he functions not as a man replete with weaknesses, but as a symbol of manliness. Through Samson, the film's creators accommodate a critique of the masculine side of their fantasy of gender conflict. Tondra's claim that all men are weak owing to their addiction to corruption finds ample demonstration in all the characters except Samson, who functions as an incorruptible symbol of their collective strength. Samson's depiction as the lone guardian of the sort of patriarchal order which would allow the smooth transfer of biopower over Diana from the condescending Orloff to the tyrannical George affords the critic a glimpse at the "much more" Carrasco mentions. According to this film, what lies just below the surface of patriarchy's institutional control is a wrestler who enforces order not through outmoded reason but brute physical strength, masculinity's biologically based edge in the conflict of genders.

Toward the film's close, the vampire women execute a plan to deal with Samson by sending one of their wrestling slaves to take the place of Samson's next opponent, the Black Mask. After dispatching the Black Mask, the slave dons his tights and mask and takes his place in the ring. This bout constitutes one of the genuine highlights of the film. Samson is sore pressed as the slave knows karate! "He could kill me with a single blow," Samson whispers to his ring man. The ring man encourages Samson to give up the bout, but the silver-masked man resolutely insists on seeing this terrible match to its conclusion. During the second fall, the villain nearly unmasks Samson (a dreadful humiliation in the world of Mexican professional wrestling); however, it is Samson who unmasks his foe, inexplicably revealing not a man, but a werewolf! Pandemonium ensues until the slave transforms from a werewolf to a bat and flees the arena.

Samson follows the bat and discovers the lair of the vampire women. Initially Samson finds himself captured and in grave jeopardy as Tondra insists that his identity be revealed. She seems to understand that transforming Samson from the masked symbol of manliness to an individual man would effectively destroy him as a threat to her transgressive plans. Yet before she can unmask him, the sun begins to rise. The vampire women retreat to their coffins. Nature itself, as represented by the sun, symbolically forms a tag-team partnership with Samson, allowing him to set all the vampire women on fire. As Samson thrusts his burning torch into each of the coffins, we hear the vampire women moan and howl as they begin to burn. The symbolism of Samson's phallic victory with its abundant sexual metaphors over the vampire women cannot be mistaken.

The film succeeds in a sense where Tondra does not in that it unmasks the power behind patriarchal control. Samson, the living embodiment of masculine force, props up the social order which allows George to subjugate Diana so unapologetically and with the full sanction of her father. Patriarchy in all its forms depends upon an improbable *deus ex machina* to liberate it from the threat posed by the vampire women. The classic use of the *deus ex machina* not only resolves dramatic conflicts, but reveals that the rescued characters continue to enjoy their measures of security and control by dint of grace rather than merit. Historically this technique served monarchical power with its irrational basis in divine right. Showing that patriarchal order depends on grace provides viewers with a striking contrast to most genre pictures where men rule through merit, not grace; and in turn weakens rather than reinforces masculine order. The film's drastic retreat from reason; in short, the rapidity with which the scientists and government officials give up on their mechanisms of asserting reason's control over society surrenders considerable patriarchal power. In the last analysis, these enlightened institutions and social conventions of normalcy depend not on reason for their sustenance, but on a masked wrestler.

In revealing all this, the film's third phase of the classic horror structure is interestingly altered. Instead of a tripartite structure of order-disorder-order, we see that the third phase is just an alternate disorder masquerading (in this case literally) as order. For critics of patriarchal authority, masculinity itself poses no problem. But hegemonic masculinity that assumes its own superiority and subjugates through the manufacture of binaries such as masculine-feminine, normal-other—in short, patriarchy—needs exposure for the irrational thing it is.[9] By showing patriarchy propped up by a man in sequins and tights, a miraculously improbably *deus ex machina*, rather than an enlightened or democratic institution, the sciences, or any other masculinist rational structure; *Samson versus the Vampire Woman* participates in a dazzling form of what appears to be unintended critique, although Alfonso Corona Blake's intentionality remains unknown. The film so consistently depicts the impotence of the patriarchal realm to defend itself, that we could conclude from evidence within the text that Blake may have actually intended the critique his film achieves.

Sadly, *Samson versus the Vampire Women* cannot fully take its place as what film scholar Robin Wood might call a "progressive text."[10] While demonstrating that patriarchal power depends not on enlightened institutions or scientific reason but a man in a mask and tights lends the film a certain critical valence, the film fails to offer a credible alternative. Despite their compelling vampire make up in early sequences and hubba-hubba good looks thereafter, the vampire women fail to offer the viewer a viable or attractive alternative to patriarchy. Not only are the vampire women all destroyed at the film's close, even while they are functional, their power structure leaves much to be desired. Sorina is a tyrant who reigns through fear. In one sequence, she learns that Tondra and the male slaves have failed to abduct her successor owing to the intervention of Samson. In a childish huff, Sorina transforms two peripheral vampire women into dust with an imperious gesture and a puff of flame and smoke. Moreover, their goal is not to liberate Diana from her father and fiancé's tyranny, but to forcibly bend her to theirs (although we should note that Diana is marked to assume the leadership role currently held by Sorina). The progressive task of providing an attractive alternative to patriarchy will be left to other films born of more progressive ambitions.

Beyond its peculiar brand of critique, the film affords many charms; not the least of which is watching a man in a sequined robe, tights and a silver mask conduct a serious discussion about contemporary anxieties including the proliferation of nuclear weapons with Prof. Orloff in yet another scene in which patriarchal failings find themselves subject to criticism. But for film fans whose taste may run more toward Luis Buñuel than El Santo, *Samson versus the Vampire Women* surrenders more ground in admitting the sham of patriarchal power than perhaps any other film of comparably modest ambitions. For this alone, the film deserves to be cherished as a cultural artifact of real interest.

NOTES

1. See Carl Mora's fifth chapter of *Mexican Cinema: Reflections of a Society 1896–1988* (Berkeley: University of California Press, 1989) and *Mexican Cinema*, Paulo Antonio Paranaguá ed. Ana López tr. (London: British Film Institute Publishing, 1995).
2. Mora, p. 102.
3. Mora, p.104.
4. Bruce Austin, "The Development and Decline of the Drive-In Movie Theater," *Current Research in Film: Audiences, Economics, and Law, Volume 1* (Norwood NJ: Ablex Publishing, 1984), p. 64.
5. Quoted in Austin, pp. 69–70.
6. The film was lampooned on the television show *Mystery Science Theater 3000* indicating that, at the very least, that show's producers think *Samson versus the Vampire Women* a poor film.
7. For an excellent and systematic discussion of narrative patterns in horror films see Andrew Tudor, *Monsters and Mad Scientists: A Cultural History of the Horror Movie* (Oxford: Basil Blackwell, 1989).
8. Jorge Carrasco "Superhéroe a la Medida" *Hispanoamericano*, September 20, 1982, p. 56. Translated in Mora, p. 146.
9. For feminist critics, the ideas of psychoanalyst Jacques Lacan serve extremely well. Lacan identifies the manufacture of binary oppositions as the strategy which allows the Law of the Father, masculinity's dominance over the symbolic order, to perpetuate itself. For a fine introduction to Lacan's applicability to the study of texts, see Toril Moi, *Sexual/Textual Politics: Feminist Literary Theory* (New York: Routledge, 1985).
10. To read Wood's interesting thoughts on progressive ideology and horror films, see *The American Nightmare*, Robin Wood and Richard Lippe, eds. (Toronto: Festival of Festivals, 1979).

Understanding Cultural Currents

14

Monsters and Mayhem Below the Mason-Dixon

Stephen Budney

Imagine a mansion on the evening of a party. The atmosphere is electric—charged with gaiety, excitement and brightness. The sound of a clarinet playing Dixieland jazz wafts out of wide opened doors to echo into the heavy night air. Elegantly dressed young women adorn the arms of attentive young men who bring them offerings of punch. Just outside the kitchen entryway, servants labor hurriedly to open cases of liquor, struggling to keep up with the demand. In his haste, one young servant makes a clumsy attempt to pry open a case of champagne using a meat cleaver. Distracted by the noise of the crowd and the strains of the music, he sets down the cleaver and momentarily turns away to listen. When he turns back to his task, the cleaver is gone.

Nearby, yet removed from the social whirl, another young man sits alone in the mansion's summer house contemplating the gravity of the act that he has just committed. He has jilted his lover. He sits quietly at a table among the carved cherubs and caged white birds that decorate the room and sniffs a floral bouquet, his lover's bouquet, which she has just hurled at him in her hasty, wounded departure. As he ponders, he hears someone quietly enter the room. "Charlotte?" he queries. A meat cleaver falls, severing at a stroke his right hand which had rested on the table. The young man screams and raises his stump in a defensive posture. It is to no avail. Again and again the cleaver falls, splattering the surrounding alabaster cherubs with gore.

People who enjoy horror films will recognize this vignette from Robert Aldrich's 1964 production *Hush ... Hush, Sweet Charlotte*. The young paramour who was dispatched so rudely was portrayed by Bruce Dern. David J. Skal has described this scene as "the first Grand Guignol moment in American film." It is a moment that, along with Alfred Hitchcock's *Psycho* (1960) and William Castle's *Strait-Jacket* (1964), helped usher in the era of the splatter movie.[1] That distinction aside, *Hush ... Hush, Sweet Charlotte* is also interesting because of where it situates the action. For the mansion where these gruesome events occur is ensconced firmly in the American South—in Louisiana, to be precise.

The South, with its brooding mansions and moist, reptile-infested swamps, would seem to naturally lend itself as an atmospheric setting for an entire subgenre of gothic horror cinema. But such has not been the case. Horror films such as *The Evil Dead* (1983) or *The Beast Within* (1982) have used the South as the provenience of their action without exploiting

Southernness to enhance their depictions. Location in these films is unimportant; they could have just as easily been set in any of the 48 contiguous states or Canada. The protagonists of these movies exhibit neither regional nor stereotypical traits and so these films are excluded from this examination. Ignored also, but of equal importance, is the not inconsiderable body of films set in the South that deal in voodoo and magic. These films raise different questions and demand a separate examination.

For the purposes of this cinematic inquiry, three films will be examined. The works have been chosen with no consideration for production budget, but with the following criteria in mind.[2] First and foremost, each must rely upon the American South for their regional context. More succinctly put, some aspect of the personality of the South—real or imagined—must be integral to their method of emplotment. Having set this standard, it will then be possible to speculate upon the fears within us these movies appeal to. Do viewers find the characters portrayed in these films compelling enough to identify with them? If so, is it because the depictions are ones that viewers are comfortable with and can subscribe to?

The first film, the aforementioned *Hush ... Hush, Sweet Charlotte*, represents the high-rent district of this trilogy. It was directed by Robert Aldrich, who described the film as "cannibal time in Dixie."[3] Just two years earlier, Aldrich had directed *What Ever Happened To Baby Jane? Baby Jane* had been such a success that the same formula was thought to be viable for *Charlotte*, right down to some members of the original cast. The obstacle to renewed success was the fact that the stars of *Baby Jane*, Joan Crawford and Bette Davis, hated each other deeply and satisfyingly. Their constant, open warfare on the set of that film is the stuff of Hollywood legend.

Crawford was originally cast as Davis' co-star in *Charlotte,* but her monumental ego had met its match. She simply could not withstand another confrontation with the imperious Davis. Crawford sought a way out of the film, claiming—or feigning—exhaustion, and was replaced by Olivia deHavilland.[4]

As the title suggests, the story centers upon Charlotte (Davis), the indulged daughter of a possessive father. It was Charlotte who had allegedly murdered her boyfriend by cutting off his right hand and then decapitating him. Among the locals, the hand and head were rumored to have never been found. Thirty-seven years after the murder, Charlotte is, save for a sloppy but faithful maid (Agnes Moorehead), the only occupant of the vast mansion that was the scene of the crime. Charlotte rambles about its many rooms in the middle of the night, singing the song her departed lover penned for her and, on occasion, she hears voices and sees things. Her only visitors are the local urchins, who dare each other to enter the "haunted house." Charlotte's world is representative of the Old South. On the interior of the mansion, the old ways are clung to in fond memory, but on the outside that traditional world is in decline and threatened by the encircling noose of modernity. There, on the perimeter, just outside the gates of Charlotte's abode, bulldozers await orders from Baton Rouge to build a new road right through the ancestral property. The only impediment to progress is Charlotte's refusal to leave.

Charlotte's character has obvious antecedents in Southern literature. Perhaps an aging woman living alone can exhibit strange behavior not unlike that of Miss Minnie Cooper in Faulkner's *Dry September*. It would be possible to imagine an angry Scarlett O'Hara committing the act which Charlotte stands accused of. Surely a faithless lover deserves little better fate than a Yankee freebooter. But the most compelling literary comparison is between Charlotte and the tragic heroine of Tennessee Williams' *A Streetcar Named Desire*, Blanche DuBois. Charlotte and Blanche are women are who long for a more genteel age and exhibit a pathetic vulnerability. So too, both women are besieged by outside forces that seek to sow the seeds of their destruction. The reasons for their mental instability differ, however. Blanche is convinced that the cruel words she spoke to her young homosexual husband caused him to take his own life; Charlotte suffers from the uncertainty of her involvement in her lover's murder.

The fictional figures of Charlotte and Blanche indicate that American filmgoers were comfortable with the image of the vulnerable Southern belle regardless of the accuracy of that image. Even if the rest of the nation had not suspected that the praise of Southern womanhood was disingenuous in the nineteenth century, the concept had come under full assault from within the South itself by the twentieth. Not only did activist Southern women shake the traditional stereotype, but Southern intellectuals such as W.J. Cash derided the concept.[5] The image of Southern womanhood was transformed, but the fictional ideal retained a powerful appeal. Similarly, the forces of change were closing in upon Charlotte, who fought to defend the interior and familial boundaries of her sphere.

Charlotte has received most of the attention thus far, because she is the primary character and the one through which Southerness is conceptualized in the narrative of this film. But regional pretensions aside, this film must also be viewed in a larger subset of films shot in the 1960s-70s which not only use mental derangement to elicit a response of fear, but also neurotic gender.[6] Coming off the success of *Baby Jane*, and realizing that this film contrived to fit in the same category, 20th Century–Fox undoubtedly thought another collaboration between Davis, Crawford and Aldrich would be a hit. The problem was Davis' performance. She should have tried for pathos, but played her part with the same croaking malevolence as her character in *Baby Jane*. There was, therefore, something unsympathetic and rehashed about Davis' performance.

Hush ... Hush, Sweet Charlotte is a story about social moral, and mental decay. It depends upon *film noir* lighting to promote tension, and the introduction of some occasional body parts to evoke horror. The film strives to reproduce Southern atmosphere through its visual imagery, and it succeeds. Almost every actor who graces the screen in this film is recognizable and in various stages of career ascent and descent. The characters whom they portray are, for the large part, not stereotyped and possess a certain dignity—a happy circumstance that shall not manifest itself again in the context of this inquiry.

If viewers found themselves squirming in their seats during screenings of *Hush ... Hush, Sweet Charlotte*, it was more a consequence of the movie's length—well over two hours—than a tribute to its special effects. The next film to be examined, *Attack of the Giant Leeches* (1959), did not break the compulsory 90-minute duration barrier for B films. Despite its brevity, *Leeches* opens up different avenues of exploration and might just be a more interesting film, while being far more simplistic in its pretensions.

The premise of this film is easy enough to divine from the title. Huge, bloodthirsty leeches suddenly appear in the Florida Everglades and begin sucking the locals dry. The storyline is formulaic in that it utilizes two extremely recognizable methods of emplotment. The first is that the monster leeches are mutants.

They have been transformed because radiation from nearby Cape Canaveral (Kennedy) has contaminated their environment. This cinematic evidence of Cold War angst has been described as "atomic trauma," and is frequently, and understandably, realized in Japanese horror cinema.[7] The second vehicle, the mentor complex, is a horror film standard that has spanned decades. Most viewers will associate it with the portrayal of the relationship between Dr. Van Helsing and Jonathan Harker depicted in *Dracula* (1931). In *Attack of the Giant Leeches*, as in *Dracula*, it works this way. *Leeches*' young, ineffective hero, Steve the Game Warden, has difficulty contending with the terror that grips the swamp. As the hero struggles to find a solution, he is taken under the guidance of an older man.[8] In this instance, tutelage is provided by the father of Steve's girlfriend, the pragmatic Doc Grayson. Together they find a way to rid the swamp of the giant blood-suckers. Again the man of science comes to the rescue.

While Steve and Doc Grayson might exhibit some superior qualities, the same does not hold true for the rest of the cast. These particulars consist almost entirely of ne'er-do-wells who hang around the general store, wear bib-overalls, suck corn cob pipes and imbibe from jugs. When prompted to hold forth, they mouth platitudes such as "Everyone knew Cal and Liz had a hankerin' for each other" or,

Attack of the Giant Leeches **(1959) features monsters in the Florida Everglades.**

upon observing some of the monstrous leeches, opine "It was plumb awful!" These human denizens of the swamp might be far removed from the dignity of those characters depicted in *Hush ... Hush, Sweet Charlotte*, but they are also characters that, for reasons to be examined, American moviegoers might find more interesting.

Unquestionably the most intriguing character in this film is the wife of the owner of the general store where the yokels congregate. Liz, played to the hilt by Yvette Vickers, fits no convenient category. She is at once a temptress in the mold of Stupefyin' Jones, and a woman who has been treated poorly by the men in her life. She is the woman other women sing about in country songs; afraid that she will steal their man because they cannot bring themselves to admit that their men behave little better than rutting boars.[9] If Liz has the redolence of the honky-tonk about her, most viewers find it hard to hold against her. Having had little time or use in her life for coquettishness, Liz provides an interesting, appealing, lower-class examination of a stereotype of Southern womanhood, and she benefits from the best character development in the film. Vickers herself is an interesting figure. She seems to have been typecast as the other woman, for she played a very similar role in the classic *Attack of the 50 Foot Woman* (1958). An interesting sidelight to Ms. Vickers' career occurred in July 1960, when she graced the pages of *Playboy* Magazine as that publication's "Playmate of the Month" centerfold.

Leeches was actually directed by a Southerner—Bernard Kowalski of Texas—whose list of credits also included such drive-in fare as *Night of the Blood Beast* (1958). Kowalski also helped warp innumerable young minds by directing hundreds of television episodes in the 1960s, and later moved on to the made for television movies (telefeatures) that were so popular in the 1970s.[10] The film also featured an actor who has become somewhat of a cult figure, Bruno VeSota, as Liz's corpulent, cuckolded husband. *Leeches* is included in this examination because it fits our criteria admirably in its depiction of Southerners both noble and ignoble, character developed and caricatured. Further, *Leeches* provides a perfect piece in this trilogy, a buffer between the respectable and the dreadful. For the latter it will be necessary to travel to the fictional town of Pleasant Valley, Georgia.

Seems as though the Yankees paid a visit to Pleasant Valley in 1865, burned the town and slaughtered the inhabitants. Naturally the restless spirits of these tortured souls cry out for vengeance and thirst for Yankee blood. Thus, 100 years after the massacre, the inhabitants of the town rise from the dead to extract their pound of flesh. In order to expedite their vindictive designs, the townsfolk rearrange road signs on the interstate highway so that unsuspecting Yankees on their annual pilgrimage to Florida will be rerouted through the town. Once there, they will be the guests of honor at a "party" being organized by locals Rufus and Lester. Little more need be said about the outcome.

Trailers for this bit of cinematic fare, entitled *2000 Maniacs* (1965), describe Pleasant Valley as "A Town of Madmen Crazed for Carnage! Brutal ... Evil ... Ghastly Beyond Belief!" In fact, the townsfolk of Pleasant Valley resemble the same bunch that congregates at the general store in *Leeches*, except that their credentials as crackers and peckerwoods are even more readily verifiable. Lester, for example, wears a rope belt and observes that the upcoming party will be "more fun than a beagle dog at a coon hunt!" In addition, the townsfolk of both sexes exude some sort of primal sexual attractiveness that their slow-witted Northern guests seem unable to resist. Their primal sexuality will prove an invaluable asset in helping to lure those libidinous visitors to the various "events" in which they will participate.

2000 Maniacs did not rely upon star power to entice an audience. The sole luminary that the film proclaimed was *Playboy* Playmate Connie Mason. Sad to say that Ms. Mason was no Yvette Vickers; a mere stint as a Playboy centerfold could not endow her with either Vickers' acting talent nor her sensuality. The director of the film was Herschell Gordon Lewis, the same estimable director who presented cinemagoers with such entertaining films as *Mooshine Mountain* (1964) and *The Wizard of Gore* (1972). So maladroit was Lewis' direction and cinematography in an earlier film, *Blood Feast* (1964), that a *Variety* review dismissed his work as "incredibly crude and unprofessional," and the film itself as "an insult even to the most puerile and salacious audiences."[11]

2000 Maniacs might sound like bad film fun, but potential viewers should be aware that its employment of stereotypes and symbols exceeds sensory overload. There are repeated, some would say blasphemous, invocations of Jeff Davis, Stonewall Jackson and other Confederate icons. The Confederate battle flag is displayed copiously, and the singing of "Dixie" after one visitor is dismembered at the horse race is shameful. Stir in some "pickin' and grinnin'," along with some jug-swilling, and it is hard to tell if this film is exhibiting self-deprecation or self-loathing. The motif of this film is revenge, and what humor it does exhibit is through its attempted parody of the old maxim that "the South's gonna rise again!" Perhaps thanks should be given that the rising of the Pleasant Valley dead at 100 year intervals mercifully precludes a sequel.

Because these three films are purely American, the question of whether or not Americans find the depictions of characters in movies such as *Attack of the Giant Leeches* and *2000 Maniacs* compelling must be reviewed. The answer, for the vast portion of the population which would take the time

to view these films is unequivocally yes. In two of these films, the characters are essentially hillbillies. In his book *Hillbillyland*, J.W. Williamson has shown that motion pictures have promoted the image of the hillbilly practically since the inception of the medium. For its part, the American public has embraced that image.[12] The characters in the last two films fit the hillbilly image in their dress, props and nuances of personality, being simultaneously sexual, violent, foolish and primitive.

2000 Maniacs can also be viewed as a transitional film. Although the characters exhibit hillbilly traits, they are also the product of an American cinematic trend in the cynical 1960s. Even as Americans guffawed at the buffoonery of television's *Beverly Hillbillys* or went to the drive-in to see *Hillbillies in a Haunted House* (1967), the hillbilly was being remolded. Moviemakers kept his, or her, violent nature and ignorance, but they crafted it into the more menacing character of the redneck. Gone was the sense of humor; the squeezins jug was replaced with a can of beer. The Model T jalopy with the steaming radiator was junked in favor of a Hemi-Cuda or Chevelle. The redneck image would later be sanitized and made acceptable in films such as *Smokey and the Bandit* (1977), but for a time it was epitomized by the leering shotgunner of *Easy Rider* (1969). As the redneck image became generic, many more viewers (regardless of region) would identify with it than would ever have identified with the loutish hillbilly. And, in fact, the image of redneck has transcended regional bias. The film *I Spit on Your Grave* (1977) reveals rednecks living as comfortably in Long Island, New York, as they would be lurking amongst the undergrowth along the banks of the river in *Deliverance* (1972).

Williamson also contends that the landscape, or the "mountains as monstrous," has much to do with how viewers interpret horror.[13] Here he seems to miss his own point. The landscape itself is nothing without its inhabitants. Yes, nature might indeed be capable of insensate evil, but it cannot be perceived as such unless interpreted through the lens of human experience. Unless the hillbillies Williamson writes about people the landscape, then that landscape becomes a sterile milieu. True, viewers might sense some innate horror in a film's setting, but unless they hear a Southern accent in what is supposed to be Tennessee, then the setting might as well be the Adirondacks.

Hush ... Hush, Sweet Charlotte plays upon viewers fears because it suggests a loss of identity through an impending loss of heritage and control, the trauma of which is portrayed in Charlotte's transition to madness. Her fear is ultimately enhanced by betrayal, thus prompting some viewer empathy. But what about the protagonists in the other two films? How do their fears translate into our own? Both films use variations on well-worn themes. In spite of their rural coarseness, the townsfolk in *2000 Maniacs* are able to outwit "city slicker" Yankees. Their urban guests are powerless to alter their fate, and that powerlessness is uncomfortably depicted. In the end, the Northerners fall prey to being the butt of the same joke that has impaled innumerable traveling salesmen upon the horns of bucolic cunning.

Leeches is a far more insidious film because it takes the theme of rural superiority and stands it on its head. American legend has it that country boys possess superior attributes to their urban counterparts. They can shoot straighter, track game better and subsist for interminable periods of time on next to nothing in the wild. They are intimately acquainted with their environment. So innate is their knowledge of their surroundings that they are frequently viewed as masters of their environment extending their mastery over the simple, instinctive brutes that share their wilderness domain. But in *Leeches*, the inhabitants of the Everglades have lost the power to subdue nature that is essential to their survival. They are now isolated. Even the clever poachers are picked off one by one. They are, to add a category to Williamson, hillbillies in peril.

Except for the opening of *Hush ... Hush, Sweet Charlotte*, African-Americans are absent in these films. They are thus spared the indignity of being viewed through the stereotypical lens. Depiction of stereotypes requires no imagination on the part of a writer or filmmaker. Yet stereotypes hold an undeniable appeal for the undiscriminating viewer. In the context of the films just discussed, stereotypes can be either imbecilic or possess a certain dignity. The horror film can escape too much scrutiny for its depictions because it is not considered a serious medium. But if horror films play upon our fears, perhaps they also appeal to our latent prejudices. One of the strengths of the horror genre is its ability to depict controversial material that much of the public wants to ignore, and thus would shun in a film with more serious credentials. The genre reveals social fears throughout the decades; the effects of exposure to radiation being a prominent and popular theme in the 50s and 60s. A horror film is essentially a fantasy. And whether these films make people think, or viewers laugh and accept their depictions uncritically is incumbent upon the individual.

Regional stereotyping is low on the controversy list. Does this mean it is acceptable to impugn a location and its inhabitants? Does this provide a catharsis, a safety valve for some darker impulse? Questions abound. Inwardly movie viewers should know that not all Yankees are taciturn, as well as they know that the American West is not the front of fierce American independence. Rightly or wrongly, the three films just discussed would be nothing without some utilization of stereotypical images. Hopefully they can be viewed with a sense of humor.

NOTES

1. David J. Skal, *The Monster Show: A Cultural History of Horror* (New York: W.W. Norton & Company, 1993), p. 311-12.

2. Carol J. Clover, *Men, Women, and Chain Saws: Gender in the Modern Horror Film* (Princeton: Princeton University Press, 1992), p. 20. Clover makes then the cogent point that budget is irrelevant in horror films, with some of the lower spectrum films providing greater energy and creativity than their well-financed counterparts.

3. Various, *World Film Directors* (Two volumes, New York: W.W. Wilson Company, 1988), p. II, 11.

4. James Spada, *More Than a Woman: An Intimate Biography of Bette Davis* (New York: Bantam Books, 1993), p. 351-59. During one scene in *Baby Jane*, Davis was supposed to drag her invalid sister, played by Crawford, out of her bed and down the hallway. Before shooting, Crawford fastened a 50-pound weightlifter's belt under her clothes to make the scene as difficult as possible for Davis. It worked. Davis hurt her back.

5. Marjorie Spruill Wheeler, *New Women of the New South: The Leaders of the Woman Suffrage Movement in the Southern States* (New York: Oxford University Press, 1993), p. 10-11; W.J. Cash, *The Mind of the South* (New York, Alfred A. Knopf, 1941), p. 84-87.

6. James B. Twitchell, *Dreadful Pleasures: An Anatomy of Modern Horror* (New York: Oxford University Press, 1985), p. 59, 257.

7. Skal, p. 248.

8. Rhona J. Berenstein, *Attack of the Leading Ladies: Gender, Sexuality, and Spectatorship in Classic Horror Cinema* (New York: Columbia University Press, 1996), p. 91-93.

9. John Shelton Reed, *Southern Folk, Plain and Fancy: Native White Social Types* (Athens and London: University of Georgia Press, 1986), p. 53-58. Reed deals with the subject of hillbilly or "good ol' gals" very nicely.

10. Welch Everman, *Cult Science Fiction Films: From the Amazing Colossal Man to Yog—Monster From Space* (New York: Citadel Press, 1995), p. 25.

11. *Variety Film Reviews, 1907-1980* (16 vols., New York: Garland Press, 1983), II. *Moonshine Mountain* was also released under the title *White Trash on Moonshine Mountain*.

12. J.W. Williamson, *Hillbillyland: What the Movies Did to the Mountains and What the Mountains Did to the Movies* (Chapel Hill NC: University of North Carolina Press, 1995).

13. Williamson, p. 149-51.

15

Italian Cinema Goes to the Drive-In: The Intercultural Horrors of Mario Bava

Karola

> Images live a life of their own; they stimulate our creative abilities; they agitate the whole world of our experiences; they recall far away echoes of things past which renew and affirm themselves vigorously in the act of our reading....
> —*Antonio Gramsci*[1]

Italian neo–Marxist scholar Antonio Gramsci saw individual, group and cultural texts as inherently heterogeneous undertakings.[2] First writing during the time of early greatness for Italian film, Gramsci understood the importance of the then-new medium, joining other Italian scholars in being among the first to take film seriously[3] (indeed, it was Italian Ricciotti Canudo who placed film as the "seventh art" in a 1911 pamphlet.)[4] Always a collaborative effort both of production and consumption, film evokes meaning through particular cultural symbols and meaning structures, yet simultaneously does so through a set of interculturally established conventions.[5] Italian film admirably illustrates the complex "life of their own" afforded motion picture images; it, especially, has exhibited the culturally specific-interculturally aggregated nature of the medium from its inception. The horror films of Mario Bava, both because of their artistic blending of cultural and intercultural conventions and their frank catering to international commercial tastes, provide a particularly rich example of how this heterogeneity manifests in cinematic experience.

Bava follows a long tradition of Italian filmic blending. Although Filoteo Alberini patented a kinetograph a few months after the Lumieres,[6] Italians did not do much cinematically until about a decade later when, free from the derided fairground atmosphere that often accompanied turn-of-the-century film, they began emulating U.S., British and (above all) French style and technological advancement.[7] Yet they did so with a distinctively Italian stamp. Drawing heavily on such national traditions as the *commedia dell'arte* and opera,[8] Italian cinema developed a passionate narrative feel and visual appeal marked by a love of spectacle that curiously represented the desire to capture a more realistic worldview.[9] Commenting on Italian film in 1911, French director Victorin Jasset wrote:

"The Italian producers constantly imitated developments in the French school, but with a lavishness of staging that we never attained."[10] Though criticizing the frequent lack of accuracy in the popular historical dramas (a perennial fixation of Italian cinema[11]), Jasset acknowledged the distinctiveness of the Italian style: "It aimed at impact rather than nuance, and delighted in shock tactics: its masses of sets and crowds of extras were directed with zest, often to great effect."[12] Audiences agreed—on an international scale. Italy quickly became an early center for international film production and distribution, establishing firm footholds in Europe and the Far East, as well as heavily influencing American filmmaking.[13] By the late 1910s, however, the Italian reign was ebbing, giving way to an American dominance that staggered the Italian industry.[14] Ever after influenced by American trends—whether through imitation or resistance[15]—and continued international collaboration on production and distribution,[16] Italian cinema nevertheless retained a distinctive cultural voice.[17]

Understanding Italian cinema necessitates an intercultural approach; likewise, understanding cinema as an intercultural phenomenon benefits from examining the Italian case. With a few notable exceptions, Italian film scholarship in the United States has largely focused upon the "high culture" works of the neorealist and 1960s innovative cinema.[18] The debate over high versus low culture aside,[19] more pedestrian, explicitly commercial works potentially may yield more insight into how film is at once culturally specific and interculturally constituted, especially those intended for international distribution. As sociologist Raymond Williams points out, production for a market invests any artistic project with a commodity status, which leads to control of and selection among cultural representations. In particular, "the great bulk of market production is solidly based on known forms and minor variants of known forms ... the market ... either determines or emphasizes and de-emphasizes, prevailing types of production."[20] Certainly more esoteric creations play upon their audiences' knowledge paradigms; many of the acclaimed Italian movies of the 1960s, for example, assume a spectator versed in Italian cultural and filmic history (especially from the postwar period).[21] Yet it is just this assumed sophistication that is lacking in populist efforts, which must pull in a meta-communal field of experience to reach the widest possible public.[22] When the market under consideration is both a domestic and foreign one, then the control and selection of images must conscientiously attempt to appeal to an intersection of cinematic tastes, themselves formed through past cultural-intercultural overlap and interaction at varying levels of awareness. In the case of Italian audiences, this overlap and interaction would be an explicit one, as film imports (particularly Hollywood productions) and international co-productions have remained popular even during periods of increased domestic production and attendance.[23] At the other extreme, U.S. audiences constantly witness the fruition of international influences in domestic production, but generally lacking the Italian lifelong inundation by imports,[24] and tend not to have the cultural awareness and taste for mass intercultural interpolation. In addition to/because of the need for convergence with variegated audiences' semiotic expectations, films patently designed as commodities for an international market typically use—and highlight the use of— international locations, casts, crews and producers; hence the always already present collaborative nature of filmic images acquires a further intercultural feel. Although their artistic merits may not always be apparent, the Italian films designed for international popular consumption frequently have managed to construct their requisite blendings in interesting fashion.

From Italy's early days as an worldwide cinematic giant, commercial films produced predominantly for profit and mass appeal (though not necessarily for export) have been a mainstay of the industry; even at the zenith of neorealism, they never lost their popularity.[25] However, their quality has shifted greatly (compare, say, a historical epic such as 1913's *Cabiria*[26] to a peplum[27] such as 1959's *Hercules Unchained*) as has their reception by critics, who have tended to either malign those not from the golden silent era or ignore them altogether. In many cases, this dismissal of Italian populist works has been too hasty. James Hay, for example, gives a fascinating re-reading of the much-reviled "white telephone" films of the Fascist era, revealing how these escapist popular pieces played out tensions in national identity construction.[28] And "spaghetti Western" master Sergio Leone now receives growing scholarly recognition as a major Italian filmmaker despite the explicitly market-driven nature of the majority of his oeuvre.[29]

One area of popular Italian production that has received very little scholarly attention (even negative scholarly attention) is the Italian participation in the international horror cycle of the late 1950s-early 1970s.[30] Yet the movies of this phase are excellent examples of the heterogeneous nature of filmic images. They show how expressly marketing to both foreign and domestic audiences with international productions combines with artistic processes to bring out the best and worst in culturally and interculturally derived forms of representation. Bava's films are in many ways typical of the Italian contribution to the horror cycle: Usually shot on very low budgets, often financed or at least distributed by foreign backers (especially American International Pictures) who released multiple versions edited for specific markets, they featured international stars (typically known for their horror roles, like Christopher Lee and Boris Karloff, though sometimes including others with a broader base, like Elke Sommer and Massimo Girotti[31]), dubbed dialogue and reworkings of familiar horror themes along distinctively Italian lines.[32] At the same time, Bava stands out among his peers for his artistic blends of convention and personal style (especially cinematographically), influencing not only later horror directors such as Dario Argento and John Carpenter,[33] but also such divergent directors as Federico Fellini[34] and Martin Scorsese.[35]

Bava injects the incredible into the mediocre. Horror is a genre renown for rather staid, formulaic films,[36] made with more of an eye toward finance than finesse; while Bava's films do not transcend their pedestrian origins, they have an imaginative flair that make them among the best of the genre, Italian or otherwise.[37] Bava's movies combine interculturally established horror forms with specifically Italian narrative and cinematographic traditions against a backdrop of international commercial production, and they do it in a way that reflects not only popular concerns but artistic sensibilities—making them a sound resource for analyzing the textual layering inherent in film image. Accordingly, the latter part of this chapter will highlight aspects of Bava's horror output as instances of cultural interaction; first, however, it is necessary to consider in more detail the horrific and Italian elements he drew upon to achieve these instances.

Horror Conventions

Although one of the most enduring and popular cinematic forms, horror tends to be dismissed by film scholars at best, openly reviled at worst.[38] As film scholar David Sanjek notes, horror films often are viewed as the "junk food of the imagination, trivially dispensable cultural artifacts undeserving of critical attention and devoid of artistic or intellectual sophistication."[39] To the extent that it has not been ignored, critics have mixed versions of what horror *is*—some dub it a tight, inflexible genre,[40] others an elusive one to the point of claiming horror is less a genre *per se* and more a set of "modes of address," Wittgensteinian "family resemblances" or narrative "generators."[41] Regardless of how it is labeled, horror decidedly draws upon the awareness, participation and attitude of an audience "seasoned" to particular narrative and filmic conventions,[42] in part as a result of the commercial nature of much horror cinema.[43] In order to secure their appeal, the images in popular works often "are constituted by or inscribed with those signs and structural features that the 'film community' holds most vital and hence that are most easily recognized or read."[44] In the case of Bava's horror films, the signs and structures which would have had the widest resonance in fact evolved from their inception in an intercultural cinematic milieu:[45] the fantastical works of the French filmmaker Melies; the Gothic and Romantic traditions feeding Expressionism; Hollywood horror films of the 1930s and 1940s, themselves informed by Expressionism and frequently directed by Europeans; the mid-century resurgence of horror production in England, Spain, Mexico, Japan, Italy and the U.S. Horror is a solid selection for a film aimed at an international market, since the filmmaker can be fairly certain of audience receptiveness given enough conventions are included; at the same time, having such a highly recognizable form allows for some leeway in including elements that will resonate specifically with domestic audiences.

The international appeal of horror is perhaps linked to its tendency to favor symbolic situations over particular ones. Characters are usually recognizable types:[46] psychopaths, victims, monsters, horrid children, scientists/doctors. Different kinds of horror, like Gothic or slasher films, move in and out of vogue, but similar narrative patterns recur. The ancient archetype of a journey is common,[47] as is the depiction of a threat to normalcy from an abnormal outsider.[48] There is an emphasis on the grotesque and extreme, which actually links horror to comedy and necessitates a balance between the two that is not always achieved,[49] especially since the simple stories most conducive to a horrific atmosphere are often least conducive to a believable atmosphere (dialogue particularly suffers).[50] The grotesque ties into the visceral element of horror;[51] the dreaded suspense and fear of curiosity generated by the gap in awareness between character and audience[52] is repaid half as often with a false start by the filmmaker as with a genuine shock. Shock and sensationalism have grown into a graphic fixation, making grand guignol[53] violence increasingly common from the 1960s onward as movies began to try to shock their quickly acclimated audiences in new ways. One result of more extreme narrative and visual brutality was that the sex-death connection, always a popular horror structure, became a blatant device, exploited to the full through thematic contributions like lesbian vampires and erotically staged murders.[54] Indeed, psycho-serial killer narratives in general are steeped in sexuality, as film scholar Steffen Hantke sums in a familiar description: "The killer's overwhelming power induces a lustful yet guilty submissiveness in the victim. The climactic moment of masochist submission often comes after a prolonged stalking sequence which itself has all the characteristics of a seduction."[55]

The point of view of the stalking serial killer as captured by a prowling camera creeping up to an unaware victim[56] illustrates how easily the cinematographic signification of horror is conveyed. Oddly enough, the visual markings of horror movies are at once their most conventional and most original elements, as inventive filmmakers can employ seemingly trite iconography and *mise en scene* to great effect in otherwise wretched productions.[57] Sometimes, the semiotic traces of horror images predate their cinematic appearance by millennia; for example, the stairways, corridors, windows, arches and descents favored by Murnau, Cocteau and Bergman in their dark fantasies—and adopted by nearly every horror director since—hearken to labyrinth passageways of the underworld depicted from ancient Egyptian and Sumerian civilizations onward.[58] Other evocative images are specific to the cinematic age, like the motion picture stars who become so known for horror roles that their mere appearance in a film may be sufficient to designate it as a horrific one to perspective audiences.[59] Most iconography in horror movies is well-known to even occasional viewers, frequently drawing upon the same European folkloric symbols of death and the supernatural developed to a fever pitch in Gothic novels and Expressionism: carriages, coffins, blood, crucifixes, mirrors, knives, decay, castles, demonic possession, silver, wooden stakes, full moons, eyes, doppelgangers, fire (especially in the hands of angry peasants) and so forth.[60]

Beyond representational props, horror films owe their greatest debt to Expressionism for its rich cinematographic heritage. Framing, lighting, camera movement, and the like are crucial to indicate mood and genre;[61] the Expressionists set the standard for a "ciné-vérité of the spirit," using compositions drawn from painting and techniques new to cinema to capture a feeling of the uncanny.[62] Not surprisingly, the Surrealists were reportedly fond of U. S. horror movies, which derived much of their look from Expressionism.[63] Now the heavy chiaroscuro, distortion, wide angles, filters, low-key lighting and unnatural tinting/hyperreal color of Expressionism are all so completely ingrained in the visual appearance of horror films that their appearance in other types of films can herald the approach of a horrific scene.[64]

Italian Cinema[65]

Bava and his Italian contemporaries self-consciously utilized horror conventions as much as anyone in the international cycle, yet their films retained a "distinctively Italian style."[66] A cursory review of Italian film up to Bava's work makes it seem to fall into neat chronological and stylistic categories: first the golden age silents, with their operatic sensibilities and epic scope[67]; then the huge slump in the industry beginning during WWI and dominating the 1920s, in which the few formulaic Italian releases could not compete with the massive onslaught of imports, especially from Hollywood[68]; the fruition of the Fascist investment in film production through popular, escapist pictures that emphasized melodramatic style over substance and often as not imitated Hollywood[69]; neorealism's brief but brilliant reign, rejecting spectacle and genre in favor of social criticism and an attempted verism culled from a minimalist approach that emphasized stark locations, lower class characters, stereotypical physiognomies, mid-distance shots and improvised scripting often with nonactors[70]; the 1950s and 1960s art films which overturned neorealist convention through excess, decadence, self-reflexivity and abstraction[71]; and, finally the underside of the high culture cinema of the 1950s and 1960s, the cheap, commercial, "American-style ventures" marketed both in Italy and abroad, including "spaghetti westerns," peplums, and, of course, horror movies.[72]

Upon closer inspection, however, such a discrete, linear taxonomy of Italian style breaks down. Neorealism, for example, is traditionally placed between 1943–45 and 1950–53, depending on the movies selected as "authentically" neoreal[73]; however, neorealist concerns with social justice and verisimilitude can be traced to the 1910s,[74] and can appear even in the most outlandish, decadent films of the 1950s and 1960s[75] (whose decadence, it must be added, typically represented a cultural critique rather than a endorsement[76]). Rather than a set of easily discernable periods, Italian film is better considered as a heterogeneous collection of works with internal and external influences that shows some common narrative and visual themes demarcating it, for all its variety, as a distinctive national voice. Interestingly enough, many of these themes dovetail nicely with the stipulations of horror, although prior to 1956's *I Vampiri*, there were few Italian films that could be properly termed supernatural, let alone horror movies.[77]

Foremost among Italian filmic elements is a feeling for space, a fascination with perspective, a willingness to include landscape and set as active agents (more often than not filled with figures or strikingly desolated).[78] Even neorealism, which sought to break with the epic scope so beloved of past productions,[79] has a sublime feeling for tying character and situation to environment, and makes the most of the long shots it does include, like when De Sica sets up the desolate poverty of his hero Ricci in *The Bicycle Thief* (1949) through a landscape of ugly, barren modern buildings. Nonetheless, the most distinctive Italian treatment of space is a lavish one, drawn from the richness of Italian art (especially Renaissance painting and Neapolitan landscape pieces) and opera staging.[80] It often slides into spectacle, reveling in an excessive mode of layered composition and overflowing forms, textures and colors. In this, Italian cinematography is well-matched by the popularity of melodrama, a narrative structure so prevalent in all types of Italian films that Italian film scholar Manuela Gieri refers to it as a national "hypergenre."[81] Although occasionally decried as escapist in times of political upheaval, melodrama in Italy has never received much scorn from critic or public.[82] Visconti considered melodrama the best type of spectacle, drawing on both the "natural predisposition of the people" as well as their intellectual and historical inheritance.[83]

Visconti also considered melodrama as suited to not only Italians but "the tastes of the European public because its structure is so united and direct."[84] And certainly, as Gramscian film scholar Marcia Landy points out, a "fundamental feature of mass cultural forms is their dependence on melodrama."[85] At the same time, the expressive pathos and violence of melodrama, as well as its development from the Attic stage through Italian Renaissance poetry and the growth of opera in the Baroque period, lends itself to explicit (though not exclusive) application as an Italian national form.[86] That many of the elements of melodrama coincide with those of Catholicism—notably an emphasis on the family and the (sexual) ecstasy of suffering—reinforces the structure for a culture steeped in its religious traditions. Melodrama imparts its love for archetypical characters to the *commedia dell'arte,* as well as its streamlined storytelling and fascination with physicality, and the grotesque buffoonery of the *commedia dell'arte* is prominent in Italian cinema (perhaps reaching its height with Fellini).[87]

But the ultimate expression of melodrama must be the morbid tragedy of Italian grand opera, and the sex, violence, betrayal, madness, lost hope, mistaken identity, family trauma and revenge it features have worked their way through Italian cinematic forms from classical epics to sophisticated satires to westerns.[88] Another token of lyrical melodrama, promoted to the fullest in the halcyon days of the Italian silent epic, is woman in the role of supreme tragic figure—the bereft mother, betrayed lover, fallen sinner—whatever the case, in Italian melodrama, she is the "wonderful, terrible, worthy and unworthy" diva.[89] Thus, while Italian female characters may not always (or often) win, they nevertheless get more praxis in playing than most of their European and American filmic counterparts. This aspect of melodrama in particular stands out among the many Bava employs in his horror films, as it represents a departure from the conventional female-as-victim role seen especially in American and English productions.[90]

Bava's Films as Intercultural Interaction

Born to sculptor and cameraman Eugenio Bava at the peak of Italian silent film greatness in 1914,[91] Mario Bava grew up inundated by the visual arts. Fascinated early by color (he used to play with the potassium cyanide in his father's lab because he liked its red[92]), Bava trained as a painter.[93] However, the influence of the elder Bava, who for a time headed the optical effects department of LUCE[94] (L'Unione Cinematografica Educativa, established by the Fascists in 1924), was such that the son dropped painting in favor of cinematography.[95] His talents proved equal to the task, and he became a "highly respected cameraman,"[96] with stints as director of photography starting around 1939[97] and cemented with the 1943 *L'Avventura di Annabella*.[98] Bava never intended to move beyond cinematography into the central role of director; rather he was handed the chance after filling in repeatedly for directors who walked off pictures he was filming.[99] Interestingly, the first of these pictures he "rescued" was the first film of the European horror cycle, Riccardo Freda's *I Vampiri*. Bava's choice to do a horror film for his first solo project (*Black Sunday/La Maschera del demonio*, 1960) was a calculated commercial venture designed for export as well as Italian screenings, founded on the international success of Britain's early contributions to the cycle, particularly Hammer's *The Curse of Frankenstein* (1957) and *Dracula* (1957, released in the U.S. as *Horror of Dracula*).[100] At the same time, horror would prove a showcase for Bava's visual creativity (he continued to be involved as director of photography for most of his movies), and he returned to it repeatedly throughout his career,[101] with his last work as visual effects designer for *Inferno* (1980), a horror film by admirer and emulator Dario Argento.[102] In many ways formulaic in respect to both horror and Italian cinema, Bava's work nevertheless creatively plays the conventions off of each other to provide access and meaning for domestic and foreign audiences alike, producing if not high art, at least highly interesting (and entertaining) intercultural texts.

Bava held that "photography in a horror film is 70 percent of its effectiveness; it creates all the atmosphere,"[103] and he reveled in the visual development of fright. Befitting his painting and cinematographic background, Bava's films, regardless of their other merits, feature invariably masterful image composition. Like all good visual stylists, Bava establishes the environment as an active narrative element alongside the human characters.[104] In this he hearkens to the best of both horror and Italy. The gloomy depictions of the uncanny in German Expressionist films were eagerly devoured by a public who had linked terror tales to Teutonic culture through Romantic literature, and were constantly imitated by filmmakers who recognized the power of visuals inspired by Romantic and Expressionistic painting. So imitated, in fact, that the horrific look betokened by German Expressionism lost its grounding as a cultural specific and became an international standard.[105] Like most horror movies of the period—especially Gothic pieces—Bava's movies partake of this by-then formulaic imagery. Yet they do so in a way that makes most of their contemporaries look "rather stolid" in comparison.[106] When Bava depicts feeling through environment, it is dramatic and unmistakable to any even passingly acquainted with horror conventions. If the shadows of evil are looming, they are pitch black. If there has been neglect, spider webs have taken over in every scene. If the characters are corrupt, they are surrounded by sickly green, ruined buildings and symbols of decadence and shattered innocence. All the expressionistic horrific standards are blended into the filmic composition with bold strokes, resulting in a constant richness of image where competitors would content themselves with a few redolent touches and moments.

Bava achieves the sumptuous presence of his cinematography by imparting his visuals with the sensibilities of his training in Italian representation. Like the German Expressionists, early Italian filmmakers evoke the feel of painting in their pieces. The artistic influences most at work, however, come from their own cultural experiences, chiefly the Catholic Church and the Italian Renaissance.[107] Church iconography and love of allegory contribute to the strong symbolism used by Renaissance artists, who also showed a fascination for physicality, space and spectacle.[108] These elements became "central to the native cinema" of Italy.[109] Thus as a cameraman, as well as a painter, Bava was trained to make the visual vividly convey thematic information. Accordingly, his compositions are arranged to maximize viewing experience: deep focus, long long shots, drawn-out pacing, pans and zooms not only play with perspective in their own right but also provide the ongoing framework for Bava's rich infusion of Italian visuals. Bava's more artistically recognized co-nationals made the Italian cinematic look an internationally celebrated part of the 1960s avant-garde through their imaginative use of scene and spectacle. While Bava does not aspire to the style of his celebrated peers, he does draw upon the same cultural traditions to give generic commercial pictures virtuoso atmospheric finesse, particularly through his manipulations of space and lighting. Indeed, considering that Bava typically worked with budgets under $150,000,[110] he may have been spurred to greater creativity in maximizing what impact he could get from the materials available (somewhat like the way the neorealists turned lack of funding into stylistic exploration in veristic cinema[111]).

Setting and landscape, among the most enduring visual characteristics of Italian art since the Renaissance obsession with perspective,[112] are a primary source of ambiance for Bava's films. Imposing locales, shot wide and filled with extras, were an early norm for Italian screen images[113]; while filmmakers by Bava's time had branched out in their explorations of cinematic space, an emphasis upon the scenic and a predilection for grand scope remains in Italian film, whatever its audience niche. For example, in his surreal 1966 film *Blow-Up*, Antonioni uses the wide spaces in a park to heighten and symbolically underscore his main character's ambiguity of perception.[114] At the other end of production, Sergio Leone uses the vast desolate landscapes of his Westerns to complement the melodrama of their epic narrative style. Working in horror, Bava already had a normative framework for expressionistic environments; when coupled with the Italian feeling for space, the results lead one to believe that not just horror aficionados should consider Bava "one of Italy's finest visual stylists."[115] Creepy settings are practically required in horror movies, especially Gothics, and are typically delivered through visual tropes like shadowed exterior shots, forbidding-castle-in-the-distance stills, and depictions of nature as hostile (violent storms, eerie woods, crashing seashores, etc.). Such conventions, however, are usually backgrounded; in Bava they are foregrounded.

Bava masterfully works in environmental devices from the beginning in his movies. In *Kill, Baby, Kill/Operazione paura* (1966), part of the credits roll over a village damned by its own decadence to the ravishes of a ghost child who forces her victims to kill themselves. The darkened, crumbling stone walls and their environs look more like uninhabited ruins than active habitats, and the camera pans dizzily, giving them a surreal aura. Completing the image, the hero enters the village—and the world of the fantastic—through an archway, and works his way through narrow passages between the buildings. The surreal disjunctures of *Lisa and the Devil/Lise e il diavolo* (1972, theatrically unreleased) likewise are manifested early through environment, when tourist Elke Sommer arrives in an old village and becomes lost in labyrinth streets and disoriented by Telly Savalas' friendly/menacing appearances almost as soon as she gets off the bus. In the opening action of *Blood and Black Lace/Sei donne per l'assassino* (1964), the screen is initially filled with a baroque red and gold sign reading "Christian/haute couture" that is snapped away by the wind to reveal a fountain and chateau. The dangling sign then foregrounds a long shot of a woman looking out of the chateau, and it remains in the picture for the next few sequences as she meets with a man lingering at the gate. Both are part of the high-class, corrupt group of characters who populate this horrific thriller; the fashion house placard blowing askew gives an initial visual cue to the murderous decline traced throughout the movie.

Blood and Black Lace/6 Donne Per L'assassino, as the title appears in the U.S. and the Italian trailers.

The best expressionistic cinematography in Bava's films is achieved through the use of atmospheric lighting. So striking is the chiaroscuro in his first movie *Black Sunday*, filmed in black and white to be "more conducive to fright,"[116] that he practically became stereotyped immediately as a black-and-white director (though a masterful one).[117] However, Bava did not abandon chiaroscuro in the least when working in his showcase medium, color film—he knew the stylistic impact of it too well. Shadow has long been a constant for evoking fantastical menace in horror. *The Cabinet of Dr. Caligari* (1919) features painted darkness to capture its abstraction of human darkness, and *Nosferatu*'s (1922) title character's shadow oozing across the wall remains one of its most potent images. Even if Bava's audiences were not directly familiar with the Expressionist works of early horror, they would have been familiar with the 1930s and 1940s Hollywood films that used their tradition of shadowing to set the scene (e.g., *Dracula*'s [1931] decrepit castle entrance hall), introduce characters (e.g., Karloff's backlit first appearance in *Frankenstein* [1931]), suggest supernatural presence (e.g., the panther shadow stalking Alice in the pool in *Cat People* [1942]) and depict horrific acts (e.g., Erik the gorilla's murder of Bela Lugosi in *Murder in the Rue Morgue* [1932]). French director Jacques Tourneur, whose moody contrasts for the 1940s RKO–Val Lewton productions make them stand out as among the most sublime and artistic of horror movies, may have been particularly influential on Bava's shadowing technique,[118] as Bava worked with him (and seems to have co-directed for him) on the 1959 *La Battaglia di Maratona/The Giant of Marathon*[119] Certainly Bava, like Tourneur, does not shy away from strong mixing of light and dark. True, the horror paradigm calls for expressionistic shadowing, and true, most of Bava's contemporaries were sure to include some marked usage of chiaroscuro (e.g., Christopher Lee's first appearance as Dracula is *de rigueur* backlit). However, Bava's movies go beyond their norm. The twilit filtered effect used for many a Hammer and Amicus production nightscape literally pales in comparison to Bava's impenetrable blackness. For example, in *Blood and Black Lace*, the first stalking-murder takes place in woods so dark that the movements of the actors through it are not always discernable—until the strangulation occurs, still shaded, but brutally visible. In *Lisa and the Devil*, title character Elke Sommer takes a tense car ride with a strange couple and their chauffeur. The shot of them in the interior is framed all around with black, emphasizing the weird, silent atmosphere, and reinforcing the horror trope of a journey to a fantastical realm isolated from normal time and space.[120]

Consummate as the shading is in Bava's movies, the effects he achieves with color are staggering. Beyond the cliché of red blood, color is not as associated with horror as, say, malingering shadows and menacing darkness are. It is a mistake, however, to therefore dismiss its potential power as an atmospheric element of terror, as the Expressionist horror-makers knew quite well: *The Cabinet of Dr. Caligari*, for example, was originally tinted green, steel blue and brown to enhance its surreal mood.[121] All the same, color remained mostly out of the horror realm until Hammer's Technicolor showed it to be a highly profitable addition. After that, it became fairly common for horror movies to be *in* color, but the use of color to evoke atmosphere does not appear frequently as an ongoing element. There are exceptions, of course: For example, *Peeping Tom* (1959) switches from black-and-white to color to great effect, *The Mummy* (1959) gives its ancient Egyptian tomb an eerie green glow, and *Pit and the Pendulum* (1961) uses filters of orange, blue, violet and red to heighten the terror of a young child watching his father kill his (the child's) mother and uncle. So moviegoers might expect some colorplay beyond regular Technicolor vividness, but ones outside of Italy would not expect the dramatic use of color featured in Bava's films. This is not to say that the color is obtrusive—the entire cinematography (as well as narrative) in Bava is melodramatic spectacle, and the rich coloration works right along with it. In this he joins such filmmakers as Antonioni, Fellini, Bertolucci and Visconti, all noted for their use of color as an integral, necessary part of the image and story.[122] Indeed, Italian audiences for Bava's films were likely to appreciate his color usage, given not only their filmic intake, but also their non-screen artistic traditions. As a painter, Bava would have been exposed in his training to theories on coloration, many of them probably from earlier Italian masters, who were obsessed from medieval times by color and tonality. Bava's use of color in many ways seems derived from Alberti's late fourteenth-early fifteenth century writings on the "friendship of colors" which recommend juxtapositioning contrasting colors to achieve harmonious distinction among elements in a composition.[123] At the same time, the blending of colors with shadows in his films is more like later Renaissance valuation of tonality over solid blocks of hue.[124] All of this is not to say that Bava's color influences were solely Italian—he could have easily studied the color theories of Russian artist Kandinsky, who considered contrast as "the most important principle in art at all times."[125] The point is that as an Italian, especially as a painter, Bava had a different sensibility toward color than his international competitors, and it enhances his work immensely.

Completely unnatural lighting, often in contrasting hues, is one of Bava's favorite color devices, especially when the movie or the scene broaches the supernatural. In one of the best illustrations of this, "A Drop of Water" (one of the three vignettes in *Black Sabbath/ Il tre volti della paura* [1963]), Bava uses strong colored lighting in a way more reminiscent of the stage than the screen to paint his creepy scenes. At the climax, the central character, a nurse who has thieved a ring from a dead medium, experiences growing apprehension, then outright fear as she is visited by increasing manifestations of the medium's vengeful spirit. The psychological terror of isolated individuals was apparently held in much esteem by Bava for its expressive possibilities,[126] and he builds a masterfully oppressive atmosphere for the nurse through lighting. When she first comes home and admires her new ring, the light is warm and golden, with just an undertone of flashing, opaque, bright blue from some source, ostensibly outside her window—ostensibly because the light source and angle are by no means consistent (Bava shows little concern in any of his movies for realistic lighting consistency, instead switching colors, angles, and so forth whenever it serves dramatic purpose—or perhaps budgetary exigency). As the nurse begins to dread, the warm gold light turns rosier, and the blue becomes more evident. Bava fakes out the audience in classic horror form a few times as ominous drippings prove to be from faucets and a banging from a loose window; at these times the light is a stark "naturalistic" white, matching the stark kitchen and bathroom interiors, themselves redolent of neorealism's barren interiors. As soon as the nurse exits the thresholds of these spaces of normality, however, the interplay of strong rose and blue across her disconcerted features resumes. As the tension builds, so does the blue lighting usage, until it predominates (narratively achieved through the lamp seemingly popping off), mixed in with some violet and just enough yellow, orange and pale white touches to highlight the contrast.

Even if such surreal, highly saturated color lighting is not present in a scene, the vividness of its contrast is. Where Bava uses more cinematically normal lighting, the surroundings and characters carry the color—the effect is similar to that in Visconti's *Senso* (1964), in which the warm, rich coloration matches the passionate storyline of love, war and betrayal.[127] Every color Bava movie—whether additionally featuring highly saturated lighting hues or not—displays an understanding of tonal mixing that mere filming in Technicolor cannot match. For example, the outdoor expanses in *Hercules in the Haunted World/Ercole al centro della terra* (1961) and *Twitch of the Death Nerve/Ecologia del delitto* (1971) are not merely green backdrops, they are resoundingly alive, lavish in their displays of verdure. The tainted heroines of *Whip and the Body/La Frusta e il corpo* (1963) and "The Telephone" (another *Black Sabbath* vignette) have dark hair, the perfect offset for their pale faces and voluptuously scarlet lips. The characters in *Planet of the Vampires/Terrore nella spazio* (1965) are wearing midnight blue and yellow accented uniforms that match the midnight blue and yellow edged walls of their ships. And the opulent residences in *Hatchet for the Honeymoon/Il Rosso segno della follia* (1969) and *Lisa and the Devil* are full of gold baroque fixtures and furniture set against white and sickly green.

Green is sometimes associated with decay and menace—Cennini, an early Renaissance artist, recommended greenish tones for dead bodies,[128] and stage light designers tend to avoid the hue unless they deliberately wish to create an eerie effect.[129] Green appears in many of Bava's horror films, sometimes as the color for key lighting, more often as a component of the environment; like all of the vivid tints favored by Bava, green not only enhances the atmosphere but also forms a vital part of it. Bava at times seems to choose colors simply for their aesthetics: the contrasting colors of yellow and blue are a favorite in this regard. As lighting expert Graham Walters notes, "A cool blue tint from the left and a warm yellow from the right help to create interesting highlights and shadows" on characters and sets.[130] Contrastive use of color also helps divide up the spatial plane[131]; according to Kandinsky, warmer colors move toward the spectator, while cooler move away, thus fostering the illusion of depth.[132] At other times though, the colors in Bava's films are decidedly symbolic. Whether this was always conscientiously done is debatable—artists may often match color with mood or desired effect without rational consideration of the symbolism thus conveyed.[133] Still, in so doing, artists reflexively draw upon their past training in color composition and meaning,[134] and Bava certainly would have had exposure to color symbolism formally through training and informally through everyday exposure to Italian manifestations of it, especially religious art.

In considering what the colors in his movies may mean, it is important not to impute absolute correlations. As Wittgenstein notes, "someone who speaks of the character of a color is always thinking of just one particular way it is used."[135] Color symbolism varies not only across cultures, but within them, shifting in meaning over time and context.[136] Also there may be oppositional meaning in a single color, even a single shade.[137] Yet there are some established trends, even if contradictory, and it is evident that the color composition in Bava's films follows these recurrently, if selectively. For example, green is traditionally presented in Christian art as the color of Epiphany, vegetation, spring and good works.[138] However, it also has a folkloric tradition of menace,[139] and Kandinsky imputes it with passivity, "tainted by a suggestion of obese self-satisfaction."[140] It is the latter associations that show up in Bava's symbolic use of green as it occurs in conjunction with decadent settings and corrupt characters. In the sadomasochistic *Whip and the Body*, green lighting appears much more markedly than in other Bava films, including a particularly unnatural flash on Christopher Lee's face as his ghost leans lasciviously over Daliah Lavi after viciously whipping her. Decadence is reflected through the foliage

Bava embraced the need to include familiar components of horror film iconography in his Italian films, such as casting stars well-known to U.S. audiences. Boris Karloff is seen here in *Black Sabbath/Il tre volti della paura* (1963), which exploited both his image as horror film star through his portrayal of the wurdalak and his image of horror film host, which he had cultivated on NBC's *Thriller*.

that surrounds the double-crossing, degenerate characters in *Twitch of the Death Nerve*; at one point, the film foreshadows the depravity of a group of seemingly innocent teenagers by introducing them driving through sickly yellow-green woods. Bava returns to more of a Judeo-Christian tradition, in a sense, with the use of bright, opaque blue for fantastical atmospheres: In both the Kabbalist and Catholic meaning systems (especially the cult of the Virgin Mary), blue is associated with the heavens and unearthly beings.[141] Admittedly, the beings who emerge out of Bava's blue beyond to stare in at windows, like the vampire family in *Black Sabbath* or little Melissa's deadly ghost in *Kill, Baby, Kill*, are not there for heavenly visitations. In this respect, the symbolism draws more from other associations of blue with cold and estrangement.[142] Juxtaposed frequently against this blue simply for its striking visual contrast, golden yellow sometimes appears to be next to it in Bava's films to emphasize more of a symbolic contrast — the cold supernatural versus the warm vitality.[143] Red occasionally likewise heralds vitality, particularly when mixed in with the gold. More often though, red evokes its widespread connotations of passion and violence.[144] Vivid red mannequins are positioned throughout the fashion house in *Blood and Black Lace*, anticipating the slaughter of the models, as well as foreshadowing the murderer's identity by appearing next to him right after he kills.

Once Bava has set his scene, he tends to linger in it. It is not unusual for characters to move into and then out of a frame, especially in a way that emphasizes its depth, or to be shot from such a distance as to appear quite small in the scene, like the tiny human figures in classic Neapolitan landscape paintings. Bava also draws on the Italian tradition of filled space, though typically not with crowds of humans like the grand casts of hundreds in the silent era. Interestingly, there is some visual homage to that through inhuman mimicry of the human form, such as the red mannequins, wicker dressmaker's dummies and statues that pervade the salon rooms in *Blood and Black Lace*, and the scores of bridal mannequins that play silent witness to Steven Forsyth's homicidal insanity in *Hatchet for the Honeymoon*. For the most part, however, Bava fills space with simple objects from the surroundings: branches fly by between the audience and the carriage driven by the undead Javutich in *Black Sunday*; rafters frame and cross the overhead shots of the incantation scene in *Baron Blood/ Gli Orrori del castello di Norimberger* (1972), lending the disquieting impression that the house is watching and waiting for the summoning of its deceased ancient owner; and boulders (probably the same ones[145]) strew the fantastic landscapes of *Hercules in the Haunted World* and *Planet of the Vampires*.

The latter two movies additionally illustrate well how the imagery in Bava's films works as a genre-spanning device, allowing blendings and new forms to emerge smoothly. Combining genres was certainly nothing new for the drive-in market, which capitalized on the broader appeal, nor for Italian cinema, which did it both for artistic purposes as well as commercial draw, depending on the production.[146] Obviously Bava's films intermingle forms for the increased international market appeal, but here again they do so with an artistic style that makes the conventions blossom. *Hercules in the Haunted World* was one of the first of many sequels to the 1959 original (which Bava served on as director of photography), and it targeted horror fans just as much if not more than museleman/peplum fans.[147] In addition to featuring Christopher Lee, by then an internationally known Hammer horror star, *Hercules in the Haunted World* features many recognizable horror norms (including a distinctively Italian contribution to genre: the 1909 masterpiece *Inferno*'s landscape definitely influences the look of *Haunted World*'s Hades scenes). For example, Hercules' beloved, Deianira, is under a spell reminiscent of the *Trilby*-style hypnosis so effectively absorbed as an attribute of vampiric thrall in horror iconography. As if to cement the connection, she even arises at Lee's command from a sarcophagus in straight-backed *Nosferatu* form. Lee also summons wraiths for Hercules to fight. The emphasis on battling is peplum, but the wraiths' slow emergence from their graves, their funereal appearance and their supernatural persistence answers horror expectations raised by the movie's advertising, which was so weighted toward horror in some places that audiences were led to believe Lee portrayed a vampire (he doesn't).[148]

Planet of the Vampires is in many respects typical of the common sci-fi/horror crossover, but achieves more of an overall blend of the genres than most movies of the time because of Bava's more direct injection of horror elements. The undead astronauts emerging from their graves by throwing off the metal covers and breaking out of their plastic wrappings are just like classic ghouls escaping their tombs and sloughing off spider webs. The environment is alien, but its heavy fog, whistling wind and forlorn cries for help are reminiscent of any terrestrial supernatural setting. The overall tense atmosphere inspired 1979's *Alien* to likewise infuse sci-fi with horror, sometimes through directly emulating scenes from *Planet of the Vampires*.[149]

By far the most "Italian" blending with the horror paradigm is the slick thriller-killer subgenre that dominated much of the late 1960s and early 1970s Italian horror output, the *giallo*, so named for the yellow covers borne by the Italian pulp sensationalist novels that inspired the movies.[150] Bava, in fact, is credited with setting the standard for what became the *giallo* on-screen form, first in the movie *The Girl Who Knew Too Much/La Ragazza che sapeva troppo* (1962), then more definitively with "The Telephone" short story sequence in *Black Sabbath* and with the movie seen as the "seminal *giallo*," *Blood and Black Lace*.[151] In some respects, *gialli* can be seen as more referential of Italian cultural conventions than other horror types. The settings are typically modern and elegant, and the characters are typically models, designers, photographers, aristocrats and the like. The linking of violence to the world of high fashion and wealth plays off of the image of Italy as cosmopolitan and the popularity of Italian style worldwide in the 1960s and early 1970s. It also follows the Italian tradition of decadence, though, like many films in the time of the nation's economic boom, *gialli* seem to be more inveighing against decadence than celebrating it, especially since the sophisticated, luxurious characters are usually depicted as corrupt and frequently criminal (drugs and blackmail are popular), if not outright murderous. At the same time, the *giallo* form decidedly partakes of international horrific conventions, especially the exploitive linking of sexuality and death. In *Blood and Black Lace*, for example, shots linger on bra-clad female corpses. One homicide depicts the victim writhing sexually while she is being smothered by the black-costumed masked murderer. Although the melodramatic tone and decadence generally stayed with the Italian versions, *gialli* proved highly influential to horror productions in other countries. By popularizing the faceless serial killer archetype and blatantly eroticizing brutal murder, *giallo* films are sometimes seen as the "missing link" in the slasher horror subgenre, connecting the "proto-serial killer narratives of Frederic Brown and Cornell Woolrich"[152] with the mid-to-late 1970s U.S. full-fledged products. Indeed, Bava's *Twitch of the Death Nerve*, sometimes classified as *giallo*, sometimes as slasher, definitely inspired the "body count" approach to massacre in later movies; *Friday the 13th Part II* (1981) even steals a murder from it featuring two lovers *in flagrante delicto* being run through by a spear.[153]

Scenes like this earned Bava's films a reputation for sensationalized brutality; the *Aurum Film Encyclopedia* even refers to him as "perverse."[154] Such labeling, however, not only overlooks the narrative context of Bava's violence (and the fact that he is not always explicit in every movie), it also shows a lack of understanding of the violence's cultural context. For quite a while, Italian horror films were more readily graphic both in terms of adult situations and violence than most of their English and American counterparts.[155] England's Hammer productions were actually renowned early on in the horror cycle for their increased use of sex and violence. But where Hammer offered low-cut peasant blouses and bright blood from woundings rarely shown,[156] Italian directors like Freda offered *The Horrible Dr. Hichcock* (1964) and his necrophiliac urges. Bava's *Black Sunday* was banned in Britain for eight years—and only then released as the quite tame *Revenge of the Vampire*—for its brutal imagery, including blood spurting from a spiked mask being hammered into Barbara Steele's face.[157]

For U.S. distributors, horror meant "scary kiddie fare" and they cut their imports accordingly. For Europeans, especially on the Continent, horror was adult entertainment.[158] Most of Bava's films are clearly constructed with the latter audience in mind as far as maturity level for their material; thus many have at least minor cuts in their U.S. incarnations.

Different editions for different markets is nothing new or unusual for the international film scene, especially during this time.[159] Some changes are simply a matter of pandering to the assumed consumers' taste, like AIP substituting Roberto Nicolosi's original soundtrack in *Black Sabbath* with their own Les Baxter music,[160] which at one point combines a variety of unrelated tunes (e.g., the Duke Ellington signature closing and *The Star Spangled Banner*) into an unbelievably tacky amalgamation. However, in a couple of cases, the U.S. editing completely changed the meaning of Bava's Italian versions. In addition to the music switch in *Black Sabbath*, the order of the three vignettes is changed, and more seriously, the dubbing on one of them, "The Telephone," completely revamps the storyline. Admittedly, as film scholar Antje Ascheid points out, any dubbing converts "a finished and culturally specific text to that of a transnational denationalized raw material, which is ... reinscribed into a new cultural context."[161] But "The Telephone" is extreme: Essentially, the original Italian story is a *giallo* featuring two lesbian ex-lovers, Rosy and Mary, and Rosy's murderous pimp Frank, who has escaped from prison. The AIP story not only eliminates all reference to prostitution and lesbianism (making Rosy the other woman that unspecified criminal Frank left Mary for), but also positions Frank as a vengeful undead, giving the vignette a supernatural element completely absent from the Italian version and removing a fair amount of its style and sense.[162] A similar overhauling of *The Whip and the Body* resulted in a movie so incoherent that it truly deserves its alternate release title of *WHAT?* The sadomasochistic scenes in the film of Christopher Lee whipping Daliah Lavi to the obvious sexual enjoyment of both were either majorly truncated or deleted altogether, and without them, the rest of the movie loses most of its *raison d'être*.[163]

If Bava's horror movies seem excessive in comparison to British and American ones in the 1960s, it is in part because they come from a tradition that values the excessive in artistic expression.[164] In Italian film, Fellini, especially, is known for taking cultural traditions of lavishness and excess to exaggerated heights to play out his personal opuses symbolically on the screen. As Pasolini observes about Fellini's *La Dolce Vita* (1960), "There is not one significant communication in his film which is presented purely functionally; it is always excessive, overcharged, lyrical, magical, or too violently veristic."[165] The operatic tradition that encourages this love of spectacle also fosters its manifestation in melodramatic morbidity. Commenting on the Neapolitan silent cinema, Italian film historian Guiliana Bruno observes, "Violence, love, and the physicality of desire are represented in all their immediacy and brutality and expressed in the mode of excess."[166] Titles of Italian populist dramas from Bava's production period frequently revolve around female sin, blood and death.[167] Moreover, it is important to recall the prominence with which Italian religious art has portrayed the ecstasy of suffering—while Catholicism proscribes sex for purposes other than procreation, martyrdom is frequently illustrated as a sexualized experience through the expressions and body poses of martyrs in their death throes.[168] Given all this cultural emphasis on sex, violence and spectacle, it is not surprising—nor perverse—that Bava would lay heavy on these elements in his depictions of horror, itself a melodramatic form that exploits them.

Another melodramatic convention that horror partakes of and Bava embraces to the full is the use of standard visual icons and narrative themes. Bava's pieces would have been received by foreign and domestic audiences ready to imbibe familiar character types and accoutrements, though from different traditions. Accordingly, Bava introduces different symbolic elements that are likely to resonate with horror tastes generally as well as Italian tastes specifically. In some cases, the horror iconography is obviously pandering to the need to include familiar components. This comes out most strongly in the movies' stars. Not only are well-known horror actors like Boris Karloff and Christopher Lee cast, but they are also displayed on the screen in ways that maximize their trademark images. Karloff's presence in *Black Sabbath*, for example, exploits both his image as horror star through his portrayal of the vampiric wurdalak patriarch (with pathos and shuffling walk evocative of Frankenstein's Monster) and his image as horror host through his vignette introductions (directly inspired by Karloff's gig as host of NBC's *Thriller*, an *Alfred Hitchcock Presents* imitation in the early 1960s[169]). Although none of the characters he portrays is a vampire, Lee is generally costumed in a flowing cloak like Dracula, and given similar scenes of menacing approach—he even opens his mouth when his ghost closes in on Daliah Lavi. Not all horror icons are presented so hackneyed, however. The image of the staring eye, for example, is beautifully blended with another horror standard, the moon, in a scene transition that fades the moon in the trees into a girl's eye in *Twitch of the Death Nerve*. Reflections in Bava's films transcend the formulaic mirror: the blood of his murder victim reflects Christopher Lee in *Hercules in the Haunted World*, the murder weapon does the same for Stephen Forsyth in *Hatchet for the Honeymoon* and a spilled puddle of red wine framed by its broken bottle shows an impish Telly Savalas in *Lisa and the Devil*. Even when conventional mirrors are used, the effect can be unconventional, like the triple reflection in "A Drop of Water" that traces the passage of the nurse and caretaker to the room of the dead medium even after their bodies have left the hallway. Another rather unusual way Bava handled iconography is taking symbols for other things and subverting them to horrific purpose, especially symbols of purity and innocence. Toys and dolls, emblematic of childhood, add to the creepy atmosphere when juxtaposed with an adult psychopath (*Hatchet for the Honeymoon*), an adult spiritualist ("A Drop of Water") or a child long-dead (*Kill, Baby, Kill*). Even more disconcerting is when the toys and dolls appear out of thin air, heralding contact with the supernatural ("A Drop of Water" and *Kill, Baby, Kill*). The ultimate examples of this subversion of meaning are the murderous children of *Twitch of the Death Nerve* and *Kill, Baby, Kill*.

The use of child as destroyer likely resonated with both foreign and domestic audiences; deadly youngsters were rare but not unheard of in horror at this time. However, it is possible that Italian viewers got more out of the image than others did—indeed, more out of *Kill, Baby, Kill* overall (Visconti apparently gave it a standing ovation at its premiere[170]). In the first place, in addition to the traditional ascriptions of innocence, purity and family, "nearly all the major neorealist films" feature the child as an icon for the future of Italy.[171] Thus making a malicious ghoul a young girl would convey a more radical intensity. Perhaps this is why Fellini was supposedly moved by *Kill, Baby, Kill* to likewise use a little blond girl bouncing a ball to embody wickedness—specifically the Devil—in his "Toby Dammit" section of the Poe film *Histories Extraordinaires/Spirits of the Dead* (1968).[172] Moreover, Melissa, the undead child, is potentially even a more horrific cultural figure in that she is the daughter of a Germanic aristocrat and compels her victims to suicide. Her family name of Von Graps,[173] her mother's position as baroness and her family's fair, northern look juxtaposed to the peasantry's darker southern one (the hero-coroner, an outsider, is the only other character with a relatively similar look) all suggest the Austrian occupation of Italy, still a popular topic for Italian film a century after *Risorgimento* finally drove out the Hapsburgs.[174] This is not to say that Bava necessarily intended the Graps to represent a decadent Austria preying upon Italy—certainly in the English-language version of the film, the entire village is supposedly Germanic, headed by a burgomaster. Still, the iconic resonance is there. More likely a deliberate play on Italian cultural horrors is Melissa's method of dispensing with her victims by making them kill themselves. Although the characters in the movie seem reluctant to unambiguously term it suicide, that is the apparent action, and it is automatically damnable in the eyes of the Catholic Church—thus all the more terrifying for an audience with a lifelong societal immersion in Catholic traditions.[175]

As noted previously, Catholicism works its way symbolically into several of Bava's movies (e.g., color usage, ecstasy of suffering). However, they tend to avoid portraying the Church in the exoticizing, formulaic way seen in horror films from America and England. For example, the few times priests appear in Bava's films they resemble not so much Roman Catholic clergy as Eastern Orthodox, a more fantastical religion for a Catholic country. Indeed, Catholicism works occasionally as a symbol of the non-fantastic, like the "real" everyday lifeworld represented by the playing Catholic schoolgirls who call Elke Sommer a ghost when she finally emerges (or so she thinks) from her surreal adventures in *Lisa and the Devil*. The everyday Catholic emphasis on the family likewise features prominently in Bava's movies (though often subverted to horrific purpose), as it does in many Italian productions regardless of genre. To be sure, the family is an international plot ingredient, but it takes on a more potent role in the cinema of Italy.[176] The family commonly appears in horror movies, especially before the rise of the slasher made isolated teenagers the favorite characters (and even in these there sometimes appear brothers, sisters and cousins in the absence of older relatives). Yet not many from Bava's time can match his movies' narrative exploitation of the family as a source of fright (though there are a few very notable exceptions, like the father's twisted devotion to his daughter in Franju's *Les Yeux Sans Visage* [1960], which leads him to macabre means to restore her beauty). A case in point is the Boris Karloff vehicle in *Black Sabbath*, "The Wurdalak." While Bava (who had a taste for Russian literature) may have drawn the story from an Alexei Tolstoi tale,[177] the way he plays on themes of family devotion and duty seems more inspired by Italian Catholicism and melodrama. The entire premise behind "The Wurdalak" is a family one: Wurdalaks are vampires who prey on their loved ones, and Karloff, the elderly father, comes home to his family changed into such a creature. In one climactic scene, Karloff and other family members, now wurdalaks too, surround the fleeing daughter Sdenka with accusing stares as their whispering voiceover asks, "Why did you leave us?" Earlier in the piece, Sdenka's sister-in-law cannot resist the plaintive cries of her undead child for her, and even stabs her husband to get to the boy.

The violent pathos of a wife murdering her husband for the sake of her child hearkens to another way Bava's horror films target their domestic audiences—or at least naturally draw from their shared signification systems—by incorporating operatic narrative themes. Murderous betrayal is a favorite for the *gialli*. In *Twitch of the Death Nerve*, the killers double-cross each other so complexly and with such fatal results that it is hard to keep their motives for murder straight upon first viewing. *Blood and Black Lace* of course features betrayal, bringing it to a dramatic peak when the Countess Christina shoots the treacherous lover for whom she has killed. Revenge is most interestingly carried out in Bava's films by the undead. In *Baron Blood* the murder victims of Joseph Cotten (portraying an evil, formerly deceased baron) arise from the dead to destroy him. And in one of the most original horror treatments of ghosts, the nagging wife whom Stephen Forsyth kills in *Hatchet for the Honeymoon* comes back to haunt him; the twist—and her revenge—is that everyone can see her (and thus assume she is alive) except for him, so he is never truly rid of her. Laura Betti as the wife gives a nice strong performance in a role that allows her to do so. Strong female characters are a hallmark of Italian dramatic tradition, and their inclusion in Bava's work truly sets it apart from most productions of other countries.[178] Whether evil or good, the female is typically subordinate in horror movies to the male. Although feeble females certainly do populate Bava's films, the role of woman is often a powerful one. Reminiscent of opera's ingénues and divas, weak and strong women are sometimes juxtaposed. For example, in *Black Sunday* while the good Katja (Barbara Steele, in the dual role that typecast her in horror) is relatively vulnerable and dependant on male protection, her evil counterpart Asa is fully in charge; indeed, rather than being a subservient drone for a head male vampire, Asa has her own male ghoul to do her bidding. Daliah Lavi in *Whip and the Body* is a classic diva—beautiful, passionate, sinful, treacherous and self-destructive. Next to her, the good female cousin, who is more the stereotypical B-movie romantic interest, seems bland and ornamental. More useful is Monica, the ingénue in *Kill, Baby, Kill* who purportedly studies "natural science" at a distant university and assists the hero coroner in his autopsy; however, when the supernatural pressures start to mount, she runs to the coroner with classic horror heroine helplessness. Not in the least helpless is Ruth, the local witchcraft practitioner who sacrifices herself to save the village from further harm. It is she, not the male authority figures, who defeats the forces of evil, themselves manifested as female (the ghost child Melissa and her mother, the decadent and vengeful Baroness Graps).

The character of Ruth represents another major Bava departure from most horror movies of the time period: positioning witchcraft as a beneficial, as well as legitimate, source of power. Not all depictions of witchcraft in Bava are good; though apparently also possessing vampiric attributes, *Black Sunday*'s Asa is condemned as a witch, and it is an incantation that brings the evil Baron Blood back from the grave. However, in *Baron Blood* the Baron's supernatural power is in part countered by the good magic of the witch Christina, summoning the spirit of another witch who fought the Baron in the past. Odd as it may sound, witchcraft appears almost casually in Bava's movies— like the seer in the neorealist film *The Bicycle Thief*, those with psychic powers are just part of the terrain. In *Twitch of the Death Nerve*, one character's tarot card reading and vocal concerns about bad omens seem as much means to aggravate her entomologist husband as attempts to evoke a frightening supernatural atmosphere (like Peter Cushing's more representative use of the tarot in the Amicus production *Dr. Terror's House of Horrors*, 1965). The husband mocks her revelations, but they do turn out to be correct. Indeed, tying in with a greater cultural acceptance of and affinity for everyday magic, witchcraft is accorded an unusual degree of legitimacy by many of Bava's characters. Usually, horror protagonists either openly discount beneficial mysticism as superstition or absorb it for use through established religion or Van Helsing-style science. Certainly the "man of science" trope appears in Bava, but this authority figure may act to uphold the pagan and irrational rather than reject or absorb it. For example, the coroner in *Kill, Baby, Kill* does wreck one of Ruth's spells by freeing a girl from a vicious "leechvine" wrapped around her (and thus sends her to her doom), but as he does he declares, "This isn't sorcery, it's torture"—in other words, he rejects the pain the spell causes, not necessarily the validity of spellcasting itself.

Interestingly, while it is likely that such inclusion of Italian cinematic and narrative elements may have helped Bava's horrors achieve greater resonance with his domestic market, Bava apparently hid his shared Italian origin sometimes on account of this same audience. The impact of opera imparted a flair for depictions of violence, angst, suspense and terror; however, as noted previously, Italian film did not have a marked history in horror *per se*. Thus it was Freda's contention, and Bava agreed, that Italian filmgoers were convinced that good horror movies could only come from Britain or America. Accordingly, for some of his films, Bava gave himself Anglo-sounding pseudonyms like Mickey Lion and John M. Old.[179] Ironically, while Bava nowadays is looked to for imparting a particularly Italian feel to his contributions to the European horror cycle, he tried to efface that impression at the time.

Afterword

Including conventions from specific cultural, artistic and performative traditions works to infuse variation into aggregated horror conventions. In so doing, Bava's movies carry on the cross-fertilization that makes horror an international cinema both in terms of production and appeal. Notably, while Bava's most direct influence has been upon other Italian filmmakers (especially Dario Argento), his work has inspired filmmakers from other countries, often without them being aware of it: horror critics readily acknowledge Bava "initiated stylistic and thematic trends in the genre."[180] Like more acclaimed pieces of Italian cinema throughout the twentieth century, Bava's movies have tripped the imaginations of American directors in particular, including those working outside of horror, even as they have imitated Hollywood. The intercultural layering that inherently characterizes Bava's horror films may not be sufficient to raise their worth in every critic's estimation, but it does justify giving them further consideration for how their images have partaken of and shaped the overall motion picture form. Antonio Gramsci recognized the power of the cinema to move the populace through its rich imagery. Often derided as the most commercial and pedestrian of market-driven productions, horror movies are surprisingly deep when it comes to how embedded their power is to evoke collective meaning, wherever their intercultural origins are located.

NOTES

1. Gramsci, Antonio. "The Light Which Went Out," in Pedro Cavaleanti and Paul Piccone, Eds. *History, Philosophy, and Culture in the Young Gramsci*. St. Louis: Telos Press, 1975, 27 [Collection of early works; essay originally published in *Il Grido del Popolo*, November 20, 1915].

2. Landy, Marcia. *Film, Politics, and Gramsci*. Minneapolis: University of Minnesota Press, 1994, 13.

3. Italian film criticism dates at least as early as 1910. Leprohon, Pierre. *The Italian Cinema*. Roger Greaves and Oliver Stally Brass, Trans. New York: Praeger 1966/1972, p. 15.

4. Gieri, Manuela. *Contemporary Italian Filmmaking: Strategies of Subversion*. Toronto: University of Toronto Press, 1995, p. 4.

5. Lund goes so far as to claim that today it is "confusing to speak of national cinema"; noting the elusiveness of assigning a film's nationality in the first place (e.g., does one base it on the language, actors, directors, producers or audience?), he positions cinema as inherently transnational. Lund, Daniel Manny. "Writing Film History: The Struggle for Synthesis," in Sari Thomas, Ed. *Film/Culture: Explorations of Cinema in Its Social Context*. Metuchen NJ: Scarecrow, 1982, p. 14. See also: Fischer, Dennis. *Horror Film Directors, 1931–1990*. Jefferson NC: McFarland & Co., 1991, p. xiii; Gieri, p. 84; Roberts, Martin. "*Baraka*: World Cinema and the Global Culture Industry," *Cinema Journal*, vol. 37, Spring 1998, p. 62; and Saxton, Christine. "The Collective Voice as Cultural Voice" *Cinema Journal*, vol. 26, Fall 1986, p. 20–23.

6. Gieri, 19.

7. Starting prior to 1910, the Italian film company Cines was importing French technicians, as were other companies; around the same time, the French filmmaker Pathé set up his subsidiary Film d'Art Italiano. Leprohon, p. 12–26.

8. Vacche, Angela Dalle. *The Body in the Mirror: Shapes of History in Italian Cinema*. Princeton, NJ: Princeton University Press, 1992, p. 254.

9. Leprohon, p. 27.

10. Quoted in Leprohon, p. 26.

11. Vacche, p. 3.

12. Quoted in Lephrohon, p. 25.

13. See for example, Lund, p. 15. Pastrone's *Cabiria* (1913) is widely acknowledged as a influence on D.W. Griffith and Cecil B. DeMille, e.g., Leprohon, p. 29, Vermilye, Jerry. *Great Italian Films*. New York: Citadel Press, 1994, p. 9.

14. Landy, Marcia. "The Narrative of Conversion and Representations of Men in the Italian Pre-War Cinema." *Journal of Film and Video*, vol. 37, Spring 1985, p. 30.

15. See for example, Sitney, P. Adams. *Vital Crises in Italian Cinema: Iconography, Stylistics, Politics*, Austin: University of Texas Press, 1995, p. 43–44, 89–90.

16. By the 1960s, Italian films "as often as not" featured international casts; international co-production was likewise very common by this time. Vermilye, p. 13, 185, 196.

17. Indeed, Gieri maintains that it is not accurate to speak of American imitation in the Italian industry, because the Bakhtinian carnivalization given to traditional Hollywood genres by Italian filmmakers makes even adaptations visibly Italian phenomena. Gieri, p. 87.

18. Hay, James. *Popular Film Culture in Fascist Italy: The Passing of the Rex*. Bloomington: Indiana University Press, 1987, p. 30; Muscio, Giuliana and Roberto Zemignan. "Francesco Casetti and Italian Film Semiotics," *Cinema Journal*, vol. 30, Winter 1991, 23; Sitney, p. 9

19. Not only is the debate over the relative merits of so-called high or low culture/art or non-art beyond the scope of this piece, I am inclined to agree with the claim that any distinction between the two is inherently the result of social structuration rather than intrinsic/eternal artistic processes. For an excellent discussion of this claim and other aesthetic issues, see Williams, Raymond. *The Sociology of Culture*. Chicago: University of Chicago Press, 1981.

20. Williams, p. 107.

21. Sitney, p. 8–9.

22. Hay, p. 244.

23. See for example, Sitney, 121; Sorlin, Pierre. "Popular Films or Industrial Byproduct? The Italian Melodramas of the 1950s," *Historical Journal of Film, Radio, and Television*, #3, August 1995, p. 349; Wasko, Janet. "Film Financing and Banking," in Sari Thomas, Ed. *Film/Culture: Explorations of Cinema in Its Social Context*, Metuchen NJ: Scarecrow, 1982, p. 30.

24. Fellini, for example, has commented on growing up with a constant exposure to Hollywood movies; for further insight see Fellini, Federico, *Fellini on Fellini*, Isabel Quigley, Trans. New York: Delacorte Press/ S. Lawrence, 1976. In addition to general aesthetic influence, Hollywood iconography directly appears in many Italian films; for example, in De Sica's *The Bicycle Thief* (1949), the protagonist Ricci finds a job hanging Rita Hayworth posters.

25. Leprohon, p. 87.

26. Most film titles throughout this chapter are given in either Italian or English, depending on standard usage in sources. The titles of Bava's films are given in both English and Italian upon first mention to provide additional information for those with access to the Italian versions; subsequent mentions are in English.

27. The term peplum refers (somewhat inaccurately) to the costumes affected in the cheap epic adventures produced in the late 1950s and 1960s, also called "sword-and-sandal" movies.

28. See endnote 18 for full citation.

29. For an excellent discussion of Leone, see Frayling, Christopher. *Sergio Leone: Something to Do with Death*, London: Faber & Faber, 2000.

30. There are a few notable exceptions to this; see, for example, Leon Hunt's genre analysis, "A (Sadistic) Night at the Opera: Notes on the Italian Horror Film," *The Velvet Light Trap*, #30, Fall 1992, p. 65–75; and the historical-biographical pieces on Mario Bava by Tim Lucas (*Mario Bava—All the Colors of the Dark*) and Troy R. Howarth (*Inner Darkness Made Visible: The Films of Mario Bava*), both in progress at the time of this writing.

31. A star of Bava's *Baron Blood*, Girotti appeared in Pasolini's *Teorema*, Dassin's *Medea* and Bertolucci's *Last Tango in Paris*. Lucas, Tim, liner notes to the 1999 Image Entertainment DVD release of *Baron Blood* (1972), directed by Bava and produced by Alfredo Leone.

32. For a collection of plot synopses from over 60 Italian horror movies from the 1960s, see Lawrence McCallum's guide, *Italian Horrors Films of the 1960s*, Jefferson, NC: McFarland & Co.

33. Lucas, Tim, biography feature on Mario Bava from the 2000 VCI Home Video DVD release of *Whip and the Body* (orig. 1963), directed by Mario Bava and produced by Elio Scardamaglia.

34. Supposedly, Bava's use of a vengeful

child ghost in *Kill Baby Kill* (1966) inspired Fellini to make the Devil a similar small blond girl with bouncing ball in his "Toby Dammit" episode for the Poe anthology *Histoires extraordinaires/Spirits of the Dead* (1968). Fischer, p. 76; Hunt, p. 70.

35. Howarth, Troy R. *The Mario Bava Web Page: A Tribute to the Master of Darkness and Light.* Last updated October 21, 2000, Accessed March 1, 2000. Available: http://members.tripod.com/mariobava/index.htm.

36. The admission that horror has seen more than its share of poor and mediocre movies is not at all uncommon, even among its greatest aficionados. See for example, Dickstein, Morris. "The Aesthetics of Fright," in Barry Keith Grant, Ed. *Planks of Reason: Essays on the Horror Film*, Metuchen NJ: Scarecrow, 1984, p. 68–69; Fischer, p. xi; Sobchack, Vivian. "Genre Film: Myth, Ritual, and Sociodrama," in Sari Thomas, Ed. *Film/Culture: Explorations of Cinema in Its Social Context*, Metuchen NJ: Scarecrow, 1982, p. 150.

37. "What distinguished Bava's films among others of the genre was his flair for visual style and his sense of humor in handling the cinematic clichés of horror." Vermilye, p. 111. Bava himself acknowledged that his films were motivated by monetary necessity, and once reportedly declared, "I've shot some incredibly stupid movies." Fischer, p. 65. Bava long-time biographer Tim Lucas claims that Bava referred to his films as "a bunch of bullshit." Lucas, Tim liner notes to the 2000 Image Entertainment DVD release of *Twitch of the Death Nerve* (1971) directed by Bava and produced by Giuseppe Zaccariello.

38. Etchison, Dennis. Foreword to Kim Newman, *Nightmare Movies: A Critical Guide to Contemporary Horror Films*. New York: Harmony Books, 1988, p. ix; Wood, Robin. "An Introduction to American Horror Film," in Barry Keith Grant, Ed. *Planks of Reason: Essays on the Horror Film*, Metuchen NJ: Scarecrow, 1984, p. 173.

39. Sanjek, David. "Fans' Notes: The Horror Film Fanzine," *Literature/Film Quarterly*, vol. 18, 1990, p. 150.

40. Grant, Barry Keith. "Rich and Strange: The Yuppie Horror Film," *Journal of Film and Video*, vol. 48, Spring/ Summer, 1996, p. 4.

41. See for example, Lowry, Edward. "Genre and Enunciation: The Case of Horror," *Journal of Film and Video*, vol. 36, Spring 1984, p. 13–20; Prawer, S. S. *Caligari's Children: The Film as a Tale of Terror*, Oxford: Oxford University Press, 1980, p. 33; Tohill, Cathal and Pete Tombs. *Immoral Tales: European Sex and Horror Films 1956–1984*, 1995, p. 21–22.

42. For a more thorough discussion of the interaction between convention and viewer, see Giles, Dennis. "Conditions of Pleasure in Horror Cinema," in Barry Keith Grant, Ed. *Planks of Reason: Essays on the Horror Film*, Metuchen, NJ: Scarecrow, 1984, p. 38–40; Kawin, Bruce. "The Mummy's Pool," in Barry Keith Grant, Ed. *Planks of Reason: Essays on the Horror Film*, Metuchen NJ: Scarecrow, 1984, 5; Pinedo, Isabel. "Recreational Terror: Postmodern Elements of the Contemporary Horror Film," *Journal of Film and Video*, vol. 48, Spring/ Summer, 1996, 28; Telotte, J. P. "Faith and Idolatry in the Horror Film," in Barry Keith Grant, Ed. *Planks of Reason: Essays on the Horror Film*, Metuchen NJ: Scarecrow, 1984 p. 23.

43. Prawer, p. 46.

44. Hay, p. 21.

45. Prawer, p. 32–45.

46. Friedman, Lester D. "Canyons of Nightmare: The Jewish Horror Film," in Barry Keith Grant, Ed. *Planks of Reason: Essays on the Horror Film*, Metuchen NJ: Scarecrow, 1984, p. 127.

47. Bunnell, Charlene. "The Gothic: A Literary Genre's Transition to Film," in Barry Keith Grant, Ed. *Planks of Reason: Essays on the Horror Film*, Metuchen, NJ: Scarecrow, 1984, p. 82.

48. Wood, p. 175.

49. Conger, Syndy M. and Janice R. Welsch. "The Comic and the Grotesque in James Whale's Frankenstein Films," in Barry Keith Grant, Ed. *Planks of Reason: Essays on the Horror Film*, Metuchen NJ: Scarecrow, 1984, p. 304; Prawer, p. 41.

50. Dickstein p. 69; Prawer, p. 218.

51. Lowenstein, Adam. "Films Without a Face: Shock Horror in the Cinema of Georges Franju," *Cinema Journal*, vol. 37, Summer 1998, p. 37.

52. Hantke, Steffen. "'The Kingdom of the Unimaginable': The Construction of Social Space and the Fantasy of Privacy in Serial Killer Narratives," *Literature/Film Quarterly*, vol. 26, July 1998, p. 180; Kawin, p. 8.

53. The Grand Guignol was a form of French theater that ran from 1897–1962 featuring "unflinching depictions of sensational acts of violence." Lowenstein, p. 45.

54. See, for example, Tohill and Tombs' work delineating the sex-death trend in European exploitation cinema at this time.

55. Hantke, p. 180.

56. Giles, p. 44.

57. Dickstein, p. 76.

58. For a fascinating discussion of the use of labyrinth underworld symbolism in early filmmaking, see Smith, Evans Lansing. "Framing the Underworld: Threshold Imagery in Murnau, Cocteau, and Bergman," *Literature/Film Quarterly*, vol. 24, July 1996, p. 241–54.

59. In any genre, audiences frequently use actors as a basis for movie selection. Jarvie, Ian. "The Social Experience of Movies," in Sari Thomas, Ed. *Film/Culture: Explorations of Cinema in Its Social Context*, Metuchen NJ: Scarecrow, 1982, p. 257. Recognition of horror stars was an international phenomenon; from Conrad Veidt to Boris Karloff to Christopher Lee, actors commonly crossed national lines to portray macabre characters. Prawer, p. 40–45, 203.

60. For more discussion on horror icons see Eisner, Lotte H. *The Haunted Screen: Expressionism in the German Cinema and the Influence of Max Reinhardt*. Roger Greaves, Trans. Berkeley: University of California Press, 1965/1990; also, Fischer, p. xx–xxi; Prawer, p. 32, 167; Smith, p. 250; Telotte, p. 25.

61. See for example, Bunnell, p. 82; Lowry, p. 18; Walters, Graham, *Stage Lighting*. Cincinnati, OH: Betterway Books, 1997, p. 72.

62. Eisner, p. 151–55, 219; Prawer, p. 29.

63. Wood, p. 174–75.

64. Lowry, p. 20.

65. Many excellent pieces have been devoted to various aspects of Italian cinema; accordingly, this section seeks only to provide a glance at Italian filmic traditions, in order to contextualize elements in Bava's movies that reflect his cultural heritage.

66. Newman, p. 188.

67. Leprohon, p. 16, 24–25; Lund, p. 15; Vacche, p. 254; Vermilye, p. 9.

68. Gieri, p. 21; Leprohon, p. 51–59.

69. Probably the most extensive recent treatment of this period is Hay's *Popular Film Culture in Fascist Italy* (see note 18 for full citation).

70. Landy, *Film*, p. 160–64; Vacche, p. 28, 166, 194, 252–54.

71. I use the term "art film" here loosely, referring more to the U.S. reception of and venues for higher quality Italian productions at this time. Sitney claims there is no appropriate blanket term for Italian cinema at the time of the nation's mid-century economic boom; Pasolini labels both the boom and the cinema a "vital crisis" (Sitney, p. 1).

72. Stephen Gundle gives an interesting treatment of American influences on Italian pop culture in "Sophia Loren, Italian Icon." *Historical Journal of Film, Radio, and Television*, vol. 15, August 1995. See also Leprohon, p. 174–79; Vermilye, p. 173, 185.

73. Leprohon, p. 88–89; Vacche, p. 97.

74. Bruno, Giuliana. *Streetwalking on a Ruined Map: Cultural Theory and the City Films of Elvira Notari*. Princeton: Princeton University Press, 1993, p. 15–21; Leprohon, p. 40.

75. Landy, *Film*, 162; Perricone, Joseph. "...And the Ship Sails On: A Reviewing of Fellini." *Literature/Film Quarterly*, vol. 15, #2, 1987, p. 83; Sorlin, p. 356.

76. Guido Aristarco has an excellent brief interrogation of Visconti's stance on decadence, "Luchino Visconti: Critic or Poet of Decadence?" (translated reprint in *Film Criticism*, vol. 12, Spring 1988, Luciana Bohne, translator), as does Giorgio Bertellini, "A Battle d'Arrière-Garde: Notes on Decadence in Luchino Visconti's *Death in Venice*" (*Film Quarterly*, vol. 50, Summer 1997). See also Gieri, p. 168; Leprohon, p. 168; Vacche, p. 162–67.

77. Only a handful of pre-1956 Italian films can be considered horror movies, and those only if the definition of what constitutes a horror movie is fairly loose: *Inferno* (1909), an adaptation of the Dante classic and a masterpiece of silent cinema; *Rapsodia Satanica* (1912), a melodrama about Satan turning an old woman into a youthful but destructive diva; *L'Atketa Fantasma* (1919), a story of a fighter against the forces of evil; *Il Mostro di Frankenstein* (1920), a lost version of the Frankenstein tale; and *Toto all'Inferno* (1954), a comedy pitting Toto against the Devil (pt. Hunt, p. 70).

78. Landy, *Film*, p. 166; Leprohon, p. 19, 27; Sitney, p. 138.

79. Landy, *Film*, p. 160–64.

80. Bruno, p. 210; Hay, 168; Lund, p. 15.

81. Gieri, p. 87.
82. Leprohon, 96; Sorlin, 350.
83. Visconti quoted in Sitney, 130–31; see also Aristarco, p. 59–60.
84. Visconti quoted in Sitney, p. 130–31.
85. Landy, *Film*, p. 99.
86. Cumbow, R. C. *Once Upon a Time: The Films of Sergio Leone*. Metuchen NJ: Scarecrow, 1987, p. 213–215; Gieri, p. 87; Leprohon, p. 34.
87. Cumbow, p. 215; Stubbs, John C. "The Fellini Manner: Open Form and Visual Excess." *Cinema Journal*, vol. 32, Summer 1993, p. 56–58; Vacche, p. 254.
88. Casetti, Francesco. "Cinema in the Cinema in Italian Films of the Fifties: *Bellissima* and *La Signora Senza Camelie*." *Screen*, vol. 33, Winter 1992, p. 390; Cumbow, p. 185, 214–15; Vacche, p. 239.
89. Cigognetti, Luisa, and Lorenza Serretti. "'On Her Side': Female Images in Italian Cinema and the Popular Press, 1945–1955." *Historical Journal of Film, Radio, and Television*, vol. 16, #4, 1996, p. 562.
90. Hunt, p. 71.
91. Fischer, p. 61; Lucas, biography of Mario Bava, *Whip and the Body*.
92. Lucas, Tim, liner notes to the 2000 Image Entertainment DVD release of *Hatchet for the Honeymoon* (1969) directed by Bava and produced by Manuel Caño.
93. Fenton, Jay, liner notes to the 2000 VCI Home Video DVD release of *Whip and the Body* (1963), directed by Mario Bava and produced by Elio Scardamaglia.
94. Lucas, liner notes, *Twitch*.
95. Howarth.
96. Vermilye, p. 110.
97. Lucas, biography of Mario Bava, *Whip and the Body*.
98. Fischer, p. 61.
99. Fischer, p. 61–62; Lucas, biography of Mario Bava, *Whip and the Body*; Newman, p. 196.
100. Howarth; Lucas, biography of Mario Bava, *Whip and the Body*; Newman, p. 189.
101. Bava made commercial export movies from genres other than horror, like peplum and the perennial "spaghetti Western"; though of course some stylistic devices overlap, all references in this chapter to Bava's movies are intended to apply only to his horror films.
102. Lucas, biography of Mario Bava, *Whip and the Body*.
103. Quoted from a Bava *Fangoria* interview with Tim Lucas in Fischer, p. 69.
104. Internationally renowned director of photography Darius Khondji (whose credits include Bertolucci's 1996 *Stealing Beauty*) notes that cinematography can bring a great deal to a film, working "as if it were another main character" (quoted in Calhoun, John. "Madonna With Cinematographer: DP Darius Khondji Brings *Evita* from Stage to Screen." *Lighting Dimensions*, vol. 21, January/February 1997, p. 58).
105. Prawer, p. 32, 108–09, 167.
106. Prawer, p. 241.
107. Bruno gives an especially interesting overview of the link between religious art and imagery in the silent films of Elvira Notari (see Chapter 17 in particular); see also Sitney, p. 11; Vacche, p. 4.
108. See, for example, Moshe Barasch's excellent discussion on Italian Renaissance style in *Light and Color in the Italian Renaissance Theory of Art*. New York: New York University Press, 1978.
109. Sitney, p. 11.
110. Lucas, biography of Mario Bava, *Whip and the Body*.
111. Sitney, p. 3, 7.
112. Bruno, p. 210; Gardner, Helen. *Art Through the Ages*. New York: Harcourt, Brace and Co., 1948, Chapter 27; Hay, p. 168.
113. It is important, however, not to generalize the idea of the silent Italian epics to all early Italian films. According to Bruno, George Kleine, the "most prominent distributor of Italian silent films" in the U.S., typically selected big epics for circulation, which were not representative of the overall industry output.
114. Harris, Thomas. "*Rear Window* and *Blow-Up*: Hitchcock's Straightforwardness vs. Antonioni's Ambiguity." *Literature/Film Quarterly*, vol. 15, #2, 1987, p. 82.
115. Fischer, p. 61.
116. Vermilye, p. 111.
117. Lucas, biography of Mario Bava, *Whip and the Body*.
118. Prawer notes that Bava's "visual imagination is at least the equal of that shown by Tourneur" though Bava tends to blatantly display the shocks that Tourneur veiled, p. 29.
119. Leprohon, p. 221; Fischer p. 61–62.

120. Thanks to Trevor Torralba for bringing this scene to my attention.

121. Eisner, p. 21.

122. Leprohon, p. 204–06; Sitney, p. 208.

123. Barasch, p. 32.

124. Barasch, p. 51, 73–75, 101–09.

125. Kandinsky, Wassily. *Complete Writings on Art: Volume One (1901–1921)*. Kenneth C. Lindsay and Peter Vergo (eds.) Boston: G.K. Hall & Co., 1982, p. 194.

126. Lucas, Tim. "*Black Sabbath*: The UnMaking of *The Three Faces of Fear*." *Video Watchdog*, #5, May/June, 1991, p. 52

127. Leprohon, p. 150.

128. Barasch, p. 7.

129. Walters, p. 87.

130. Walters, p. 82.

131. Wurmfeld, Sanford. "Color in Abstract Painting," in Kurt Nassua, Ed., *Color for Science, Art, and Technology*. Amsterdam: Elsevier, 1998, p. 177, 181.

132. Kandinsky, p. 179, 181.

133. The sixteenth century color theorist Lomazzo, for example, held that while color symbolically conveyed feeling and atmosphere, artists achieved their expressions with it through "intuitive experience" (discussed in Barasch, p. 159–68).

134. Thanks to artist Diane Doty for her perspective on the relationship between training, inspiration and execution.

135. Wittgenstein, Ludwig. *Remarks on Colour*. G.E.M. Anscombe (ed.) Berkeley: University of California Press, 1951/1977, Linda L. McAlister and Margarete Schättle, translators, p. 12e.

136. Hutchings, John B. "Color in Anthropology and Folklore," in Kurt Nassua, Ed., *Color for Science, Art, and Technology*. Amsterdam: Elsevier, 1998, p. 200, 205–07.

137. Barasch, p. x, 166; Vacche, p. 169.

138. Ferguson, George. *Signs and Symbols in Christian Art*. London, Oxford University Press, 1976/1954, p. 151.

139. Hutchings, p. 203.

140. Kandinsky, p. 183.

141. Halevi, Shimon. *Kabbalah: Tradition of Hidden Knowledge*. Slovenia: Thames and Hudson, 1979/1997, p. 40; Ferguson, p. 97, 151.

142. For discussion of blue as emotionally cold and distant, see Gerstner, Karl. *The Forms of Color: The Interaction of Visual Elements*. Cambridge MA: MIT Press, p. 114, 125; Gillette, J. Michael. *Designing with Light*. Mountain View, CA: Mayfield Publishing Co. 1978/1989, p. 130; Kandinsky, p. 181–82.

143. Golden yellow can represent the sun and divine presence in traditional Christian iconography (Ferguson, p. 153), and Venetian Renaissance painters were fond of infusing their work with golden glowing light (Gardner, p. 516). Kandinsky considers yellow "the typical earthly color ... like the reckless pouring out of the last forces of summer" (p. 181).

144. Red is widely correlated with energy, both positive and negative. Kandinsky, for example, calls it a "highly lively, living, turbulent color" (p. 186). Stage lighting designers employ red to evoke moods ranging from love and happiness to defiance and aggression (Gillette, p. 130). In Christian symbolism, red is the color of the Crucifixion (Hutchings, p. 203) and Divine Love, but it also can connote strong emotion in general, and represent love or hate (Ferguson, p. 97, 152).

145. The rocks in *Planet of the Vampires* came from peplum set leftovers (Lucas, biography of Mario Bava, *Whip and the Body*).

146. Gieri, p. 84–85, 160.

147. McCallum, p. 114–15, 118–20.

148. McCallum, p. 119.

149. Sanjek, p. 156.

150. Fischer, p. 5; Hunt, p. 72; Lucas, "Unmaking," p. 41.

151. Fischer, 74; Hunt, p. 71; Lucas, "Unmaking," p. 41–43.

152. Hunt, p. 71.

153. Lucas, liner notes, *Twitch*.

154. Hunt, p. 65–66.

155. Vermilye, p. 112.

156. For a thorough discussion of the Hammer style and its reception with critics and public, see Hutchings, Peter. *Hammer and Beyond: The British Horror Film*, Manchester: Manchester University Press, 1993.

157. Hunt, p. 67; Prawer, p. 250.

158. Lucas, "Unmaking," p. 34.

159. Sanjek notes that internationally targeted horror films were usually released in several versions, p. 153.

160. Lucas, "Unmaking," p. 54.

161. Ascheid, Antje, "Speaking Tongues: Voice Dubbing in the Cinema as Cultural Ventriloquism." *The Velvet Light Trap*, #40, Fall 1997, p. 33.

162. For a detailed account of the changes made in *Black Sabbath*, including a comparison of the Italian and English scripts of "The Telephone," see Lucas, "UnMaking."

163. Howarth; Lucas, biography of Mario Bava, *Whip and the Body*; McCallum, p. 237–38.

164. Barasch, p. 112; Bruno, p. 21, 98; Gardner, p. 516; Leprohon, p. 25–27; Vacche, p. 31, 267.

165. Pasolini, p. 195. See also Perricone, p. 83; Stubbs, p. 51–61.

166. Bruno, p. 21.

167. Sorlin, p. 351.

168. See for example, Bruno, Chapter 17.

169. Lucas, "UnMaking," p. 36. Around the same time, Karloff also hosted the British anthology series *Out of this World* (Lucas, Tim, liner notes to the 2000 Image Entertainment DVD release of *Black Sabbath* (1963), directed by Mario Bava and produced by Paolo Mercuri and Alfredo Leone.

170. Lucas, biography of Mario Bava, *Whip and the Body*.

171. Sitney, p. 68.

172. Fischer, p. 76; Hunt, p. 66.

173. At least, in the English version of *Kill, Baby, Kill*, Melissa's family name is Von Graps; it seems likely though that it is the same in the Italian version, as it is featured in medium long shots on a portrait caption and a tombstone. Usually in Bava's movies when English writing is substituted in for Italian (or something else), it is in close-ups on pieces of paper.

174. Hay, p. 168; Vacche, p. 3.

175. This is not of course to imply that scenes like the suicides in *Kill, Baby, Kill* would not carry extra resonance for non–Italian Catholics. Nor is it meant that all Italians are practicing Catholics or even raised Catholic. It is simply that the strong presence of the Catholic Church in Italy invariably leaves its stamp on the overall culture, and thus horrific scenes playing off of Catholic conventions would carry overall cultural weight.

176. Sorlin, p. 351.

177. Lucas, "UnMaking," p. 36. The story is misattributed in the movie to the non-existent Ivan Tolstoy.

178. Hunt, p. 71.

179. Fischer, p. 65; Howarth; Newman, p. 188.

180. Sanjek, p. 155–56.

Examining Technology In, Behind and Beyond the Drive-In

16

The Threat of Materialism in the Age of Genetics: DNA at the Drive-In

David A. Kirby

Film theorists have long debated the nature of "horror" as a film genre. Many genre critics have attempted to establish a set of "horror film" elements which can be used to distinguish a horror film from all other genre types. These attempts are complicated by the fact that critics have grouped together seemingly disparate films as horror films: "Gothic" horror, science fiction horror, slasher, psychological horror and supernatural horror films. Although no general agreement has been reached as to a single set of elements which can cover all of these diverse film types, scholars agree that the goal of a horror film is to incite fear in the audience.

In his book *Monsters and Mad Scientists: A Cultural History of the Horror Movie*, Andrew Tudor analyzed plot narratives of 990 horror films from 1931 to 1984 and found that horror films elicit fear by introducing a "monstrous" threat into a stable situation.[1] Given this narrative structure, filmmakers will maximize the number of potential filmgoers by choosing fearsome elements that are recognizable as "threats" by the largest number of people rather than elements that are based on the fears of a limited number of people. Therefore, we should be able to examine the threats in horror films in order to learn about the subjects which the general public experience as "frightening."

By examining the mechanisms used in horror films to create "monsters," we can gauge what the public found frightening about science and technology. An analysis of recent "monster movies" reveals that from the mega-hit *Jurassic Park* (1993) to the mega-bust *Bats* (1999), genetic engineering has become the preferred way of creating cinematic monsters. Exploration of these films does not give a complete picture about what is frightening about genetic engineering, however, because the fear in these films is driven by recent progress in bio-engineering. To truly understand what is frightening about the use of genetic technologies, we need to investigate how horror films first grappled with genetics itself. My research into the use of genetics in horror films shows that the first films to incorporate the concept of genetics were 1950s drive-in monster movies. Although the initial use of genetics in horror films is in relation to the threat of radiation, this threat later gives way to concerns caused by the discovery of the double helical structure of deoxyribonucleic acid (DNA) by James Watson and Francis Crick in 1953. Investigation of several low-budget horror films from the late 1950s, such as *She Demons*

(1958) and *The Killer Shrews* (1959), reveals that anxiety over the discovery of DNA centered around the materialistic nature of DNA.

Scientific materialism is an ideology built upon the assumption that all knowledge to which humans have access can be known solely through scientific inquiry and experimentation. Scientific materialism has two precepts: 1) there is only one reality, the natural, and 2) science has a monopoly on the knowledge we have about nature. DNA represented the ultimate in scientific materialism because it claimed that a single double helical molecule could explain the nature of life itself. Watson and Crick's revelation of the structure of DNA had given rise to a new form of scientific materialism: genetic materialism. Segments of the American public perceived DNA and genetic materialism as a threat in two ways: 1) materialism is in direct opposition to the ideology of theism, or the belief that the world cannot be understood exclusively in terms of its material components, and 2) DNA provided a substance which scientists could precisely manipulate to affect biological change, a contrast to the randomness of radiation-induced mutations.

Horror films of the late 1950s incorporate these threats through a scientist character who claims to posses knowledge of a molecule, referred to euphemistically as "Character X" or as "inherited factors," which explains the way we look, how we age and even our personality traits. By attempting to make directed genetic changes in living organisms, these scientists evoke our fears that real scientists could change humanity itself with their knowledge of DNA. Additionally, their claims that life can be explained by a single "substance" is a threat to those who believe that theistic explanations are also necessary to explain the nature of life. Ultimately, the cinematic experiments go astray, exploiting our fears of both threats within the films.

One can build a timeline of important genetic findings in the 1950s and media coverage of these events, as well as key films which feature genetics. I consider films, from *The Creature Walks Among Us* (1956) to *Konga* (1961), to represent transitional films with regards to the mechanisms used to create genetic monsters in horror cinema. In the early and mid–1950s, random radiation-induced mutations accounted for the dominant mechanism of biological change. In the transitional films, filmmakers replaced this mechanism with the process of making directed modifications to genetic material. The progression in genetic mechanisms of horror films throughout the 1950s was essentially one from random mutation to controlled genetic manipulation. I regard the first film in this mechanistic transitional period to be *The Creature Walks Among Us* (1956), the third in the *Black Lagoon* series. *The Creature Walks Among Us* features a scientist, Dr. William Barton, who changes the Creature's genetic material in order to create a new race of humans which could survive in outer space. What separates *The Creature Walks Among Us* from other transitional films discussed in this essay is the fact that Dr. Barton does not need to "discover" what the genetic material is before he makes changes. In the early 1950s, it was known that whatever made up "the" genetic material, it was housed inside the nucleus of the cell. Therefore, the filmmakers most likely included the only genetic material with which they would have been familiar: the nucleus.

The difference between *The Creature Walks Among Us* and other transitional films actually highlights the difference between the transitional films and later genetic engineering films of the 1960s and 1970s. The concept of genetic materialism

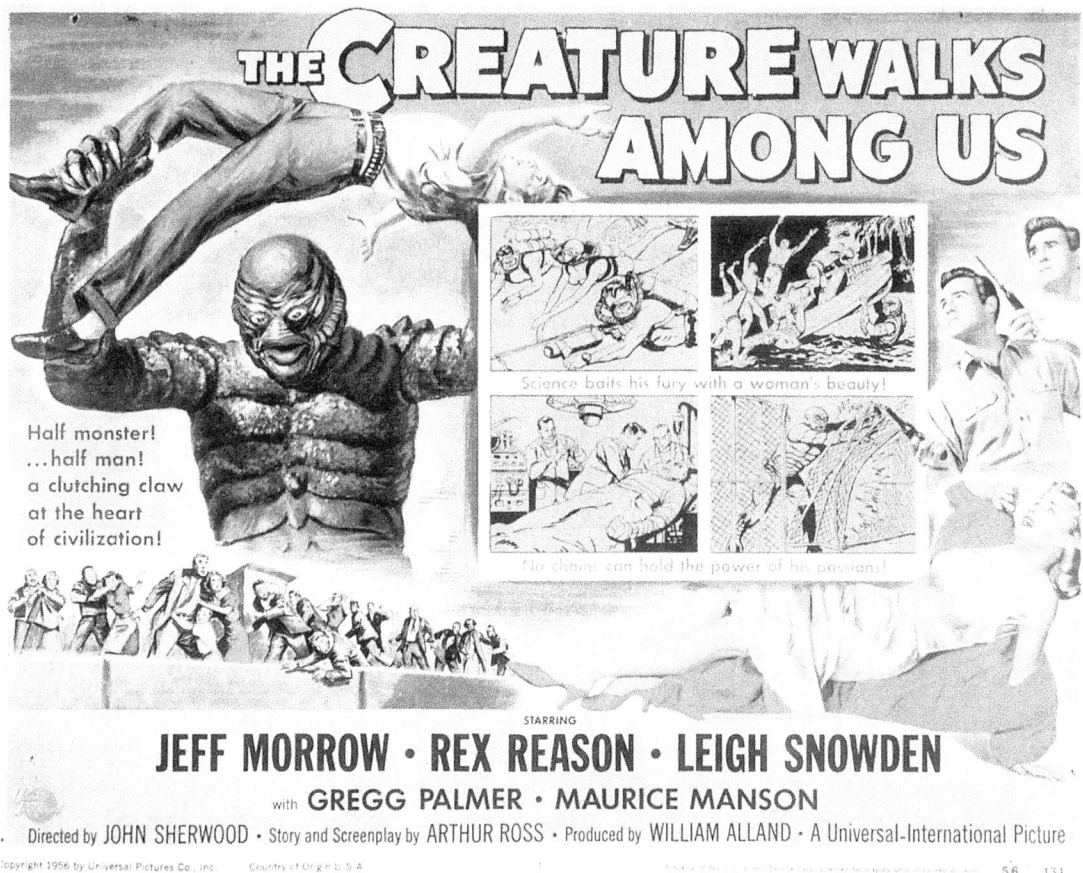

Transitional films like *The Creature Walks Among Us* (1956) were among the first to use genetics as a means by which to create or alter monsters.

was a new fear for people in the 1950s; transitional films capitalize on this anxiety by containing a scientist who in essence discovers a molecular basis for heredity. After Watson and Crick won the Nobel Prize in 1962, horror films which included genetic engineering bypassed the "discovery" aspect of the transitional films and went straight to the creation of genetic monsters through the manipulation of DNA. In essence, these transitional films are unique because they include threats from both science and technology. Science is a process by which scientists gain knowledge about the laws which govern the natural world. Technology is the manipulation of the natural world through the application of this knowledge. It is science, not technology, which is in direct opposition to theism. Theism and scientific materialism have traditionally been at odds because they both attempt to explain the nature of the world. For many theists in the 1950s, this new threat of scientific materialism, genetic materialism, seemed to be an even more insidious threat to theism: if DNA explains the nature of life itself, then theistic explanations become unnecessary. (This threat assumes, of course, that there is only a single explanation for life and that there is no way to reconcile the two ideologies.)

As scientists re-affirmed the nature

of DNA in the late 1950s and early 1960s, it was no longer necessary for genetic horror films to show scientists discovering the molecular "nature of life." Eventually, the threat of genetics in horror films shifted away from the theistic to the technological. By the mid–1960s, biologically based films such as *The Satan Bug* (1965) featured applications of genetics in bio-warfare. In 1973, genetic engineering became a reality when bacterial DNA from two different species was combined by Stanley Cohen and Herbert Boyer. In addition to theological concerns about DNA and the nature of life, this new technology has ushered in the very real and very problematic experiments DNA which consume us today: human cloning, genetically engineered food, human gene therapy, etc.

Genetics and Drive-In Horror Films

Genetics and DNA have routinely been ignored when scholars discuss horror films of the 1950s. Rather, film scholars have interpreted horror films of the 1950s as reflecting concerns about three threats: 1) the Cold War and Communism, 2) suburbanization and social conformity, and 3) the atomic bomb and nuclear catastrophe. One of the problems with these interpretations is that they generalize from a narrow set of films which were produced by major studios, such as *Them!* (1954), *Invasion of the Body Snatchers* (1956), *The Incredible Shrinking Man* (1957), and *The Fly* (1958). Focusing on these "classic" films gives us a restricted account of the threats which provoked fear in 1950s American society. This view has led people to believe a simplistic rhetoric of common fears—a scholarly mantra which is called up whenever anyone mentions 1950s horror films: Communism, conformity and catastrophe. I argue that we need to expand the number and types of films critically analyzed in order to get a more complex view of 1950s society and the cinema it produced.

One class of films which are regularly neglected in cultural analyses of the 1950s are drive-in horror movies. Most drive-in horror films are considered "B" movies (or lower), and few of the movies would be regarded as "masterpieces" of the art. It is often assumed that these films are merely inferior copies of the "classic" films mentioned previously. However, the mediocrity or obscurity of these films in no way undermines their usefulness as cultural texts. The principal interest in these movies is not, after all, whether they are aesthetically or commercially successful. Whether the quality of the final film is "good" or "bad," all drive-in horror films were created with the intention of returning at least some money to the company which produced them. Motion picture production is a business and the appeal of any product, such as a fictional film, depends on its resonance with consumer experience and popular belief. In fact, I contend that drive-in horror movies reflect society to a greater extent than other movies because their success is due more to resonance with its audience than to critical acclaim, studio publicity, star power or aesthetics.

My goal in looking at drive-in films is not to refute previous interpretations, but rather to offer a broader view of the fears expressed in 1950s horror films especially with regards to science and technology. According to Andrew Tudor's research, the most frequent type of threats (251 out of 990, or 25 percent) in horror films is scientific in nature. Due to this extremely high number, Tudor concludes that "the belief that science is dangerous is as central to the horror movie as is a belief in the malevolent inclinations of ghosts, ghouls, vampires, and zombies."[2]

Contemporary scientific discoveries have provided horror filmmakers with a means for creating monstrous threats. 1950s drive-in horror film audiences would likely be familiar with scientific discoveries that popular magazines of the time (*Time*, *Life*, *The Saturday Evening Post*, etc.) reported weekly. Drive-in filmmakers recognized two advantages in using current scientific discoveries in their films. First, contemporary discoveries offered plausible justifications for the creation of monsters in a film. Audiences which recognized a scientific discovery were more willing to accept that monsters could be created through the plot outlined in the film. Secondly, and more importantly, the use of current scientific discoveries made the scientific threats more tangible to the audience and thus more frightening. An audience which recognized the science on the screen as something they had just read about in *Reader's Digest* was more likely to be afraid of the monster created by this science. Many revolutionary genetic discoveries occurred in the 1950s, in particular the structure of DNA; all the popular magazines covered these events. Therefore, it is not surprising that genetics first makes its entrance into horror cinema in the 1950s.

Drive-in filmmakers of the decade commonly utilized a "straight out of today's headlines" approach when including a scientific mechanism. In several instances it is possible to follow the appearance of a scientific discovery in the popular press to its appearance at the drive-in. For example, the plot of Roger Corman's drive-in classic *The Wasp Woman* (1959) revolves around a cosmetics executive who stops the aging process by using "enzymes" from royal jelly. Several cosmetic firms in the mid–1950s promoted royal jelly (the substance which turns a bee larva into a queen bee) as an "elixir of youth." (As the title suggests the jelly in *The Wasp Woman* comes from wasps, not bees. This is clearly a flaw in the script, as wasps do not produce royal jelly. It is possible that the filmmakers thought wasps would be scarier than bees because wasps have a more potent venom.) A myriad of popular media articles catalogued the royal jelly craze. For example, *Consumer Reports* reviewed the many royal jelly-related cosmetics in "It Must Be Royal Jelly" (January, 1958). Business journals also discussed the commercial use of royal jelly by cosmetics firms. For example, a 1958 article in the business magazine *Changing Times* discusses the use of royal jelly as an anti-aging cosmetic.[3]

The Wasp Woman even has a meta-reference about the use of "headline" science in horror films. One of the scientists in *The Wasp Woman*, who is opposed to the use of the royal jelly, remarks that "30 years ago a bunch of quacks were treating people with monkey glands. It seemed to work for awhile. Then the deterioration set in." In the early 1920s, monkey glands were seen as a "revolutionary" scientific discovery which could reverse the aging process. The endocrinologist Dr. Serge Voronoff became an international celebrity in 1919 for convincing wealthy, elderly men that implanted monkey glands would make them younger and give them the potency of 20–year-olds. As was the case with royal jelly, monkey glands showed up as a plot element in several horror films of the early 1920s, including *The Screaming Shadow* (1920) and the classic Lon Chaney, Sr., film *A Blind Bargain* (1920).

Radioactive Mutants Run Wild: Genetics Enters the Cinema

Perhaps no link between headlines, science and film is more evident than the use of radiation in drive-in horror films of the 1950s. The standard assumption by horror film scholars has been that the inclusion of radiation in a horror film is a reaction to the dropping of atomic bombs on Hiroshima and Nagasaki, and the potential for nuclear destruction during the Cold War. Certainly the threat of nuclear destruction is evident in many films in which the destructive power of the atomic bomb is visualized as a city-devouring monster who awakens after an atomic explosion as in *The Beast from 20,000 Fathoms* (1953), *It Came from Beneath the Sea* (1955), *Godzilla* (1956) and *Rodan* (1957). A more comprehensive analysis of 1950s drive-in films reveals, however, that the possibility of nuclear catastrophe was not the only threat from radiation presented to 1950s audiences. The threat to our genetic material through radiation-induced mutations represents the earliest incorporation of genetics in horror cinema. As I will later show, this threat of radiation-induced mutations is later supplanted by the materialistic threat of DNA as a plot element in drive-in horror films. The word "mutation" simply describes any change in the genetic material of an organism. Because a mutation changes the genetic material which controls an organism's physical traits, mutations change an organism's physical characteristics. Exposure to radiation increases the rate at which mutations occur. Therefore, radiation increases the number of physical changes in an organism. Since mutations are almost never beneficial, radiation is seen as having a negative effect on an organism.

Although it is useful to talk about mutations changing the physical nature of a fully grown individual, these mutations are not likely to create "monsters." Instead it is more probable that mutations will cause cancerous growths rather than monstrous deformities. Indeed, the threat of radiation-induced cancer is depicted in several drive-in horror films where exposure to radiation causes out-of-control cellular growth, as in *The Amazing Colossal Man* (1957). It is possible to produce "monsters" through radiation, but this is due to the heritable nature of the genetic material. Because an organism's genetic material is inherited, mutations in the sex cells (sperm and egg) will be passed down to the next generation. A developing organism starts off as a single cell, so inherited mutations will affect every subsequent cell of an organism as it grows. Therefore, the threat of radiation is not merely to current humanity, but to the genetic material we leave to future generations.

Popular media in the 1950s were filled with dire warnings about the degradation of the human genetic pool from continued atomic testing. Several popular science books, such as eminent geneticists Bruce Wallace and T.H. Dobzhansky's *Radiation, Genes, and Man* (1959), warned that exposure to radiation would alter humanity's genetic material in such a way as to "produce death, disease, monstrosity, invalidism, or simply delicate health in the descendants of the irradiated individuals."[4] By the 1950s, photographs of disfigured children born to parents exposed by the atomic blasts in Japan supported the fears of genetic destruction from radiation. Throughout the 1950s, articles on the dangers of radiation to the human race appeared in many of the most popular magazines of the day, including *Time*, *Life*, *Look* and *The Saturday Evening Post*. The *Ladies Home Journal* had an article on "Radioactivity and the Human Race" (Sep., 1956), while the *Saturday Review* had an article on "Race Poisoning by Radiation" (Jun. 9, 1956) by H.J. Muller, who won the Nobel Prize for his studies of radiation-induced mutations in fruit flies and bacteria.

Anxiety over radiation's long-term

genetic effects is clearly evident in the plots of 1950s drive-in horror films. For example, in *Terror from the Year 5,000* (1958) the genetic material of human colonies has been damaged irreparably by radiation in the atmosphere. One of these colonies attempts to replenish their gene pool with undamaged genetic material by bringing a human from the "present" into the future. The concern over radiation's detrimental effects on future generations is also seen in the Sam Katzman–produced film *The Werewolf* (1956). In the film, the "mad scientist" Dr. Forrest explains the need to protect humanity's genetic material from radiation:

> Some day it will happen. The human race will destroy itself. Not quickly, but slowly. The wolfman is proof. Radiation creates mutants. People who become monsters, no longer human.
> They'll make the Hydrogen Bomb more powerful, then more powerful again. Enough to change every person on the face of the Earth into a crawling, inhuman thing through fallout radiation.

Their solution to radiation's gradual genetic threat is to "immunize" humanity by exposing them to small amounts of serum made from a radioactive "mutant wolf."

Although the scientists in *The Werewolf* express concerns about the long-term genetic effects of radiation, the werewolf in the film is created by an "instantaneous mutation." In drive-in films, the spontaneous creation of monsters is much more common than the scientifically accurate process of inheritance. The slow process of mutation and inheritance through multiple generations does not make for gripping cinema. Instead, drive-in horror films visualized the threat of radiation to our genetic material as monsters instantaneously created through exposure to radiation. In *The Cosmic Monster* (1958), for example, several types of insects exposed to radiation from cosmic rays immediately mutate into giant monsters. While the public feared mutational effects of radiation on other organisms, the more dangerous threat was to our own genetic material as portrayed in *The Cyclops* (1957) and *The Hideous Sun Demon* (1959). With the exception of *Them!*, however, these mutation films ignore the necessity of heritable changes and instead rely on the more exciting instantaneous genetic mutations. Given that drive-in films thrived on immediate visual gratification, it is not surprising that most filmmakers choose instantaneous monsters over inherited monsters.

Despite the concern about radiation in the environment emanating from either natural sources, atomic testing or new nuclear power plants, many scientists actually used radiation with the specific intent of changing genetic material. Control of heredity had been a goal for scientists since humans first domesticated plants and animals. Before the 1950s, farmers and scientists used selective breeding as the only way to cultivate new breeds of animals and new varieties of plants. Selective breeding is limited as a technology because it requires a large amount of variation at the genetic level; the only way to produce genetic variation is through the slow, natural process of mutation. Starting in the early 1950s, biologists increased the amount of genetic variation available for selective breeding by using radiation to increase mutation rates in plants and animals. By the late 1950s, several popular science magazines heralded the practical applications of radiation in agriculture. "New Plants Produced by Radiation" (April 1957) in *Science Digest* touted the advantages of "applied radiation" for "speeding up evolution" through an increased mutation rate. *Reader's Digest* (November 1958) condensed the article "The New Age of Atomic Crops" from *Popular Mechanics* (October 1958) for even broader public consumption.

For the first time, humans could actually control heredity by applying gene altering technologies through the use of radiation in agriculture. However, drive-in filmmakers did not share the same optimism as popular science magazines and portrayed the agricultural applications of radiation as a new threat. In addition to the threat of radiation itself to our genetic material, there was the fear associated with scientists who felt that they could control these genetic changes. In the Bert I. Gordon film *Beginning of the End* (1957), for example, scientists at a USDA facility use radiation to create giant tomatoes and strawberries which they hope will be the "future of the American farmer." Unfortunately, the USDA scientists are not able to control their new gene-altering technology, and giant locusts threaten Chicago as an outcome of their experiments. As has been the case with all new biotechnologies, the general public suspected that scientists would try to use radiation to change humanity. These fears show up in several drive-in films where radiation is used to create "supermen." For example, in *The Gamma People* (1956) the scientist ruler of the fictitious Central European country of "Gudavia" uses radioactive "gamma rays" to create a race of human geniuses. Although the threat of scientists creating supermen was not new to horror films, the threat became more and more frightening with our growing knowledge of genetics.

The fear expressed in these films, that radiation would be used to change humanity's genetic material, was not based on any real experiments. Scientists understood that their use of radiation to improve crops was an illusionary "control over heredity."

Radiation only allowed scientists to produce new breeds by increasing the random process of mutation. For every "beneficial" mutation there were thousands of mutations which resulted in death or genetic abnormality. The only way for gene-altering technologies to be of practical use in improving humanity's genetic material was if scientists could make directed mutations. Until the early 1950s, scientists could not make directed mutations, because they did not know the exact nature of the "genetic material." This all changed in 1953 with the discovery of the double helical structure of DNA by Watson and Crick. The abstract concept of a 'genetic material' became a concrete and material reality with the resolution of the DNA double helix. The knowledge that a single molecule, DNA, coded for all the traits in an organism (including humans) created a new threat for 1950s American society: the threat of the materialistic ideology. For the rest of this essay, I will explore the new threat of genetic materialism and how it was incorporated into two drive-in horror films, *She Demons* (1958) and *The Killer Shrews* (1959).

The DNA Revolution Begins: Genetic Materialism Enters the Mainstream

The discovery of the DNA double helix had an enormous impact on both biologists and the general public. Throughout the first half of the 20th century, biologists had been searching for the "genetic factors" which could explain the biological processes controlling the stability, survival and reproduction of organisms. Watson and Crick proposed a molecular structure for these "factors" that was so simple and elegant, the scientific community readily accepted it. Although the genetic code would not be worked out until the late 1950s, the pairing of the four complementary DNA bases (A, T, G and C) made it clear how DNA stored the information which coded for all of an organism's traits and characteristics. In addition, Watson and Crick's double helical model immediately depicted how the DNA molecule could replicate itself, providing a mechanism for transmission of genetic information from generation to generation.

By 1958, DNA had made its way into all of the major popular magazines. Popular science magazines first discussed DNA as the "ultimate genetic material," as in an October 1956 *Scientific American* article entitled "The Gene." Other popular magazines soon featured articles referring to DNA as the "ultimate explanation" for life, as in the article "Alphabet of Life" in the *Saturday Review* (January 5, 1957). What may have pushed DNA into the American public consciousness was a cover story called "The Secret of Life" in the widely read national magazine *Time* (July 14, 1958) which refers to the DNA molecule as "the carrier of heredity and the chemical master of all life." In his 1988 autobiography *What Mad Pursuit*, Francis Crick recalls an anecdote involving the DNA chemist Paul Doty which illustrates the extent to which DNA had permeated the American public. In the late 1950s, Doty saw a man selling lapel buttons in New York, one of which had the letters "DNA" on it. When Doty asked the vendor what the letters meant, the vendor replied in a strong New York accent, "Get with it, Bud. Dat's the gene."

It is clear from a multitude of popular magazine articles that the public acknowledged DNA as "The" genetic material and recognized the potential benefits of directed mutations. Nevertheless, a survey of these magazines also reveals that discussions of DNA and the possibilities of genetic manipulations were not limited to its potential benefits, but also reflected the fear created by the materialistic nature of DNA. Oftentimes the same articles which hailed DNA as the "stuff of life" denounced the threat of scientists using the "new genetics" to create "monsters" or "supermen." Additionally, numerous articles warned the public against embracing a materialist definition of life to the detriment of theistic explanations. Therefore, it was only a matter of time before the threat of genetic materialism began appearing in drive-in horror films.

Unlike the fear of scientists using radiation on humans, the notion that scientists would use their knowledge of DNA to make directed changes in humans was a very real "threat." Although scientists' primary concerns were for curing inherited disorders, many people saw gene altering technologies as a way of attaining the goal of eugenics. Eugenics is defined as the improvement of the genetic make-up of the human species. According to eugenicists, humans are "de-evolving" because individuals with "defective" genetics (whom natural selection would have kept from breeding) are "contaminating" the human gene pool. Although the extreme eugenic measures taken by the Nazis completely discredited the eugenics movement, many prestigious scientists of the 1950s (including longtime eugenicist H.J. Muller, Nobel Prize–winning chemist Linus Pauling and Aldous Huxley's brother Julian Huxley) supported the theory behind the eugenics movement. The understanding of DNA as the genetic material meant that scientists could "improve" human genes through directed mutations without the need for selective breeding of humans, sterilization or other extreme measures. For example, Nobel Prize–winning geneticist George W. Beadle, whose face adorned the cover of the aforementioned 1958 *Time* magazine cover story on genetics, claimed in an interview with the *Saturday Review* ("Genes and Geopolitics," November 14, 1959) that not only would our knowledge of DNA allow humans to change their genetic makeup, but that this knowledge should "be applied to directing our own evolutionary futures."

Genetic engineering was even seen as a way to protect humans from the detrimental genetic effects of radiation. Bruce Wallace and T. H. Dobzhansky conclude their 1959 book *Radiation, Genes, and Man* with the idea that someday the detrimental genetic effects of radiation may not matter because "we will soon have the ability to control and direct biological evolution."[5] These claims were bolstered by experiments in which injected DNA changed the genes of viruses and bacteria ("Man-Made Genes," *Scientific American*, February 1957), and ducks ("Heredity by Injection," *Time*, June 10, 1957). Perhaps no written work made it more clear to the American public the possible uses for the new genetics than the best-selling 1959 English translation of biologist Jean Rostand's 1956 book *Can Man Be Modified?* Like many other scientists, Rostand felt that "contrary to popular belief, man has long since ceased to evolve." Based on the burgeoning knowledge of DNA and successful experiments in cloning frogs, Rostand believed that we would soon be able to make "precise hereditary changes—controlled mutations" in the human genetic material.[6]

Many people felt threatened by the possibility of scientists manipulating human genetic material, and this fear permeated most reviews of Rostand's book. Indeed, nearly every article which discussed the new discoveries in genetics brought up the apprehension of scientists making directed mutations in humans. *The New York Times Magazine* article "Small Wonder Called the Gene" (November 23, 1958), for example, praises the determination of the genetic material in one paragraph, while in another paragraph the article makes comparisons to Aldous Huxley's novel *Brave New World* and the use of genetic technologies to create "supermen." Several drive-in horror films of the late 1950s and early 1960s incorporated the threat of scientists, armed with new knowledge of a physical genetic material, making changes in humanity's genetic makeup. In both *She Demons* and *The Killer Shrews*, scientists have discovered a material resembling DNA, referred to as "Character X" or "inherited factors," which they claim codes for all the characteristics of a living organism including humans. In each film, these cinematic scientists attempt to "improve" the human race by using this knowledge to make "directed mutations," evoking our fears that real scientists could change the human race itself by manipulating our DNA.

In addition to the fears that scientists were going to manipulate our genetics, DNA's threat to theology played out in drive-in horror films. Theism is the belief that the world cannot be understood exclusively in terms of its material components. According to theism, there are realities outside the natural that can never be explained scientifically. Scientific materialism is in direct opposition to the ideology of theism, because scientific materialists make the claim that the world can exclusively be known through its physical makeup. Theists considered Watson and Crick's uncovering of the structure a major blow for their ideology, because scientists claimed that it explained the nature of humanity itself. For example, George Beadle claimed that the double helix allowed humans to "define life in objective terms—ability to replicate in the manner of DNA," and that Watson and Crick's research meant that the "understanding of the nature of life is thus replacing mystery."⁷ Even human qualities which were traditionally thought to require theistic explanations, such as morality, intellectual potential and ethics, could be attributed to our genetics. In "Alphabet of Life" (*Saturday Review*, Jan. 5, 1957), for example, biologist Dean Fraser claims that "it's the nucleic acids [DNA] that account for the difference between Jack the Ripper and a buttercup, that distinguish between the potential of an Einstein and the village idiot."

Religious authorities responded to the threat of genetic materialism by writing articles for popular religious magazines, such as the interdenominational Christian magazines *The Christian Century* and *The Ecumenical Review*, and the Catholic magazines *America* and *Catholic World*. Lay persons also responded to the characterization of DNA as the "molecule of life" or the "stuff of life." For example, the *Time* magazine cover story on "The Secret of Life" provoked several harsh letters to the editor (August 4, 1958). One letter contained a single question indicating the writer's shock that scientists could make such claims, "'The Secret of Life': Come again?" Another respondent wrote that they were "profoundly amazed that geneticists can seriously entertain the theory of chance rendezvous of DNA producing the complex human being." The threat that theists felt about scientists claiming a material "essence of life" can best be summed up in the response of former Vice-President Henry A. Wallace, a world-renowned plant breeder, to George Beadle's assertion that DNA is the "definition of life." According to Wallace, "pure materialism" is destroying the human "spirit." Furthermore, Wallace believed that "the scientist will never have tools with which to work in this dimension [the spiritual] but I trust that in his efforts to push the tower of Babel to the skies he does not destroy that ultimate factor [the love of God]."⁸

She Demons and *The Killer Shrews* incorporate the tension between materialism and theism as a fear based on the hubris of scientists. Scientist characters in these films claim that life can be explained by a single "substance." They then try to use this knowledge to change the nature of living organisms. Ultimately, in each film the scientist's genetic manipulations go dangerously wrong, exploiting our fears of materialistic scientists who claim that the ultimate answer to nature and life can be summed up in the physical world.

She Demons

Except for a pseudo-newscast which opens the film, the action of *She Demons* takes place on an "unknown" island in the Pacific Ocean which is used by the U.S. Navy for practice bombing runs. Hero Fred Maklin, Jerrie Turner (whose wealthy father has financed Fred's research trip) and crewmen Kris and Sammy are stranded on the island by "Hurricane Emily." Kris is killed early in the film, and the group discovers the corpse of a "She Demon" who has the "body of a woman, but the face of a demon." Based on the She Demon's physical appearance, Fred concludes that he has discovered the island of "animal people." Fred and the others run across a group of dancing women who are dressed like the dead She Demon, but whose faces are "normal." The women's dance routine is broken up by the "Nazi Gestapo" who put the women back into bamboo cages. After a series of fights and chases, Fred, Jerrie and Sammy are captured and taken to meet Col. Karl Osler. Osler is performing a multitude of experiments on the island, including an experiment to repair his wife Mona's face. We learn that this experiment is what transforms the women into the She Demons. Thanks to timely bombing by the U.S.

Navy, Osler and his laboratory are destroyed and the heroes escape the island.

In many ways the plot structure and the characters in *She Demons* are a throwback to the heyday of the "mad scientist" film in the 1930s. In fact, it is hard to come by a "madder" scientist than *She Demons*' ex–Nazi Col. Karl Osler. The filmmakers appear to have at least partially based Osler, who is also known as "The Butcher," on real-life Nazi scientist Dr. Josef Mengele, known as the "Angel of Death." Mengele is perhaps the most infamous Nazi doctor for his so-called "medical" experimentation in the Auschwitz Death Camp. According to Fred, Osler, like Mengele, "earned his nickname by using unfortunate Nazi prisoners as human guinea pigs." Also, like Mengele, Osler is "one of the most wanted men by the War Crime Commission." Mengele and other Nazis escaped Germany after the war, and there were rumors in the 1950s that Mengele was still conducting his gruesome experiments.[9]

As in every mad scientist film, *She Demons* contains a scene in which Osler explains to the heroes (and to the audience) the nature of his scientific experiments. This scene in *She Demons* is incredibly long, accounting for almost 16 percent of the entire film (a 12-minute scene in a film which is only 77 minutes long). One of the reasons for such a lengthy scene is that Osler explains the whole history of his research program. During World War II, his experiments were aimed at fulfilling the Nazis' eugenic goal of perfecting a "master race." Osler claims that the "Fuhrer believed that since we were developing a master race, there would be no place for scarred war veterans. Every Nazi was supposed to be a perfect human specimen." His initial attempts to remove scar tissue using radiation were unsuccessful. They did, however, lead to his discovery that volcanic heat could be used as an unending source of power.

During one of his experiments, Mona's face was scorched by "exhaust from the lava." Having previously failed to remove scar tissue with radiation, Osler switches his efforts towards a genetic solution. Osler goes beyond the "theory" of a genetic material to discovering a physical substance, "Character X," which has the same properties as DNA. Like real scientists of the 1950s, Osler makes extraordinary claims that his genetic material codes for all human traits, saying that Character X is "a chemical quality composed of genes that gives us our personal appearance, our individual character." Since Character X is responsible for all traits, it cannot be removed without killing the person. Osler, therefore, has devised a system for the exchange of Character X from one person to another, a "gene transfer" experiment which he hopes will transfer the physical characteristics of the women in the cages to Mona. Likewise, the Character X from Mona transfers her disfigured appearance to the women.

Although Mona's Character X explains the She Demons' mutilated faces, her Character X cannot explain the "fangs" and "claws" of the She Demons. Osler explains to Fred that in addition to Mona's Character X, he has used Character X from animals:

Fred: Those creatures out there are a reflection of your wife's disfigurement. But the fangs, the claws, their animal instincts?

Osler: Ah, well. Unfortunately, a full transfusion of Character X from Mona would be so devoid of character genes that it might be fatal. Therefore, it was necessary to reinforce the substance passing from Mona to the girls by Character X from a combination of animals.

Fred: So, in addition to your wife's genes, those poor girls are being injected with gene cells, or Character X as you call it, from animals!

The She Demons, therefore, contain the genetic material of more than one species. This makes them the first organisms created through recombinant DNA technology on the screen. Osler further believes that humans can be improved through these genetic alterations. When he is accused of being "insane," Osler responds that "only the unimaginative cannot believe that Man is capable of improving on nature."

Although Character X from Mona and animals transforms the dancing women into She Demons, Character X from the dancing women does not seem to have any effect on Mona. In one of the film's best-known scenes, Mona removes her bandages, revealing that her face is just a skull with two eyeballs. The fact that Mona's face remains mutilated clearly indicates that Osler's genetic experiments have been a complete failure. Even his "successes," the She Demons, are only temporary because they "regenerate" Character X over time and revert back to their original appearance. In the end, Osler's claims that Character X codes for everything about humans, including "individual character," are not supported by the results of his experiments. Theists would argue that Osler's experiments to change humanity were doomed to fail because humanity cannot be summed up exclusively by a single molecule like DNA or Character X.

The Killer Shrews

As with *She Demons*, a hurricane strands the protagonists of *The Killer Shrews* on a remote island. Capt. Thorne Sherman and his first mate Rook are bringing supplies to Dr. Milo Craigis when a hurricane forces them to anchor their boat in a lagoon near the island. Dr. Craigis, his daughter Ann, her fiancée Jerry Farrell and geneticist Dr. Radford Baines are using the island as a base to conduct genetic research on shrews. Knowing that a "mutant" breed of giant shrews is loose on the island, Craigis was hoping to send Ann back on the boat with Sherman. Since they are unable to leave on the boat, Ann tricks Sherman into staying at their house-laboratory that night. Giant shrews kill Rook, who has been waiting by the dock in the lagoon. During the night, a shrew gets into the house and bites the hired hand Mario, who, surprisingly, dies instantly from the bite. Radford discovers that the shrews have "assimilated" the poison Craigis put out for them into their saliva. After an aborted attempt to reach the boat, shrews start to enter the house through several holes. During this shrew invasion, Radford is killed by a shrew bite. Sherman comes up with the idea of welding several 55-gallon steel drums together, and Craigis, Sherman and Ann (Jerry refuses to join them and is killed by the shrews) duck-walk to the beach in their "human tank" where they swim out to the boat.

In the same way that *She Demons* is reminiscent of 1930s horror cinema, *The Killer Shrews* shares a great deal with horror films of the 1970s. I found that *The Killer Shrews* is not only the first film to accurately portray genetic research and the uses of genetic technologies, it also is the first film to include the issue of human overpopulation, which is a staple of 1970s eco-horror films. Rather than seeking cultural solutions to overpopulation (i.e., lower human birth rates or less consumption of limited resources), Craigis tries to solve the problem by genetically modifying humans, saying to Sherman, "Think of what would happen if you could isolate and identify the inherited factor in each gene." Like real-life biologists, Craigis understands that it is necessary to know what the genetic material is before he can make directed mutations. Craigis informs Sherman that prior to Sherman's arrival, Craigis had discovered these "inherited factors" and had made genetic changes in the shrews which reduced their size, lowered their metabolism and increased their lifespan. Radford interrupts their conversation to proclaim "progress" in their experiments. He brings in a shrew (actually a mouse) and claims the shrew "maintains low metabolism" while its age is equivalent to an 140-year-old human. Ultimately, Craigis wants to solve the problems of overpopulation by making the same genetic changes in humans.[10]

Despite their success in manipulating the shrew's "inherited factors," an unforeseen "mutation" occurs which causes one strain to grow much larger than a normal shrew.[11] Although the scientists' made directed genetic changes, they were not able to predict how these changes would interact with the normal process of mutation. As Craigis explains to Sherman, "In controlling the size factor, we seemed to have crossed some of the other characteristics." Craigis is so focused on a materialistic explanation of life that he never takes into account possible theistic factors. He believed that because he understood the shrew's genetic material ("inherited factors"), he understood the entire shrew. According to *The Killer Shrews*, material explanations are not enough because a shrew is more than just its inherited factors.

Unlike *She Demons*, the genetic manipulations in *The Killer Shrews* are permanent and, even more importantly, they are inheritable. Alterations made to the shrews' genetic material are passed on to the shrews' offspring, allowing Craigis to "establish traits" and "trace the progressions through a number of generations." Unfortunately, the giant shrews escape from the laboratory. The danger faced by the characters is magnified, because the giant shrews can pass down their engineered genes to their offspring. According to Craigis, a month after the shrews escaped, "we saw one of their offspring. They were multiplying." Rather than a handful of "mutant" shrews loose on the island, the shrews have mated and produced "hundreds" of new giant shrews. Not only did the giant shrews inherit the genetic changes made by the scientists, "they inherited all the negative characteristics of their breed." Among the "negative characteristics" of shrews is the fact that they must "eat three times their own weight in food every 24 hours or starve."

Ultimately, the giant shrews produce so many offspring that they use up all the resources on the island. Craigis and Radford point to the overpopulation of the shrews as justification for their genetic intervention. Radford maintains that "very soon, right here on this island, there's going to be a miniature reproduction of an overpopulated world and you'll see the importance of what we're working to avoid." Likewise, Craigis views the giant shrews as an "excellent example of overpopulation," and he predicts that the shrews will either starve or resort to cannibalism. Unfortunately, as Sherman points out, Craigis is unable to foresee that he, Ann, Sherman and the others represent an alternate food source. The giant shrews, therefore, provide an appropriate metaphor for our genetic creations coming back to "consume" us. This is not the only error that Craigis makes in the film. Again and again, Craigis is forced to admit that his incomplete knowledge has led to "mistakes in judgment." For example, Craigis admits to Sherman that he "didn't know about the hurricane. I didn't anticipate the effect it would have on the shrews. I thought the house would be safe

The Killer Shrews (1959) is apparently the first film to accurately portray genetic research and the uses of genetic technologies, as well as the first horror film to include the issue of human overpopulation.

through the crisis." In addition, Craigis admits to Radford that he did not anticipate that the shrews would assimilate the poison he set out for them.

Even Craigis' few preparations for possible disaster indicate that he believes that he is in total control of his scientific experiments. According to Craigis, he chose the island because "it's isolated. Miles of open water in any direction." Since shrews "do not swim," Craigis is convinced that the "world is in no danger" from his genetic experiments. What Craigis fails to understand is that shrews may not swim, but they also do not weigh 100 pounds either. What *The Killer Shrews* asks us, then, is: Who is Craigis to say that his genetic manipulations have not led to shrews who can swim? Craigis assumes that his knowledge of the material world is sufficient to predict the consequences of his experiments. The fact that his experiments go out of control indicates that according to *The Killer Shrews* this assumption is wrong.

Conclusions: Food for Shrews?

Although it may be a coincidence that *She Demons* and *The Killer Shrews* take place on islands, it is clear that both films demonstrate the influence of H.G. Wells' 1896 novel *The Island of Dr. Moreau*. The island of "animal people" in *She Demons* is obviously a reference to Moreau's island of "Beast-People." The Moreau story is a powerful allegory about a scientist who attempts to manipulate nature in order to fit his vision of humanity. Fictional scientists who alter the genetics of living beings derive their iconography from the Wells' narrative. As is the case with his cinematic descendants Col. Osler and Dr. Craigis, Moreau takes an intensely materialistic view on the nature of humanity. Even though he was not a theist, Wells expressed his discontent with strict scientific materialism in several articles around the time he wrote *The Island of Dr. Moreau.* Instead of a strict materialistic view of humanity, Wells supported an ideology in which humans are the products of complex interactions between heredity, environment, the individual and society. Therefore, it is not surprising that, like Moreau's Beast-People, Osler's physical changes to the She Demons are not permanent. According to Wells, Moreau's inability to create humans from animals is a direct result of his refusal to acknowledge that humans cannot be summed up as merely material objects of flesh and blood.

In addition to their shared island setting, both *She Demons* and *The Killer Shrews* contain the element of a hurricane. (It is of note that one of the most influential horror films of the last ten years, *Jurassic Park* [1993], also includes an island, a hurricane and genetically engineered monster mayhem.) The inclusion of a hurricane may, like the island setting, be coincidental—just a plot convenience to keep the protagonists from escaping the island. I would argue, however, that hurricanes are an ideal metaphor for unknowable theistic factors which prevent scientists from controlling nature. Hurricanes are commonly referred to as "Acts of God." Likewise, the phrase "playing God" is frequently applied to scientists who manipulate living organisms. Both phrases imply the existence of theistic factors (God) in the realm of the natural (hurricanes and living entities). The use of hurricanes in conjunction with the genetic manipulations reminds the audience that there are some segments of the natural world which materialistic science cannot completely explain or control.

Watson and Crick's double helix may have ushered in the unique threat of genetic materialism, but the ideology of materialism itself was not new for 1950s American society. It could be argued, in fact, that materialism underlies all the themes of 1950s horror films including the triple-c threats of conformity, catastrophe and Communism. Many cultural critics argue that the prosperity of 1950s America led to rampant consumer materialism and suburban conformity. For theists of the time, this emphasis on material objects came at the expense of spirituality. For example, in "Materialism and Man" (*Saturday Review*, December 26, 1959), Prince Bernhard of the Netherlands writes a critique of the U.S. saying that "never and nowhere has any person been immune to the temptations of materialism. The temptation to give too much prominence to material goods and all things connected with them has always manifested itself very strongly in times and places of prosperity and affluence."

In addition to conformity, many theists blamed the threat of nuclear catastrophe on scientists who believed that the answers to all the world's problems could be found in the material world. For example, an editorial in *The Christian Century* ("Scientists Not Asked to Play God," May 27, 1959) advocated that Congress immediately ban nuclear testing rather than "dropping this responsibility into the laps of the scientific elite" who had caused the problem in the first place. Dialectical materialism is a form of scientific materialism and is the underlying philosophy of Communism. According to dialectical materialism, the goal of a perfect human society will inevitably be achieved by the action of forces operating according to scientific laws. Articles linking scientific or dialectical materialism to the threat of Communism invading American society filled many of the popular magazines of the 1950s. For example, the article "Asia and Scientific Materialism" in *The Christian Century* (June 9, 1954) cautions that the teaching of scientific materialism in "American colleges and universities" was leading to a "weakening" of Christianity and is "preparing the way for communism." The author further argues that scientific materialism "determines the character of men's behavior towards his fellow-men, as is so clearly shown in present-day communism. For the genuine materialist, man is nothing more than a complicated material mechanism." Although this article does not mention DNA or genetics, this argument foreshadows concerns about genetic materialism. It is evident that the public apprehension of genetic materialism in the late 1950s was a continuation of the fears already expressed about dialectical and consumer materialism throughout the 1950s.

The threat of genetic materialism is still very much present in American society. In today's cultural atmosphere, it would be very unusual to find a scientist who does not believe that DNA is the "stuff of life." Although there are many vocal critics of genetic materialism, including biologists Richard Lewontin, Stephen Jay Gould and Ruth Hubbard, many sociologists feel that the American public has become more accepting of the genetic materialist ideology. In their 1995 book *The DNA Mystique*, sociologists Dorothy Nelkin and Susan Lindee show that this growing public acceptance of genetic materialism has translated into a "cult of the gene" which increasingly appears in popular cultural narratives.[12] Nelkin and Lindee cite numerous examples of popular cultural texts from the 1980s and 1990s which include images of the gene as omnipotent, concluding that "these popular images convey a striking picture of the gene as powerful, deterministic, and central to an understanding of both everyday behavior and the 'secret of life.'"[13]

I maintain that the horror film is one form of popular culture which has not embraced the genetic materialist philosophy. In fact, a quick survey of horror films of the 1990s demonstrates that they contain similar plot elements as 1950s drive-in which warn against complete societal acceptance of genetic materialism. In the film *Mimic* (1997), for example, Dr. Susan Tyler eradicates a deadly cockroach-born disease by creating genetically engineered insects from the DNA of termites and praying mantises. Just like Dr. Craigis in *The Killer Shrews*, however, Dr. Tyler is forced to admit, "We changed its DNA. We don't know what we did!" As in *The Killer Shrews*, Tyler is unable to control her genetic changes and the engineered insects terrorize New York City. Likewise, in the 1996 film *The Island of Dr. Moreau*, Moreau's claim that DNA contains all the "destructive elements of the human psyche" is reminiscent of Col. Osler's belief in the properties of Character X in *She Demons*. Similarly, Moreau's genetic manipulations fail and he is killed. Despite the similarities there is a critical difference between genetic films from the 1950s and today: Genetic engineering was only a concept in the 1950s; today, genetic engineering is a reality. As evidenced by the cloning of Dolly the sheep and the near-completion of the Human Genome Project, our technology has caught up with our science. As biotechnology continues its rapid expansion into the twenty-first century, horror films will continue to warn us of the dangers of genetic manipulation. Otherwise, we will all end up as food for giant shrews.

NOTES

1. Tudor, Andrew. *Monsters and Mad Scientists: A Cultural History of the Horror Movie*. Oxford: Basil Blackwell, 1989.
2. Tudor, p. 133.
3. "And Now the Queen Bee Sells Cosmetics." *Changing Times*. July, 1958. (The royal jelly fad was revived in the 1980s, and royal jelly is still promoted today for its "age-defying" abilities.)
4. Wallace, Bruce and T. H. Dobzhansky. *Radiation, Genes, and Man*. New York: Holt, 1959, p. 8.
5. *Ibid*, p. 75.
6. Rostand, Jean. *Can Man Be Modified?* Trans. by Jonathan Griffin. New York: Basic Books, 1956, p. 91.
7. Beadle, George. *Science and Resources: Prospects and Implications of Technological Advance*. Ed. by Henry Jarrett. Baltimore: John Hopkins, 1959, p. 17.
8. Wallace, Henry A. *Science and Resources: Prospects and Implications of Technological Advance*. Ed. by Henry Jarrett. Baltimore: John Hopkins, 1959, p. 28.
9. Human bones found in Brazil in 1985 have been identified by authorities as Mengele's; however, many people still believe that he is not dead.
10. Exactly how this solves the problem of overpopulation is not clear. Humans with half the metabolism who live twice as long would still use the same amount of resources.
11. A normal shrew weighs less than one ounce, while the mutant shrews weigh between 50 and 100 pounds.
12. Nelkin, Dorothy and Susan Lindee. *The DNA Mystique*. New York: W.H. Freeman, 1995, p. 3.
13. *Ibid*, p. 2.

17

Wizards of Gore, Dances of Life and Hidden Dimensions

Gary D. Rhodes

The history of the horror in motion pictures is replete with bizarre filmmakers and bizarre films, from the works of Georges Melies to F.W. Murnau, from Tod Browning to Roger Corman, and from Al Adamson to Wes Craven. But a strong contender for the most unusual, the most eccentric, is Herschell Gordon Lewis and the trail of films left in his path. Like the dismembered bodies he glorified, Lewis' films are choppy mélanges of violence and black comedy, innovation and ineptitude.

At the dawn of a new millennium, however, Herschell Gordon Lewis is a little-known name to most filmgoers. His films are generally not studied in university courses, and his name is generally little known to professors who profess to know film. Even Ephraim Katz's seemingly all-encompassing *Film Encyclopedia* does not give Lewis a biographical entry.[1] Yet he is a hero to famed film director John Waters, and movie posters of his films sell for high prices at auctions and on the Internet. The reason is in part the subgenre of horror he invented: the splatter (or "slasher") film.

Lewis began making movies in 1960, his first being *The Prime Time*. Veteran producer David F. Friedman, already involved in exploitation films, was a production supervisor on the movie. He and Lewis quickly developed a business relationship that led them to collaborate on numerous exploitation films. Many were "nudies," featuring threadbare plots and threadbare costumes to support adult-oriented visuals.[2]

In 1963, the duo moved into the horror genre with *Blood Feast*, a color film that starred actors Mal Waldron and Connie Mason, the latter best-known at the release of the film for having been a June 1963 *Playboy* playmate. *Blood Feast* featured some nudity, but centered on visceral images of gore. Human dismemberment and mutilation were displayed in detail. "Barf bags" bearing the name *Blood Feast* were distributed to many audiences, seemingly suggesting what response audiences should give to it. Censors in some areas were outraged, but the film was a major success. The slasher-splatter era was born. And Lewis' career as the "Godfather of Gore" began.[3]

To capitalize on *Blood Feast*'s success, Lewis and Friedman made *2000 Maniacs* (1964) and *Color Me Blood Red* (1965). Both films relied heavily on gore imagery. Neither was as financially as successful as *Blood Feast*, and Lewis' relationship with Friedman came to an end. However, Lewis continued making gore films throughout the 1960s and early 1970s, including *Gruesome Twosome* (1967), *A Taste of Blood* (1967), *Something Weird* (1967) and *The*

Gore Gore Girls (1972). Even some of his non-horror films incorporated gore elements, including *Moonshine Mountain* (1964) and *She Devils on Wheels* (1968). Some of the gore scenes in Lewis films even used animal entrails to heighten the realism of the respective special effects.

To read plot synopses of Lewis' horror films makes them sound so violent as to be almost unbearable viewing experiences. A woman's face being pushed into a boiling pan of French fries on a hot stove. Another woman's face disfigured beyond recognition by a meat cleaver. A third woman's face charred by a clothing iron; her nipples are then clipped, causing milk to spew forth. These death scenes in *The Gore Gore Girls* read on paper as incredibly violent and degrading, the kinds of images against which a variety of groups would rail. However, viewing these sequences yields a different experience than might be expected. An overt sense of black comedy pervades a great many Lewis film scenes, as well as a kind of cinematic shoddiness that makes them difficult to view with a strong degree of seriousness.

Humorous or not, Hershell Gordon Lewis' horror films feature some remarkable moments. Lewis may even qualify as an auteur, or force a re-investigation of the underlying assumptions of that term. For many of his films, Lewis wrote, directed, produced, photographed and scored. The minuscule budgets with which he worked gave him a large degree of artistic control on one level, yet limited his freedom due to constraints of time, equipment and the caliber of talent which he could afford. Forgetting conscious intentionality and adopting instead a structuralist vision of the auteur, we can find in Lewis' horror films an extremely consistent style. True, some aspects of his work are derivative, such as the lengthy, static shots highlighting the female (and often nude female) form that are influenced by the exploitation and "nudie" films that were produced even before his collaborations with David F. Friedman. But a unique and codified style clearly emerges in his horror movies. In addition to the repeated use of gore effects, the Lewis style features coherent and repeated texture and feeling. His films *do* feature bad acting, inane dialogue, flat visual composition, poor lighting and uneven editing, at least according to traditional critical standards. And yet there is a surprising and almost incredible consistency to these problems from scene to scene and film to film. They are signifiers of a Lewis style, a style which knowingly or not broke from the parameters of the classical Hollywood style.[4]

The Wizard of Gore (1970), produced and directed by Lewis, is a paradigm of the Lewis style on many levels. The plotline, which at first seems to be a thinly veiled excuse to highlight scenes of blood and gore, features Ray Sager as "Montag the Magician," whose nightly magic shows have him seemingly gutting female volunteers who are then able to return to their audience seats seemingly unscathed. The methods of mutilation vary from chainsaw and railroad spike to sword swallowing and industrial punch press. After each performance, however, the volunteers later die of wounds like those received on stage.

Local TV talk show host Sherry Carson (Judy Cler) is spellbound by Montag's show, trying with some difficulty to get him to appear on her program *Housewives' Coffeebreak*. He finally agrees not to an interview, but to a live TV performance of a new "fire" trick. But Montag doesn't know that Sherry's boyfriend Jack (Wayne Ratay), a sports writer, understands that a connection exists between the magic tricks and deaths of the volunteers. He involves the police, who agree to be on hand at the TV studio for the broadcast.

Once the program begins, Montag

hypnotizes the studio audience and home viewers in a master plan to kill everyone. The hands of everyone who see his mesmerizing eyes inexplicably begin to bleed. Jack knows better than to watch, and pushes Montag into a fire meant for Sherry and others. He appears to burn alive, and yet the obligatory and seemingly "happy" closing scene between Jack and Sherry proves otherwise. Just as Sherry proclaims everything that has happened to be "impossible," Jack pulls off a mask to reveal that he is actually Montag. He quickly pushes his hands into Sherry's torso and pulls out her intestines. But instead of dying like his prior victims, Sherry laughs and makes her own revelation to Montag: he is merely a thought of hers, and in reality he is about to give a performance, the first performance of the film. "The End — or The Beginning?" is appended to the closing credits, making clear that the narrative has come full circle.

Despite its low-budget qualities and emphasis on splatter effects, *The Wizard of Gore* has various narrative features that give it distinction. The film certainly employs the Lewis style in its acting, dialogue, cinematography and editing, but its plotline possesses somewhat more depth than most of Lewis' earlier films. For example, witness Montag's opening speech:

> Torture and terror have always fascinated mankind. Perhaps whatever drove your predecessors to the sadism of the Inquisition and the gore of the gladiators' arena is the same thing that compels you to stare at bloody highway accidents.... Today, television and films give us the luxury of seeing grisly dismemberments and deaths without anyone ever getting harmed.

In another scene, Sherry Carson complains to her TV audience about the glut of cheap "exploitation" films inundating viewers. At these moments, *The Wizard of Gore* comments on itself and the splatter subgenre that historically had not yet reached maturity; the wry self-critique almost prophetically envisions the slasher-splatter-gore movement of the 1980s horror film.

Interesting though its self-reflexivity is, a much larger percentage of the plot — indeed, the very hinge of its climax — develops out of the issue of reality vs. unreality. Montag even taunts the audience with this conflict in his opening speech:

> What is a magician? A person who tears asunder your rules of logic and crumbles your world of reality, so that you can go home and say, 'Oh, what a clever trickster he is! What a sly deceiver!' and go to sleep in the security of your own *real* world? What is real? Are you certain you know what reality is? How do you know that this second you are not asleep in your bed dreaming that you are here in this theater! Ahh yes, it all seems *too* real.

The conflict he invokes has deep roots in the history of horror films; that is, dreamlike plot frameworks that either question what really happened or make clear that what the audience believed was happening was merely a character's dream. Dreamlike unrealities are also a convention of gothic fiction that predated the advent of the horror film. On the level of its plot, little is made of the reality vs. unreality issue that has not been explored in dozens of other films and novels. In fact, it is true that *The Wizard of Gore*'s narrative uses this device in a very heavy handed manner.

However, the cinematic signifiers of the reality vs. unreality question in *The*

Wizard of Gore break with traditional Hollywood film form and convention in a unique fashion. Though a "Lewis style" has been discussed and identified, this essay will not argue that Lewis the man intentionally and consciously pursued a break with Hollywood tradition. In fact, it is likely that—given time constraints, talent constraints and economic considerations (e.g., getting booked into theaters that were not art houses), etc.—Lewis the man would not have desired or necessarily been *consciously* able to create a film with an eccentric cinematic structure.

And yet, through use of shot composition, editing and music, *The Wizard of Gore*—intentionally or not—generates a highly unusual sets of rules regarding time and space. These spatio-temporal concerns help signify the reality vs. unreality question through cinematic means, reinforcing the points made narratively through the character Montag. Furthermore, these cinematic constructs create a unique viewing position for the spectator, a zone in which the standard Hollywood rules of time and space do not apply.[5] The work of theorist Edward T. Hall can provide the tools to understand better these facets of *The Wizard of Gore*. Hall spent much of his life in pursuit of unlocking the doors of how time and space are understood by humans in different environments and cultures.[6]

Time

Twice did Edward T. Hall examine the subject of time in a book-length study, first in his 1959 text *The Silent Language* and then in the 1983 *The Dance of Life*. Both studies investigate the many different ways that humans experience time, as well as the many different kinds of time that exist. For example, Hall draws a sharp line between monochronic time (that which is used by "low-involvement peoples who schedule one thing at a time and become disoriented if they have to deal with too many things at once"[7]) and polychronic time (that which is used by peoples who "keep several operations going at once, like jugglers"[8]). Furthermore, he makes distinctions between personal time, profane time, sacred time, physical time, micro time, biological time, sync time and—most importantly for our understanding of *The Wizard of Gore*—metaphysical time.[9]

To begin our own discussion, we need to realize what appears to happen with time in *The Wizard of Gore* that is different from a traditional film in the classical Hollywood style. Most Hollywood films follow a timeline in which each shot replaces a prior shot and each scene replaces a prior scene to move the chronology of the story forward in a linear pattern. The exceptions are those that employ specific narrative means (e.g., dialogue) or cinematic conventions (e.g., a closeup of a person's eyes or face to suggest they are thinking) to convey flashbacks or flashforwards, but even these exceptions generally occur for the exposition of an otherwise linear narrative. This essentially chronological use of narrative time exemplifies what Hall in *The Silent Language* describes as a kind of U.S. time, in which Americans "think of time as a road or a ribbon stretching into the future, along which one progresses."[10]

Editing styles impact this flow of chronology in the sense that series of shots of more lengthy duration (i.e., slower paced editing) suggest what Hall would call slow-moving personal time, which he defines as the manner by which people experience time in "different contexts, settings, and emotional and psychological states."[11] In this case, the "person" is the film character(s) and/or the film spectator; likewise, shot sequences of more short duration (i.e., faster paced editing) suggest fast-moving personal time of the film character(s) and/or film spectator.[12] Other cinematic conventions have also developed during the twentieth century to impact further the power of editing over personal and narrative time (e.g., lap dissolves suggest the passage of time, even if of an imprecise duration, and fade-to-blacks represent the end of time in a given scene or depicted event or entire story). Thus, editing and other film language mediate the linear ribbon of narrative time against the manner or "speed" by which is experienced.

While the treatment of time in the classical Hollywood style has generally been of a simple "one thing after another" chronological nature (despite notable exceptions like Quentin Tarantino's 1995 *Pulp Fiction*), in other ways Hollywood has employed more complex notions of conveying narrative time, most notably parallel editing. Some debate exists over the advent of this convention, in which the audience witnesses two or more simultaneous events through editing, showing part of one event and then part of another, understanding that both (or three or four or more) are unfolding more or less concurrently. Regardless of who should receive credit for its advent, parallel editing quickly became a cinematic convention in Hollywood through which audiences could understand that multiple narrative events are occurring at the same time. Editing causes the audience to shift and reorient themselves from place to place, while still understanding the overall narrative flow. Some more complex films feature a large number of characters and settings must be juggled by the spectator. Precisely because of parallel editing, whether in simple or advanced usage, we can employ Hall's term polychronic (again, that time in which people keep many activities going at once) as a further description of time as used by the classical Hollywood paradigm, even if the multi-scene form is subsumed under a more general linear structure.

Given that time in traditional Hollywood films is generally linear and polychronic, it is possible to ascertain how strongly Lewis' film presents a contrasting time schema. To begin broadly, *The Wizard of Gore* is essentially monochronic in its narrative structure. The film uses a number of settings to advance the story, from the quartet that constitute the bulk of the film (Montag's Theater, Montag's dressing room, Sherry's apartment and Sherry's television studio) to those seen more briefly (e.g., a restaurant, a police station, a cemetery, a morgue, a few exteriors, etc.). However, *The Wizard of Gore* does not generally intermingle the time of more than one event. In other words, though the spectator sees Sherry and Jack at Montag's show and then see a female victim collapse at a restaurant, the narrative makes clear that these are *successive* events, not concurrent ones. Only when Montag is broadcasting his hypnosis over TV and Jack is attempting to rouse his friends from the trance do we see anything resembling parallel editing and polychronic time. Even then, it is the intermingling of only two events, rather than anything more complex. But this finding is not particularly illuminating in and of itself, because more simple Hollywood films and especially low-budget movies sometimes work with monochronic time. "B" movies of the '30s and '40s, as well as of the drive-in era, often use monochronic time. Lewis' other films, for example, generally use monochronic time as well.

What highlights *The Wizard of Gore*'s uniqueness is the juxtaposition of the very simple and easy-to-follow monochronic time narrative with the bizarre use of time at Montag's theater. The four gore segments during his performances do not follow a simple monochronic process. They follow a polychronic structure, but they are not similar to the use of time in traditional Hollywood feature films. Furthermore, the pacing of the gore segments is much faster than in the other segments of *Wizard of Gore*'s narrative. For example, only four shots are used to visually convey the first four minutes of *The Wizard of Gore*; in the first gore segment, however, 17 shots are seen in only one minute and 35 seconds. The juxtaposition of these different pacings and use of time as a concept create Lewis' unique style of filmmaking.

When the bloody chainsaw mangling occurs during the first gore segment (hereafter "Segment A"), a wild, plungered trumpet sound with brass accompaniment is heard and many (though not all) of the shots are handheld and thus a bit shaky. As already noted, the pacing of the editing is much faster than any other non-gore scene. Shots A1–A8 (i.e., the first eight shots in Segment A) and A12–A15 illustrate these moments.[13] When the woman's body appears unharmed and we see the audience, the music uses a calm, chime-like sound (perhaps from a xylophone) and the shots employ use of a tripod and are thus very balanced and steady. (See, for example, Shots A9–A11 and A16–A17.) The music thus helps make the transition back and forth from the violent bloody mess to the apparently untouched and healthy female form.

Though this discussion has already discarded the notion of a conscious auteur acting with intent to create film form, it is worthwhile to consider what Herschell Gordon Lewis himself has said about Segment A. In an audio commentary he recorded for a DVD issue of *The Wizard of Gore*, Lewis said of the chainsaw segment: "Now we have two sets of reactions. That's the whole idea. One is where he literally saws the guts apart. And there's also what the audience sees, which is not the same thing at all."[14] Presumably he is referring to the two alternations between the female character being harmed/unharmed, apparently suggesting that the first is what kills the character (who dies from chainsaw wounds after Montag's performance is over) and the second is an illusion the filmed theater audience witnesses. That interpretation suggests the film audience doesn't even see the first alternation. While an interesting intention, no secondary cues—such as dialogue or visuals—support Lewis claim or make it understandable to a film spectator. Furthermore, the subsequent gore segments feature more than two alternations; the result convolutes Lewis' intention further, as it would be even more difficult to understand when the film audience sees the gore and when it does not.

What of those other gore segments? The other three do bear marked similarities to the first, all using polychronic time. Handheld, shaky camera shots generally convey the victim being harmed. However, they become increasingly complex and do not adhere to the same rhythmic structure as one another. For example, the second gore segment ("Segment B")—which has Montag harming his victim by hammering a spike into her head—unfolds in the following manner:

1. Shots B1–B7=victim harmed
2. Shots B8=victim unharmed
3. Shot B9–B13=harmed
4. Shot B14=unharmed
5. Shots B15–B17=harmed
6. Shot B18=unharmed
7. Shots B19–B23=harmed
8. Shots B24–B29[15]=unharmed

As the above shot breakdown indicates, the level of complexity in the gore segment has increased over Segment A, the chainsaw episode. In Segment B, the

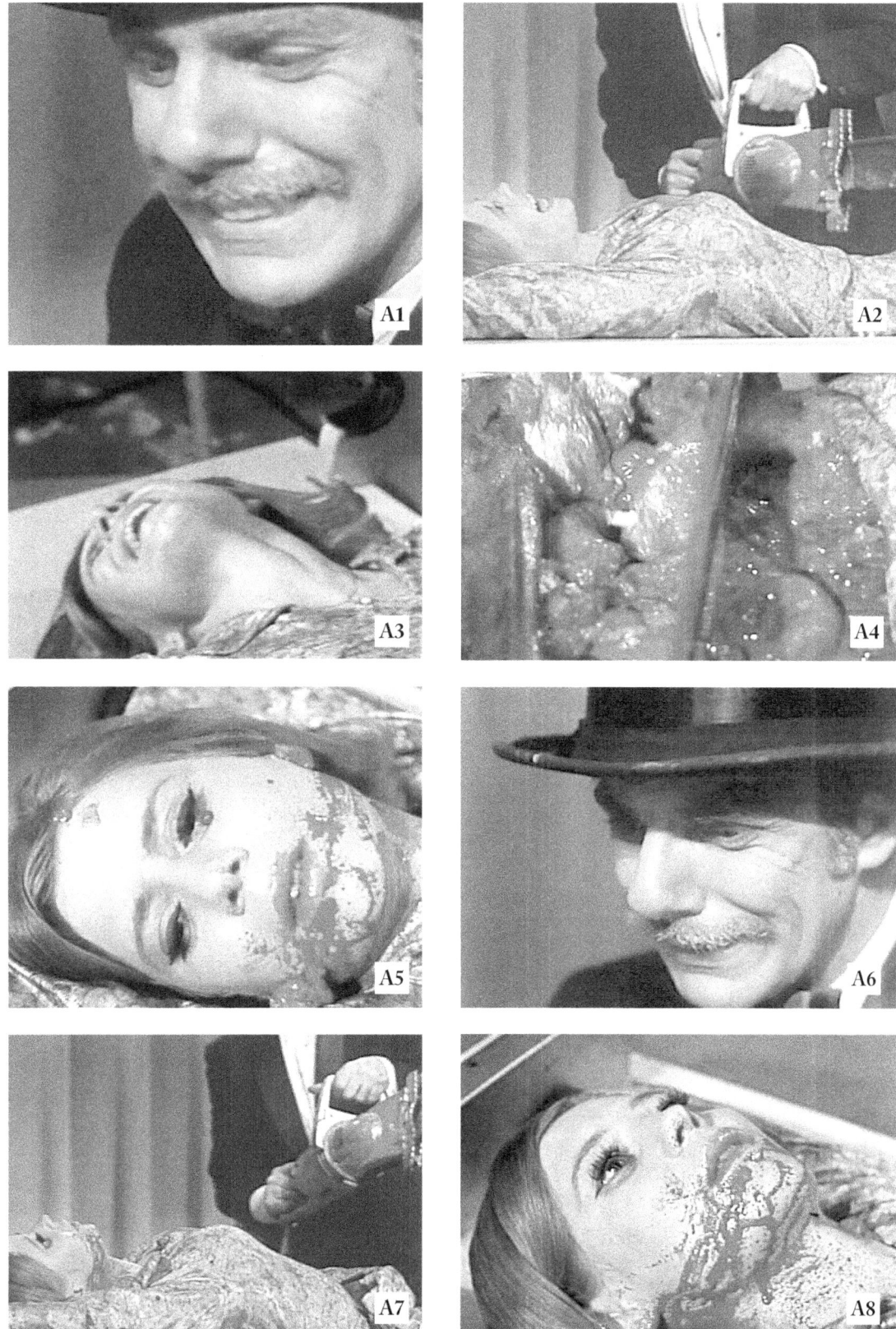

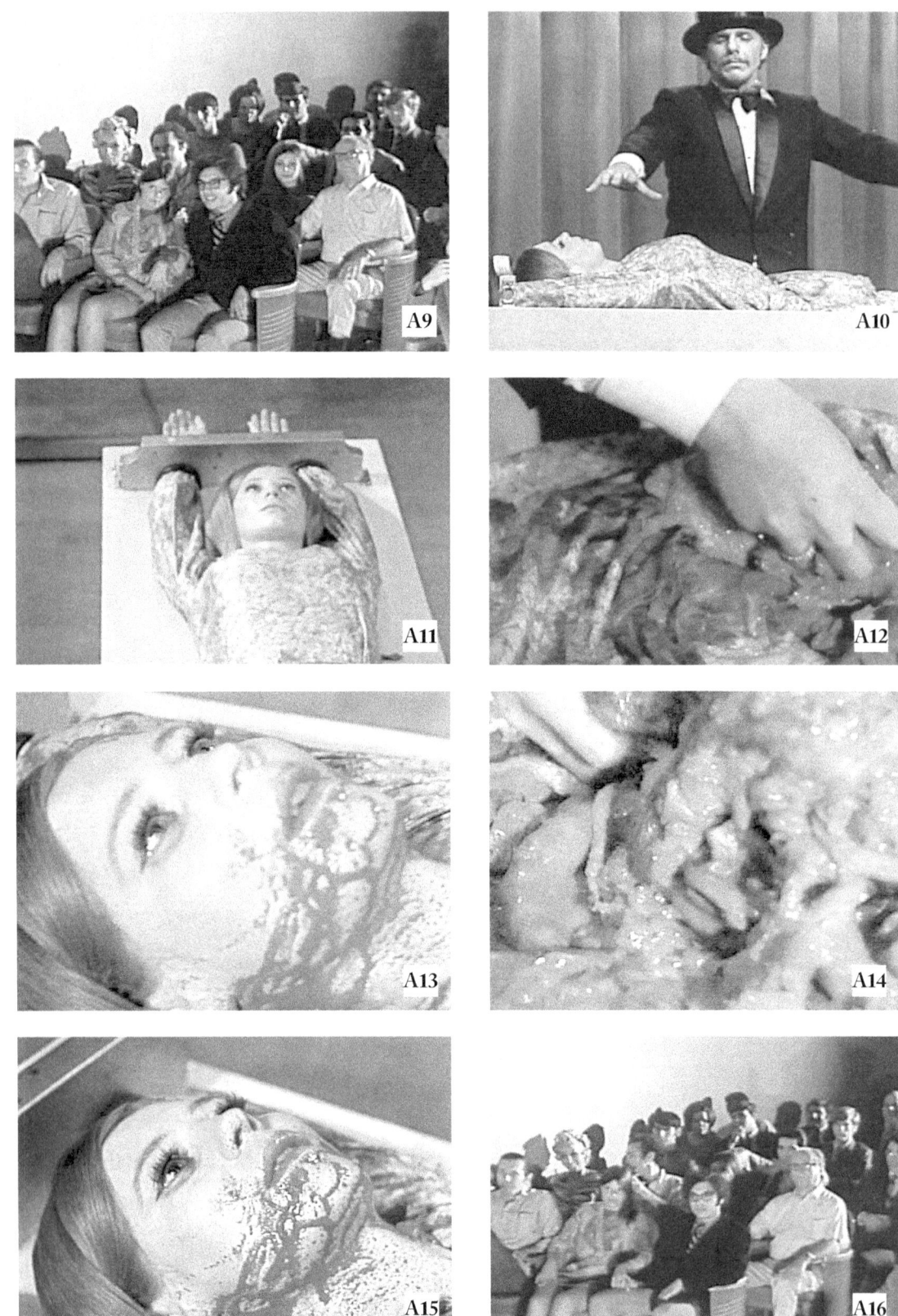

alternation between harmed/unharmed status occurs four times in eight series of shots, which occur in the following combinations: 7 (i.e., B1–B7) then 1 then 5 then 1 then 3 then 1 then 5 then 6. No internal pattern or similarity to Segment A is evident. Even the gore does not get progressively more bloody or profane; indeed, Shots B1–B7 (which show the removal of the victim's brain) and Shots B19–B23 (which show both of the victim's eyes pushed back into their sockets and then the removal of one) are arguably gorier than Shots B9–B13 and B15–B17 (the two middle "harmed" groups of shots). The pacing is quite rapid in the "harmed" series of shots, most of which run two to five seconds in length. The major exception is Shot B22, which for several seconds shows the removal of the victim's right eyeball. The overall

segment runs three minutes and two seconds.

The third gore segment ("Segment C") follows a different pattern in terms of the alternation between depicting the female as harmed/unharmed, which occurs this time from an industrial punch press.

A shot from Gore Segment B.

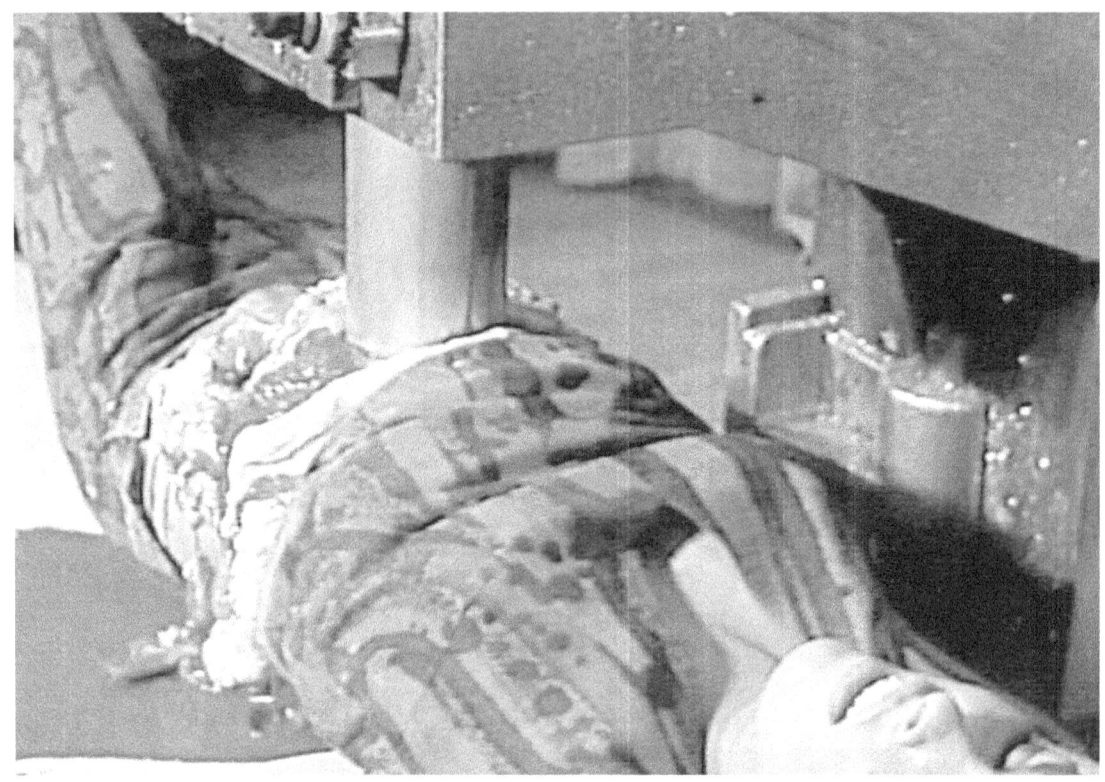

A shot from Gore Segment C.

The following breakdown illustrates the shot sequence:

1. Shots C1–C6=harmed
2. Shots C7–C8=unharmed
3. Shots C9–C13=harmed
4. Shots C14–C16=unharmed
5. Shots C17–C20=harmed
6. Shots C21–C24[16]=unharmed

On this occasion, the alternation between harmed and unharmed occurs three times, with the shots in each sequence grouped as follows: 6 then 2 then 5 then 3 then 4 then 4. Again, no internal pattern or similarity to Segment A or B exists. Probably the goriest of the harmed shots is the second group (C9–C13), in which we see various organs of the victim that Montag then touches with his hands. The pacing of harmed shots is rapid, with most running two to four seconds each. The overall segment lasts two minutes, 20 seconds.

The fourth gore segment ("Segment D") features not only a different alternating pattern of harmed/unharmed shots (which occur from sword swallowing), but also perhaps the most complex sequence of all four gore segments. The following chart illustrates the shot breakdown:

1. Shot D1=harmed
2. Shot D2–D3=unharmed
3. Shot D4=harmed
4. Shot D5–D7=unharmed
5. Shot D8–D12=harmed
6. Shot D13–D15=unharmed
7. Shot D16=harmed
8. Shot D17=unharmed
9. Shot D18=harmed
10. Shot D19–D20=unharmed

This segment then features an alternation between harmed/unharmed five times, with the ten groups of shots as follows: 1 then 2 then 1 then 3 then 5 then 3 then 1 then 1 then 1 then 2. No pattern exists in these groupings of shots, either internally or by comparison to Segments A, B or C. The goriest group of shots is probably the last (D18), in which unidentifiable chunks of flesh comes out of the mouth

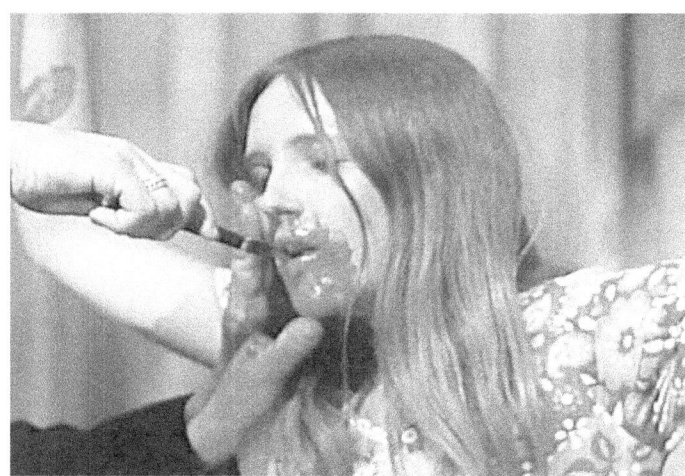

Two shots from Gore Segment D.

of one of the two victims. Segment D runs approximately five minutes, six seconds. The pacing, while faster than the general narrative of the film, is less rapid than the prior three gore segments. Harmed shots last from four to eight to 15 seconds each.

Tallying up both the number of shots and the number of alternations between harmed/unharmed in the gore segments, no pattern emerges. The greatest number of shots comes in Segment C, but the greatest number of alternations occurs in Segment D. And yet it is not a cumulative building, for Segment B features more alternations than Segment C. The groupings of shots and the running times of the segments show no constancy or evolving pattern either. In other words, it is not as if the complexity of either the alternations or shots consistently increases from segment to segment. While similarities are present (e.g., the alternations of harmed/unharmed, the use of handheld camera for most harmed shots), time in the gore segments seems generally instable and unpredictable, fostering a kind of uncertainty for the spectator.

The use of time in the gore segments is not compliant with the norms of time as generated by the classical Hollywood paradigm. Indeed, the temporal depiction onstage in the gore segments is all the more striking when viewed against the film's otherwise generally simple, straightforward, monochronic use of time. So how can the use of time be reconciled with the narrative? What sense can be made of them? Rejecting Herschell Gordon Lewis' explanation as unacceptable allows for the ability to consider again the work of Edward T. Hall. Of the many streams of time he explores in *The Hidden Dimension*, it is the metaphysical which best explains the phenomena experienced by both Montag's theater audience and *The Wizard of Gore* spectator. Hall's discussion of metaphysical time invokes—along with the occult and *deja vu*—time warps and offers examples of people who had on one or more occasions "transcended time and space."[17] During their metaphysical encounters, those persons apparently existed outside or apart from other kinds of time which he catalogues, such physical time (i.e., the time generated by the revolutions of the Earth around the sun), and were apparently unable to describe precisely how metaphysical time worked. Hall concludes that metaphysical time is a very difficult concept to understand or explain, partially due to the intimate and personal way it is experienced.

Wittingly or not, Lewis in the gore segments of *The Wizard of Gore* creates a cinematic representation of metaphysical time, clearly differentiating it from more standard markers of time in the Western world and in the classical Hollywood paradigm. The four gore segments are simulcra of the metaphysical, juxtaposed sharply against the more standard and linear flow of time seen in the rest of the film.

The understanding of time, due to apparent repetitions of events in the harmed/unharmed alternations, is skewed from being understood by the viewer. Rather than being cued by some narrative or visual device (such as the filmed audience at Montag's theater), we are left to experience the jarring and inexplicable movement without explanation. Nor are we even able—as Hall would say—to "pin down"[18] any firm conclusions about the film's metaphysical time by scrutinizing the four gore segments; no real patterns of time or shot sequencing occur. As audience members, we are left to grasp for meaning out of mystery; the lack of a clear understanding is indeed what helps the metaphysical to develop. To borrow another phrase from Hall, these segments are very definitely "extraordinary occurrences," in terms of the non-gore segments of *The Wizard of Gore*, Lewis's other film output and the classical Hollywood paradigm.

Space

In his book *The Hidden Dimension*, Edward T. Hall examines what he calls the "social and personal space and man's [sic] perception of it."[19] Hall devotes the text to proxemics, which he defines as "the interrelated observations and theories of man's [sic] use of space."[20] The analysis goes so far as to posit that "virtually everything that man [sic] is and does is associated with the experience of space."²¹ Hall's observations will prove a valuable guide in charting *The Wizard of Gore*'s unique use of space, particularly in the theater where Montag performs gore Segments A–D.

The first scene in the film constructs what will become a repetitive use of spatial distinctions and features: the theater stage. In Shot 1, Montag's assistant places a sign reading "Montag the Magnificent" on an easel directly facing the camera, which in turn directly faces the magician's stage. When Montag appears on stage and speaks (also Shot 1), he speaks directly to the camera and then is decapitated by a guillotine. During this sequence, frames of film are occasionally frozen, upon which onscreen film credits appear.

When the credits conclude, Montag (with his head back on his shoulders, the prior illusion at an end) continues speaking to the camera, though we soon see cutaways of live audience members. But those images of the live audience are always shown at a distinct 45 degree angle, meaning that—in terms of shot juxtaposition—they are all grouped in a small number of seats to Montag's left. And that orientation can be witnessed most clearly in the following diagram, which attempts to show the approximate layout and use of space in Montag's theater:

```
------------(stage)---
         Montag
--(stage)-------------
         Film      Theater
         Spectator Audience
```

Given that the spatial aspects of Montag's theater exist in the manner shown above, important questions remain. What is the result of this use of space? What meaning, even if unintentional, does it hold? Occasionally his head turns to his left to speak to them, but generally he looks straight ahead, in the direction not of the audience but instead to *their* left, which is the location of the camera.

To begin, one might argue that the intent of this spatial orientation is for Montag to be looking at the audience members clustered to his left, and that the difference in camera placement and Montag's gaze is a mistake. With regard to spatial connections between characters in narrative film, theorist Edward Branigan would suggest that—despite the spatial difference between the vision represented in the shot and the location of a given character—the composition is still likely linked to a given character. He believes:

> The act of 'telling' or representing is first of all a creation of space, a display of the visual through acts of vision.... Subjectivity in film depends on linking the framing of space at a given moment to a *character* [author's emphasis] as origin. The link may be direct or indirect. In the POV structure it is direct, because the character is shown and then the camera occupies his or her (approximate!) position, thus framing a spatial field derived from him or her as origin. In character 'projection,' however, ... there is no coincidence of space, rather space is joined to a character by other logical or metaphorical, means. What is important, therefore, in determining subjectivity is to examine the logic which links the framing of space to a character as origin of that space.²²

Branigan refers to indirect, "character projection" structures as "deviant"²³ point-of-view shots, with character origin made clear through "secondary cues [that] reinforce spatial orientation."²⁴ Secondary cues could be dialogue or other visuals, such as long shots that would show a wider field of vision and help the viewer understand better where objects and/or characters "are" within the given setting. But within *The Wizard of Gore*, no secondary cues are present, and spatial orientation between, say, Montag and the audience (when he is looking straight into the camera) are so awry geographically that little exists to "reinforce."

Given that Branigan's comments are not helpful for understanding Montag's theater, we can turn towards spectator theory for other possible explanations. As theorist Nick Browne suggests, "Film [tries] not just to direct the attention but to place the eye of the spectator inside the fictional space, to make his presence integral and constitutive of the structure of views."[25] *The Wizard of Gore* takes the enterprise addressed by Browne discusses to an extreme. It is the emergence of what I have termed the *spectator-as-character*: that rare instance in Hollywood films (especially outside of self-reflexive comedy film sequences) in which, however subtly, the film spectator is incorporated into the narrative plot.[26] Here the *spectator-as-character* occurs due to subject positioning resulting from camera placement, reinforced by the direct gaze of Montag at the spectator.

Since this phenomenon occurs in Scene 1, an examination of the film reveals that the *spectator-as-character* occurs in the scenes (especially the gore segments) which take place in Montag's theater. The result of this use of space and its meaning (even if unintentional) can be better understood by Edward T. Hall's theories on proxemics. Hall suggests that:

> ...people from different cultures not only speak different languages, but, what is possibly more important, *inhabit different sensory worlds* [emphasis in original]. Selective screening of sensory data admits some things while filtering out others, so that experience as it is perceived through one set of cultural patterned sensory screens is quite different from experience perceived through another. The architectural and urban environments that people create are expressions of this filtering process. In fact, from these man-altered environments, it is possible to learn how different people use their senses. Experience, therefore, cannot be counted on as a stable point of reference, because it occurs in a setting that has been molded by man [*sic*].[27]

Hall's comments suggest that experience and understanding is at least to a degree instable due to spaces designed by humans, or, we can add, spaces as visually constructed by the filmmaking process. In particular, the use of space in Montag's theater erupts out of the instability of experience as that stable point of reference, placing the spectator into a position unlike one s/he is used to occupying in a traditional Hollywood film.

The spatial orientation in *The Wizard of Gore* also invokes another aspect of Hall's discussion of proxemics: the dynamism of space, in which he suggests that a person's "perception of space is dynamic because it is related to action—what can be done in a given space—rather than what is seen by passive viewing."[28] Much discussion in film studies has occurred on whether the spectator is passively viewing, actively watching or both. For the present discussion, that distinction is less important than the application of Hall's analysis to the spatial orientation of Montag's theater. In other words, a live and active viewer may offer any number of reactions, even to the degree of closing his/her eyes or leaving the movie theater. Certainly more options are open to the live viewer than being cued by the reactions of the filmed theater audience, who seem wholly intrigued by Montag's onstage show, rather than, say, disgusted or sickened. An attentive viewer of *The Wizard of Gore*, regardless of his/her reaction, is nevertheless confined by the space created for the spectator. In other words, his/her perception of space at Montag's theater is guided more by a lack of ability to take action than by, say, variant emotional responses. The place in which the spectator is positioned is unchangeable; the gore segments must be witnessed.

The only occasion during which the spectator is given a more unique set of positions is during groups of harmed shots in Segments A–D. When the grisly violence occurs, many of the shots offer close-ups, which keeps the spectator in the position of watching unfolding action but given them a better vantage point. Coupled with the change in proximity is a change in visual style. Most of the harmed shots are filmed with a handheld, shaky camera, offering a (potentially) more realistic texture due to their similarity to the handheld shots a viewer may associate with newsreels or TV news. Despite the stylistic variance, however, the spectator's position remains fixed: the gore must be witnessed.

Of the many kinds of space described by Hall, that which best represents the world of Montag's theater is "fixed-feature space—one of the basic ways of organizing the activities of individuals and groups. It includes material manifestations as well as the hidden, internalized designs that govern behavior as man moves about on this earth." Hall believes that perhaps the most important point of fixed-feature space is that "it is the mold into which a great deal of behavior is cast."[29]

A theater automatically represents fixed-feature space because of the clear activity/purpose for which it is built. Material manifestations in it include of course theater seats which generally are not moved (or a fixed location for an automobile, in the case of a drive-in theater), as well as a stage and/or movie screen. The difference in design between the two places—for the viewer and the viewed, the audience and the performer—creates a hidden, internalized line between them as much as it creates a material and geographical line. Behavior, as Hall suggests, is governed by the mold of space; that is to say, the space dictates than an audience takes their seats and watch what unfolds. Regardless of whether one defines watching as passive or active, it is the requested behavior that occurs at a theater, be it indoor or outdoor.

The Wizard of Gore creates a doubling of this fixed-feature space in the scenes of Montag's theater. A live viewer is positioned in a single theater seat in a given movie theater or a given automobile location at a drive-in theater. That mold governs behavior while watching the film; one is not generally apt (or at least *expected*) to move from seat to seat in a theater or hop from car to car while viewing a film, for example. But *The Wizard of Gore*—at least in the scenes taking place at Montag's theater—creates a position for the live viewer that places it as a character in the film narrative, an audience member at Montag's theater, a second fixed-feature space. The use of the actual theater (for exhibition purposes) and Montag's theater (for narrative purposes) thus means the spectator plays the dual role of actual audience viewer and a positioned character. The duality reinforces the rigidity of space in the filmed and actual viewing environment, most overtly if the latter is an indoor theater, but also in the case of a drive-in, whose ostensible purpose (to view films) is much the same.

True, a film could, for example, show a theater interior using so many shots, including moving camera, as to illustrate a traditionally fixed-feature space without anchoring the spectator to a particular location or set of locations in it. Such a film could illustrate these many shots without truly incorporating the live viewer into the role of *spectator-as-character*. But *The Wizard of Gore* chooses not that path, but instead one which so thoroughly anchors the audience that during the gore segments only two major points-of-view are available to them. Montag on stage and brief shots of the in-film audience are the main images available to the spectator.

Indeed, the rigidity of space is so confining that—despite playing a similar role as the in-film audience—there exists what Hall would call "sociofugal" space, meaning that space which keeps people from interacting to any great degree.[30] The line between the spectator and the in-film audience is almost as sharp as the line between the spectator and Montag onstage. The result means the *spectator-as-character* has no one with which to identify onscreen, being left instead to remain a character silently watching the gore within the spatial confines created by the film.

Conclusion

To make more sense of what *The Wizard of Gore* creates in its four gore segments, we need to reconsider the spatiotemporal as a single concept, given the irrevocable tie in the film between time and space. As has been established, time is relatively instable in the gore segments, with violence to victims happening over and over again. The lack of a clear pattern of harmed/unharmed alternations in the gore segments helps reinforce the unfixed temporal structure, as does the unusual use of polychronic time juxtaposed against the film's otherwise monochronic chronology.

It is in these respects that the metaphysical takes hold in the gore segments.

Furthermore, the use of metaphysical time interacts with space not only due to the fact that visuals are seen during a temporal progression, but also in the use of handheld camera. When the harmed shots occur in their bizarre time structure, the spectator is forced close to the action through handheld camera shots that mimic the supposed realism of newsreel or TV news cinematography. The spatial construct in Montag's theater also forces the spectator to be a witness to the graphic depictions of violence to the degree of becoming the *spectator-as-character*, who is repetitively acknowledged by the magician's gaze. The limited number of visually composed angles in the theater fortifies the spectator's confined status within the sociofugal environment, as does the doubling of the fixed-feature space (i.e., the theater within the film and the theater/drive-in in which actual viewers watch the film).

The result of time and space in the gore segments is the creation of a cinematic zone in which a spectator's understanding of events is forever skewed. Under scrutiny, structural patterns do not emerge to help guide us. We are simply confined in a set spatial environment, being forced to watch action unfold again and again and again. In Bermuda Triangle-like fashion, we drift in and out of understandable monochronic time, repeatedly experiencing the mangling of human bodies and their unharmed appearance. The metaphysical acts as a basis for the use of time, but that factor alone suggests to Edward T. Hall that knowledge of exactly what is transpiring and exactly *when* it transpires is outside of our grasp. Film conventions of the classical Hollywood paradigm have not prepared us for *The Wizard of Gore* and its singular use of the spatio-temporal.

Deeply flawed in many respects, the film output of Herschell Gordon Lewis does contain much aesthetically that is very worthy of study. Intentionally or not, his films reject standard Hollywood traditions, pursuing instead a unique cinematic vision. Though indebted stylistically in some ways to the history of exploitation film, Lewis created a filmic world that was distinctively his own. From a historical materialistic perspective, we might even bestow the title "auteur." Regardless, his movies are in need of further examination and study, as they remind us of how wonderful and original film can be when it escapes the dominant and repetitive structures of Hollywood.

Notes

1. Katz, Ephraim. *The Film Encyclopedia*. 2nd Ed. New York: HarperPerennial, 1994.

2. Examples include such films as *Nature's Playmates* (1962), *Bell, Bare, and Beautiful* (1963) and *Goldilocks and the Three Bares* (1963).

3. For an overview of Lewis' gore films, see Randy Palmer's *The Godfather of Gore*. Jefferson NC: McFarland, 2000.

4. Here I refer to the kind of traditional Hollywood style as explored by David Bordwell, Kristin Thompson and Janet Staiger in *The Classical Hollywood Cinema: Film Style and Mode of Production to 1960*. New York: Columbia University, 1985.

5. In this essay, I will use the term "spectator" to identify the theoretical construct/position created by film, whereas I will use "viewer" and "audience" to identify live filmgoers.

6. Edward T. Hall

7. Hall, Edward T. *The Hidden Dimension*. Garden City NY: Doubleday and Co., 1966 p. 162.

8. Hall, p. 162

9. Hall, Edward T. *The Dance of Life: The Other Dimension of Time*. Garden City, NY: Anchor/Doubleday, 1983 p. 13–27.

10. Hall, Edward T. *The Silent Language*. Garden City, NY: Doubleday, 1959, p. 28.

11. Hall, *The Dance of Life*, p. 19.

12. *Ibid*, p.24.

13. Here I am counting shots in the gore sequence as they exist on the Image DVD *The Wizard of Gore (Special Edition)*.

14. Hershell Gordon Lewis quoted on the audio commentary of the Image Entertainment DVD *The Wizard of Gore (Special Edition)*, released in 2000.

15. All of these shots have been compiled, examined, and numbered based upon the film print released by Image Entertainment on the DVD *The Wizard of Gore (Special Edition)*.

16. All of these shots have been compiled, examined, and numbered based upon the film print released by Image Entertainment on the DVD entitled *The Wizard of Gore (Special Edition)*.

17. Hall, *The Dance of Life*, p. 23.

18. *Ibid*, 23.

19. Hall, *The Hidden Dimension*.

20. *Ibid*.

21. *Ibid*.

22. Branigan, Edward. *Point-of-View in the Cinema: A Theory of Narration and Subjectivity in Classical Film*. New York: Mouton, 1984: p. 73.

23. *Ibid*, p. 83.

24. *Ibid*, p. 106.

25. Browne, Nick. "The Spectator-in-the-Text: The Rhetoric of *Stagecoach*." In *Film Theory and Criticism: Introductory Readings*. Leo Braudy and Marshall Cohen, eds. Oxford: Oxford University, 1998: p. 223.

26. See Chapter One of Gary D. Rhodes' *White Zombie: Anatomy of a Horror Film* (McFarland, 2001) for a lengthy discussion on the *spectator-as-character*.

27. Hall, *The Hidden Dimension*, p. 2.

28. *Ibid*, p. 108.

29. *Ibid*, p. 100.

30. *Ibid*, p. 101.

18

Drinking Blood with Walter Benjamin and David Durston

Karola

When I first approached this essay, it seemed straightforward enough. Gary Rhodes loaned me a horror movie and told me about its intriguing and probably unique background. Liking the film and sensing its analytic possibilities, I eagerly volunteered to write about it. Assuring him I would be done rapidly, I set out to, only to discover as I went along that I had flipped overboard into depths unimagined. I decided to swim with the undercurrent instead of float to a surface analysis. My original intent was to write a brief essay, remaining mainly within the familiar, pulling in a few established concepts to guide discussion of the film. That this was a myopic approach only occurred to me much later, when this analysis had drifted me down to wrestle with conceptual sea monsters whose understanding wriggled and slipped in my grasp. I'm not sure I won the battle, but it's been an enlightening struggle.

To begin with, the movie, *I Drink Your Blood*, appeared to be the first (and possibly the only) movie that the Motion Picture Association of America had assigned an X rating solely on account of violence.[1] As a result, it had gotten some new, more innocuous footage added by its creators, and had been cut who-knows-how-many different ways by theater projectionists in a last-minute scramble to make it R-rated and legal for exhibition after it had already been shipped out to them (following a lost appeal to the MPAA).[2] Arguably, no two locations had had the same screening material. Indeed, at least eight versions of *I Drink Your Blood* circulated in the decades after its 1971 release—a plethora for what had been on release a rather obscure picture, and surely a testimony to how many versions must have been edited at the time. Nearly 30 years later, having achieved an underground following and surviving to an era no longer shocked by graphic depictions, the movie was re-cut by its director drawing from his still-intact collection of all the footage shot for the film, and given new life as a DVD.[3] With its history of multiple (random) edited versions and current cult status, *I Drink Your Blood* seemed to me a popular culture vehicle perfectly suited for analytic inquiry.

For one thing, there was the X rating, the movie's nemesis (or serendipity, depending on how you looked at it). I knew 1971 fell right in the midst of the Motion Picture Association of America's struggle over its revised ratings system, and I felt sure that looking into that a bit could yield some interesting perspective on *IDYB* as part of a greater social turmoil. For another thing, there was the result of the X rating—the multitude of tinkered copies and the later recutting. These seemed to call into question the very idea of an original or authentic version of the film (especially since the "first" version shown to the MPAA was itself a re-edit of the director's initial foray, cut to please the producers). Copies, originals, authenticity, cult following, director's cuts ... they all suggested to me Walter Benjamin's seminal 1930s essay "The Work of Art in the Age of Mechanical Reproduction." A favorite among philosophers of varying stripes and inquiry, as well as a regular citation in most film journals, Benjamin's essay delves into the impact of standardized mechanization on the unique aura of art, and into the relationship between original and copy. Therefore I had a perfect grounding, I thought, for claiming *IDYB*'s deeper import. Completing the picture of good, ready-to-hand analysis in the making, Gary had set up an interview for me with David Durston, *I Drink Your Blood*'s director and writer. Social conflict, theoretical/phenomenological linkage, the perspective of the artist—I imagined this essay should have my fingers flowing over my keyboard in no time.

But no. As I tried to skim over them, each portion of my investigation attached weight to my inquiry, presenting me with new information, concepts, questions that pulled me deeper. The first insight to draw me in was the movie itself, especially after I had talked to Durston (who proved wonderfully articulate about his film's development and broader implications). His details pushed me to delve further, exploring *IDYB*'s 1971 context in contemporaneous newspapers, magazines and—lucky find—MPAA rating board member's memoir. Not that my explorations were by any means exhaustive; yet they revealed an interesting current of social events swirling around Durston's film.

This is not to say that the low-budget *I Drink Your Blood* made headlines itself; both *The New York Times* and *Variety* passed it over in their reviews. It did get bookings in theaters in New York and Los Angeles, as well as about 360 others across the country. In some it teamed with *I Eat Your Skin*, a pairing which continued in drive-in revivals, and which led *IDYB* to be widely regarded as a movie about cannibalistic hippies. It actually features no cannibalism and, despite its title, no blood-drinking (the movie's producer, Jerry Gross, gave it its misnomer label to make it sound scary[4]). There are hippies in it though—evil Satan-worshipping hippies, who descend on a near-deserted town and feed LSD to a kindly old veterinarian who confronts them about raping his granddaughter. The vet's grandson, who is just a kid but outraged at the hippies doping Grampa with "that L-whatever you call it," seeks revenge by infecting them with rabies from a dog. Soon, foaming, murderous hippies are running amok, chasing each other and whomever they can find, and infecting construction workers from the nearby dam.

Durston says he was interested in doing a horror film about something awful that might really happen, and got the main idea for the story from an actual outbreak among Iranian schoolchildren who had been attacked by rabid wolves. He spoke to the American doctor who had flown over to treat them—this interview is reminiscent in the informed, medical tone of an *IDYB* exposition voiceover describing the course of rabies in infected humans—and shaped his story with references to other cultural fears at the time. Prominent among these is the Manson family theme embodied in the hippies; one scene even features a girl painting "pig" on the stomach of a cohort being tortured. Yet the hippies are not completely vilified, and are themselves portrayed as victims to other social terrors, as one reviewer noted: "one of the prime youth nightmares of our time—a horde of literally rabid, axe-wielding hard-hats hunting down members of the younger generation."[5]

The same reviewer felt *I Drink Your Blood*, therefore, "must have some claim to redeeming social value."[6] *The Los Angeles Times*, which had deigned to review *IDYB*, concurred (though obviously to its surprise): "*I Drink Your Blood*, believe it or not, is a tour de force of a caliber not equalled since the similar *Night of the Living Dead* ... a triumph in virtually all respects."[7] While *IDYB*, like most low-budget horrors, has its cheesy moments (some consciously well-hammed for laughs), it is an entertaining and well-done film; some of its actors deservingly went on to more reputable works. This is not to say it is for everyone's tastes—*The Motion Picture Guide*, for example, refers to *I Drink Your Blood* as "bizarre" and "pretty gross."[8] However, since the L.A. reviewer must have seen a version edited by Durston himself (he cut the Los Angeles and New York versions finally given R ratings by the MPAA), I have to wonder whether some of the poor impression *IDYB* left on others was due to a random edit job. *The Aurum Film Encyclopedia*, while acknowledging "*I Drink Your Blood* had all the makings of another *Night of the Living Dead* (1968) or *The Texas Chain Saw Massacre* (1974)," felt that, because of the cuts, "as the film now stands what looks like it might have been a raw, ferocious thriller has become a frustrating exercise in splicing."[9]

Innocuous, merely restrictive or utterly ruinous for the viewer, the cuts to make *IDYB* rated R function as a manifestation of the conflict over the rating system circa 1971. The film business in general at this time appeared in turmoil; in my research for this chapter, I ran across repeated journalistic speculations, uttered with more or less confidence, that the industry was on its way to financial ruin and decrepit obsolescence. In the midst of concern over economics, concern over immoral or harmful content was likewise mounting. Finally feeling too pressured, the film industry instituted in 1968 "a self-defense mechanism designed to forestall Government interference,"[10] the four-letter rating code of G, M,[11] R, and X. While receiving praise from some quarters (e.g., many parents, neighborhood groups, movie theater owners), the system was soon criticized by others for presenting vague guidelines that practically invited the Code and Rating Administration to make inconsistent, and seemingly narrow or arbitrary, judgments about the ratings of films submitted to it. To make matters worse, "the only extended description of the rating system" made public in the early '70s was a 1968 brochure published by the MPAA to outline the official code objectives.[12] The delineation of the X rating in this brochure is about twice as long as any other, and is the only one that names specific film features for the Administration's consideration, rather than the more general concern listed for motion pictures' "theme, content and treatment." It reads:

(X) PERSONS UNDER 16 NOT ADMITTED

> This category includes motion pictures submitted to the Code and Rating Administration which in the opinion of the Code and Rating Administration are rated (X) because of the treatment of sex, violence, crime or profanity. Pictures rated (X) do not qualify for a Code Seal. Pictures rated (X) should not be presented to persons under 16.
>
> The program contemplates that any distributors outside the membership of the Association who

choose not to submit their motion pictures to the Code and Rating Administration will self-apply the (X) rating.[13]

The Administration's refusal to give a seal to X-rated films mirrored the public's reaction to them as taboo. The fact that X seemingly only appeared when explicit sex was present strengthened the onus of its label for a film. For, while the raters considered some films submitted to them (like *Midnight Cowboy* and *A Clockwork Orange*) X material because of concerns over violence, these concerns evidently were always accompanied by even stronger concerns about the films' sexual content.[14] By 1971, X equated to smut in most perspective audiences' experience, and many theater owners were accordingly reluctant to screen anything that might get their facilities labeled "dirty" movie houses. Moreover, in the early '70s many areas began to legislate restrictions regarding the exhibition of X-rated films. Importantly for a movie like *I Drink Your Blood*, a popular tactic included barring drive-in theaters from showing X-rated movies.

Thus when the MPAA gave *IDYB* an X rating, it effectively stigmatized it, hurting, if not destroying, its distribution viability — several booked theaters were on the verge of canceling its run.[15] An appeal was lodged with the Code and Rating Appeal Board to re-rate the movie as R, and not without hope: The Board had occasionally downgraded the severity of a film's rating before *I Drink Your Blood*, including changing two X-rated movies to R without requiring re-edits (*The Love Doctors* and *Medium Cool*).[16] The MPAA's apparent lack of condemnation for *IDYB*'s matter-of-fact nude scenes (the hippies like to worship Satan naked) and brief, non-explicit (and relevant) sexual content probably strengthened the hope that the movie would indeed be re-rated. After all, no film had been given an X rating strictly for violence.

But the MPAA held fast to its ruling. And approximately 360 copies of *I Drink Your Blood* were already headed for their theaters. Desperate to get them screened, director Durston recut a New York and L.A. version of the film to show the MPAA for an R rating (it got one), while producer Gross somehow managed to contact all of the theaters in two days. Gross alerted the managers to have their projectionists cut their copy in accordance with what they thought local community standards were for an R rating.[17]

Therefore, in principle, every audience for *I Drink Your Blood* then and afterwards could have seen a different version. Already a likely candidate for cult status, this made *IDYB* the veritable shoo-in: its mystique seemed to increase with the knowledge that whatever version you watched, it wasn't *the* version, because *the* version did not exist. The film's following increased over time, which at last led its DVD producers to approach Durston about issuing a director's cut. Durston, pleased and rather amazed at this interest in some movie he'd done nearly 30 years before, was even more pleased and decidedly amazed when the director's cut premiere screening in New York packed in an excited crowd, despite a midnight time slot and January blizzard. Fascinated with the movie's history, almost all of the audience had seen it before, several in differing versions (it was at the premiere that a fan informed Durston that he'd seen eight variations). Many lingered to ask Durston questions after the movie.

The allure of a director's cut of *I Drink Your Blood* for audiences three decades after the film's inception suggested the force exerted by the concept of an authentic version, *the* version, here at last — the original. While interviewing

Durston, I brought up Benjamin, who claims film to be a medium inherently without original (in the sense of an authentic masterwork—more on this later). We discussed the theory for a while, Durston endorsing my opinion that Benjamin's assertion, while interesting, didn't seem to hold up; *I Drink Your Blood*'s fascination appeared strongly linked to a search for authenticity. Perhaps, suggested Durston, film does have an original, though a somewhat different one than many artworks— the director's cut, a polyglot undertaking of many persons like all films, but one which clearly marks and unites a coherent vision, an original intentionality.

Musing on film auteur theories, I drifted along toward Benjamin, ready to re-read his essay for streams of thought I could channel to my purposes, wondering how to best to divert those I could not. Yet before I could immerse myself in the essay, the vortex of the movie sucked me in for one more whirl of conceptualization. The quandary: Benjamin's theory is on the relationship between the copy and the original for works of art. Could I legitimately consider *I Drink Your Blood*, or any cult movie for that matter, a work of art? Rarely are cult movies accorded the status of art cinema like the stark commentaries of Italian neorealists, the expressionist *oeuvre* of French New Wave or the experimental forays of recent film school graduates. A major value claim on cult movies is their status as kitsch, which is practically by definition not "high art." Moreover, any discussion on art veers dangerously toward aesthetics, and I felt extremely queasy at the thought of trying to charter that immense body of thought. I bethought a compromise. The writings of the neo–Marxist Frankfurt School philosophers, among whom Benjamin is usually counted, tend to show a marked partiality for high art and high culture elements in general.[18] The outright disdain for more pedestrian endeavors varies (Benjamin perhaps shows it the least), yet it may be easily inferred that the partiality for the "high" blinds the Frankfurt School to the potential artistic merits of the "low."[19] Given this current of snobbery, could I not escape the conceptual eddies that threatened to bring down my analysis by claiming that the dismissal of cult movies from the ranks of artworks constituted elitism? As I have discussed elsewhere in this volume in relation to Italian director Mario Bava, even the most seemingly tired and uninspired horror film can contain cinematographic mastery, visuals of stunning beauty and creativity that would surely satisfy the most rigorous superciliousness. For what it sets out to be—a low-budget, but interesting, horror movie—*I Drink Your Blood* does a great job. It's well-shot and well-acted for the most part, and whips up some weird frenzies while keeping its tongue close to its cheek. Is it art? It could be, if popular culture is allowed admittance to the category. Let the aesthetic theorists decide—I avoided the quandary and being sucked irretrievably under by reckoning that art is a floating signifier for a reason, and there may be many things that can be validly considered artworks given the right conceptualization, including a cult movie. I was drifting back toward Benjamin.

By the time the current of this analysis had swept me to "The Work of Art in the Age of Mechanical Reproduction" and the curling tendrils of my would-be philosophical argument, I realized I had already gone much deeper than I originally intended. Still, I reflected, deep is good when it comes to Walter Benjamin, at least temporarily, for he wrote with depth as a given. Benjamin wanted his readers to be actively engaged, wanted them to exert themselves in fathoming concepts as much as he did.[20] A worthy endeavor, no doubt, but Benjamin's renowned philosophical inconsistencies[21] combined with his difficult prose tend to make his conclusions rather murky.

Such murkiness lurks in abundance where "The Work of Art in the Age of Mechanical Reproduction" is concerned. The longest coherent piece Benjamin wrote, it is probably also the best-known and most debated.[22] In advance of the arguments it presents, there are contentions over its proper version and language usage. Apparently, there are four versions of the essay.[23] Each contains much of the same information, but only the second, for Benjamin, gives a "definitive" treatment of all the concepts related to mechanical reproduction and its consequences. This is the version Benjamin shared with friend and Frankfurt School colleague Theodor Adorno; following his suggestions, Benjamin edited a fourth version, which went on to become the canonical one, especially for English language readers. However, according to critical scholar Miriam Bratu Hansen, it is the inferior of the four: "The English version of the essay that appears in *Illuminations* not only suffers from an unreliable translation but also is based on the most compromised German version of the essay."[24] Unreliable or not, any English rendition of "The Work of Art in the Age of Mechanical Reproduction" suffers not only all the problems associated with any translation, but also those associated with foreign philosophical terminology. Social theorist Julian Roberts, for example, illustrates the potential for ambiguity in Benjamin's language when he spends nearly 40 pages of his book on Walter Benjamin unraveling the meaning behind the German term *Technik* (translatable as both "technology" and "technique") as it appears in Benjamin's philosophy.[25] Following the lead of these relatively more minor, but equally contentious considerations, the arguments contained within the essay offer seemingly endless, rich substance for scholarly dredging. Agreed with, applied, explained, critiqued, contested, remade—small wonder one academic began his article on Benjamin with the statement: "The argument of Benjamin's *The Work of Art in an Age of Mechanical Reproduction* [sic] is probably so familiar that there is no need to repeat it here. It has been reproduced, endlessly, within our own critical discourses, and each time we reproduce it, its aura increases rather than diminishes, as if to confute the predictions of the essay itself. That essay is notoriously ambivalent ...."[26]

The thesis (arguably) of "The Work of Art in the Age of Mechanical Reproduction" is that the advent of technology forces a radical departure for art from its traditional sociocultural place as a part of religious and, later, secular aesthetic, ritual. Mechanized copying (even just as a possibility) robs the original artwork of its aura. Thus stripped, the artwork becomes of the masses; no longer a power demanding contemplation, it becomes an object of consumptive absorption—all immanence, no transcendence.[27] Art in/through the age of the machine partakes of exhibition and shock, which pander to appetites they quickly anaesthetize, rather than of cult value and distantiation which create "a demand which could be fully satisfied only later."[28] Yet the decline in the authenticity and deeper meaning of art is not quite as dire a situation as it seems. The slow death throes of the aura leave room for the use of mechanical reproduction for the radical mobilization of the masses. Copied art has no soul—my word, not his, for Benjamin scrupulously avoids the overtly ecclesiastic—but it liquidates corrupt bourgeois conventions, and thus serves as a politicizing illuminator (if properly guided by Communism instead of fascism).

Of all of the conceptual sea monsters

prowling this thesis (and there are several), the idea of the aura of a work of art is probably the most elusive, the most slippery and—of course—the most pivotal in the essay.[29] Perhaps the best grasp of the aura is achieved by consulting other Benjamin works that mention it (e.g., "On Some Motifs of Baudelaire" and "A Brief History of Photography") and Benjamin commentaries by other people who try to explain it (although these can obfuscate as much as they illuminate). At the same time though, Benjamin gives as complete a picture of aura (arguably) in "The Work of Art" as he does anywhere else, so that's probably the best place to start tackling the concept. One of the most frequently quoted passages describing the aura explains it with reference to nature:

> The concept of aura which was proposed ... with reference to historical objects may usefully be illustrated with reference to the aura of natural ones. We define the aura of the latter as the unique phenomenon of a distance, however close it may be. If, while resting on a summer afternoon, you follow with your eyes a mountain range on the horizon or a branch which casts its shadow over you, you experience the aura of those mountains, of that branch.[30]

Indeed, the aura as the touch of a distant shadow is a useful illustration, but maybe not the wisest one to adopt in reference to the aura of an artwork, as it undercuts Benjamin's attempt to historicize the aura by positioning it as a phenomenal constant of the natural world.[31] Moreover, typical of the Frankfurt School, Benjamin's philosophy is uneasy with the relationship between "man" and "nature," generally construing nature as something to be subdued as a matter of course and process (though Benjamin is rather melancholy about this).[32] Thus the aura, as he uses it for art, cannot be construed as a simple extension of "the aura of natural" objects.

A further dive into Benjamin's usage of the term aura in "The Work of Art" (as well as in other pieces) finds the concept very much ensconced in human contexts—and simultaneously, very much estranged from them. Only an original may truly possess an aura, though Benjamin does imply that copies made by nonmechanical methods of reproduction (like foundry and stamping) may have somewhat of an aura, especially if they are old. One of the main characteristics of the original is its uniqueness, its specific existence in space and time, the *hic et nunc* (here and now) of a work that grants authenticity.[33] That unique existence grants the original a heritage of experiences, structures and meaning systems. According to Benjamin, the aura subsumes and carries these traditions—it is these traditions. At the same time, the aura encompasses and references more than the changeable traditions of mere mortals. Benjamin felt the aura was distance made present. Because of this, the aura acts as a defining part of an original artwork: The aura is what enables a given work of art to reach beyond itself to the Ideal of Art. This is where the cultic element of the aura—and thus the artwork's "parasitic" dependency on religion—emerges. In Benjamin's depiction, the core, formative function of art is a religious one: The ritualistic role of art is magical and evocative. The bourgeois secularization of religious culture could not eclipse art's transcendent reflection of the Ideal form, though it shunted it onto aesthetics.[34]

In effect, this part of Benjamin's theorizing about the aura takes on Platonic overtones, if not theological ones. Benjamin's first scholarly inclinations were deliberately religious. Benjamin, like most of the Frankfurt School, was Jewish, and Gershom Scholem claims that during the late 1910s, "Benjamin's thought revolved around a complex amplification of the concept of myth taken from Jewish religion, history and philosophy (and ethnology)."[35] Early on, the young Benjamin sought reconciliation of the woes of humanity through theology. Later, life brought the influence of Marxism and atheism. Yet despite his supernatural disavowal, he retained a mystic undercurrent in his philosophy (how strong this really is is a favorite Benjamin research debate topic). Unable to fulfill his Messianic inclinations by following obviously religious speculations, Benjamin turned to art as the repository for the transcendent and resplendent. Adorno, arguably a better Marxist and certainly a much stauncher materialist than Benjamin, claimed that this view of art led to undialectical thinking, veiled theology, and generally messy metaphysics.[36] His position has been assumed as a common criticism of the mysticism of "The Work of Art in the Age of Mechanical Reproduction."

Another popular contention is that the essay does not truly address, let alone explain, the causality and process involved in the mechanical copy's diminishment of the original's aura.[37] Just because the original is/may be exposed to technical reproduction and public exhibition, why must it therefore be cheapened? Inasmuch as a machine-produced replica may be admired, collected, contemplated, revered, etc., why do its traditions and potentially transcendent associations not qualify it for an aura?[38] Recourse to Benjamin for answers to these questions results in the (arguable) conclusion that he regarded the diminishment of the aura (and its restriction to original artworks) as a self-evident consequence of the modern technological era. Mechanized copies carry the onus of alienated production. As Julian Roberts describes, for Benjamin "capitalism prevented the integration of the spiritual with the technological—of theory with practice, in Marxist terms. Its irrational perpetuation of the division of labor made it impossible to assume the control that modern technology offered and demanded, and it plunged *Technik* into the dark of a spiritless and amoral practice."[39] Adorno and other Marxist contemporaries held that this made mechanistic processes and products worthy only of condemnation. But Benjamin, influenced by his Surrealist friends and Bertolt Brecht, looked for the redeeming qualities present in mechanical reproduction, like the politicization of art. Still, Benjamin could not concede any auratic merit to technology; he apparently believed that the reflection of the Ideal represented in pre-machine original artwork was of a finite quality—not only could it not be extended into nontraditional art manifestations, but its auratic trace could not but be lessened by them.[40]

Thus, Benjamin baldly states that photography and film inherently have no original possible and no true aura—though he does claim the cloudy and refracted impressions in the earliest photos display a lingering, decaying aura. And he is careful to warn of the false aura built up by the narcissistic industries of capitalism and fascism. The only genuine aura in film and photography is that of the natural subject being replicated, and this, according to Benjamin, is duly diminished by the process. In other words, reality itself becomes a hollow shadow which cannot compete with the replica's exposure of it, like slow motion's depiction of dimensions hidden from everyday observation or panorama's exhibition of faraway vistas in familiar settings. Years later, postmodern scholar Jean Baudrillard would take this line of reasoning to the extreme by claiming that simulation had surmounted its referential reality and effaced it:

> [Simulation] is the generation by models of a real without origin or reality: a hyperreal ... the very definition of the real becomes: *that of which it is possible to give an equivalent reproduction*.... At the limit of this process of reproducibility, the real is not only what can be reproduced, but *that which is always already reproduced ...it is reality itself today that is hyperrealist* .... And so art is dead, not only because its critical transcendence is gone, but because reality itself, entirely impregnated by an aesthetic which is inseparable from its own structure, has been confused with its own image.[41]

Benjamin does not take his work to the (in my mind) reductionist and ridiculous end reached by Baudrillard. Still, "The Work of Art" makes it clear (as Benjamin gets) that the threat posed by mechanical reproduction to the aura is a wide-ranging and irreversible one. The original is not gone as a result in Benjamin (as it is in Baudrillard), but its specialness is.

At this point in my attempt to use Benjamin to illuminate *I Drink Your Blood*, I had to come up for air. I realized I disagreed with him on some of his most important conceptualizations, and swimming against his current would require a deeper plunge. First, there was the argument that the copy, as a matter of course, degraded the original. The criticism that this lacked causal and rhetorical strength seemed a good one to me; regardless of what he claims in other essays or what his adherents write, Benjamin's position so depends upon weak, prejudicial grounds as to be untenable. Though the extent may vary with the person, it is evident from the attention famous original artworks get that their mystique is enhanced rather than detracted by their multifarious versions. Indeed, this would actually make more sense under Benjamin's plan of the aura as a repository of tradition than his exclusionary conclusion—the tradition of reproduction, and the varying circumstances of copies' circulation, would imbue the authentic, unique, first execution with increasing fetishism and enchantment—adding to its aura with each layering of repetition history—rather than "[detach] the reproduced object from the domain of tradition."[42] Of course, Benjamin's version of the aura eschews the exhibition that typically accompanies a much-copied piece of art and virtually describes film; however, his argument for why exhibition goes against the cultic *raison d'être* of art is capricious. Benjamin notes that with early ritualistic art:

> One may assume that what mattered was their existence, not their being on view.... Certain statues of gods are accessible only to the priest in the cella; certain Madonnas remain covered nearly all year round; certain sculptures on medieval cathedrals are invisible to the spectator on ground level ... by the absolute emphasis on its exhibition value the work of art becomes a creation with entirely new functions, among which the one we are conscious of, the artistic function, later may be recognized as incidental.[43]

What Benjamin leaves unsaid are all the times when exhibition to people, not spirits, is the order of the day, when the Madonna is unveiled and paraded through the streets. Certainly, the decontextualizing that museums and collectors frequently impose on works never intended as "art" (e.g., ceremonial masks, weapons and icons) does do something to them, usually exoticizes them and mutilates their deeper meaning.[44] But that this is necessarily, inherently the case is highly debatable, and at any rate to blame exhibition qua exhibition for aura reduction ignores that its regular role in art far predates perspectival display.

Diverting what essentially is one of the main arguments of the essay still wasn't enough to make Benjamin accessible for *I Drink Your Blood*; there remained his blunt denial of film having any access to original and aura. With eyes that opened some 35 years after the inception of "The Work of Art," I felt like I could see an artistry in film that would have been mostly opaque in Benjamin's time. I had seen something he probably had not—the first celluloid prints of certain movies inspiring all the wonder, reverence and valuation that attached to more traditional artworks. Although more than one was usually produced, it seemed to me that the reels of films were treated now as unique and special; therefore they might legitimately be coded as originals, especially if they were very old or the film very highly regarded. Moreover, Benjamin accords live theater the ability to have an aura— and apparently status as an original— despite the fact that theater is an inherently reproductive art form (not to mention an exhibitive one).[45] Theater takes the "same" play and performs it repetitively, in rehearsal and before an audience. True, as Benjamin points out, different audiences attend each show, and their collective energy inspires different performances from the cast and crew. This makes every enactment an irreplaceable experience. But if you only go to see a play once, you are not aware of the variation, and unless something goes awry, you may easily discuss the play with someone who saw it on a different night as if the two experiences referred to the same, unique artwork. If theater, as a serial artwork, may be considered as having an original and having an aura, then the simple fact of film's repetitive nature alone should not bar it from being likewise considered.

All of which does not mean that every showing of every copy of every movie would classify as an original. It just opens up the possibility for a filmic original. Durston's notion of the director's cut as the original seemed to me a good way to navigate Benjamin's technological prejudices and investigate the interplay of film original and copy. And *I Drink Your Blood* flowed right along with it. The excitement generated by the re-edited re-issue rippled with enthusiasm not for seeing another version but for seeing *the* version. Its cultic valuation increased by the plethora of copies that were the same yet different, whose ostensible lack of a credible, referential original fed the fascination for that original, for that authentic, authoritative artwork that was the director's cut of *I Drink Your Blood*.

Satisfied at last with the drift of my analysis and confident that only elaboration remained, I emailed the gist to a particularly perceptive sociologist I know, John Murphy, asking him to clarify a few minor points concerning Benjamin's philosophy. He answered my questions, but also made some passing comments that sank my hopes for a rapid conclusion and showed me the depths I thought I'd plumbed were really the shallow shelf of a much deeper argument on the structure of the original and mechanistic reproduction. "Actually," wrote Murphy, "there is no original—the original does not exist as a realist form. The original is a mode of praxis, and thus this modality of praxis can be systematically hidden. Praxis, in other words, can be obscured. This happens when technology (mechanical reproduction) makes claims and establishes mechanisms, that attempt to conceal praxis.... But technology is another mode of praxis (which Benjamin also seems to forget), and thus the obliteration is not complete. Technology ... is not anonymous, no matter what type of claims are made."[46] My attempt to do a three-hour philosophical tour through *I Drink Your Blood* guided by Walter Benjamin was turning out to need analytical scuba gear— I wasn't just using "The Work of Art" as a touchstone any more, I was taking its ideas and completely revamping them. Yet I felt I could not remain within more traditional waters—Murphy's claim, though it thrashed Benjamin's ontological warrant, made sense. Nothing inherently has the property of the original. To claim some object is an original, and some other object is a copy because "that's what they are," is essentialism, and removes the human factor in the perception of reality. If I draw a picture and photocopy it, both my picture and the photocopy have an independent, unique existence; both occupy a singular position in space and time; both over time will experience changing context, history and tradition. Neither my picture nor its photocopy has as a constituent, physical (or even metaphysical) element of its existence the state of being an original or being a copy. Both are formed by my creative human activity—my praxis. One is the product of my hands using a pen to create an image on a piece of paper, one the product of my hands pushing buttons to create the image using a photocopy machine (itself the product of other humans and machines). My modality of praxis—handcrafted or machine-executed—and my perception makes my drawing appear as the original and my photocopy as the copy, not the objects themselves. What this means for Benjamin and film is that Benjamin, enmeshed in the veil of anonymity shrouding technology, reduces all processes and products of mechanistic reproduction (like film) to the machine, and removes their human praxis.[47]

Benjamin describes photography (and by extension film) as a simple reflection of reality caught in a machine's aperture. In his phenomenology of photographs, Hubert Damisch reminds us, "photography is nothing other than a process of recording, a technique of *inscribing*, in an emulsion of silver salts, a stable image generated by a ray of light. This definition, we note, neither assumes the use of a camera, nor does it imply that the image obtained is that of an object or scene from the external world."[48] But for Benjamin, the whole of film reduces to the camera: The audience may think it identifies with the actors, but it really identifies with the camera; the actors themselves perform "not for an audience, but for a mechanical contrivance"; and the camera works seemingly on its own, as it "intervenes with the resources of its lowerings and liftings, its interruptions and isolations, its extensions and accelerations, its enlargements and reductions."[49] The essay does concede some human presence in photographic works, yet it is a nominal one, in which artistry "devolved only upon the eye looking into a lens," in turn producing "multiple fragments" incapable of stimulating contemplation, even when arrayed as a film.[50] Benjamin refuses to see the whole, imaginative human behind that eye guiding the camera, denying active engagement to director, editor et al., as well as actor and audience. The self-effacement of technology's praxis prevails throughout his conceptualizing (as does essentialism), and hence the argument that the "copy" diminishes the "original" naturally follows.

This rather narrow surface interpretation of technology and its relationship to humanity leaves film adrift, devalued of necessity as mere machine regurgitation. Finally deciding that the constructs of "The Work of Art" were going to remain too myopic for my analysis no matter how I wrestled with them, I turned toward the deeper explorations in the works of civilizational scholar Lewis Mumford, which offered me a better distillation of how praxis might work in the mechanistic realm, and thus in film.[51] First writing roughly at the time of Benjamin's essay, Mumford points out that technology has been intertwined with human society from the beginning—even Neolithic populations had machines. Admittedly, "Looking back over the course of Western Civilization since the fifteenth century, it is fairly plain that mechanical integration and social disruption have gone on side by side."[52] Writing in 1966, Mumford considered this a trend that over the last 100 years had led to "a radical transformation in the entire human environment."[53] Yet Mumford realizes what Benjamin apparently does not, which is that all technological innovations, in all eras, have led to a remaking of society because "all the arts and institutions of man [sic] derive their authority from the nature of human life as such ... the machine is just as much a creation of thought as the poem."[54] Society forms before, beyond, through, and with technology—mechanical is part of the cultural, something Benjamin grasps in principle, but not in the fullness of its implications for his claims.

Amazingly—or predictably—or both—*I Drink Your Blood* illustrates all of these profound concepts, giving concrete refutation to Benjamin along the way. And returning me, at last, to the investigative waters whence I started this convoluted analysis in the first place. *IDYB*, better perhaps than any other movie, shows the hide-and-seek that technology plays with its creative human element, and demonstrates that even when that praxis is evident, we still tend toward the original modality as a way of relating to it.

In one sense, *I Drink Your Blood* opens out its praxis as a mechanical (re)production. Like most performing arts, film is a collaborative effort; unlike the traditional performing arts (or at least their pre-industrial manifestations), though, film has collaborators entirely tied to the mechanistic aspects of it (indeed one could claim the audience can only access and contemplate film mechanistically). *IDYB*'s situation highlights the range of these participants. The MPAA, in rating the picture X, assumes the human presence in it. The Code and Rating Administration's very *modus operandi* working within the industry flouts film as anonymous technology centered upon the machine. Gross and Durston, like any individuals heading productions, are configured as the creative force behind the movie—and thus the ones who are expected to alter their product to appease the MPAA, if they want the Association's seal. It is interesting to note that only those whose positions tend to indicate an authoritarian role in production—in this case, the producer and director-writer—are held accountable and/or "allowed" to modify a film for reappraisal. For their part, the raters exert their will upon even those movies they pass without contestation (for movie-makers know in advance to shoot toward a desired rating), and thus enter themselves into the creative process. In the case of *IDYB*, it was a forced entry that impinged on the images fashioned by Gross, Durston and all of the others involved in the movie. No wonder *IDYB* was given over to appeal in an attempt to keep it uncut yet R-rated: The vision of the movie Durston put together obviously did not cohere with the vision the Code and Rating Administration had for it—if they had one at all. For part of the impetus behind the X rating overall would seem to be the discouragement of movies like *I Drink Your Blood*. Not quite as overt as banning them altogether or editing them directly, the

Director David Durston of *I Drink Your Blood.*

MPAA nevertheless put forth an additional human element—its own—into the creation (and attempted elimination) of movies like *IDYB*.

A far more unwitting and yet more direct group of contributors to *I Drink Your Blood* were the theater projectionists who had to cut it to meet their best estimate of R standards. Certainly projectionists in the early 1970s were far more skilled than most today (they had to be), but Gross, pressured by the MPAA, basically invested them with the roles of director and community judge as well as editor. Oddly, each projectionist theoretically contributed as much as anyone in the cast or crew to the ultimate texture of the film. Some undoubtedly slashed it beyond recognition, taking out scenes the raters didn't have a problem with (Durston's edit, the one approved by the MPAA for an R re-rating, contains scenes cut from one of the widest circulating versions of *IDYB*). Some may have left it entirely alone, and actually projected the X version under an R rating. Each theater would have had, potentially, its own unique cutting of the film. Now admittedly, every film-viewing experience can be said to be unique, changed by subtle and broad context variations. But *I Drink Your Blood* in its early distribution rounds truly represents an unusual amount of uniqueness in its viewing experience: The one context not routinely subject to variation—the film itself—would have been one of the major sources for it.

Yet it's extremely unlikely that any popular audience member at the time would have even known all the convoluted praxis that backgrounded their viewing experience. Nor, honestly, would most have cared. Although certainly some audience members enjoyed *I Drink Your Blood* (especially those who saw more coherent versions), few probably devoted any really reflective energy to it. Many probably did not devote their entire attention to it, using it as an excuse to leave home, an escape from the heat indoors, a reason to hang out at the drive-in, a soundtrack to make-out sessions, etc. I don't want to create the impression that *I Drink Your Blood* deserved such a fate; the important point here is that its pre-cult audience, arguably like most horror audiences, simply consumed it as another flick, caught up in its technological self-effacement. As with so many movies flickering across the screen, *IDYB* was an anonymous piece of mass culture to the populace.

Not so did it remain, at least for some members of the populace. The revival-drive-in circuit, then home video, led *I Drink Your Blood* to develop an interest among viewers as something more than a random mass product to be consumed and discarded. This interest goes beyond awareness of the creative human element in the movie; it is an actual appreciation. Strikingly, this appreciation for *IDYB*—a technological endeavor—manifests with a veneer of the original modality, namely, as a cult movie. That is to say, fans of *IDYB* and other cult movies acknowledge these movies as mass works, but insist on them as sometimes art, sometimes kitsch, sometimes bizarre, but always as marked with a uniqueness, a specialness that makes cult movies stand out among other movies. I'm not sure it's something mystical like Benjamin's idea of an aura (clearly it's not exactly his conception) but there's something about the social construction of certain films that endows them with a distinctiveness which gets coded like a traditional artwork, like an "original." The most evident manifestations of this semantic appropriation of the original modality are so-called art and auteur cinemas, as well as film awards and the canonization of "classic" movies and directors. Obviously, *I Drink Your Blood* and other movies of its ilk do not fall into such "high art" film categories. Rather, their cult status appears to be a weird sort of negotiation between their technical and original modes of praxis: It penetrates and even celebrates the mechanical reproductive/mass aspects (more so than say, the exaltation of art cinema, which has an originalesque worship of the vision of the auteur[55]), but simultaneously acknowledges and delights in the original aspects—the cult film is somehow "better" (or worse) than its peers, more zany or artsy or political or schlocky or whatever. For fans of cult movies, the human production is transparent; they perceive the accomplishment and/or creativity which seem the hallmark of the original praxis modality. *And* they enjoy the pop culture characteristics.

I Drink Your Blood partakes of all these cult movie frameworks; however, it also departs from them in one significant detail that's instructive for the current relationship of the original modality to film. Several cult movies (particularly horror ones) possess more than one version, differing edits for differing markets (usually distinguished by country). These variations are often rare and highly sought after. They are also finite, and, though one may be preferred to another, they are also authoritative, generally speaking. In other words, while cuts may be made on a version at the behest of, say, the distributor, to the dismay of, say, the director, very few (if any) cult movie versions have been systematically created by a group usually not considered as part of productions at all—the projectionists.⁵⁶ The multiversioning of *IDYB* is admittedly finite as well, but finite to the tune of well over 300 possibilities. Because they represent changes made by a non-authoritative source, the *IDYB* movies raise a question of authenticity that's not really an issue for most cult releases. Hence the excitement over the DVD revamping by David Durston. This director's cut, indeed all director's cuts, acts as the "original" for the film. But such a quality is not vested in the cuts or anything concrete about *IDYB* as a realist form. It comes from the authenticity that is granted to a director's cut, a leftover trapping of the traditional original modality of a singular artist exerting praxis. This modality is rather problematic and deficient as applied to films, which are rarely if ever completely the result of one human. Yet the yearning to apply such an ill-fitting conceptualization as the solo film artist exists, just as the quest for authenticity exists, spurred onward if not created in the wake of challenges to the idea of a unique, authoritative piece like that posed by *I Drink Your Blood* and, less dramatically, by film in general.

Cult movie, art cinema, director's cut—all are hybrid ways of understanding and experiencing what is always already a human artwork created as a collaboration for a collective using technology. It is likely that film will be grasped and appreciated at least in part by using non-mechanistic qualities and meanings for quite some time. As Lewis Mumford notes, "Fragments of culture continue to live long after the society that originally sustained them has passed away: often long after they have ceased to be a rational response to a situation or the expression of a need."⁵⁷ Can film, like far older artworks, outlast the society that birthed it? Who knows. Previous societies echo in our most futuristic, mechanistic endeavors, and film is no exception. There lies the original and the technological, sometimes restless in conjunction, sometimes at ease, and probably conceiving modes of experience we are not yet aware of. Certainly if *I Drink Your Blood* and Walter Benjamin show us anything, it is how complex mass cultural products and speculations can be; no matter how straightforward their relations, there is always more to explore and create. We should always take the plunge—even if the subject matter seems shallow, it can

easily lead to analytic depth and new currents of thought.

By the way, and fittingly for this discussion, the original name Durston had for *I Drink Your Blood* was *Hydrophobia*.

NOTES

1. *I Drink Your Blood* writer director David Durston claims that the film was the first to be given an X rating for violence. Motion picture anthologies consider it "one of the few" or "very few" films ever given an X rating for nonsexual content. Durston, David. Telephone interview with author. November 25, 2000. Nash, Jay Robert and Ross, Stanley Ralph. *The Motion Picture Guide: H–K, 1927–1983*. Chicago: Cinebooks, Inc., 1986, p. 1327. Hardy, Phil, Editor. *The Aurum Film Encyclopedia, Volume 3: Horror*. London: Aurum Press, 1985, p. 235.

2. It is my own extrapolation from the information available that the copies were shipped while the appeal was underway.

3. Durston.

4. *Ibid.*

5. Hardy, p. 235.

6. *Ibid.*

7. *L.A. Times*' review quoted in Frank, Alan. *The Horror Film Handbook*. Totowa, NJ: Barnes & Noble Books, 1982, p. 78.

8. Nash and Ross, p. 1327. Of course, since the entry also makes the common misattribution of cannibalism to the film, it makes one wonder how closely the reviewer regarded it.

9. Hardy, p. 235.

10. "Rating the Rating System." *Time*, May 31, 1971, p. 72.

11. M was the original gradation between G and R. M stood for "mature audiences," i.e., "adults and mature young people." According to the explanatory brochure issued by the MPAA in 1968, M included "motion pictures that in the opinion of the Code and Rating Administration, because of their theme, content and treatment, might require more mature judgment by viewers, and about which parents should exercise their discretion." In early 1970, GP ("general admission, parental guidance advised") supplanted M, and a scant two years later was supplanted itself by PG ("Parental Guidance Suggested; some material may not be suitable for pre-teenagers"). From reprint of brochure in Farber, Stephen, *The Movie Rating Game*. Washington DC: Public Affairs Press, 1972, p. 113; see also "Rating," p. 72.

12. Farber, p. 112.

13. Farber, p. 113–14.

14. Farber describes several cases in detail where it is evident that graphic or grotesque violence was a consideration for an X rating. In all these cases, however, when the final rating given was X, explicit sexual content appeared the chief factor.

15. Durston.

16. Farber provides a list of films that made rating appeals to the MPAA Code and Rating Appeal Board up to April, 1972 and the results of their reviews, p. 120–21.

17. Durston.

18. The Institute of Social Research, better known as the Frankfurt School, was an extraordinary collection of mainly German and Austrian scholars loosely united by their interest in socio-cultural issues and re-interpretations of Marxist theory. The Institute operated out of the University of Frankfurt (with branch offices in other countries) from 1923 until approximately 1933, when its mostly Jewish members emigrated under Nazi duress. Diaspora followed, with a mid-1930s re-headquartering at Columbia University in New York City. Benjamin is generally counted among the Frankfurt School, though not as one of the inner circle; he remained in Europe, mostly in Paris, following the exodus from Germany, and committed suicide in 1940 when a delay during his attempt to escape France across the Pyrenees drove him to despair. For an excellent discussion of the Frankfurt School's history and various philosophies, see Jay, Martin. *The Dialectical Imagination*. Boston: Little, Brown and Company, 1973.

19. The Frankfurt School, while not exactly reactionary neo–Luddites, nevertheless held technology and the mass popular culture it fostered to be primarily responsible for the dulling of humanity. For example, Max Horkheimer notes at the beginning of *Eclipse of Reason*, "It seems that even as technical knowledge expands the horizon of man's [sic] thought and activity, his autonomy as an individual, his ability to resist the growing apparatus of mass manipulation, his power of imagination, his independent judgment appear to be reduced."

New York: Continuum, 1947/1992, p. v–vi. In *Literature, Popular Culture, and Society*, Leo Lowenthal claims, "In popular culture, men [sic] free themselves from mythical powers by discarding everything, even reverence for the Beautiful. They deny anything that transcends the given reality ... while popular is depicted as the pursuit of relaxation or the attempt to escape reality, higher art is assumed to be a legitimate and spiritually fruitful pursuit, which ennobles the soul, and raises it to an ideal realm." Englewood Cliffs NJ: Spectrum/Prentice-Hall, 1961, p. 6, 42.

20. Wolin, Richard. "From Messianism to Materialism: The Later Aesthetics of Walter Benjamin." *New German Critique*, # 22, Winter 1981, p. 96.

21. As Jürgen Habermas writes in his profile of the philosopher, "Benjamin's intellectual existence had so much of the surreal about it that one should not confront it with facile demands for consistency.... Benjamin belongs to those authors on whom it is not possible to gain a purchase, whose work is destined for disparate effective histories." *Philosophical-Political Profiles*. Translated by Frederick G. Lawrence. Cambridge MA: MIT Press, 1981/1983, p. 130. Wolin attributes much of the debate surrounding Benjamin to discrepancies between his early and later works, as well as his changing responses to changing political circumstances: "The multiplicity of concerns and the plurality or methodological approaches that characterize the thought of the later Benjamin account for the differing portraits of Walter Benjamin that have emerged with the recent availability of his *Gesammelte Schriften* in nearly its entirety, and the often acrimonious debate over which is the *authentic* Benjamin, the 'materialist' or 'theological.' The lack of consensus accurately reflects the dilemmas posed by the conflicting political choices which forced themselves on Benjamin." Emphasis in original, footnotes deleted, p. 82.

22. See for example, Caygill, Howard. *Walter Benjamin: The Colour of Experience*. London: Routledge, 1998, p. 82, 98. Gelley, Alexander. "Contexts of the Aesthetic in Walter Benjamin." *MLN*, vol. 114, 1999, p. 943. Knizek, Ian. "Walter Benjamin and the Mechanical Reproducibility of Art Works Revisited." *British Journal of Aesthetics*, Vol. 33, # 4, October 1993, p. 357. Koch, Gertrud. "Cosmos in Film: On the Concept of Space in Walter Benjamin's 'Work of Art' Essay." Translated by Nancy Nenno. In Andrew Benjamin and Peter Osborne, Editors, *Walter Benjamin's Philosophy: Destruction and Experience*. London: Routledge, 1994, p. 205. Note that the abundance of scholarly works devoted to "The Work of Art in the Age of Mechanical Reproduction" forbids an exhaustive review for a discussion of the current scope; accordingly, all references pertaining to Benjamin and/or his essay should be seen simply as pertinent exemplars drawn from a much larger corpus.

23. Caygill considers there to have been three versions: a series of 19 numbered and titled observations on the subject completed late 1935; a French translation of this completed in Spring 1936 with Pierre Klossowski that changes some content and takes off the political edge of the 1935 work; and finally, a version completed over the next three years that deletes some of the original conceptualizing and emerges as a far more vague piece, p. 98. Miriam Bratu Hansen argues that the 1935 version was actually a second draft of an earlier hand-written formulation, though she notes that this first draft was not viewed as definitive by Benjamin. "Benjamin and Cinema: Not a One-Way Street." *Critical Inquiry*, Vol. 25, Winter 1999, p. 313–14. Both Caygill and Benjamin agree that it is the last, most truncated version, which Theodor Adorno published in his edition of Benjamin's *Schriften* in 1955, and which appears in translation in the English language collection *Illuminations*. Because it is the most widely known among English speakers, it is the final version that is used for references here.

24. Hansen, p. 314.

25. Roberts, Julian. *Walter Benjamin*. London: Macmillan Press, 1982: cf. 157–95, though the concept of *technik* appears throughout the book.

26. Baldo, Jonathan. "Narratives as Theaters and as Machines: Two Figures of Repetition in Kafka and Benjamin." *Journal of the Kafka Society of America*, # 1/2, June/December 1988, p. 11.

27. For an interesting treatment of Benjamin on immanence and transcendence, see Kaufmann, David. "Correlations, Constellations, and the Truth: Adorno's Ontology of

Redemption." *Philosophy and Social Criticism*, Vol. 26, # 5, 2000, p. 62–80.

28. Benjamin, Walter. "The Work of Art in the Age of Mechanical Reproduction." *Illuminations*. Hannah Arendt, Editor. Translated by Harry Zohn. New York: Schocken Books, 1969, p. 237.

29. Probably more has been written about the aura than any other point in the essay (for that matter, it is a concept used by other Frankfurt School philosophers as well as other critical theorists, though not necessarily in the same sense as Benjamin). For example, see Rodolphe Gasché's chapter on Kantian elements in Benjamin's concept of the aura, "Objective Diversions: On Some Kantian Themes in Benjamin's 'The Work of Art in the Age of Mechanical Reproduction,'" in Andrew Benjamin and Peter Osborne, Editors, *Walter Benjamin's Philosophy: Destruction and Experience*. London: Routledge, 1994, p. 183–204. Knizek, like other critics, dwells extensively on the looseness of the aura concept, using it to find the essay's thesis untenable.

30. Benjamin, p. 222–23.

31. Caygill, p. 104.

32. For a fascinating discussion on Benjamin, Critical Theory and nature, see Roberts, David. "On Aura and an Ecological Aesthetics of Nature." In Gerhard Fischer, Editor, *'With the Sharpened Axe of Reason': Approaches to Walter Benjamin*. Oxford: Berg, 1996, p. 55–66.

33. Jay provides a good brief commentary on the aura's "here and now" yet distant quality, p. 210.

34. For further discussion of Benjamin's view of the Ideal reflective function of the artwork as manifested in the individual form, see Kohlenbach, Margarete. "The Desire for Objectivity: Walter Benjamin and Early Romanticism." *German Life and Letters*, Vol. 48, # 1, January 1995, p. 25–38.

35. Koch, p. 210. For exploration of Benjamin's Messianic/mythic streak, see also Habermas; Jauss, Hans Robert. "Tradition, Innovation, and Aesthetic Experience." *The Journal of Aesthetics and Art Criticism*, Vol. 46, # 3, Spring 1988 cf. 385–87; and especially Wolin.

36. Habermas, p. 139–43, 152–53; Kaufmann, p. 65, 69–70. Benjamin sent the second version of "The Work of Art" to Adorno, who critiqued it in a March 18, 1936, letter. While acknowledging it was an "extraordinary study," Adorno clearly had some problems with the essay:

> In your earlier writings, of which the present essay is a continuation, you distinguished the idea of the work of art as a structure from the symbol of theology on the one hand, and from the taboo of magic on the other. But I now find it somewhat disturbing—and here I can see a sublimated remnant of certain Brechtian themes—that you have now rather casually transferred the concept of the magical aura to the 'autonomous work of art' and flatly assigned a counter-revolutionary function to the latter ... it seems to me that the heart of the autonomous work of art does not itself belong to the dimension of myth ... but is inherently dialectical.... You underestimate the technical character of autonomous art and overestimate that of dependent art; put simply, this would be my principal objection. But this objection could only be made effective precisely as a dialectic between the extremes which you tear asunder.

Adorno, Theodor. From *Theodor Adorno and Walter Benjamin: The Complete Correspondence, 1928–1940*. Henri Lonitz, Editor. Translated by Nicholas Walker. Cambridge MA: Harvard University Press, 1999, p. 129, 131.

37. Caygill, p. 105–06; Habermas, p. 139; Jayne, Richard. "The Work of Art as a Serial Reproduction: Kafka and Benjamin." *Journal of the Kafka Society of America*, # 1/2, June/December 1988, p. 27–29; Knizek, p. 357, 360–62.

38. In his excellent treatise on early modern lithography, William B. MacGregor discusses the popularity of lithograph collecting, particularly among the upper classes. Eagerly sought and creatively arranged in folios, these collections were highly prized. MacGregor notes: "For a medium that was by no means a

novel one in [the eighteenth century] the engraving's charge or *aura*—that which by Walter Benjamin's lights, mechanical reproduction was supposed to rob—was still one gathers, very much intact." MacGregor, William B. "The Authority of Prints: An Early Modern Perspective." *Art History*, Vol. 22, # 3, September 1999, emphasis in original, p. 391.

39. J. Roberts, p. 160.

40. Habermas, p. 138–39, 146.

41. Baudrillard, Jean. *Simulations*. Translated by Paul Foss, Paul Patton and Philip Beitchman. New York: Semiotext[e], 1983, emphasis in original: 2, 146–47, 151–52. For a further exploration of Baudrillard's relationship to Benjamin's work, see Krauss, Rosalind E. "Reinventing the Medium." *Critical Inquiry*, vol. 25, 1999: 290–92.

42. Benjamin, p. 221.

43. *Ibid*, p. 224–25.

44. David Carrier explores through a variety of perspectives how exhibition, change of context and the museum setting affect the work of art in "Art Museums, Old Paintings, and Our Knowledge of the Past." *History and Theory*, vol. 40, May 2001, p. 170–89.

45. For perspectives on Benjamin and the repetitiveness of theater, see Baldo: cf. 11–14, 18; and Wirth, Andrzej. "Beyond Benjamin: Performative Artwork and its Resistance to Reproduction." In Gerhard Fischer, Editor, *'With the Sharpened Axe of Reason': Approaches to Walter Benjamin*. Oxford: Berg, 1996, p. 219–24.

46. Murphy, John. Email to author, May 31, 2001.

47. Admittedly, Benjamin hopes for a humanistic usage of film for spreading emancipating knowledge and revolutionary fervor, which does reflect a certain acknowledgement of praxis. However, this praxis is not located in the medium itself. The technological is still without aura and creative human input; it can only be redeemed as praxis insofar as it can be appropriated for other active modalities.

48. Damisch, Hubert. "Five Notes for a Phenomenology of the Photographic Image." *October*, 5, 1978, p. 70.

49. Benjamin, p. 228–29, 237.

50. *Ibid.*, p. 219, 234.

51. Mumford is useful for general technology/society relations, which is the broadest concern of this essay; for more specific rebuttals of the position that film's mass technological status bars it from aesthetics and the human touch, see Jarvie, Ian. *Philosophy of the Film: Epistemology, Ontology, Aesthetics*. New York: Routledge, 1987.

52. Mumford, Lewis. *The Culture of Cities*. New York: Harcourt, Brace and Company, 1938, p. 7.

53. Mumford, Lewis. *The Myth of the Machine: Technics and Human Development*. New York: Harcourt, Brace & World, 1966, p. 3.

54. Mumford, Lewis. *Technics and Civilization*. New York: Harcourt, Brace and Company, 1934, p. 317–19.

55. At the same time though, cult movies typically do not (for obvious reasons) display the worship of self-effacing technology and mechanistic praxis seen in the exaltation of special effects.

56. Certainly other cases must have occurred of projectionists re-editing a movie on their own recognizance or in response to a community pressure, but these would have been by and large isolated incidents.

57. Mumford, *Cities*: 73.

About the Contributors

Christine Berzsenyi is an Assistant Professor of English and teaches honors composition, basic writing, technical writing and women's studies at Penn State University, Wilkes-Barre. Her research and teaching links rhetorical theory, gender studies and communication media.

Mark Bould is a Senior Lecturer in Film and Media Studies at Buckinghamshire Chilterns University College. His recent publications include a long interview with China Miéville and articles-chapters on *Blade Runner* and *Johnny Mnemonic*; *Neuromancer*, *Eve of Destruction* and *Barb Wire*; the early SF novels of Gwynneth Jones; and a Marxist critique of theories of the fantastic. He has contributed numerous entries to the *Critical Guide to Contemporary Directors*, and his reviews have appeared in *Foundation*, *Historical Materialism*, *Public Understanding of Science Fiction*, *Science Fiction Studies* and *Scope*. In addition to further pieces on Jones and Miéville, he is currently working on the films and fiction of John Sayles and on the politics of SF cinema since *Star Wars*.

J. Rocky Colavito is an Associate Professor of English and Head of the Department of Language and Communication at Northwestern State University. He received his degree in rhetoric, composition and the teaching of English from the University of Arizona. His current research agenda involves visual rhetoric, emotional appeals and advertising campaigns/media. He counts the original *Godzilla*, *Destroy All Monsters*, *X the Unknown* and *Reptilicus* as the ultimate all-night drive-in VCR experience.

Chris Cooling is a doctoral candidate in critical studies at the University of Southern California's school of Cinema-Television. He is currently working on his dissertation, which explores the cultural mythology of recent independent American film. His writing has appeared in *American Cinematographer* and the *Canadian Journal of Film Studies*.

Graeme Harper is Director of the Development Centre for the Creative and Performing Arts at the University of Wales, Bangor, and heads such research and publication programmes as "New Screen Criticism" and "Theory and Practice." His work has been published in *Sight and Sound*, *CineAction*, *Southerly*, *TimeOut Neonlit Fiction* and many other journals. As a writer, he holds the awards of NBC New Writer of the Year and the Premier's Award for Fiction and has been 1999–2000 writer–film producer fellow. His books, works of film and literary criticism and of fiction, include *Black Cat, Green Field* (Transworld) and *Swallowing Film* (Q), and he is co-editor of a book on cult cinema. His forthcoming books include *Captive and Free* (Cassell), *Fabulous and Funny* (Cassell) and *Creativity and Critical Reading* (Blackwell). He holds doctorates from the University of Technology, Sydney, and from the University of East Anglia.

Karola [Schwartz] is a graduate student in communication at the University of Oklahoma. Her research interests include intercultural communication, interpersonal relationships, political rhetoric, performance studies and social theory.

David A. Kirby is an Assistant Professor in the Department of Biology at American University where he teaches courses on the interaction between science and society. He earned his PhD. from the University of Maryland in evolutionary genetics and has published several scientific articles in *Genetics and the Proceedings of the National Academy of Sciences*. Currently he is using interdisciplinary approaches to study the intersection between science, society and popular culture, including historic representations of biological technologies in cinema. His latest article in *Science Fiction Studies* explores eugenics and gene therapy in the 1997 film *Gattaca*.

Eric Kramer, a true lover of the drive-in experience, is currently an Associate Professor of Communications as well as an Adjunct Faculty in the Department of Film/Video Studies at the University of Oklahoma. He has taught in Taiwan, Japan, Germany and England, and has been a Fulbright scholar to the College of Mass Communications, Sofia University, Bulgaria. He is the author of several books and articles: *Modern/Postmodern: Off the Beaten Path of Antimodernism and Consciousness* and *Culture: An Introduction to the Thought of Jean Gebser*.

Michael E. Lee holds a Ph.D. in Historical Musicology from the University of Southern California. Today he is a professor of Musicology at the University of Oklahoma where he also teaches for the Film Studies Program. In addition to research on experimental music and film music, he has published essays about such "B" horror films at *The Corpse Vanishes* (1942), *The Leopard Man* (1943), and *The Monster and the Girl* (1941).

Gary Rhodes is a professor in the University of Oklahoma Department of Film and Video Studios. His books include *Lugosi* (McFarland, 1997) and *White Zombie: Anatomy of a Horror Film* (McFarland, 2001). He has worked on several film restorations, provided audio commentary for DVDs and published many essays on film-related topics. A filmmaker himself, his work includes such documentaries as *Solo Flight* and *Lugosi: Hollywood's Dracula*.

John Springer is currently an Assistant Professor in the English Department at the University of Central Oklahoma. His writings on film and literature have appeared in *Genre, Iris* and *Literature/Film Quarterly*. He is the author of *Hollywood Fictions: The Dream Factory in American Popular Literature* (University of Oklahoma Press, 2000). He lives in Norman, Oklahoma, with his wife Laura and their four children.

Steven Schneider is working towards a Ph.D. in Philosophy at Harvard University, and a Ph.D. in Cinema Studies at New York University's Tisch School of the Arts. His articles on the horror genre appear in *Paradoxa, CineAction, Other Voices* and the *St. James Encyclopedia of Popular Culture*. Chapters are forthcoming in *Horror Film Reader* (Limelight Editions) and *Violated Bodies: Extreme Film* (Creation Books). Steven is presently co-editing (with Richard Allen) a volume of essays on psychoanalysis and the horror film, entitled *Freud's Worst Nightmares*.

Tony Williams is an Associate Professor of Cinema Studies in the Department of English at Southern Illinois University at Carbondale. He is the author of *Jack London: The Movies* (1992), co-author of *Italian Western: Opera of Violence* (1975), and co-editor of *Vietnam War Films* (1994). His essays have appeared in such anthologies as *The American Nightmare* (1979), *Making Television* (1991), *Inventing Vietnam* (1991), *Crisis Cinema* (1993) and *Reviewing British Cinema* (1994).

Index

*Numbers in **bold** represent photographs*

Abbott and Costello 100
Academy Awards 45
Adamson, Al 259
The Addams Family 100
Adorno, Theodor 282, 284
Agres, Stuart J. 43
Alberini, Filoteo 211
Aldrich, Robert 201, 202, 203
Alexander, Suzanne 116
Alien (1979) 225
Allied Artists 57
The Amazing Colossal Man (1957) 177, 246
America 251
American Drive-in Theatre (1997) 4, 25
American International Pictures (AIP) 53, 54, 65, 226
Amicus Studios 220, 230
Andrews, Dana 68, 73
Andrews, Nigel 156
El angel exterminador (1962) 187
Annandale, David 5, 129
Antheil, George 156, 163
Antonioni, Michelangelo 218, 221
Archaeology of Knowledge 143, 146, 147, 148, 149
Argento, Dario 213, 217, 231
The Aristocats (1970) 26
Aristotle 45, 46, 48, 50, 51
Arkoff, Samuel Z. 53, 54
Arlen, Betty 113
Arsenic and Old Lace (1944) 100
Ashcroft, Ronnie 54, 55
Assault on Precinct 13 (1976) 105
Astor, Mary 118
The Astounding She Monster (1958) 47, 54, 55, 173, 180
Attack of the Crab Monsters (1957) 57, 59, 64
Attack of the Fifty Foot Woman (1958) 177
Attack of the Leading Ladies: Gender, Sexuality, and Spectatorship in Classic Horror Cinema 170
Attack of the Leeches (1959) 203–205, 206, 207
The Aurum Film Encyclopedia 226, 279

Australian Film Development Corporation 32
Australian Film, Television, and Radio School 32
Australian National Cinema 28
L'Avventura di Annabella (1943) 217

Babuscio, Jack 114
Back from the Dead (1957) 180
Baron Blood (1972) 224, 229, 230
Barrett, Adrienne 155, 157, 158
Barthes, Roland 14
Bats (1999) 241
La Battaglia di Maratona (1959) see *The Giant of Marathon*
Bava, Eugenio 217
Bava, Mario 6, 211, 213, 214, 215, 217–231, 281
Baxter, Les 226
Beach, David 83
Beadle, George W. 249, 250, 251
The Beast from 20,000 Fathoms (1953) 246
The Beast Within (1982) 201
Bedlam (1946) 55
The Beginning of the End (1957) 248
Behind the Green Door (19) 79
Benjamin, Walter 6, 277, 281, 282, 283, 284, 285, 286, 287, 288, 291
The Benny Goodman Story (1955) 61
Benshoff, Harry 71, 72, 73
Berenstein, Rhona 170, 171
Bergman, Ingmar 81, 215
Bertolucci, Bernardo 221
Berzsenyi, Chrystine 5, 169, 297
Beverly Hillbillies 207
The Bicycle Thief (1949) 216, 230
The Big Chase (1954) 117
Birchard, Robert 152, 154
The Birth of the Clinic: An Archaeology of Modern Perception 143
Black, Louis 151
Black Panther Movement 105
Black Sabbath (1963) 221, 222, **223**, 224, 225, 226, 229

Black Sunday (1960) 178, 217, 220, 224, 229, 230
Blacktown Drive-in 26
Blair Witch Project (1999) 80, 85
Blake, Alfonso Corona 190, 196
A Blind Bargain (1920) 245
Bliss (1981) 31
The Blob (1958) **44**, 161
Blood and Black Lace (1964) **219**, 220, 224, 225, 229
Blood Feast (1964) 80, 206, 259
Blood Orgy of the She Devils (1973) 172
Blood Spattered Bride (1974) 49
Blow-Up (1966) 218
The Body Snatcher (1945) 55
Bogart, Humphrey 118
Bogdanovich, Peter 32, 33, 148
Bold! Daring! Shocking! True! 149
Bonanza 21
Bonnie and Clyde (1967) 101, 103
Bould, Mark 5, 7, 297
Boutross, Tom 55
Boyer, Herbert 244
The Brain That Wouldn't Die (1962) 129, 130, **131**, 133, 135, 136, 138, 139
Branigan, Edward 271, 272
Brave New World 250
Brecht, Bertolt 284
Brewster, Carol 116
Bride of Frankenstein (1935) 129, 172, 178, 193
"A Brief History of Photography" 283
Bringing the War Home 106
Bringing Up Baby (1938) 116
British Board of Film Censorship 81
Brontë, Emily 11
Brooks, Hal 63
Browne, Nick 272
Browning, Tod 259
Bruegel, Pieter 13
Bruno, Guiliana 227
Budney, Stephen 6
Bunuel, Luis 187, 197
Burns, Marilyn 99

301

Burton, Tim 143, 148
Byron, Stuart 153

The Cabinet of Dr. Caligari (1919) 130, 220, 221
La Cage aux Folles (1978) 153
Can Man Be Modified? 250
Canudo, Ricciotti 211
Capra, Frank 100
Captive Wild Woman (1943) 172
Carey, Peter 37
Carpenter, John 84, 105, 213
Carr, Cynthia 82, 85
Carrasco, Jorge 195
Carrie (1976) 34, 35
Carry On, Screaming (1966) 100
The Cars That Ate Paris (1974) 27, 28, 30, 31, 32, 35, 36
Cash, W. J. 203
Cassell, Sandra 81, 85
Casting the Runes 68
Castle, William 48, 86, 201
Castle of Otranto 97
Cat People (1942) 67, 69, 75, 172, 178, 220
Cat Women on the Moon (1953) 5, 113–124, 180
Catholic World 251
Chambers, Marilyn 79
Chaney, Lon, Sr. 2, 245
Chapin, Harry 84
Charisse, Cyd 121
Chester, Hal E. 69
Chevalier, Maurice 21
Un Chien Andalou (1928) 156
The Christian Century 251, 256, 257
Churchill, Winston 11
CIA 105
Cinema Under the Stars 4
Citizen Kane (1941) 42
Clark, Bob 84
Clarke, Robert 54, 55, 56, **57**, **58**, 59, 60, 61, 62, 63, 64, 65
Clarke, William 56, 57, 59, 64
Cler, Judy 260
A Clockwork Orange (1971) 280
Clover, Carol 173, 174, 181, 182
Cobra Woman (1944) 172
Cocteau, Jean 215
Cohen, Herman 53, 56
Cohen, Larry 84
Cohen, Stanley 244
Colavito, J. Rocky 5, 41, 297
Cold War 114, 118–120, 121, 122, 123, 124, 204, 244, 246
Color Me Blood Red (1965) 80, 86, 259
Come Next Spring (1956) 113
The Comedy of Terrors (1963) 100
Confessions of a Blue Movie Star: The Evolution of Snuff (1976) 91
Consumer Reports 245
Cooling, Chris 5, 141, 297

Corber, Robert 119, 123
Corman, Roger 3, 5, 18, 32, 245, 259
The Cosmic Monster (1958) 247
Cotten, Joseph 113, 229
Cottonpicken' Chickenpickers (1967) 114
Countess Dracula (1970) 172
Crabs (1974) 31, 32
Craven, Wes 33, 79, 80, 81, 84, 85, 86, 87, 88, 90, 91, 92, 93, 259
Crawford, Joan 202, 203
Creature Walks Among Us (1956) 242, **243**
Creed, Barbara 172, 173, 177
Crick, Francis 241, 242, 243, 248, 259, 250
Cronenberg, David 84
Crossfire (1947) 117
Cult Movies magazine 6
Cult of the Cobra (1955) 175
Cummins, Peggy 73
Cunningham, Sean S. 79, 80, 83, 84
Curse of Frankenstein (1957) 217
Curse of the Cat People (1944) 172
Curse of the Demon (1957) 67, 68, **69**, 73, 74, 75
Curtis, Alan 118
Cushing, Peter 230
The Cyclops (1957) 247

Damisch, Hubert 287
The Dance of Life 262
Daniel, Leslie 136
Dark Star (1973) 105
Darwin, Charles 11
A Date with Death (1959) 65
Daughter of Horror (1956) 5, 155–168
Daughters of Darkness (1971) 172
Davis, Bette 202, 203
Davis, Jefferson 206
Day, Doris 21
The Day the Earth Stood Still (1951) 113
Dead Alive (1992) 80
Dean, James 22
Death Race 2000 (1975) 28, **29**
Deleuze, Gilles 131, 138
Deliverance (1972) 207
Dementia (1953) see *Daughter of Horror*
Denham, Maurice 68
De Niro, Robert 34
DePalma, Brian 26, 33, 34, 35
Dern, Bruce 201
Descartes, Rene 13
De Sica, Vittorio 216
Destination Moon (1950) 113
Destroy All Monsters (1968) 41
The Devil Bat's Daughter (1946) 172

Devil Girl from Mars (1954) 49, 120, 171
The Devil's Nightmare (1971) 172
The Devil's Wedding Night (1973) 172
Dickens, Charles 11, 13
Diller, Barry 153
Discipline and Punish: The Birth of the Prison 143
Dmytryk, Edward 117
DNA 241–246, 248–251, 253, 257
The DNA Mystique 257
Dobzhansky, T. H. 246, 250
Dr. Jekyll and Mr. Hyde (1932) 55, 61
Dr. Tarr's Torture Dungeon (1972) 46, 50
Dr. Terror's House of Horrors (1965) 230
Doctor Zhivago (1965) 21
La Dolce Vita (1960) 227
Doyle, Blue 56, 57, 62, 64
Dracula (1931) 55, 204, 220
Dracula (1958) see *Horror of Dracula*
Dracula's Daughter (1936) 172, 192
Dragnet 61
Dread of Difference: Gender and the Horror Film 173
"Drive-in Movies and Theaters" 4
Drive-in Theaters: A History Since Their Inception in 1933 (1992) 4, 54
Durant, John 189
Durning Charles 33
Durston, David 6, 277, 278, 279, 280, 281, 286, **289**, 291, 292
Dwork, Steve 85

Earth vs. the Spider (1958) 43
Easy Rider (1969) 102, 103, 207
Ebert, Roger 80, 85, 86
Ecologia del delitto see *Twitch of the Death Nerve*
The Ecumenical Review 251
Ed Wood (1994) 147
Edward Scissorhands (1990) 148
Ellington, Duke 226
Eloquence: A Rhetorical Bestiary 51
Eppler, Dieter 130
Ercole al centro della terra see *Hercules in the Haunted World*
Espy, Willard 51
Everett, Linda 4
Evers, Herb 129, 135
The Evil Dead (1983) 80, 201
Experimental Film and Television Development Fund 32
Exploitation Pictures 155

Farrell, Thomas 50
Farrell, Timothy 145

Faulkner, William 202
FBI 105
Fear and Loathing in Las Vegas 102
Fellini, Federico 213, 216, 221, 227, 228
Film Encyclopedia 259
Fire Maidens from Outer Space (1956) 173, 180
Fitzgerald, F. Scott 18
The Fly (1958) 176, 244
Force of Evil (1948) 117
Foucault, Michel 141, 142, 143, 146, 147, 149, 150, 151, 152, 154
Fowler, Gene, Jr. 67, 70, 71, 72
Fowley, Douglas 113, 115, 117
Franju, Georges 229
Frank, Horst 129
Frankenstein (1931) 55, 220
Freda, Riccardo 217, 226, 320
Freud, Sigmund 11, 21
Friday the 13th (1981) 79, 92
Friday the 13th Part II (1981) 80, 226
Friday the 13th Part III (1982) 80
Friedman, David F. 259
Frogs (1972) 51
La Frustra e il corpo see *Whip and the Body*
Fujiwara, Chris 70

Galindo, Alejandro 187
The Gamma People (1956) 248
Garbo, Greta 121
Gebser, Jean 10
The Ghost (1963) 177
Giallo films 225, 226
Giant of Marathon (1959) 220
Gieri, Manuela 216
Gigi (1958) 21
The Girl Who Knew Too Much (1962) 225
Girotti, Massimo 213
Glen or Glenda (1953) 141–154
Gli Orrori del castello di Norimberger (1972) 224
God Told Me To (1977) 84
Godzilla (1956) 246
Godzilla (1998) 51,
Godzilla vs. the Thing (1964) 41
Goethe, Wolfgang 13
Goliath Against the Vampires (1961) 190
Gordon, Bert I. 248
The Gore Gore Girls (1972) 260
Gould, Stephen Jay 257
Gramsci, Antonio 211, 216, 231
Grant, Barry Keith 173
Grant, Cary 116
Grantham, Lucy 79, 81, 85
Gray, Fabian 195
Greenberg, Roy 172
Greetings (1968) 33, 34
Grey, Rudolph 143
Grisham, John 190

Gross, Jerry 278, 288, 289
Gruesome Twosome (1967) 259
Guattari, Felix 131, 138
Gunsmoke 91

Halberstam, Judith 173
Hall, Edward T. 262, 263, 270, 271, 272, 273, 274
Hallmark Releasing Corporation 79, 82, 83, 86, 87
Halloween (1978) 80, 84
Halloween H$_2$O (1998) 80
Hammer Studios 217, 220, 224, 225
Hansen, Gunnar 100
Hansen, Miriam Bratu 282
Hantke, Steffen 214
Hardy, Phil 85
Harper, Graeme 5, 25, 297
Hart, Lynda 174
Hasselhoff, David 46
Hatchet for a Honeymoon (1969) 222, 224, 227, 228, 229
Hawks, Howard 116
Hay, James 213
He Knows You're Alone (1980) 173
The Head (1961) 129, 130, 133, 135, 136, 138, 139
The Headless Ghost (1959) 180, **181**
Henry: Portrait of a Serial Killer (1986) 92
Hercules in the Haunted World (1961) 222, 224, 225, 227
Herrier, Mark 33
Hess, David 81, 85
Hi Mom (1970) 34
The Hidden Dimension 270
The Hideous Sun Demon (1959) 47, 53–65, 247
Hill, Jack 3
Hillbillies in a Haunted House (1967) 207
Hillbillyland 207
Hilton, Arthur 117, 120
Hiroshima 246
Hiss, Alger 121
Histories Extraordinaires see *Spirits of the Dead*
The History of Sexualtiy: Volume One 143, 150, 151
Hitchcock, Alfred 33, 34, 119, 156, 201
Hollinger, Karen 178
Hollywood from Vietnam to Reagan 99
Hooper, Tobe 85
Horrible Dr. Hitchcock (1964) 226
Horror of Dracula (1958) 217
Horror High (1974) 49, 50
Horton, Andrew H. 6
Hot Rods to Hell (1967) 35
House Beautiful 106
House By the Lake (1976) 93
The House By the River (1950) 117

House on the Edge of the Park (1979) 85
House That Dripped Blood (1970) 93
Hubbard, Jim 84
Hubbard, Ruth 257
Hudson, Rock 21
Human Genome Project 257
Hurwitz, Vic 84
Hush, Hush ... Sweet Charlotte (1965) 6, 201, 202–203, 205, 207, 208
Huxley, Aldous 249, 250
Huxley, Julian 249
Hydrophobia 292

I Bury the Living (1958) 5, **43**,
I Drink Your Blood (1971) 6, 277–292
I Led Three Lives 120
I Married a Monster from Outer Space (1958) 56, 67, 68, 70, 71, **73**, 76
I Passed for White (1960) 122
I Spit on Your Grave (1977) 207
I, the Jury (1947) 121
I, Vampiri (1956) 216, 217
I Walked with a Zombie (1943) 67, 75
I Was a Communist for the FBI (1951) 120
I Was a Teenage Frankenstein (1957) 54
I Was a Teenage Werewolf (1957) **10**, 54, 67
Imitation of Life (1959) 122
In Cold Blood 102
In the Name of National Security 119
Incredible Melting Man (1978) 41, 48
Incredible Shrinking Man (1957) 244
Inferno (1980) 217, 225
Infra-Man (1976) 1, 5
Invasion of the Body Snatchers (1956) 28, 73, 76, 244
Invasion of the Saucer Men (1957) 56
Invasion of the Star Creatures (1962) 180
Ireland, John 117
The Island of Dr. Moreau 255–256, 257
It Came from Beneath the Sea (1955) 246

Jack Maggs (1997) 31
Jackson, Stonewall 206
James, Montague R. 68
Jasset, Victorin 211, 212
Johnny Quest 41
Johnson, Lyndon B. 106
Jones, Duane 36
Jory, Victor 113, 115, 117, 118, 121

Joyce, James 11
Jungle Woman (1944) 172
Jurassic Park (1993) 241, 256

Kahn, Herman 108
Kandinsky, Wassily 16, 221, 222, 223
Karloff, Boris 2, 32, 33, 36, 55, 148, 213, 220, **223**, 227, 229
Karola 6, 211, 277, 298
Katz, Ephraim 259
Katzman, Sam 247
Kennedy, Robert 107
Kernke, Karin 130
Kerouac, Jack 103
Kesey, Ken 103
Kidder, Margot 33, 34
Kill, Baby, Kill (1966) 219, 224, 228, 230
The Killer Shrews (1959) 248, 253–255, 256, 257
The Killers (1946) 117, 118
King, Alyce 54, 57, 64
King, Gary 169, 170
King, Martin Luther 107
King Kong (1933) 43
King Sisters 54, 56
Kingswood Country 29
Kirby, David A. 6, 241, 298
Kirkwood, Robin 56
Koerner, Charles 69
Konga (1961) 242
Kotcheff, Ted 28
Kowalski, Bernard 205
Kramer, Eric Mark 5, 9, 298
Krawitz, Jan 4

Ladies Home Journal 246
Lady from Shanghai (1948) 157
Lafflan, Patricia 120
Lamont, Adele 129
Lancaster, Burt 118
Landy, Marcia 216
Lang, Fritz 117
Lapenieks, Vilis 55
Last House on the Left (1972) 5, 50, 86, 87, **89**, 90, 92, 93
Last Year at Marienbad (1961) 151
Lavi, Daliah 226, 227, 229
Lawrence of Arabia (1962) 21
Leary, Timothy 105
Lee, Christopher 21, 213, 220, 223, 224, 225, 226, 227
Lee, Jack 28
Lee, Michael 5, 6, 67, 187, 298
The Leech Woman (1960) 180
Leith, Virginia 129
Lennon, John 11
Leone, Sergio 213
Lewis, Herschell Gordon 3, 6, 80, 85, 86, 206, 259, 260, 261, 262, 263, 264, 270, 275
Lewton, Val 55, 67, 70, 75, 76
Life magazine 106, 246
Lili (1953) 21

Lincoln, Fred 81, 85
Lindee, Susan 257
Lisa and the Devil (1972) 219, 220, 222, 227, 228
Lisa e il diavolo (1972) see *Lisa and the Devil*
Litvak, Anatole 156
Look magazine 246
The Los Angeles Times 279
Los Olvidados (1950) 187
Love Bug (1969) 26, 28
Lugosi, Bela 2, **144**, **147**, 148, 149, 151, 220
Lumiere Brothers 211

McCarthyism 119
MacGinnis, Niall 68, 73
McGovern, George 103
McKeon, Elizabeth 4
McLuhan, Marshall 45, 51
McMahon, Ed 155, 156
McReynolds, Bill 60
Mad Max (1979) 27, 28, 29, 30, 31, 32, 35
Madness and Civilization: A History of Insanity 143
Mailer, Norman 106, 107, 109
The Maltese Falcon (1941) 118
The Man from Planet X (1951) 55, 61
Manson, Charles 91
Marcuse, Herbert 100, 105, 108
Marx, Karl 11
Mason, Connie 206, 259
Maybach, Christiane 130
Medium Cool (1969) 280
Medved, Michael 190
Melies, Georges 214, 259
Mellencamp, John 19
Mesa of Lost Women (1952) 180
Meyer, Russ 92
Midnight Cowboy (1969) 280
Milland, Ray 44
Miller, Dr. George 27, 29, 31, 37
Miller Consolidated Pictures 65
Mimic (1997) 257
Miner, Steve 80
Mitchum, Robert 118
La Momia Azteca (1957) 188
Monet, Claude 13
Monroe, Marilyn 22
Monsters and Mad Scientists: A Cultural History of the Horror Film 241
Monsters in the Closet: Homosexuality and the Horror Film 71
The Monstrous-Feminine 172, 173
Moonshine Mountain (1964) 106, 260
Moore, Charles 194
Moorehead, Agnes 202
Mora, Carl 187
Morrow, Susan 116
Morton, Jim 156
Motion Picture Association of America (MPAA) 80, 277, 278, 279, 280, 288, 289
The Motion Picture Guide 279
Motorcycle Gang (1957) 35
Mulcahy, Russell 27
Muller, H. J. 249
Mulvey, Laura 118
Mumford, Lewis 288
The Mummy (1932) 193
The Mummy (1959) 221
Murder a la Mod (1967) 35
Murders in the Rue Morgue (1932) 220
Murnau, F.W. 215, 259
Murphy, John 286, 287
Murray, George K. 189, 190
Museum of Jurassic Technology 148
My Fair Lady (1964) 21
My Son John (1952) 120
Myrick, Daniel 85
The Mysteries of Udolpho 97
Mystery Science Theatre 3000 130

Nagasaki 246
Naron, Lynn 6
Narrow Margin (1952) 117
Natural Born Killers (1994) 92
Nelkin, Dorothy 257
The New York Times Magazine 250
Nicholson, James H. 53
Nicolosi, Roberto 226
Nietzsche, Friedrich 13, 14, 16
Night Evelyn Came Out of the Grave (1971) 50
Night of the Blood Beast (1958) 205
Night of the Lepus (1972) 51
Night of the Living Dead (1968) 4, 26, **27**, 33, 35, 36, 80, 107, 192, 279
Night Tide (1961) 5, 180
Nightmare of Ecstasy: The Life and Art of Edward D. Wood, Jr. 143, 145
A Nightmare on Elm Street (1984) 30, 92
Niland, John 50
Ninotchka (1939) 121
Nixon, Marni 156
Nixon, Richard M. 103, 107
Norms of Rhetorical Culture 50
Nosferatu (1922) 33, 220, 225

O'Dea, Judith 36
O'Kelly, Tim 32
The Old Dark House (1932) 100
"On Some Brief Motifs of Baudelaire" 283
On the Road 102
Ondracek, Jack 169
Operazione paura (1966) see *Kill, Baby, Kill*
O'Regan, Tom 28

Oscar and Lucinda (1988) 31
Otto, Rudolf 16
Out of the Past (1947) 118
The Overlanders (1946) 28
The Overlook Film Encyclopedia 85

Pacino, Al 35
Panic in the Year Zero (1962) 44, 49
Paramount Studios 142, 153
Paranagua, Paulo Antonio 187
Parker, Clifton 68
Parker, John P. 155, **157**
Pasolini, Pier Paulo 227
Pauling, Linus 249
Peary, Danny 90
Peckinpah, Sam 91, 118
Peeping Tom (1959) 221
The People Under the Stairs (1991) 93
Peterson, Nan 56, **57**, 60, 61, 62, 63, 64
Pettersson, Birgitta 81
Phantom Lady (1944) 117, 118
Phantom of the Opera 64
Phipps, William 115, 117, 118
Pinky (1949) 122
The Pit and the Pendulum (1961) 221
Plan 9 from Outer Space (1959) 141
Planet of the Vampires (1965) 222, 224, 225
Playboy magazine 205, 206, 259
Popcorn (1991) 33
Popular Mechanics 248
Powell, Michael 28
Price, Michael F. 6, 64, 65
The Prime Time (1960) 259
Prince, Stephen 91
Prom Night (1980) 80
Psycho (1960) 201
Pulp Fiction (1995) 263

Queen of Outer Space (1958) 173, 180

Radiation, Genes, and Man (1959) 246, 250
La Ragazza che sapeva troppo see *The Girl Who Knew Too Much*
Rain, Jeramie 81, 85
Ramos, Jose Ortiz 190
Ratay, Wayne 260
Razorback (1984) 27
Reader's Digest 245, 248
Reagan, Ronald 153
Re-Animator (1985) 80
Red Planet Mars (1952) 148
Redmond, Liam 74
Rembrandt 13
Renoir, Pierre-Auguste 13
Reptilicus (1962) 41, **42**, 47, 49
The Return of Jesse James (1950) 117

Rhodes, Gary D. 53, 259, 277, 278, 298
Rilke, Marie Rainer 13
Rin Tin Tin 76
Riviere, Joan 174
RKO Studios 67, 69
Robles, German 188
The Rocky Horror Picture Show (1975) 83
Rodan (1957) 246
Rodeo Tri Drive-in 169
Roeg, Nicholas 28
Rogers, Shorty 156, 165
Romero, George 26, 33, 35, 36, 80, 107
Roosevelt, Franklin Delano 121
Rosler, Martha 106
Il Rosso segno della follia see *Hatchet for a Honeymoon*
Rossitto, Angelo 159
Rostand, Jean 250

Sager, Ray 260, **265**, **266**, 267
St. James, Gaylord 82, 85
Salt, Jennifer **34**
Samson versus the Vampire Women (1965) 6, 187, 189–197
Sanchez, Eduardo 85
Sanders, Don and Susan 4, 25
Sanjek, David 214
Santo, El 6, 187, **188**, **189**, 190, 191, 192, 195, 197
Santo contre el asesino de la TV 188
Santo contre les mujeres vampiro 190
Santo versus the Diabolic Brain (1961) 187
Santo y Blue Demon vs. el Dr. Frankenstein **189**
The Satan Bug (1965) 244
The Saturday Evening Post 189, 245, 246
Saturday Review 249, 251, 256
Savalas, Telly 219, 227
Scaife, Tod 68
Scarface (1983) 35
The Scarlet Letter 97
Schaeffer, Eric 148, 150
Schlesinger, Arthur, Jr. 120
Schneider, Steven 5, 79, 298
Schwartz, Karola see Karola
Science Digest 247
Scientific American 249, 250
Scooby Doo 41, 97
Scorcese, Martin 213
Scream (1996) 33
The Screaming Shadow (1920) 245
The Screaming Skull (1958) 5
Sea Hunt 61
Secret Agent (1907) 108
Seeley, E. S., Jr. 55
Segrave, Kerry 4, 54, 85
Sei donne per l'assassino (1964) see *Blood and Black Lace*

Senso (1964) 222
The Seven Year Itch (1955) 113
Seyler, Athene 68
Shared Pleasures: A History of Movie Presentation in the United States 54
Sharrett, Christopher 98, 107
She-Creature (1956) 175
She Demons (1958) **175**, 241, 251–253, 254, 255256,
She Devil (1957) 180
She Devils on Wheels (1968) 260
She-Wolf of London (1946) 172
The Silent Language 262
Silk Stockings (1957) 121
Simon, Michael 130
Simon del desierto (1965) 187
Siodmak, Robert 117
Sisters (1973) 25, 26, 33, 34, **35**, 36
Skal, David J. 201
Skyview Drive-in 1, **2**, **3**
Smokey and the Bandit (1977) 207
The Snake Pit (1948) 156
The Snake Woman (1961) 177
Snuff (19) 80
Something Weird (1967) 259
Something Weird Video 46
Sommer, Elke 213, 219, 220, 228
Song of the Thin Man (1947) 117
Sontag, Susan 114
The Sound of Music (1965) 21
Spacek, Sissy 34
Spectator-as-Character 272, 274
Spellbound (1945) 156
The Spider Woman Strikes Back (1946) 172
Spillane, Mickey 118, 121
Spirits of the Dead (1968) 228
Springer, John Parris 5, 6, 155, 298
Star Wars (1977) 1, 21
Stedow, Jim 100
Steele, Barbara 226, 229
Step Right Up! I'm Gonna Scare the Pants Off America 49
The Stepford Wives (1974) 28
Strait Jacket (1964) 86, 201
A Streetcar Named Desire 203
Streiner, Russell 36
Students for a Democratic Society (SDS) 103, 105
The Suspect (1944) 117
Szulkin, David 81, 83, 87, 93

Talbot, Lyle 145
Talbott, Gloria 71
Tarantula (1955) 43
Targets (1968) 32, 33, 35, 148
Tarrantino, Quentin 263
Tascosa Drive-in Theatre 56, **59**, 60, 65
A Taste of Blood (1967) 259
The Tax Inspector (1991) 31
The Terror (1963) 32

Terror from the Year 5,000 (1958) 175, 177, 247
Terrore nella spazio see *Planet of the Vampires*
The Texas Chainsaw Massacre (1974) 5, 80, 82, 85, 92, 97–110, 279
Them! (1954) 244, 247
They're a Weird Mob (1966) 28
The Thing (1951) 193
Thompson, William 157
A Thousand Pleasures 131
Thriller 223, 227
Time magazine 246, 250, 251
Together (1971) 79
Toho Studios 52
Tolstoi, Alexei 229
Tootsie (1982) 153
Tormented (1960) 178, **179**, 180, 181, 182
Touch of Evil (1958) 157
Tourneur, Jacques 67, 68, 69, 70, 74, 75, 178, 220
A Town Like Alice (1956) 28
Il tre volti della paura see *Black Sabbath*
Trevor, Claire 61
Trilby 225
Tryon, Tom 70
Tudor, Andrew 172, 174, 241
Tufts, Sonny 113, 115
"The Turn of the Screw" 97
Twain, Mark 13
Twitch of the Death Nerve (1971) 222, 224, 225, 227, 228, 230
Twitchell, James B. 88, 89
2000 Maniacs (1965) 6, 82, 205–207
2001: A Space Odyssey (1968) 21

Ulmer, Edgar G. 55
The Undertaker and His Pals (1967)
L'Unione Cinematografica Educativa (LUCE) 217
Universal Studios 64, 65, 187
University of Oklahoma 4
Unknown 97

The Vampire Lovers (1970) 172
Van Gogh, Vincent 13
Variety 82, 206
Vendelin, Carmen 183
VeSota, Bruno 155, 160
Vickers, Yvette 205, 206
Victor/Victoria (1982) 153
Vietnam War 15, 36, 85, 101, 103, 105, 106, 107, 109, 148
Village Voice 142, 153
The Virgin Spring (1960) 81, 84, 85, 86, 91, 92
Viridiana (1961) 187
Visconti, Luchino 216, 221, 222, 228
Voodoo Woman (1957) 173, 180
Voronoff, Serge 245

Waiting for Godot 14
Wake in Fright (1971) 28
Waldron, Mal 259
Walkabout (1970) 28
Wallace, Bruce 246, 250
Wallace, Henry A. 251
Walters, Graham 222
The War of the Worlds (1953) 113
Warner Brothers 65
Warren, Bill 135
The Wasp Woman (1959) 176, 177, 245
Watergate 103
Waters, John 92
Watson, James 241, 242, 243, 248, 249, 250, 256
Watts, Harry 28
Weaver, Tom 6
Webb, Alex 6
Weir, Peter 27, 28, 31, 37
Weird Tales 97
Weiss, George 151

Welles, Orson 12, 156
Wells, H. G. 255, 256
The Werewolf (1956) 247
Weschler, Lawrence 148
West Side Story (1961) 21
Whale, James 100
What Mad Pursuit 249
Whatever Happened to Baby Jane? (1962) 202
Whip and the Body (1963) 222, 223, 226, 229
Whitman, Charles 148
Why Are We in Vietnam? 106, 109
Wieland 97
Wilder, Billy 113
Wilkinson, R. N. 64
Williams, Raymond 212
Williams, Tennessee 203
Williams, Tony 5, 113, 299
Williamson, J. W. 207
Windsor, Marie 115, 117
Withrow, Clay 6
Wittgenstein, Ludwig 223
The Wizard of Gore (1970) 4, 6, 82, 206, 259–275
Wood, Edward D., Jr. 5, 18, 141, 142, 143, **144**, 145, 147, 148, 150, 151, 152, 153, 154
Wood, Robin 80, 86, 90, 99, 100, 101, 109, 117, 197
"The Work of Art in the Age of Mechanical Reproduction" 278, 281, 282, 283, 284, 286, 287
World War I 215
World War II 9, 176, 252
Wright, Bruce Lanier 169, 170

X: The Man with X-Ray Eyes (1963) **44**, 46, 48

Les Yeux Sans Visage (1960) 229

www.ingramcontent.com/pod-product-compliance
Lightning Source LLC
Chambersburg PA
CBHW081540300426
44116CB00015B/2701